BLAKE

MORRISON

CAMP CUBA

PENGUIN BOOKS

PENGUIN BOOKS

Published by the Penguin Group. Penguin Books Ltd, 27 Wrights Lane, London W8 5TZ, England. Penguin Books USA Inc., 375 Hudson Street, New York, New York 10014, USA. Penguin Books Australia Ltd, Ringwood, Victoria, Australia. Penguin Books Canada Ltd, 10 Alcorn Avenue, Toronto, Ontario, Canada M4V 3B2. Penguin Books (NZ) Ltd, 182–190 Wairau Road, Auckland 10, New Zealand · Penguin Books Ltd, Registered Offices: Harmondsworth, Middlesex, England · These extracts are from *And when did you last see your father?* by Blake Morrison, first published by Granta Books 1993. Published in association with Penguin Books 1994. This edition published 1996 · Typeset by Rowland Phototypesetting Ltd, Bury St Edmunds, Suffolk. Printed in England by Clays Ltd, St Ives plc ·
10 9 8 7 6 5 4 3 2 1

I

A hot September Saturday in 1959, and we are stationary in Cheshire. Ahead of us, a queue of cars stretches out of sight around the corner. We haven't moved for ten minutes. Everyone has turned his engine off, and now my father does so too. In the sudden silence we can hear the distant whinge of what must be the first race of the afternoon, a ten-lap event for saloon cars. In an hour the drivers will be warming up for the main event, the Gold Cup – Graham Hill, Jack Brabham, Roy Salvadori, Stirling Moss.

My father does not like waiting in queues. He is used to patients waiting in queues to see him, but he is not used to waiting in queues himself.

A queue, to him, means a man being denied the right to be where he wants to be at a time of his own choosing, which is at the front, now. Ten minutes have passed. What is happening up ahead? What fathead has caused this snarl-up? Why are no cars coming the other way? Has there been an accident? Why are there no police to sort it out? Every two minutes or so my father gets out of the car, crosses to the opposite verge and tries to see if there is movement up ahead. There isn't. He gets back in and steams some more.

In the cars ahead and behind, people are laughing, eating sandwiches, drinking from beer bottles, enjoying the weather, settling into the familiar indignity of waiting-to-get-to-the-front. But my father is not like them. There are only two things on his mind: the invisible head of the queue and, not unrelated, the other half of the country lane, tantalizingly empty.

'Just relax, Arthur,' my mother says. 'You're in and out of the car like a blue-tailed fly.'

But being told to relax only incenses him. 'What can it be?' he demands. 'Maybe there's been an accident. Maybe they're waiting for an ambulance.' We all know where this last speculation is leading, even before he says it. 'Maybe they need a doctor.'

'No, Arthur,' says my mother, as he opens the door again and stands on the wheel-arch to crane ahead.

'It must be an accident,' he announces. 'I think I should drive up and see.'

'No, Arthur. It's just the numbers waiting to get in. And surely there must be doctors on the circuit.'

He sits there for another twenty seconds, then leans forward, opens the glove compartment and pulls out a stethoscope, which he hooks over the mirror on the windscreen. It hangs there like a skeleton, the membrane at the top, the metal and rubber leads dangling bow-legged, the two ivory earpieces clopping bonily against each other. He starts the engine, releases the handbrake, reverses two feet, then pulls out into the opposite side of the road.

'No,' says my mother again, half-heartedly. It could be that he is about to do a three-point turn and go back. No it couldn't . . .

My father does not drive particularly quickly past the marooned cars ahead. No more than twenty miles an hour. Even so, it *feels* fast, and arrogant, and all the occupants turn and stare as they see us coming. Some appear to be angry. Some are shouting. 'Point to the stethoscope, pet,' he tells my mother, but she has slid down sideways in her passenger seat, out of sight, her bottom resting on the floor, from where she berates him.

'God Almighty, Arthur, why do you have to do this? Why can't you wait like everyone else? What if we meet something coming the other way?' Now my sister and I do the same, hide ourselves below the seat. Our father is on his own. He is not with us, this bullying, shaming undemocratic cheat. Or rather, we are not with him.

After an eternity of – what? – two minutes, we are up level with the cars at the head of the queue, which are waiting to turn left into the brown ticket holders' entrance, the plebs' entrance. A steward steps out of the gateway towards us, but my father, pretending not to see him, doesn't stop. He drives ahead, on to a clear piece of road where, two hundred yards away, half a dozen cars from the opposite direction are waiting to turn into another gateway. Unlike those we have left behind, these cars appear to be moving.

Magnanimous, my father waits until the last of them has turned in, then drives through the stone gateposts and over the bumpy grass to where an armbanded steward in a tweed jacket is waiting by the roped entrance.

'Good afternoon, sir. Red ticket holder?' The question does not come as a shock: we have all seen the signs, numerous and clamorous, saying RED TICKET HOLDERS' ENTRANCE. But my father is undeterred.

'These, you mean,' he says, and hands over his brown tickets.

'No, sir, I'm afraid these are brown tickets.'

'But there must be some mistake. I applied for red tickets. To be honest, I didn't even look.'

'I'm sorry, sir, but these are brown tickets, and brown's the next entrance, two hundred yards along. If you just swing round here, and . . .'

 'I'm happy to pay the difference.'

'No, you see the rules say . . .'

'I know where the brown entrance is, I've just spent the last hour queueing for it by mistake. I drove up here because I thought I was red. I can't go back there now. The queue stretches for miles. And these children, you know, who'd been looking forward . . .'

By now half a dozen cars have gathered behind us. One of them parps. The steward is wavering.

'You say you applied for red.'

'Not only applied for, paid for, I'm a doctor, you see' – he points at the stethoscope – 'and I like being near the grandstand.'

This double *non sequitur* seems to clinch it.

'All right, sir, but next time please check the tickets. Ahead and to your right.'

This is the way it was with my father. Minor duplicities. Little fiddles. Money-saving, time-

saving, privilege-attaining fragments of opportunism. The queue-jump, the backhander, the deal under the table. Parking where you shouldn't, drinking after hours, accepting the poached pheasant and the goods off the back of a lorry. 'They' were killjoys, after all – 'they' meaning the establishment to which, despite being a middle-class professional, a GP, he didn't belong; our job, as ordinary folk trying to get the most out of life, was to outwit them. Serious lawbreaking would have scared him, though he envied and often praised to us those who had pulled off ingenious crimes, like the Great Train Robbers or, before them, the men who intercepted a lorry carrying a large number of old banknotes to the incinerator ('Still in currency, you see, but not new so there was no record of the numbers and they couldn't be traced. Nobody
 got hurt, either. Brilliant, quite brilliant'). He was

not himself up to being criminal in a big way, but he was lost if he couldn't cheat in a small way: so much of his pleasure derived from it. I grew up thinking it absolutely normal, that most Englishmen were like this. I still suspect that's the case.

My childhood was a web of little scams and triumphs. The time we stayed at a hotel situated near the fifth tee of a famous golf-course – Troon, was it? – and discovered that if we started at the fifth hole and finished at the fourth we could avoid the clubhouse and green fees. The private tennis clubs and yacht clubs and drinking clubs we got into (especially on Sundays in dry counties of Wales) by giving someone else's name: by the time the man on the door had failed to find it, my father would have read the names on the list upside-down – 'There, see, Wilson – no Wilson, I said, not Watson'; if all else failed, you could try slipping the chap a one-pound note. With his innocence, confidence and hail-fellow cheeriness, my father could usually talk his way into anything, and usually, when caught, out of anything.

He failed only once. We were on holiday, skiing, in Aviemore, and he treated us to a drink in one of the posher hotels. On his way back from the lavatories, he noticed a sauna room for residents near a small back entrance. For the rest of the week, we sneaked in to enjoy residents' saunas. On the last day, as we were towelling ourselves dry, an angry manager walked in. 'You're not residents are you?'

I waited for some artless reply – 'You mean the saunas aren't open to the public, like the bars? I thought . . .' – but for once my father stammered and looked guilty. We ended up paying some exorbitant sum *and* being banned from the hotel. I was indignant. I discovered he was fallible. I felt conned.

Oulton Park, half an hour later. We have met up with our cousins in the brown car park – they of course got here on time – and brought them back to the entrance to the paddock. My father has assumed that, with the red tickets he's wangled, we are entitled to enter the paddock for nothing, along with our guests. He is wrong. Tickets to the paddock cost a guinea. There are ten of us. We're talking serious money.

'We'll buy *one*, anyway,' my father is saying to the man in the ticket-booth, and he comes back with it, a small brown paper card, like a library ticket, with a piece of string attached to a hole at the top so you can thread it through your lapel. 'Let me just investigate,' he says, and dis-appears through the gate, the steward seeing the lapel-ticket and nodding him through: no stamp on the hand or name-check. In ten minutes or so my father is back. He whispers to my Uncle Ron, hands him the ticket and leads the rest of us to a wooden-slatted fence in a quiet corner of the car park. Soon Uncle Ron appears on the other side of the fence, in an equally quiet corner of the paddock, and passes the ticket through the slats. Cousin Richard takes the ticket this time and repeats the procedure. One by one we all troop round: Kela, Auntie Mary, Edward, Jane, Gillian, my mother, me. In five minutes, all ten of us are inside.

'Marvellous,' my father says. 'Three pounds eleven shillings and we've got four red tickets and ten of us in the paddock. That'd be costing anyone else twenty guineas. Not bad.'

We stand round Jack Brabham's Cooper, its bonnet opened like a body on an operating table, a mass of tubes and wires and gleamy bits of white and silver. Later, Moss overtakes Brabham on lap six, and stays there for the next sixty-nine laps. A car comes off the circuit between Lodge Corner and Deer Leap, just along from where we're standing. There is blood, splintered wood and broken glass. My father disappears – 'just to see if I can help.' He comes back strangely quiet, and whispers to my mother: 'Nothing I could do.'

2

She will sleep with him tonight. She worries that it's macabre, but I encourage her: she must do what feels right. And she says this is the last night she'll ever have him here, and she wants them to spend it together.

We are sitting on the bed round midnight, and

she is stroking his hand and kneading his face and then she tweaks his nose and says: 'Icy. But you never did complain of the cold, did you?' We have kept the window open, which is just as well because we've not been able to turn the radiator off and from time to time I catch a whiff of something I don't much want to think about. His face, the chin propped up on its T, is still perfect. He has always been a great sleeper ('I was really hard on,' he'd say when he woke from an afternoon nap or evening pre-pub zizz), and all this sleeping he is doing now seems his apotheosis – the hardest sleep of all. 'No, the easiest,' says my mother when I try this conceit on her: 'No dreams, no worries about oversleeping, nothing.'

She leaves the room and I lift back the sheet. It isn't him in quite the same savoury way now. There is a deep blackberry bruise spreading either side of the stomach scar – the skin looks papery-thin and in danger of oozing or bursting. Little red lines have appeared on parts of his bleached hands. The back of his neck, from what I can make out, has gone purple and discoloured, all the blood gathering there. I admire her for sleeping with him, but hope she won't slip between the same sheets, that she'll find a way to fold them so that her warm flesh isn't up against his cold.

When I come in at seven next morning, she's breathing beside him. Later, when I return, I find she's been crying.

'I've just been talking to my little man.'

'What about?'

'Oh, I've been telling him he shouldn't have gone and left me alone like this – not so soon.'

'I'm sure he didn't want to.'

'No, I know, I don't mean to be nowty. But the fact remains: he's upped and gone.'

She berates him some more, and I think of Cleopatra berating Antony:

> Hast thou no care of me, shall I abide
> In this dull world, which in thy absence is
> No better than a sty.

This is the way the world goes, the men running out on the women, running out *before* the women. A shorter life-expectancy: there's one great inequality men can brandish on their placards, can grumble about to women, who endure most of the others. But perhaps even in this women – as the ones left painfully behind while their husbands move beyond pain – end up suffering the most.

3

Sunday breakfast in the dining-room, the sun riding down from Embsay Moor. On the side-plates my father has laid out a series of vitamin pills: he has become fanatical about minding his As and Bs, his Cs and Ds, newly convinced that we can avoid colds and flu if we adopt a regime of tablets and capsules. Some of the pills are hard to swallow, others star-burst oilily when you nip their skin with your teeth. The family, not for the first time, is acting as a controlled medical experiment: what we are swallowing today, every patient in Earby will be swallowing tomorrow.

After toast and marmalade, my father and I retire to the two tip-back chairs which face out through the sash windows towards the moor. He is checking the share market, I the sports pages of the *Sunday Express*, where I stare for hours at the blurred anguish of a backward-arching goal-keeper. My mother, having cleared the breakfast stuff, is back again now with two mugs of coffee: 'Made with hot milk, Mummy? Smashing.'

It is my father who says this, not me. All through our childhood he has called his wife 'Mummy', never Agnes, her actual name, which he hates because it sounds drab and old-fashioned, never Kim either, the name her friends use and which he persuaded her to adopt not so much to seem chic and fifties – was it plagiarized from Kim Novak? – as to erase her rural Irish past. She has shed her name, abandoned her country and buried her Kerry accent; in return he calls her 'Mummy'.

'It's your half-term coming up,' he says.

'Hum.'

'I've been thinking. It's time we went camping.'

'Camping?'

'You know, fathead – tent, poles.'

'Hum.'

'Just the two of us, boys together – or *men* together.'

I have just had my twelfth birthday. This is what he must mean by 'men'. The thought of a camping holiday with my father fills me with dread.

'It's good to get away sometimes, you know – we love Mummy and Gillian, but there are things we're better off doing on our own, no faffing about or worrying if they're cold: you can't imagine them enjoying three nights in a tent like we will.'

'Hum.'

'Under the stars, fresh air and exercise – marvellous.'

A week later, on a hill above Lake Windermere, we're listening to the six o'clock news: there is something about Fidel Castro, with his big beard, and President Kennedy, who is so young and smily and perfect, and President Khrushchev, who my father says you can't trust. 'Secret installations', the newsreader says several times, and I think how difficult it must be to hide bombs: I have seen pictures of them and they are huge, or at least the clouds they give off are huge. Below, a rowing-boat chops and stitches its way across the water. The sheep on the green hills opposite are dotted tinily up to the summit, then evaporate into cumuli. 'Marvellous,' my father says. 'Couldn't have picked a better day. Fresh air, blue sky, not a soul in sight – makes you glad to be alive.'

I sit on the tartan rug while he reaches into the boot, then dumps the heavy, rope-necked canvas swagbag on to the turf beside me. He undoes the rope, then slides the bag along the length of tent and yanks it up, like a mother removing the dungarees from her flat-on-its-back, nappy-heavy toddler. It must be years since the tent was last up, on the beach at Abersoch or in the back garden, but at once a familiar smell rises from it – the smell of canvas and sand-dunes and grass cuttings and suntan oil and dead earwigs.

'Funny,' my father says, and goes back to the boot of the car. I get up, and fiddle with the guy-ropes, their heavy wooden adjustables.

'Is there a bag anywhere under the tent?' he shouts, as he opens the car door and peers under the back seat. I lift one corner and find a small blue canvas holdall.

'Yes,' I call.

'What's in it?'

‘Pegs,’ I shout back, pulling out a clunky handful of them – they look like primitive-man sticks of firewood, with little notches axed into the side.

‘No poles?’

‘No.’

I can remember what the poles are like – thick, wooden, three feet long, with large metal spears and slots at each end. I search the bracken, the canvas, under the car.

‘I must have put them in,’ my father says, without conviction.

‘Couldn’t we break some branches off and make do with those?’

‘Don’t be daft. It’ll be dark in half an hour.’

‘What are we going to do?’

‘Pack up and go home.’

On the drove-road back down, though, he has another idea. ‘We could stay in a hotel, I suppose.

And ring Mummy, and get her to drive up with the poles tomorrow and meet us halfway.'

Monday evening, with poles. After the misfortune of the night before – soon enough converted by my father into a huge joke against himself, the sort he could afford once he'd found the cosy hotel, with its log fire, consommé and roast duck – we have spent most of the day in the car. First we drove to meet my mother and sister in Kirkby Lonsdale, and had lunch. Then we came north again, nosing through the drizzle round Grasmere and Rydal Water, listening to the car radio, the weather forecast, the latest on Cuba. 'It's bound to clear up soon,' my father says, who is never one to complain, whose meteorology is a science of optimism. To him, rain is the natural order of things, which in the Yorkshire Dales is about right, and anything other than rain is a blessing.

'Lucky with the weather,' he'll say when it's heavy and overcast. 'Marvellous day' denotes high cloud. 'Miraculous, like being on the Riviera' is when the sun, however briefly, gets through the clouds.

At five we begin looking for a good pitching spot – 'I suppose there are official sites, but it's not the same as camping wild, and you have to pay.' We drive to Ambleside and Windermere: nothing. We take a left turn to Skelwith Bridge: the fields by the river are fenced off with barbed wire. We go back to Grasmere, through Chapel Stile, to the Dungeon Ghyll Hotel (trying not to notice the word Hotel), and as darkness begins to fall we settle on a spot by a stream. It is a low, unsheltered strip of flat grass. The farmer, though apparently surprised when we ask, has no objection to our being here. As my father's torch dims

 from a bright stare to yellow myopia – 'Bloody

batteries gone already' – we get the last guy-rope secured, the last bendy leg of the camp-bed into its slot. It is only, what, seven-thirty, but I want to climb into my sleeping-bag.

We tie the tent flaps and set off for the pub, leaving the shaky house by the stream. As we drive, the Home Service is taken up with Presidents Kennedy and Khrushchev: the smily young hero has blockaded Cuba; Russian ships are sailing towards it. There are words I don't understand – diplomatic manoeuvres and retaliatory risks – and words that need no explanation, like World War Three. Will my father be too old to fight this time? I've had this daydream for years that if he's called up for war we'll keep him in the attic, like that picture I've seen at school of the Cavalier concealed in a tree-trunk. And if they send someone looking for him and ask me do I know where he is, when did I last see him, could they just look round, I'll not give him away, I'll keep his secret safe . . . Now the next war's nearly here, though, my plan seems childish. Maybe this time no one will have to fight, it can all just be push-buttons. We slam the car doors and step into the pub car park. Annihilation must look like the sky does now, blindness and blackness.

It's quiet inside, and the barman doesn't seem to notice my juniority (does he take me for fourteen? eighteen? is he pretending not to see?). The warmth and cigarette smoke and sawdusty floorboards create a fug of sociability, but it's hard to settle into, knowing we have to drive back to the cold tent, knowing the world may end. There are only men in here, big, smoking, laughing men jawing about war.

'Them bloody Russkies need a taste of their own medicine,' says the fat one with sideboards from his bar-stool. 'This Kennedy's called their tune. He's the first to stand up to 'em like we should have long since. I take my hat off to him.'

'Nay, Frank,' says the barman, 'the Reds an't been that bad. They've not dropped their bombs on anyone.'

'Maybe so, but they've got as far as Cuba, and this Castro bugger is standing there with open arms saying come on in, there's plenty room for thee, you can hide your nuclear weapons in my beard.'

'What a world it's coming to,' my father pipes up from our pock-marked brass table by the log fire, shaking his head, hoping some neutral, uncontentious remark like this will let him in on the conversation, will be the right kind of admission fee. The fat man with sideboards shuts up now, the barman goes off to serve another

customer, and my father is left hanging there, at the edge of someone else's talk, wanting to insinuate himself, to be accepted. I know how it will go from here, because it's happened before in other pubs. My father will pick up our glasses, order another pint, start chatting to the man in sideboards, buy me shandy and crisps and say: 'Marvellous part of the world: wish I knew it better. What's your poison? Theakstons?' I am beginning to miss my mother. I don't want to watch what's going to happen happening: my father slowly winning over the suspicious locals; the conversation turning from world politics to legends of local brawlers, womanizers, con artists; the pint after pint, the whisky chasers, then the one for the road, and the next one for the road and the last one for the road. I stare at the smoke rising from the logs and imagine one wisp of it
 journeying up the chimney and out through the

stack into the night, to dissolve in the immense black spaces and be gone from sight if anyone were looking, and yet not be gone, for surely nothing can be lost forever, every trace of whatever happened on the earth is recorded somewhere, even the dimmest or shortest life must have its immortality: the stars are shooting us for someone.

It seems very late, but perhaps it's no later than closing time when we leave, my father belatedly guilty at the sight of me sitting alone by the fire, a collage of deconstructed beer-mats across the brass table. The cold drizzle in the car park comes as a shock, and as we drive back the radio spits and crackles over the whish-whosh of the wipers – 'crisis', 'urgency', 'ultimatum'. Soon the headlights are picking out our frail little homestead: it looks like a story-book picture of the first pig's house, the one made of straw. The wind is getting up now, not to wolf-howl strength, but enough to growl and yank at the guy-ropes. We stoop inside, relieved to be out of the rain, but even my father's cheeriness can't make this a homely place, let alone home. He hands me a flask of coffee, with whisky added. 'That'll help you sleep,' he says, as my throat implodes, my stomach seethes with fission. I hear the rain beat the canvas. I hear the stream getting louder, more confident. I look up into the blackness and imagine Russian ships steaming across the dark sea and meeting American ships and all the bright final skies. There seems no kindly light that will lead us out of this, my father and me, here in our paper bag amid the encircling gloom.

We wake very early. The stream has burst its banks, and our tent, which has no groundsheet,

 is standing in an inch of water. Outside it's raining

still and the wind whines to be off its leash. We drag ourselves out of our sleeping-bags and into our shoes, and splosh about in a sort of panic to be gone, breaking up the camp-beds, uprooting the pegs, dismantling the poles, tearing the canvas from its frame. It seems extraordinary, in the light of day, that we should have chosen this site – the stream looks higher than the fold of grass we pitched the tent in. But at least the tedious rituals of tent-packing can be dispensed with: we just dump the stuff higgledy-piggledy in the boot, and by eight o'clock are on the road.

It stops raining round four – 'Told you our luck was in' – but it's too late by then to think of drying the tent, even if the sun had come out, which it hasn't. There's nothing to stop us putting it up damp, of course, which is what my father seems determined to do. He gets the map out. 'Got it, just the spot,' he says, and we drive on through more flooded lanes, damp hedgerows, mist-obscured fells. 'Must ring surgery,' he says, pulling up by a red telephone box, not for the first time on this holiday, or others. Surely it's too early for surgery? Who can he be ringing? Through the mist of panes, I can see his head nodding. Any sane person would have called it quits by now, would have turned round and gone home, but here we are, proving ourselves hardy and hearty, pointlessly.

An hour later, I am sitting in front of a hotel lounge fire. My father fetches me a whisky mac: 'You're all right, they'll not notice, it'll help you thaw out. My feet are like ice.'

'Thanks, Dad.' He is still gloating at the trick he has pulled on me – trick or treat, I'm not sure which.

‘Happier now?’

‘Yes.’

‘Maybe it’s soft, but I didn’t see any point sleeping in that sodding tent with the forecast for more rain.’

‘You’re right.’

‘And it is our last night, and we’re still boys away together. If I’d been on my own, or with Uncle Ron, I’d have stuck it, but there was no point making you miserable – I sometimes forget, you *are* only twelve.’

I let this go, too relieved to be here to argue. There is a television in the corner of the room, a little grey window high in a walnut tower, and when the news comes on there are pictures of a smiling President Kennedy: the Russian ships have turned back, the newsreader says, and Mr Khrushchev has agreed to dismantle all his missile bases in Cuba. A man with a microphone stands in front of the White House and says: 'No one here yet knows what precisely made the Russians back down.'

My father and I clink glasses.

'Here's to Kennedy,' he says.

'To Kennedy,' I reply, my eyes watering over.

4

He is dead and I feel an odd triumph about it. He is dead, the thing (when I was small) I used to dread more than any other, but I'm still here, my mother's still here. I can hear her breathing, the world has ended but we've survived, we're OK. He is dead – no rage against the dying of the light, no terror and delirium, only a night-light smothered in its own wax. Sitting here, the body silent between us as we peer into it for a sign of some kind, I'm on a shock-induced high. If I listen hard enough, I know I'll hear his own count-your-blessings verdict: 'Well, that wasn't so bad, was it? When I think how it could have been – drawn-out, or abrupt and messy, or in hospital rather than here – it makes me feel lucky. A good death and a good life too: who could beat it?'

'The GP said to lay him flat.' My mother rises, icy calm, and we lift his head and remove some of the pillows from under it, straighten him on his back, pull his right leg up from its dangling position, and draw the covers up to his chest – why would anyone, except in the movies, draw them over the head, and shut out before time what will soon be unseeable forever? I'm crying quietly through this, and then leave my mother alone with him, and cry more noisily at the kitchen window. Outside is a tree-stump he left as a bird-table, with frills of white fungus growing out of its side.

I keep shooting back to see how she is, to see how he is. I feel a lifetime has passed, but the clock says seven-thirty, and here I am in the living-room, twenty, thirty minutes after his death, wading in boxes and boxes of photographs. It's something I do every Christmas, but Christmas has come a little early this year. Even now I can see it's some futile struggle to resuscitate and preserve him. His face swims up from the bendy sheens of black and white, the cardboard transparencies, the tiny sepia squares – in RAF uniform in the Azores; in his wedding suit in 1946; with a litter of twelve labrador pups, with babies, with toddlers, with his leg in plaster; being carried downstairs 'fresh' by a collection of male friends at his retirement party. There is something boyish and little in these that won't do, won't measure up. Then I find something better: a photograph of him outside our old rectory, leaning dandyishly against the side of his black Mercedes, a cigarette dangling from his right hand, his beautiful wife, fortyish then, posed beside him – an image of wealth and health and substance to set against the poverty and sickness we've lived with for the past month; an image, too, of the aspirations and affectations death has snuffed out.

There he lies, solid on his bed. I touch his skin. An hour after his death his forehead has cooled to marble already, but when I slip my hand under the covers and across his huge ribs, the chest is hot.

And it is still warm when the GP comes at nine: 'Poor Arthur, you didn't deserve this,' he says. And it is not much cooler – I know. I check – when Malcolm, the undertaker, arrives at eleven. He is fortyish, remembers me from school, is gangly in a grey suit with a Rotary Club badge on his left lapel: 'Oh dear, oh dear, Arthur,' he says and doesn't know where to put himself.

He asks for a bowl of water, and while my mother is out of the room uses a long tweezery implement to shove a piece of cotton wool into my father's open mouth, where it rests (visibly) at the back of the tongue – 'to stop any gases coming up,' he explains. My mother returns with the warm water. Malcolm takes a razor and for the next hour or so works away at my father's week-old stubble, 'just tidying him up.' I look at my mother and see that she is thinking what I am thinking – why bother with these cosmetics? Who will see him in the coffin? And even if he were to lie open for public viewing in a chapel of rest, who would mind the stubble? He might, I suppose: he was always a great one for checking whether I'd shaved. But he didn't like this sort of shaving himself – used only an electric razor – and would have resented the waste of manpower: better to have got Malcolm out doing something useful in the garden. If he'd been here, *really* been here, that's what he'd be arranging.

But my mother and I are new to all this, and yield to Malcolm's sense of etiquette. And at least it gives him something to do while he chats:

'I've done forty-eight this year – about one a week it works out. It's a sideline, the undertaking. My main business is joinery. But I don't get much call for that these days, and you've got to make ends meet. There's nothing special you want, is there? No? Fine. Of course some people want the works, you know, the whole waxworks. It's amazing what you can do these days – inject the client with formalin by sticking this tube into the neck artery, or drain the blood and urine off with an electric pump, and put caps under the eyelids to make the eyes more rounded, sleep and peace, like. I don't hold with that: making a corpse like a plum instead of a prune, it's not right. No embellishing, nothing fancy, simple and clean: that's my philosophy.'

I wait for the moment when he will nick my father's chin – do the unpumped dead bleed less profusely than the living? – but he does it all spotlessly. I help him roll my father on to his side, so he can remove the pads from under him, wash his bottom and put a fresh nappy between his legs: it's dirty work, but someone has to do it, and 'there may be more fluids,' he says. My father's body is a little stiffer now, but his back, as I hold him, is still warm, the skin red and corrugated where the sheet has wrinkled under him. 'This is why we come in fairly sharpish,' says Malcolm, 'before the rigor mortis. After twelve hours they can be very stiff and hard to move. After four or five days they go floppy again.'

My father said that he'd never wear a shroud in his coffin; and he would not have wanted to waste a good suit. So now I help dress him in a pair of fawn cotton pyjamas. Malcolm hasn't batted an eyelid yet, any more than my father has, but suddenly he seems flustered. I hold the body upright for him. He puts the right arm in the left sleeve, only realizing his mistake when he finds the pyjama buttons are underneath my father's back. We lift the body, and get the pyjamas off then on again the right way. They won't button up over the swollen stomach and zip scar, so we leave them open. There's one final cosmetic act: the chin support, a small white plastic T to keep the jaw from dropping too far open.

Once Malcolm has gone I sit with my father again and touch the little pacemaker box in his chest, sliding it about under the skin. My mother sits across from me, holding his hand. She has not cried properly yet: with each phone call – and as the day wears on there are more and more of these – her eyes water and her lips tremble, but she does not howl. Now, finally, she throws herself across him and sobs into his cold neck and chest.

5

When did you last see your father? Was it when they burnt the coffin? Put the lid on it? When he exhaled his last breath? When he last sat up and said something? When he last recognized me? When he last smiled? When he last did something for himself unaided? When he last felt healthy? When he last thought he might be healthy, before they brought the news? The weeks before he left us, or life left him, were a series of depletions; each day we thought 'he can't get less like himself than this,' and each day he did. I keep trying to find the last moment when he was still unmistakably there, in the fullness of his being, *him*.

When did you last see your father? I sit at my desk in the mortuary-cold basement of the new house, the one he helped me buy, his pacemaker in an alcove above my word processor, and the shelves of books have no more meaning than to remind me: these are the first shelves I ever put up without him. I try to write, but there is only one subject, him. I watch the news: Yugoslavia, the General Election, the royal separations – the news he didn't live to see. I've lost sight not only of his life, what it meant and added up to, but of mine. I feel as if an iron plate had come down through the middle of me, as if I were locked inside the blackness of myself. I thought that to see my father dying might remove my fear of death, and so it did. I hadn't reckoned on its making death seem preferable to life.

When did you last see your father? A friend says: 'You know it's a painting, of course. Something to do with Charles the Second, I think. It hung on the stairs in my boarding-school, the first thing you'd see each term, just what you needed when your father had dumped you like a sack of potatoes. You know the one – it's incredibly famous.' I don't know it, or if I do I've forgotten. But suddenly everybody I meet seems to allude to it, or parody the phrase: variations on it are the stuff of sitcoms or Whitehall farce. I turn up the painting shortly afterwards, a Victorian tableau of the Civil War, the Cavalier boy stand-

 ing stiffly on a stool before a table of Puritan

inquisitors – 'And When Did You Last See Your Father?'

I feel like an inquisitor myself. 'When did you last see *your* father?' I want to warn people: don't underestimate filial grief, don't think because you no longer live with your parents, have had a difficult relationship with them, are grown up and perhaps a parent yourself, don't think that will make it any easier when they die. I've become a death bore. I embarrass people at dinner parties with my morbidity. I used to think the world divided between those who have children and those who don't; now I think it divides between those who've lost a parent and those whose parents are still alive. Once I made people tell me their labour stories. Now I want to hear their death stories – the heart attacks, the car crashes, the cancers, the morgues.

The cursor pulses on the screen in front of

me. Some of my friends and contemporaries have written moving elegies for their fathers. Even when my father was in the best of health, I used to sit mooning and tearful over these poems as if they were for me, as if I'd written them myself. I wanted my father to hurry up and die so that I could join the club. I wrote an elegy for a friend of his, as preparation. I ran elegiac lines for him through my head. Now he's given me my opening, and the poems won't come.

Not that he'd mind much. He thought poetry all right in its way, so long as he didn't have to read it and I didn't suppose it a proper job. He said he couldn't understand my poems, and to me that was the ideal arrangement. I'd begun writing to escape him, to enter a world outside his control, so why would I have wanted him to get interested in my work? Perhaps the obscurity
 of some of my poems was there to keep him away

– just as, I now guiltily recognize, I put him off coming to the London newspaper offices I worked at and which he wanted to see ('It'd be nice to get an impression – how many people did you say you have under you? only two?'), and which he thought were regrettable but necessary steps towards the summit: a job in Leeds or Bradford ('just down the road from here – you could do it in fifty minutes') on the *Yorkshire Post.*

Only once, with the poetry, did I relent. It was 1985, and I'd won a prize, and invited him to the awards ceremony in County Hall. He turned up in his yellow-and-white Dormobile with stickers of the places he'd visited on the back window. It was loaded with wood he'd brought down from Yorkshire because my garden, he'd decided, was in need of some rustic fencing. In a big room overlooking the Thames, surrounded by poets, publishers, literary agents, people from the Arts

Council, he seemed small, shrunken, at a loss, a wine glass not a pint tankard in his hand. He wanted to enjoy himself, but he had a frowny, intimidated look about him, and I waited for him to make some withering remark about the company: 'Clever lot of buggers they think they are, eh?' Ken Livingstone was supposed to be there, and I knew my father had heard of *him*, but at the last minute Livingstone dropped out. Afterwards, someone asked my father what he thought of my poem, 'The Ballad of the Yorkshire Ripper', and he replied: 'The Yorkshire Ripper? Nothing very poetic about him.' He seemed to enjoy himself after that. We were supposed to go on to a meal somewhere, and he began trying to organize a large party, as if it were a midnight swim at Abersoch, everyone together, no shirkers, one big happy family. A large number of people were urged into the back of his Dormobile, between the rustic poles. I have suppressed the memory of who exactly he did give a lift to that night, but in my dreams Joseph Brodsky, Martin Amis, Craig Raine, Julian Barnes, Salman Rushdie and Dylan Thomas's daughter are driven over Westminster Bridge while my father explains that when you're putting up rustic fencing you must be sure to use six-inch zinc nails not four-inch iron.

Dreams? In truth, I don't dream of him. I dream of the vast ribcage of a bison lying on the sheet of the desert and being picked clean by vultures. I dream of blistered skin and crumbling parchment and a cyclone of paper bits, a lost masterpiece blowing about the sky. But I don't dream of him.

I tell the therapist this, as if it were a great discovery. Yes, Dad, a therapist. I know you don't approve, I know you're pretty down on analysts, male or female (and this one's female), and yes *of course* I should have shopped around and found a cheaper one, or at least should have asked this one, instead of supinely writing the cheque: 'How much for cash?' But I do have to talk to someone; I'm not going to get through this alone. Not that we hit it off together all that well, she and I. There is no couch in her room, though there are beanbags, and a baseball bat to hit them with. Myself, I don't use the baseball bat, nor scream, nor weep. I sit in a white canvas chair, the sort film directors have, and I play her back bits of my life.

She catches me smiling at critical points of my psycho-story, and this, she says, or gets me to say, is because I'm trying to distance myself ironically from my emotions. She tells me I'm a poor communicator, that I don't listen to what my body's telling me, that I give out ambivalent signals. All of this is true, and helpful – so helpful that soon, I think, I shall stop seeing her.

In July I go up to Yorkshire – the first time in seven months. The village wants to remember you, Dad. You were going to be a bench at first, but there is a bench already, for someone else. Then you were going to be a tree, but they worried that in digging the hole they'd sever gas pipes or electric cables. So you have become a sundial instead. The wind blows through the delphiniums and the roses not yet deadheaded. The rustic fencing you put up rots at its own feet. The raspberries have mildew – they're grey and ashy like a dead mouse, and dissolve in the wind.

The ashes themselves, your ashes, have been kept in a big sheeny-brown plastic jar at the bottom of the wardrobe, and we've chosen today to scatter them. I take the jar down the garden, unscrew the lid, dip my hand in and taste a few grey specks: a smoky nothingness on my tongue. You, or your coffin, or a crematorium pick 'n' mix, how can I tell? My mother and sister come, and we start to pour helpings of you among your favourite bits of the garden. We take it in turns, filling the lid of the jar with fine shale (like those upturned lids we used to fill with mouse poison and leave behind the fridge), then tossing the shale to the wind. The wind blows powder back in our faces; a speck catches in my sister's eye, her good eye; my trouser bottoms are sifted in volcanic dust. You cover the flower-bed like fine spray, every leaf variegated. We keep on scattering till the jar is tipped up for the last time. My mother hugs my sister. I walk off with the jar, which is like a giant pill-box, and hear your voice in the wind: 'Useful container that – I should hang on to it.' I stow it in the garage between the jump leads and a shrunken plastic bottle of anti-freeze.

Back in London, the therapist asks: 'How long did you say it had been now?'

'How long has what been?'

'Since the death. When did you last see your father?'

I remember the answer then. I tell her.

6

He isn't drinking, isn't eating. He wears his trousers open at the waist, held up not by a belt but by pain and swelling. He looks like death, but he is not dead, and won't be for another four weeks. He has driven down from Yorkshire to London. He has made it against the odds. He is still my father. He is still here.

'I've brought some plants for you.'

'Come and sit down first, Dad, you've been driving for hours.'

'No, best get them unloaded.'

It's like Birnam Wood coming to Dunsinane, black plastic bags and wooden boxes blooming in the back seat, the rear window, the boot: herbs, hypericum, escallonia, cotoneaster, ivies, potentillas. He directs me where to leave the different plants – which will need shade, which sun, which shelter. Like all my father's presents, they come with a pay-off – he will not leave until he has seen every one of them planted: 'I know you. And I don't want them drying up.'

We walk round the house, the expanse of rooms, so different from the old flat. 'It's wonderful to see you settled at last,' he says, and I resist telling him that I'm not settled, have never felt less settled in my life. I see his eyes taking in the little things to be done, the leaky taps, the cracked paint, the rotting window-frames.

'What's the schedule for tomorrow?' he asks, as always, and I'm irritated, as always, at his need to parcel out the weekend into a series of tasks, as if without a plan of action it wouldn't be worth his coming, not even to see his son or grandchildren. 'I don't think I'll be much help to you,' he says, 'but I'll try.' By nine-thirty he is in bed and asleep.

I wake him next day at nine, unthinkably late, with a pint-mug of tea, unthinkably refused. After his breakfast of strawberry Complan he comes round the house with me, stooped and crouching over his swollen stomach. For once it's me who is going to have to do the hammering and screwing.

I make sure there are only two light but time-consuming jobs for us. The first is to fix a curtain pole across the garden end of the kitchen, over the glazed door, and we spend the best part of two hours bickering about the best way to do this: there's a problem on the left-hand side because the kitchen cupboards finish close to the end wall, six inches or so, and you can't get an electric drill in easily to make the holes for the fixing bracket. The drill keeps sheering off, partly because I'm unnerved by him below, drawing something on the back of an envelope. I get down and he shows me his plan: a specially mounted shelf in the side wall to support the pole rather than a fixing bracket for it on the end. Sighing and cursing, I climb back up and follow his instructions in every detail – not just the size of screws and Rawlplugs needed, but how to clasp the hammer.

'Hold it at the end, you daft sod, not up near the top.'

 'Christ, Dad, I'm forty-one years old.'

'And you still don't know how to hold a hammer properly.'

Infuriatingly, his plan works – the shelf mounting, the pole, the curtain, all fine. I try not to give him the satisfaction of admitting it.

We bicker our way into the next room and the other job: to hang the chandelier inherited from Uncle Bert. At some point in the move, many of the glass pieces have become separated, and now, in the dim November light behind the tall sash-window, we spend the afternoon working out where they belong, reattaching them to the wire that joins them. 'This really needs soldering,' he says, meaning that he will find an alternative to soldering them, since to solder would mean going out and spending money on a soldering iron when he has a perfectly good one at home. I watch him bowed over the glass diamonds, with pliers and fractured screw-threads and nuts and bits of wire

– the improviser, the amateur inventor – and I think of all the jobs he's done for me down the years, and how sooner or later I'll have to learn to do them for myself.

'I think that's it,' he says, attaching a last bauble. He stands at the foot of the stepladder holding the heavy chandelier while I connect the two electrical wires to the ceiling rose, tighten the rose-cover and slip the ring-attachment over the dangling hook. He lets go tentatively – 'Gently does it' – unable to believe, since he has not done the fixing himself, that the chandelier will hold. It holds. We turn the light on, and the six candle-bulbs shimmer through the cage of glass, the prison of prisms. 'Let there be light,' my father says, the only time I can ever remember him quoting anything, though I can recall some joke he used to tell, about failed floodlights at

 Turf Moor, a visiting Chinese football team, and

the punch-line 'Many hands make light work'. We stand there gawping upwards for a moment, as if we had witnessed a miracle, or as if this were a grand ballroom, not a suburban dining-room, and the next dance, if we had the courage to take part in it, might be the beginning of a new life. Then he turns the switch off and it's dark again and he says: 'Excellent. What's the next job, then?'

PENGUIN 60s

ISABEL ALLENDE · *Voices in My Ear*
NICHOLSON BAKER · *Playing Trombone*
LINDSEY BAREHAM · *The Little Book of Big Soups*
KAREN BLIXEN · *From the Ngong Hills*
DIRK BOGARDE · *Coming of Age*
ANTHONY BURGESS · *Childhood*
ANGELA CARTER · *Lizzie Borden*
CARLOS CASTANEDA · *The Sorcerer's Ring of Power*
ELIZABETH DAVID · *Peperonata and Other Italian Dishes*
RICHARD DAWKINS · *The Pocket Watchmaker*
GERALD DURRELL · *The Pageant of Fireflies*
RICHARD ELLMANN · *The Trial of Oscar Wilde*
EPICURUS · *Letter on Happiness*
MARIANNE FAITHFULL · *Year One*
KEITH FLOYD · *Hot and Spicy Floyd*
ALEXANDER FRATER · *Where the Dawn Comes Up Like Thunder*
ESTHER FREUD · *Meeting Bilal*
JOHN KENNETH GALBRAITH · *The Culture of Contentment*
ROB GRANT AND DOUG NAYLOR · *Scenes from the Dwarf*
ROBERT GRAVES · *The Gods of Olympus*
JANE GRIGSON · *Puddings*
SOPHIE GRIGSON · *From Sophie's Table*
KATHARINE HEPBURN · *Little Me*
SUSAN HILL · *The Badness Within Him*
ALAN HOLLINGHURST · *Adventures Underground*
BARRY HUMPHRIES · *Less is More Please*
HOWARD JACOBSON · *Expulsion from Paradise*
P. D. JAMES · *The Girl Who Loved Graveyards*
STEPHEN KING · *Umney's Last Case*
LAO TZU · *Tao Te Ching*
DAVID LEAVITT · *Chips Is Here*

PENGUIN 60s

LAURIE LEE · *To War in Spain*
PATRICK LEIGH FERMOR · *Loose as the Wind*
ELMORE LEONARD · *Trouble at Rindo's Station*
DAVID LODGE · *Surprised by Summer*
BERNARD MAC LAVERTY · *The Miraculous Candidate*
SHENA MACKAY · *Cloud-Cuckoo-Land*
NORMAN MAILER · *The Dressing Room*
PETER MAYLE · *Postcards from Summer*
JAN MORRIS · *Scenes from Havian Life*
BLAKE MORRISON · *Camp Cuba*
VLADIMIR NABOKOV · *Now Remember*
REDMOND O'HANLON · *A River in Borneo*
STEVEN PINKER · *Thinking in Tongues*
CRAIG RAINE · *Private View*
CLAUDIA RODEN · *Ful Medames and Other Vegetarian Dishes*
HELGE RUBINSTEIN · *Chocolate Parfait*
SIMON SCHAMA · *The Taking of the Bastille*
WILL SELF · *The Rock of Crack As Big As the Ritz*
MARK SHAND · *Elephant Tales*
NIGEL SLATER · *30-Minute Suppers*
RICK STEIN · *Fresh from the Sea*
LYTTON STRACHEY · *Florence Nightingale*
PAUL THEROUX · *Slow Trains to Simla*
COLIN THUBRON · *Samarkand*
MARK TULLY · *Beyond Purdah*
LAURENS VAN DER POST · *Merry Christmas, Mr Lawrence*
MARGARET VISSER · *More than Meets the Eye*
GAVIN YOUNG · *Something of Samoa*

and

Thirty Obituaries from Wisden · SELECTED BY MATTHEW ENGEL

ANTHONY BURGESS

CHILDHOOD

PENGUIN BOOKS

PENGUIN BOOKS

Published by the Penguin Group. Penguin Books Ltd, 27 Wrights Lane, London W8 5TZ, England. Penguin Books USA Inc., 375 Hudson Street, New York, New York 10014, USA. Penguin Books Australia Ltd, Ringwood, Victoria, Australia. Penguin Books Canada Ltd, 10 Alcorn Avenue, Toronto, Ontario, Canada M4V 3B2. Penguin Books (NZ) Ltd, 182 – 190 Wairau Road, Auckland 10, New Zealand · Penguin Books Ltd, Registered Offices: Harmondsworth, Middlesex, England · This extract is from *Little Wilson and Big God* by Anthony Burgess, first published by William Heinemann Ltd 1987. Published in Penguin Books 1988. This edition published 1996. · Typeset by Rowland Phototypesetting Ltd, Bury St Edmunds, Suffolk. Printed in England by Clays Ltd, St Ives plc · 10 9 8 7 6 5 4 3 2 1

Wedged as we are between two eternities of idleness, there is no excuse for being idle now . . .

I was born when the war was at its grimmest, on February 25, 1917. Unrestricted submarine warfare had begun at the beginning of the month, though food rationing was not to come in until my first birthday. England was still stunned by the death of a finger-pointing icon: Lord Kitchener had been drowned on June 5, 1916, when the *Hampshire* struck a mine. The battle of the Somme, which had begun a month later, had whimpered to an end on November 13, with 420,000 British losses – a figure as hard to visualize as great wealth. But the Americans declared war on April 6, 1917, and on June 26 their first contingents arrived in France. I was not quite a month old when the Leningraders rehearsed the October Revolution. My birth thus coincided with that of the modern age – American world hegemony, the dissolution of Christendom. I yelled my Otto Rank anger at the light just as the Sunday pubs were opening. A child of the Fishes, I was thirsty as a fish: the lactal ducts could never refill fast enough.

February 25 is the feast day of saints and martyrs not much regarded – Victorinus and his companions, Caesarius of Nazianzus, the virgin Walburga, the bishops Tarasius and Gerland, Ethelbert of Kent. In 1601 it was an Ash Wednesday and the day of the execution of the Earl of Essex – one of those historical dates I can never forget. It is the birthday of musicians – Caruso, Myra Hess, of the impressionist painter Pierre Renoir, above all of the dramatist Carlo Goldoni, with whom I have always felt a faint affinity. The day before is the birthday of George Moore and of Arnold Dolmetsch, the day before that of George Frederick Handel. The day after honours Victor Hugo, Honoré Daumier, and Buffalo Bill. How much truth there is in astrology I do not know, but the first fortnight of Pisces certainly presides over arts to which I was attracted about equally in my youth. I spent too long deciding which art to follow – music, writing, drawing, the popular stage. It was not until I was thirty-seven that I became a writer. Certainly I had to be an artist of some kind or other. My father breathed beer on me and said: 'He may be a new Napoleon.' Not Wellington. The Catholic North-West, like Ireland, had looked to the French being on the sea, and the decay of the Orange.

One's first memories are often vicarious: one is told that one did something or was involved in something; one dramatizes it and folds the image falsely into the annals of the truly remembered. So, less than two years old, I am sitting on a shoulder in Manchester's Piccadilly while a flag-waving crowd cheers the Armistice. Then the lights go out. In early

1919 my father, not yet demobilized, came on one of his regular, probably irregular, furloughs to Carisbrook Street to find both my mother and sister dead. The Spanish influenza pandemic had struck Harpurhey. There was no doubt of the existence of a God: only the supreme being could contrive so brilliant an afterpiece to four years of unprecedented suffering and devastation. I, apparently, was chuckling in my cot while my mother and sister lay dead on a bed in the same room. I should not have been chuckling; I should have been howling for food; perhaps the visiting neighbour who had herself just been stricken had provided me with a bottle of Glaxo. My father's attitude to his son must now have become too complicated for articulation. It would have been neater if all three in that room had been obliterated. When I was old enough to appreciate his mingled resentment and factitious gratitude at my survival, I was able to understand his qualified affection, his lack of interest in any future I might have, the ill-considered second marriage which was a way of getting me off his hands.

Of my sister Muriel he passed on no memories. My mother survived briefly in vague reminiscences of the Manchester music hall – a voice that could ride over a restive audience, the shining abundant hair, the neat ankles. When she herself became part of an audience she was a comedian's gift: her laugh was loud and primed general laughter. As a housewife she had no further duty to the lissom shape that had been her professional pride. She took to Guinness and boiled puddings. It would be easier to recreate her in fiction, relating her to Molly Bloom and Rosie Driffield, than to wrestle with a virtually non-existent reality. It is difficult to know how far we have an obligation to the dead. I sometimes resent my father's failure to introduce me even to her insubstantial after-image, but he spoke little of her. She joined the great boneyard of the war and its aftermath. My father went back to Swift's Beef Market, bought a straw hat, took heavily to draught Bass, and waited for the cleansing 1920s.

I come to full consciousness in a terraced house on Delauneys Road, Higher Crumpsall, in the care of my mother's sister, Ann Bromley. She was a war widow with two daughters, Elsie and Betty. Opposite the house was a great infirmary where, I learned, people were cut open. This gratuitous slashing and slitting seemed reasonable to me, who must have absorbed by osmosis the ethos of the times. My father was a lodger, visible mainly on Friday evenings, when he brought home a prime joint from the beef market. For the rest of the time he drank or tried to cut down on his drinking by playing the piano in one of the local cinemas. He then combined both diversions by becoming the regular pianist at the Golden Eagle, a huge pub on Lodge Street, Miles Platting. There he met his second wife, who was the widowed landlady. In 1922 I was told that she was my new mother. Before then I called my aunt mother.

There is no magic in the word: it is the name a child will happily give to any woman who looks after him. It did not follow that Elsie and Betty were my sisters. I hear myself calling at the age of three and a half, with a Lancashire vowel: 'Mother, mother – there's a donkey on the road.' A workman had knocked on the door asking for hot water for his tea can. He said: 'You're a big baby, shouting for your mother because you see a donkey.' I did not know what he meant – fear of the donkey, wonder at it? How, anyway, did I know it was a donkey? Across the road, behind that gaunt façade of many windows, the cutting up of living bodies was calmly proceeding.

I slept alone in a cold room with one picture on the wall. It was of a gipsy woman looking balefully and pointing a finger. I was told that the legend beneath it was 'Beware'. When I thought I was asleep the picture would open on loud hinges and disclose the world of cutting up live but uncomplaining bodies. It was lighted by fire. I was given the choice of joining the bodies or else remaining where I was, in the big lumpy flock bed which was steadily filling with horse shit and turning into Delauneys Road. The turds were turning into aromatic serpents with teeth. I would scream and scream, and my aunt would come in her night-dress to see what the trouble was. The trouble was the picture, but it was not removed. I was never taken into her bed. After so much public horror, what was a mere child's nightmare?

The house was damp and looked out on a damp back garden which was full of slugs and, I feared, snakes. I was shown a picture of Christ being laid in his tomb. I asked what was happening. A male voice said: 'They're going on a journey.' It must have been the voice of a local boy named Stevie, who sometimes had dinner with us. Among the peas on his plate was a black one. He impaled it on his fork and said: 'My name is Stevie Blackpea.' Blackpea had to be some relation of Blackpool, where I must sometime have been taken. I can remember only a railway compartment with a black pool outside it: etymology was drawing me slowly to a life of words. I had new dreams in which Christ was laid in a black snaky pool in the back garden. I did not know that he was Christ. He was merely a man inexplicably naked. Nakedness had something to do with going on a journey.

There was a piano in the front room, as there seemed to be in all the front rooms of that period, but I never heard my father play it. Elsie did. There was a volume of popular songs that must have been called the *Star Folio*, for there was a star on the cover and a couple dancing. I would take the cat on my knee and sing to it – a rigmarole about dancing on a star. I hear the vowel in 'dancing': the short front one of Manchester. I draw the external world into senseless recitatives: couch dance star cat fire dinner. One Friday my father brought with the weekend joint a large new cash book and a thick-leaded pencil. I began to transfer the external world to its pages in vigorous pictograms. It became a matter of urgency, like going to the lavatory. I saw in some newspaper a heart transfixed by a dart. I had to rush to the cash book and scribble it in before it disappeared.

This early life of fragments has little meaning. There is murk with occasional dull flashes of things and people. It is the lack of continuity that disconcerts, as though one were perpetually dying and being reborn to trivialities. My life as yet had no religion in it. My aunt and cousins were Protestant but did not go to church. My father had probably lost his faith. All his life long he said: 'When you're dead you're finished with.' Nobody taught me how to pray. I do not remember visits from the other Wilsons, who had nothing to mourn and retained a certain devoutness. In 1921 I was taken prematurely to school by little girls who lived two or three doors down. One Friday afternoon I, or they, showed up late. I knew it was Friday, because we had had shop fish and chips for the midday meal, which we called dinner. 'Why are you late, Jack Wilson?' the teacher asked. 'Too many chips,' I said, wondering why I said it. Then we were set to draw a teacup, and the teacher emphasized the slight tapering of its shape. One boy, with modish logicality, drew a perfect inverted cone. I crayoned a multicoloured jack-in-the-box. I think it was a Protestant school, because I half-remember hearing a Protestant hymn sung as the winter twilight settled down. It began 'Herb, hide with me.' Childish religion was full of shadowy characters like Herb. God was Harold on both sides of the fence. His brother Will was cooked till done.

But as yet I had no need of God. My night-time world was terrifying enough without him. Snakes persisted. I remember a dream which may be a distortion of a memory of seeing a film with Mary Pickford in it: she, the young girl, sat on the knee of an old man in a white suit and hat in a garden. They looked calmly at a writhing mass of monsters which prefigured the pythons and hamadryads I was to know in Malaysia. They were all dead white. Where did they come from? I had not at that time been taken to the Belle Vue Zoo. My snakes may have been the Kundalini serpents of the collective unconscious – forms of white female flesh which lived in the base of the spine, already sexual, ready to be transformed into the *prana* or inner life force. They related to bleached dog turds on the road. They were garden worms terrifyingly magnified. A healthy human bowel movement, so I was later to be told in the Royal Army Medical Corps, went 'twice round the pan and was curly at both ends'. The snake as vitalized faeces is still a frightening presence of my dreams. Sometimes I dream that Sigmund Freud and Carl Jung are together, looking at my snakes and coming to no conclusion about them. They have no resemblance to real snakes, which I have found to be graceful, warm, and intelligent. They disappeared from my dreams in Delauneys Road when, after a bout of night hysteria, the picture of the gipsy was removed from my room by my father. But they came back later.

8 Nineteen twenty-two was a key year in modern literature.

It saw the publication of *The Waste Land* and *Ulysses* – a denial of life and a celebration of it. I got out of the waste land of my aunt-mother's house into the vital labyrinth of a huge pub. Nineteen twenty-two was the year of my father's marriage into the Dwyer family. The Dwyers were successful immigrants from Dublin. There was no Irish brogue left in them, and their speech was pure Manchester. The troubles of their native country – the heavy fighting in the capital, with the blowing up of the Four Courts, which followed on the setting up of the Irish Free State in 1921 – aroused little interest. One of the Dwyer women who had stayed behind cursed the curse of Cromwell on the Black and Tans but ended up marrying one of them. Other Dwyers crossed the water later on odd visits, with Irish Sweepstake tickets for illegal sale tucked in their bloomers. The Manchester Dwyers were adoptive Mancunians, though very Catholic in the Irish manner. The greatest member of the family is George Patrick Dwyer, who was to become Bishop of Leeds and then Archbishop of Birmingham. It was he who, in a television discussion, cured Malcolm Muggeridge of his atheism and initiated his long climb to sanctity. When George was installed as archbishop, the novelist Olivia Manning said to me: 'John, I did not realize you were so well connected.' When I told her that Birmingham was merely a Catholic archdiocese, she said: 'Oh, that explains it then.' The economic substructure of the Dwyer passion for turning sons and daughters into bishops and mother superiors was a flourishing greengrocery and poultry business. There was, however, a George Dwyer who went to Australia and became a millionaire. He was involved in sexual irregularities scandalous in a great Catholic family. His son Dan became aide-de-camp to General Blamey.

The woman my father married had herself married into the Dwyers and became one of them. She had been Maggie Byrne, again Manchester Irish, and her husband, Dan Dwyer, had been landlord of the Golden Eagle. She took over the licence when he died – not in the war and not of influenza. She had two grown daughters, Agnes and Madge, of exceptional beauty, though she herself had run to fat in the acceptable mode of pub landladies and suffered from spectacular pains in the feet and back. She was not, in other words, an attractive woman. She was also virtually illiterate and drew her name on a cheque as though from a memory of Egyptian hieroglyphics. Her marrying a Wilson entailed long instruction in the carving of new signs. She needed the strong arm of a husband, whom she called a 'usbint, in the management of a large and rowdy pub in a slum neighbourhood, but the licence was hers, and hers the name in the legal legend over the front door. She was to be boss. My father, once the wedding was over, was bold in rejecting the inferior status proposed and revealed that he had not resigned from Swift's Beef Market. I saw him now even less

 than previously, and my seclusion in a remote corridor of

the labyrinth was perhaps what he sought. He played the piano in the huge music saloon in the evenings, accompanying performers like Tim Carlisle, whose sister Elsie became a famous radio crooner with Ambrose's band. I, as a minor, was not allowed in there, and I was always asleep when the pub closed.

The Golden Eagle of Miles Platting was well known, a boozer of Victorian amplitude, gleaming with brass. The brass sign with its spread wings on the façade was much coveted by local Protestant clergymen. There were three singing rooms, a vast spit-and-sawdust, and a number of snugs. The beer came from the Cornbrook Brewery, which owned the premises and rendered the title landlord or landlady a misnomer. An era of limited drinking hours had been initiated by the Defence of the Realm Act, represented in newspaper cartoons as Dora, a repressive dragon of a female in black, but before the war the pub had opened at six in the morning and did not shut until eleven at night. Workmen came in early for rum and coffee; some came in early and stayed till closing-time. One man died on the premises of delirium tremens, after several days of seeing snakes and Germans leering from the ceiling. There was a legend that an American soldier, not yet demobbed, had come in to boast: 'Waal, I guess and calculate your lil asshole of a country had to call on us to fight your goddam war for you,' and been stabbed to death, his body, by common consent, being deposited in the middle of the night in the middle of

Queen's Road. There was a fearsome character known as Nancy Dickybird, whose violent approach was signalled by runners – 'Nancy's coming.' The main bar would clear on her entrance, and my stepmother would greet her with a truncheon and knuckledusters. There was an extensive armoury available for defence, including two army revolvers complete with ammunition. Nancy would sail into an ecstasy of foulness, urinate on the floor, and then leave.

Lodge Street was a tough street in a tough area. I had moved a short way south from my birthplace to the northern segment of Miles Platting, with Collyhurst to the west, but the Queen's Road where my mother had shopped was the tram-clanging artery which fed all these districts. I was in an ugly world with ramshackle houses and foul back alleys, not a tree or a flower to be seen, though Queen's Park and a general cemetery were available to the north-west if a breath of green was required. If the beer-intake of an urban area is an index of its prosperity, then Miles Platting was not badly off, but heavy patronage of the Golden Eagle often meant neglect of domestic responsibilities. A husband came into the public bar one evening in need of his pint. He was shaken. His wife, dead out from a debauch with her cronies, had left the bathing of the children to him. He conscientiously sluiced them all in a tin tub, dressed them for bed, then asked one girl: 'Where's your nightdress, love?' The girl said: 'I don't live here.' It was a district where the women did most of the fighting, usually because of suspected or discovered adultery. For a small transgression, it was enough to smash the delinquent's downstairs windows with a house key. But in bar or street or alley there could be hair-tearing and even breast-slashing. Children played barefoot not because they had no shoes but because they had grown out of them.

The old Lancashire mythology of clogs and shawls and morning knocker-up was to be looked for now more in towns like Rochdale than in Manchester districts like Miles Platting. The clatter of clogs was infrequent, but black shawls were plentiful. My stepmother and stepsisters put them on when they went shopping. The knocker-up was dying out because of the advent of cheap alarm-clocks. My Uncle Billy had once taunted an old woman knocker-up with her long pole that could tap at upper windows: 'Hallo, missis, art going fishing?' He was chased and swiped with 'I'll give you fishing, you young bugger.' It was he who had given the lying excuse for being late for work one summer morning: 'I slept with my pillow on the window sill. Knocker-up knocked pillow and I couldn't hear.'

I was brought to the Golden Eagle without warning of what was in store for me. There was no attempt to prepare me for a change of ménage. I was brought into the pub by my father between three o'clock closing and five-thirty reopening, trod sawdust and tried to take in brass beer engines and swabbing barmen, then toddled left down a corridor to a bright kitchen-living-room where the three females of my new life were waiting for me. They had not seen me before. I wanted my mother. 'This is your mother now, love, and these are your sisters. Her you called your mother is now your Auntie Annie.' I was thin, small, pale, undernourished. Annie, my new mother said, had done her best but it hadn't been good enough. As an earnest of a more nutritious regime she handed me a fairy cake. I knocked it out of her hand. The younger daughter, Madge, said, without rancour: 'You'll be buried with your hand sticking up out of the grave, and everybody that passes by will hit it and say: There lies the boy that knocked a fairy cake out of his mother's hand.' My stepmother should have swiped me but did not. She was pretty tolerant. The introduction of a snivelling lad into her household meant a new gratuitous responsibility, and she had a pub to run. I was to sleep in the little downstairs room of Harry the chief and resident barman, on a little trucklebed. Shortly afterwards a proper child's bed was bought for me, and it was placed in the corner of the master bedroom where my father and his new wife slept. I have no recollection of waking up to amorous noises.

I remember going to bed in the summer light, unable to sleep because of the downstairs racket. I wandered that upper floor, which, corresponding to the ground-floor drinking palace, was vast and had a huge drawing-room with eight windows looking down on Lodge Street and one of its slummy tributaries. I would go into all the bedrooms and micturate in all the chamberpots. I would return to the drawing-room and try to leave some residuary golden drops on the carpet. Then I would bang the piano. Nobody heard. Down below three pianos thumped and tinkled simultaneously, like something by Charles Ives. Across the road from the window by my bed a gramophone played 'Margie' or 'The Holy City'. I looked out of another window, which dominated an outdoor women's lavatory and its yard. One black-shawled crone said to another. 'He sent me this letter, the false bastard.' And she showed it before taking it into the closet to befoul.

My stepmother, whatever else she was, was a good plain cook, skilled at mutton stews, meat and potato pies, classical hotpots, fruit tarts, nutmeggy custards. My fattening began with butties spread with home-made damson jam. Breakfast was bacon and a fried egg, with bacon fat poured all over the plate: this was for the dipping of bread and was called dip. I ate but was perpetually angry. I expressed my anger in drawings of my stepmother wearing a chef's toque, beating a pudding batter, and displaying male genitals. These were the only genitals I knew about, and I always scrawled the penis as an icon of foul insult. I lacked the comforting contact of female flesh, and when I was offered it by my stepsisters I was unwilling to accept it. I would be called into their bedroom in the morning while they were dressing and told to give them 'a kiss and a love', but I was shy of touching their exposed arms and backs. They noted the shyness and giggled at it. They were well-shaped girls with fine Irish creamy flesh, a year or so between them, in their very early twenties. Agnes was coal-haired and showed the blood of a wrecked Armada; Madge was prettily mousy. They were pure and deeply Catholic. They took me to mass, which was boring and incomprehensible, but the Gregorian line of a priest (the mass must have been high and sung) stuck in my head: '*Per omnia saecula saeculorum.*' A queer kind of English, a sort of code, the *orum* dangerous magic.

I was a fidgety child, and, as a revenge for my transplanting, fidgeted odd coins off the kitchen dresser into my pockets. I see myself, fidgety, being told to lie still on the kitchen sofa, the pub cat in my arms, while the two-minute silence of November 11, 1922 was observed. If I moved, I was told, the war would start again. I did not know what the war was, but one-legged drinkers in the public bar, men coughing their lungs up, black boozing widows were the war. War was a word like 'runcible' or a termination like *orum.* In November my stepmother started mixing her Christmas puddings. In December the greengrocer-poulterer Dwyers arrived with the colossal turkey. On Christmas Day, when the licensing hours imitated Sunday, the pub closed at two and Christmas dinner was eaten at three. The turkey stuffing was herbs and pork sausage meat. No Dwyers came for Christmas, nor any Byrnes. My stepmother and her brother had quarrelled, as always happens in families, over a family will. The Dwyers kept their own green Christmas over the greengrocer's shop, laden with all the unsold holly and mistletoe, but the Wilsons were welcome at the Golden Eagle. My stepmother approved of my two uncles – the master plumber Jack, who looked like Stanley Baldwin, the common plumber Jimmy, who looked like James Maxton and whose wife Lily, my apparent godmother, she considered a shiftless slut.

My grandfather was dead by 1922, and my grandmother kept to her bed in a rented house with an imported pair of Finnegan girls to look after her. My father had taken me to visit her by tram – a clean, smiling old Irish lady sitting up in a lace mobcap – and I had begun to learn to read on the outward and homeward journeys, my primer my father's packet of Three Castles with its citation from Thackeray's *The Virginians*: 'There's no sweeter tobacco than comes from Virginia, and no finer brand than the Three Castles.' I was seeing more of my father now. He had even lifted me from sleep to be shown to some visitors in that huge drawing-room. I remember crying: 'Bugger off, you buggers,' at the same time wondering where I had learned the word and its double usage. It came from nowhere, like the chef's toque and the genital obscenity.

The visiting Wilsons were two families. My Uncle Jack and Aunt Nell spoke grammatical Lancashire English, as befitted a master plumber and his wife, and their two daughters, Joan and Winifred (who was later to sign her name Wynné), were to be taught the piano. My Uncle Jimmy and

Aunt Lily had the one daughter, named for my dead sister Muriel. She was to become a dancer with stage hopes, but she declined into being a hostess in a night club run by a former boxer. The Wilsons were revealed as a fair-haired family, except for Uncle Jimmy, who had picked up a Spanish swarthiness and Eskimo straight hair. My father and Uncle Jack were gingerish. My cousins were pale of eyelash and had translucent skins. I was to favour my Uncle Jimmy in a modified form – hair curly and dark brown, near-invisible eyebrows a half-hearted tribute to the family fairness. The family nose was assertive. '*Il est juif, sans doute*,' a French lady said of me in 1939, in a Luxembourg night club full of visiting Nazis.

These Christmas parties, beginning in the Golden Eagle, continued in the later locales to which we moved. After the afternoon torpor there was the powerful tea of my stepmother and rich iced volcanic-earth-coloured uneatable Christmas cake. The real festivities began after ten at night, when my cousins and myself were dropped food-drugged and bloated into the one double bed. There was a supper of cold turkey and ham and tongue with piccalilli, sherry trifle, charlotte russe, mince pies, the sullen reappearance of the Christmas cake, Moët et Chandon champagne. Then in the great drawing-room three pianists accompanied songs in turn – my father, my Aunt Nell, my stepsister Madge. The songs were 'Finnegan's Ball', 'Here's Another One Off To America', 'Coronation Day' (the correct version, not

Buck Mulligan's), 'Pale Hands I Loved', 'Because', 'Dear Little Shamrock', numbers from *Little Nelly Kelly*, 'Ma, He's Making Eyes At Me', 'Avalon', 'Yes, We Have No Bananas'. When my cousins and I had grown, and another pair of cousins had been added to the master plumber's ménage, we too participated, and I sang 'The Golden Vanity' with, for some reason, my trousers falling down. Trousers were called kex, which properly means the dry hollow stalk of umbellifers like cow parsnip and wild chervil.

Clad in new short kex, I was taken to school in 1923, to St Edmund's RC Elementary at the corner of Monsall Road and Upper Monsall Street. I was still weak and unmuscular through having no proper mother, though I was no longer undernourished. In the school hall, Miss Sullivan, the headmistress, a dried spinster of ferocious irritability now rarely seen in schools, ordered us to crawl in a phalanx like little mice, and I see myself still as a lone mouse laggard, all the others well ahead. There were, till the tropics ruined them, photographs of me at six, one of them as a melancholy pierrot, and the pallor under the straight fringe, the deficient vitality, the rejection of the external world were striking and terrible. But I could read fluently, apparently without much teaching. Miss O'Flaherty wrote THE CAT SAT ON THE MAT on the blackboard, and I was the only one in the class able to rattle it off, though, through a kind of surrealist perverseness more than ignorance, I transposed the nouns. Miss O' Flaherty had a short way with chatterers. She would make them stand in front of the class and paste over their mouths, using gloy from the conical gloypot, a neatly scissored strip of coloured paper. One boy, a sufferer from adenoid growths ('Dodt do it, biss, I cadt breathe') screamed at the prospect and fainted. Another boy, tall and with a courtly manner, accepted the punishment philosophically. When Miss O'Flaherty was not looking, he doffed the gag, smiled and bowed, then replaced it. It was better than the strap from Miss Sullivan.

I was now taught some Catholicism, which chiefly had to do with eternal punishment for trivial offences. We were told that each of us had a guardian angel, an invisible monitor even in the lavatory, and we sang a song to him or her or it:

Guardian angel, from heaven so bright,
Watching beside me to keep me aright,
Fold thy wings round me and guard me with love,
Softly sing songs to me of heav'n above.
Beautiful angel, so tender and mild,
Lovingly guard me, for I am thy child.

It was a harmless and charming fiction; it still is. But the Manichee in us all, even at the age of six, had to assume that there was another angel, a very bad one, hitting out at the pale epicene from heaven, and, since fighting was a sin, winning most of the rounds. One of our teachers, more Butlerian than was right for a Catholic, assured us that sins like nose-picking and incontinence of the bladder were really a disease that merited our being carted off to Monsall Isolation Hospital, which was just across the road. Presumably people were cut up there in isolation. I was sent there eventually, but it was for scarlet fever.

To be a Catholic meant primarily belonging to a minority faction which was despised by the scholars of St Augustine's C of E Elementary School, on the other side of Monsall Street. I was taught by my fellows to call them proddy dogs in response to their jeer of cat licks. The opposed canticles of abuse are still going strong in Northern Ireland.

> Cat lick, cat lick, going to mass,
> Riding to hell on the devil's ass

was answered by

> Proddy dog, proddy dog on the wall,
> A small raw spud will feed you all.
> A ha'penny candle will give you light
> To read the Bible of a Sunday night.

I did not know what the Bible was, but evidently it was a dirty book. It was confirmed for me later that not only was it dirty, it was dangerous. It was the prime cause of people losing their Catholic faith. This is, historically speaking, a sound enough judgement. There was perturbation at my secondary school when the Book of Job was a set book for the Higher School Certificate examination. My English teacher, a Xaverian brother who had not read it before, conceded that the style was sound even if the theology was shaky. Anyway, the Bible was mostly a foul book that had produced proddy dogs.

Across the street from the Golden Eagle was a little shop run by the Misses Hogan, a couple of witches in dusty black. After two days of constipation I was sent across there with a teacup to buy two pennyworth of California syrup of figs. This, the most saccharine thing, outside the films of Mary Pickford, that California ever produced, did not act at once but when it did act it acted relentlessly. I was taken short in afternoon school and bewrayed my kex shamefully. In the whole of a man's life there is no worse humiliation than the dropping of that heavy load clothed. I had to run home, accompanied by two girls, and was given by Madge for some reason a lace doily for the tersive act. I was in a deep pit of shame, but my schoolfellows, when I went back next morning in fresh kex digesting a hardboiled egg, did not point the finger. It was the sort of thing that might happen to anyone, like being bust. 'You see that lad over there? Well, he's bust.' This meant that in the playground the one remaining button at the back of his kex had snapped off. One lad to whom it happened said: 'Told my bloody mother to sew the bloody thing on proper and she didn't bloody listen. Now my bloody kex is coming bloody down. Have to walk bloody home with my bloody hands in my bloody pockets, bloody it. And there goes the blooming bell.'

There were certain school clowns who, for a halfpenny

fee, would guarantee to make you laugh. One boy had a continuing saga about a man with a dog called Bugger. The two were always travelling by rail. The guard would shout 'All change for Oldham,' and the man would say: 'Come on, Bugger, we're on the wrong train again.' On the way home from school, one little girl pointed me out to her friend as a boy that could make you laugh. I obliged with funny faces and no fee charged. The faces were funny only in the sense that they were the objective correlative of an exercise of the risor muscles. Nature was telling these children to laugh, and it would have been madness to laugh at nothing. There is nothing intrinsically funny in anything – certainly not in a man whose dog was named Bugger. One regular comedian of St Edmund's would exchange humour for cigarette cards, but he had to be given the cards first. The cards were his comic property. He would hold them up to the sun and say: 'You see them? Them's shit, them is. Ta-ta.' And he would amble off, his act finished, occasionally turning round with his tongue lolling as we collapsed in dutiful mirth. The performance was highly popular. Young learners about sex are told nowadays that an orgasm is a kind of sneeze. Laughter is the same kind of shocked release but it is less apocalyptical and, to most children, pleasurably controllable, like the action of the rectal sphincter. When I published my first novel, I was surprised to be told it was comic. Those two little girls were making a proleptic judgement on my career.

At the age of six a social function was imposed upon me that had everything to do with entertainment, though not necessarily of the comic kind. On Queen's Road there were two cinemas – the Rex and the Electric. They faced each other, like the Globe and the Rose playhouses on the Elizabethan South Bank, but not in true rivalry. Going to one on a Monday and Thursday (the day the programme changed) did not prevent your going to the other on a Tuesday and Friday, if you could afford it. The cinemagoer's criteria had more to do with hygiene than with the quality of the entertainment offered. The Rex was called a bughouse and the Electric not. The Electric used a superior disinfectant like a grudging perfume; the Rex smelt of its patrons and its lavatories. With the Rex, it was said, you went in in a blouse and came out with a jumper. So it was to the Electric that the children of Lodge Street went, clutching their pennies, on a Saturday afternoon. Because I lived at the Golden Eagle I was called Jackie Eagle, and ten or twelve boys would, after midday dinner, cry out for Jackie Eagle from the verge of the public bar the law forbade them to enter. They would hold on to me in their redolent jerseys all the way down Lodge Street and left and over on Queen's Road. I was the only one of them who could read.

The manager of the Electric did not wish too many even of his front rows to be defiled by children, and so we were jammed three to a seat, with a gaping black auditorium behind us clean for the evening's two houses. So I began a lifetime's devotion to the cinema, a one-sided love affair in which I was more bruised than caressed. In those old silent days the art was almost an aspect of literature. I heard my little treble voice crying the text aloud for the benefit of even big louts whom the reading mystery had passed by. 'Kiss me, my fool,' mouths the Spanish gipsy siren, and the caballero who proposed knifing her trembles so that his knife silently clatters to the floor. 'Came the dawn,' a regular cliché. We saw Rudolph Valentino in *The Sheik* and Ben Turpin in *The Shriek*. There was *The Four Horsemen of the Apocalypse* ('What's that mean, kid?'), with artistic camera-masks that varied the shape of the frame. There was a Chester Conklin comedy which began with lovers kissing on a doorstep. 'The end,' the legend said. There were roars of kids cheated. 'Of a perfect day.' That was all right, then, but the humour was too adult for relief: the buggers were clearly not to be trusted. There was one frightful shock for me. A character with dirty beard and gabardine spoke, and then the black screen filled with unintelligible letters. I know now it was Hebrew; I even remember a beth and a ghimel. To my illiterates it was all one, and there was bafflement and then anger at my failure to twang it off. 'Thought you said the bugger could read.' So I improvised a flight of suitable invective. No piano played in the pit: we were too cheap for music.

At Christmas 1923 my stepsisters took me to the pantomime at the Palace Theatre on Oxford Street in the heart of the city. It was *Dick Whittington* and Dorothy Ward was the principal boy. She sang 'Nothing Could Be Finer Than To Be In Carolina In The Mor–or–orning'. This was theatre, this was the real thing. The auditorium smelt of cigars and rustled with chocolate boxes. Dick and his cat soared over us in a balloon. When I got back to the family kitchen I was hysterical with wonder at the size of the proscenium arch. 'It stretched from there to there,' and I ran with trembling pointing arm from one end of the kitchen to the other. The mensuration was sound in a relative way: one kind of architectural extension was the figure of another. Dorothy Ward's song summed up the magic and still does. Where was Carolina? In America, like California. Where is America? Never mind. Carolina must have been better than California: it exported no bewraying syrup of figs. When I first went to Chapel Hill in North Carolina I found I remembered every word of the song and could even play it on the piano. 'If I had Aladdin's lamp for only a day, I'd make a wish, and here's what I'd say: Nothing could be finer than . . .'

The years become confused, obedient to Proust or Ford Madox Ford. Real time emerges with a vague chronology. I could not have been sitting in the front porch of the Golden Eagle in the enchanted days after seeing *Dick Whittington*, trying to draw a stage on a panel of a shoebox. ('What's that you're drawing, kid?' – 'A pantomime.' – 'You're bloody daft.') It must have been in the spring of

1924. But I get up from my work and toddle to the kitchen, where the women are discussing the scandal of Fatty Arbuckle, a muffled news item of 1923, which gave California a worse name than syrup of figs, or the wedding of the Duke and Duchess of York, which, as the Queen Mother will confirm, took place on April 26 of that year. I can recall no procession of the seasons, which Lodge Street could not manifest through flowery spring or russet autumn. I can remember no rain, and rain, according to the outsider's myth of Manchester, is the one thing I ought to remember. I seem to have spent a lot of time sitting in fine weather in the porch of the Golden Eagle, drawing or else playing with the sixpenny toys I could buy at the Misses Hogan's – metal fishes to be fished for with a magnetic rod, a fragile earthbound Sopwith Camel. Also reading.

The reading must have reached a fair stage of efficacy before the Saturday processions to the Electric. I had a weekly paper for children called *Chick's Own*, with Rupert the Chick as the front-page hero. This came out on Mondays. Madge said that *Tiger Tim's Weekly*, out on Thursdays, was a nice paper too, and it sounded sympathetic. I was called a weakly child, and it was comforting to think of a tiger brought down to my level. I read the balloons in the cartoons about anthropomorphic animals, and assumed that the print récit under the coloured pictures would be beyond me. But it was not: I was merely lazy. Words were helpfully split with hyphens into their constituent morphemes. There was always a full-page story that did not so condescend. This I found I could read too. 'Let us give this poor dog some of our hot soup.' 'Soup' I read as 'soap', not unreasonably, since that is how it is rendered in what Henry Higgins calls Broad Romic. The notion of comforting with hot soap was not unpleasant. Soap was at least wholesome – the whole of Miles Platting, said my stepmother, could do with more of it – and might be palatable hot.

The wicked press barons who put out these twopenny rations of kidfeed had sensible editors. The child's ideal companion would be a rational animal with his own weaknesses. Animals will take love without demanding it; they have teeth, but they will not bite with the vindictiveness of human adults. They are free and indifferent, but they will go into spasms of affection with a discontinuity the child understands. They demand no covenant and do not know the meaning of obligation. Dress them in jerseys and kex, give them a minimal vocabulary but no expressiveness in their masks, save the query marks of an occasional smile of triumph at some naughtiness, and they earn love without mawkishness. I look back at that anonymous sub-art with a genuine gratitude. I saw no implausibility in Porkyboy's eating sausages for Christmas breakfast or Tiger Tim making a stew out of bread and cheese. The gentle way out of the animal world into the human was through Marzipan the Magician, with his candy-striped wand, and the gnome

Bushybeard. Stories about human adults would have been frightening, for human adults were irrational, gross, demanding. They also rejected magic, whose power had been confirmed by the child's distortion of religion. Certain features in both of my weaklies or weeklies encouraged, like a gentle laxative, activities which would have been too costively painful in school. You became numerate through linking digits with a pencil and ending with an angular cartoon sketch. You could paste a torso and sundered limbs on a piece of card, scissor them out and assemble them with paper fasteners, so that you had a flat marionette that could walk and gesture. These publications had an acceptable moral content. Naughtiness was behovely, but all would be well.

Incoming and outgoing customers must have noted something unhealthy in this thin-legged child drawing on ragged card or gaping over *Chick's Own.* I should have been throwing stones or kicking an old tennis ball about Lodge Street with its tougher urchins, or slopping in bare feet through the mud and horse-merds. Occasionally, to oblige, I would take off my shoes and half-heartedly slop, only to have my shoes stolen. That was naughty. My stepmother would take time off from the beer pumps to clout me. I would cry and be called, as D. H. Lawrence had been called, mardarse. The clouting would then be just enough, but there was a double clouting that was not. There was a hired girl named Bertha, who turned out to be mad. She came down the stairs that led from the private quarters to the sawdust concourse that was the public bar. It was a noble staircase, and she descended with the grace of a Tolstoy princess. But she was stark naked. She had to be taken back to her parents in Collyhurst. Clothed, of course. Before then she had played on me a trick of curious malice. Every Monday we children had to take to school a coin in an envelope, a contribution to an African mission for dragging black infants to the light. I took my wrapped penny, but it turned out to be a penny-sized watch crystal. I was clouted in class and then clouted when I took home a written complaint. Bertha eventually admitted with glee that she had been responsible for the pointless substitution, but by then it was too late. The great truth of the world's injustice had been established for me.

A strange collective naughtiness came over a group of us when we were going back to school one day after the dinner break. A ragged man appeared from an alley, which was called also an entry or a ginnel, with a battered straw hat set rakishly. He danced and played a tin whistle. He was a pied piper whom we had to follow. He also sang the songs of the day – 'Margie' and 'I'm Forever Blowing Bubbles'. We joined in, we capered, we followed him from street to street. Then he doffed his cady in farewell and disappeared down another entry. We were very late for school, but, because the piper was an undoubted adult, we had felt him

 somehow to be a representative of the establishment that

regulated our education, a kind of demented school inspector. We were not walloped by Miss Sullivan: there were too many of us. There was also a sinister magic in the occasion which she must have recognized. There was a mystery to be considered: the cane did not meet the case.

My joining a group of peers, delinquent or not, was a rarity. I was grasped eagerly, even desperately, on Saturday afternoons, when the eccentricity of my being able to read was a blessing, but for the rest of the time I was either distractedly persecuted or ignored. On Saturday mornings I would stroll like a clubman down Lodge Street, turn right on Queen's Road and go into an ice cream parlour that served a penny vanilla ice in a glass dish. I was cut off from the halfpenny wafer-lickers. I was Jackie Eagle, who partook of the glory of the polished brass effigy with its spread pinions, of the wet wealth within. I was also one despised, mardarse.

In 1924 there was a change in my life. My stepmother grew tired of the stress of what she called the public business, and my father had had enough of Swift's Beef Market. It was time his book-keeping skills were employed to a more profitable end. The stock and goodwill of the Golden Eagle were sold to a new tenant, and we moved to a tobacconist's shop on Princess Road, Moss Side. This was a sizeable migration.

Moss Side, which was to become a Caribbean slum, was at that time a respectable district with decent houses, front gardens with trees in them, a bowling green, the scent of a coming seediness. It was a long way south from Queen's Road. The small boy who could reduce the stage of the Palace Theatre ('Butterflies will flutter up and kiss each little buttercup at daw-aw-awning') to the dimensions of the Golden Eagle kitchen could as easily expand a city to a world. Harpurhey and Miles Platting were now wrapped in north-eastern cold, and the bulk of Ancoats, the city centre itself, the University and Hulme kept off the Arctic winds. Moss Side is bounded by Moss Lane East and West to the north. Princess Road is to its east. In my boyhood it ran north through Hulme to the centre, as it does still, but to the south it stopped at Southern Cemetery. It was to move on to new housing estates like Wythenshawe and lead to the international airport at Ringway. Princess Road was like Queen's Road, a loud artery which fed quieter streets. These considered the impropriety of becoming slums before leafy Moss Lane East banished the thought. Trams clanged down and up Princess Road, and one of my first sights there was of an amorous dog caught in a cowcatcher. Our shop was Number 21, and Wilson's stood in gold paint over its window. The name did not represent my father's new assertiveness. It was also my stepmother's now, and M. Wilson was inked like an ideogram at the foot of cheques. Our shop was divided by a narrow alley or entry from a cinema called the Palace. On the other side of the shop was a barber, Louis Cohen. The cinema was run by Jakie Innerfield. Jews thus entered my life, admirably flamboyant ones. Innerfield had come south from Cheetham Hill, the Jewish quarter very well presented in Louis Golding's forgotten novel *Magnolia Street.* Innerfield's two daughters were Jewesses of a recognizably Cheetham Hill type – dark, scented, overdressed, dangerously erotic. Manchester Jewish speech seemed strongly adenoidal and always loud. Manchester Jews matched Manchester Catholics by getting on. They recognized an affinity.

The shop sold not only cigarettes and tobacco but boxes of chocolates: it was not a sweet shop in the sense that you could buy gobstoppers or Ogo-Pogo sticks there. Ogo-Pogo sticks were named for a mythical creature in a popular song:

> I'm looking for the Ogo-Pogo,
> The funny little Ogo-Pogo.
> His father was an earwig,
> His mother was a whale.
> I want to put a little bit of salt on his tail.

Though customers could come in for a packet of Player's or Gold Flake or Black Cat, the business was from the first trying to expand into a wholesale supply depot for smaller shops. Rough boys coming to buy their fathers a packet of Woodbines would see me proudly lifting the heavy wooden slab that was a continuation of the counter. 'You're not supposed to go in there, kid,' they would say. But I could say: 'I live here.' Beyond the shelves crammed with King George V and Gold Leaf chocolates, and cigarettes, some of them of brands now forgotten, lay the stockroom. Here parcels were made up for delivery by a straw-haired young man named Harold Smith. He taught me a song:

I want to be alone,
Yes, I want to be alone,
I want to be alone with Mary Brown.
Would I take her through the park?
Yes, I'd kiss her in the dark
And tell her she's the nicest girl in town.
Is she a raving beauty?
No, I wouldn't call her that.
Has she a form like Venus?
No, she's just a trifle fat.
But she's got a lot of dough
And she's single now, you know.
So I want to be alone with Mary Brown.

The stockroom had a strong odour of the pinewood of Swan matches and it was full of huge cartons, some empty. Harold Smith shut me in one of these and then sat on the flaps. I learned fear of darkness and asphyxiation. I think of dying even now as being shut in an empty cardboard carton. It is the panic of not being able to breathe that affects many Mancunians. The damp air, admirable for cotton spinning, brings us up bronchial. One of my earliest medicines for a weak chest was Owbridge's Lung Tonic, which had once contained opium. There were other opiates, all from the North-West – Battley's Sedative Solution, Dover's Powder, Dr Collis Browne's Chlorodyne, Godfrey's Cordial, Mrs Winslow's Soothing Syrup, Atkinson's Infants' Preservative, Street's Infant's Quietness. We needed opium up there, but doctors' lobbyings had banned it. It was at 21 Princess Road that I first became aware of Manchester's damp. It had never rained on Lodge Street; it was all reserved for Moss Side.

Behind the stockroom was a small living-dining-room at whose table my father kept the books and looked after the orders. He always wore a bowler hat while working, and he had a fine heavy ebony ruler of the kind that Bob Cratchit raises to the Scrooge whose new benevolence looks like madness. It was a dark room looking on to Louis Cohen's backyard, and the electric light was always on. Beyond it was the kitchen where my stepmother cooked. I saw more of her now, and of my father, though it was mainly his waistcoated back and his bowler, which he called a pot. My stepmother watched him at his figure-totting as though he would cheat her. But he had only an actuarial control of the money: it was she who carried the account at Williams Deacon's Bank at the corner of Princess Road and Moss Lane East.

She revealed herself now as interested mainly in money, not so much the acquisition of it as the fear of losing it. Had she done the right thing in leaving the public? Was my father competent to conserve her capital? She had little to do now but cook and brood, teeing and laying as she put it while she lay sleepless in bed. Agnes and Madge were working, both of them at the Manchester offices of Famous Lasky, which organized the distribution of Paramount pictures through the North-West. They were both courting, and soon they would marry, and there was the question of the cost of their weddings. My stepmother talked of little but her pains and apprehension about money. She was interested in other people's pains, though more pharmaceutically than compassionately, for she had a number of home-made remedies inherited from her misty Irish past. These were dangerous and contained paregoric, ipecacuanha, and a substance she called ikey-pikey. My father, given a cloudy bottle for his cough, would hide it unopened in a drawer. She made me gargle with chloride of lime. To comb one's hair with water was good for it. After all, the hair was a plant, and plants throve on water. When, run down and weak as I was, I got blood-poisoning in my left leg through carrying a pen with a rusty nib in my stocking, she exacerbated the poison with hot fomentations. But she cooked well and gave us all a fine shop tea of tinned salmon, lettuce with Lazenby's dressing, and cream horns from Price's up the street. 'Eat hearty,' she would say. 'There's half a crown's worth of food on the table.'

Upstairs was the drawing-room, with a piano hardly touched by my father. The room was used for alternate courting by the two daughters. There was a portable gramophone up there, with Layton and Johnstone ready to sing 'It Ain't Gonna Rain No More' and 'Bye Bye, Blackbird'. There was also 'Me And Jane In A Plane', played by Jack Hilton's Orchestra, and, on the other side, 'I'm Going Back To Imazaz (Imazaz the pub next door)'. Why does one remember these vapidities so well?

I'll be keeping my eye
On the man in the moon.
He's a dangerous guy
When he starts to spoon.
My kisses I'll shower
A million an hour.
No traffic cop
Will ever stop
Me and Jane in a plane.

Open on the piano was a new song which Madge played and sang. It was called 'When It's Nighttime In Italy It's Wednesday Over Here'. One of the lines ran: 'Oh, the onions in Sicily make people cry in California.' So they ought to cry, the bewraying buggers. I would take no more of their syrup of figs.

We had also a crystal set, a miracle never superseded by electronics, for music and speech of insuperable clarity came from a cat's whisker tickling a tiny nugget of carborundum pyrites. 2ZY was the Manchester call sign. We heard John Henry and Blossom. And also 'If you speak to an Eskimo his breath will freeze your ear. When it's night-time in Italy –' And then the patch of crystal would die and a new facet had to be tickled. My father was not impressed by the wonder. The only entertainment he sought was in the Alexandra Hotel, a pub opposite Williams Deacon's Bank. There he drank draught Bass with new cronies, most of them shopkeepers like himself – Lee and Aldridge, rival butchers; Price, floury and vanilla-scented from the cake shop; Flynn, smelling of fish; the manager of Seymour Meads, who looked like an undertaker; an undertaker. I saw more of him, but not much.

Visits from the Wilsons were, as before, reserved for Christmas, but the greengrocer Dwyers – Jack and Ima – came with a professional interest in the new shopkeeping venture. Other relatives, and relatives of relatives, turned up for Sunday tea. There was even a German relative of relatives named Wilhelm Froelich but called Billy Fraylish, Catholic Bavarian and headmaster of a Catholic elementary school. He told coarse jokes in a full-blooded Manchester accent. 'Why does the sea roar?' – 'Wouldn't you roar if you had crabs on your bottom?' I remained unsociable, too much the silent reader of *Chick's Own* and *Tiger Tim's Weekly*. A weakly child still, not enough devilment.

The school I was sent to was the Bishop Bilsborrow Memorial Elementary up Princess Road, next to the tram depot. Because of its religious liaison with the English Martyrs Church on Alexandra Road, which was the near parallel of Princess Road, it was sometimes itself called the English Martyrs. Nobody knew who Bishop Bilsborrow was, beside presumably being an English martyr. I have never found out. Bilsborrow sounded like bilberry, and the Protestant children called us Ripe English Tomaters: there was a flavour of Dwyer greengrocery around. We were told what martyrs were – Catholics mostly Irish unbelievably tortured by the English proddy dogs. This was to habituate us to the tortures meted out by Sister Ignatius, the headmistress. She raised the strap back over her shoulder before smiting. She never missed.

I was too young for her. I was with Mother Andrea, who looked after the juniors. I rose from the first class to the second in half an hour, being the only one who could read, with noise and fluency, the neat print script on the blackboard: 'Stop, stop, Mr Pancake. But the pancake went spinning like a wheel down the hill.' Mother Andrea had a sweet face and was kind and gentle. She taught us the Our Father and the Hail Mary and the Glory Be. We knew who Hail Mary was. There was a statue of her, in blue with a wreath of stars, in the school hall. There older boys, whose screams from the strap we could hear, were sent sobbing to kneel and beg forgiveness. We had to be satisfied with the promise of more apocalyptical punishments. Hell, gently explained by Mother Andrea, was all the more terrible for the gentleness. 'For ever, Mother Andrea?' – 'Yes, for ever and ever.

I pray to Almighty God that none of you children will ever merit his eternal fire.' The End of the World might not be far off. It might come so swiftly that sinners would not have time to repent.

One summer's day the End of the World came. A sunny morning grew, in an instant, black. It was industrial fog, encouraged by the rare lack of a western wind to settle. The classroom lights were switched on: it was the middle of the night before dinnertime. It may also, said Mother Andrea gently, be the consummation of all things. Let us pray. The prayer was efficacious. God relented. A summer's day returned to sinful Manchester. But it had been a terrible moment.

I fell in love with a girl named Joan Price. She was dark, pretty, probably of Silurian stock, and she was seven years old like myself. I fell in love with her because she was talented. She could sing 'Felix Kept On Walking' with a stylized lope, hands joined behind in the manner of Pat Sullivan's cartoon character, whom we all knew and admired in both his animated and syndicated strip forms. She was sometimes asked to perform during one of the little dancing lessons we were given when Mother Andrea was oppressed by the tedium of Sums. My love for her was expressed through the urge to make her admire her admirer through skill in her own sphere. I offered to sing the whole of 'Me And Jane In A Plane' but did not get past these lines:

In my two-seater
What could be sweeter?
I'll have St Peter
Step inside
And bless the bride.

They were considered blasphemous. 'Proddy dog,' jeered some classmates. Joan Price was our only star. I loved her without knowing what love was. Not having yet read William Blake, I told my love, though not to my love, and discovered that the rest of the boys knew what love was. Love was kissing. In the playground a gang tried to force us to kiss. The mask of fury of a girl can be terrifyingly adult. Joan Price beat me with her hard little fists. I learned, and have never unlearned, that falling in love is dangerous.

One humiliation followed another. I found that I was colour blind. That could be called a kind of unwilled patriotism, since John Dalton, after whom the complaint is named in most languages, discovered its existence while teaching at New College, Manchester. I was already known to be able to draw well, but my first trial with water paints had me making green leaves orange. My classmates saw first with awe and then with giggles, and they called on others to see and giggle. They were in the presence not of decent stupidity, like getting a sum wrong; this was a physical deformity. Mother Andrea was not teaching us; a Miss Clayton, later to be called Clayballs by her pupils, had come down from the upper school to give us what was called Art.

The crowd around my desk attracted her. She came, saw, and hit. It was a response pedagogically unsound. She shook me before the class and held up my painting for derision. She, or I, got plenty of that.

They say that about one in fifty of males is daltonian. It is a defect of the optic nerve passed on from grandfather to grandson through the female, who is rarely colour blind herself. Apparently it is due to the absence of one of the photopigments in the foveal cones. The Ishihara test shows me to have a particularly full-blooded variety of the defect. There is a kind of *pointilliste* diagram crammed with polychrome dots: a large white 2 appears in it for the normally endowed; for the daltonians there is a large white unequivocal 5. But for me there is more than a dubiety about green and the various reds, or blue and violet. I am not sure how to name any colour; I am totally without a chromatic glossary. I recognize that there is a huge variety of colours in the world, but I am dubious about saying what they are. Women, who cannot understand the defect, like to test me with their gamboges and aubergines, and end in awe, as in the presence of genius. Women, anyway, have a wider colour vocabulary than men, and no man ought to turn his back on John Dalton as on the prophet of a breed of cripples. There is more colour blindness around than is recognized.

I make a plea for the daltonians to all organizations that use a colour taxonomy on the oppository lines of a phonemic

system. At Charles-de-Gaulle airport in Paris, travellers to the United States are split up for boarding on the basis of the issue of a card of a colour of perverse subtlety, as befits the capital of *haute couture* – violet, vermilion, kelly green. There are concert halls with green areas and brown areas. If the three colours of traffic signals were displaced I should be lost. There is sympathy for the blind, but not for the colour blind. There is also an epistemological problem. If a daltonian reads green as orange, what philosopher may say that he is wrong? The secondary realities, of which colour is one, are not to be decreed by a majority vote.

Clearly, daltonianism is a barrier to the writing of fiction (less, it would seem, to the painting of pictures, where the bizarrely idiosyncratic vision may be accepted. Turner? Cézanne?). Fiction deals with the external world, where things are coloured, and the fiction-writer has to get the colours right. My first wife not only used to check the colours of my sunsets and gladioli but also would equip me with detailed wardrobes for my fictional characters. Critics would sneer at my prose and psychology but often praise the dress-sense of my women. I was cheating, but there is no art without cheating. That is why Plato and Tolstoy condemned literature.

I naturally now became shy of painting lessons and, in compensation, concentrated more on line, but drawing, especially vicious caricature, became more and more of a private activity. At the same time there began slowly to germinate what might be termed a synaesthetic faculty – a capacity to interpret the visual as the gustatory, and, much later, the auditory as the visual. I mean that I responded to a colour as if it were something to taste: this colour, which might not be that of a lemon, stung the tongue like a lemon; what might be black or deep purple nauseated like undercooked liver. When my father took me to a Hallé concert, I heard what I was told was an oboe as silver-green lemon juice; the flute was light brown and cold veal gravy. The urge to write for an orchestra, which came much later, was a compensation for painting the pictures I could not paint. Whatever the music critics say, I orchestrate well; I am in control of the tonal palette, or palate. When the tonal colours do not flash out, or when the mixture sounds wrong, it is always the fault of the conductor. I do not find a chromatic or tastebud analogy in words. I doubt if anyone does. The famous sonnet of Rimbaud, in which the vowels are given colour qualities, has everything to do with alchemy and nothing at all with visual perception.

Nineteen twenty-four was the year of the British Empire Exhibition at Wembley: I remember the commemorative postage stamp. What I most strongly remember is a newspaper photograph of the Prince of Wales sculpted in New Zealand butter. My imagination tasted the sailor prince. He smoked a pipe when he was not snapped smiling with a fag in his teeth, and the tobacco he smoked was called Baby's Bottom (smooth as a). We had this tobacco, its tin crawling with bare infants, on our shelves. My schoolmates doubted that such a proddy dog obscenity was possible. I brought five of them to the shop to prove that it was, but we happened to be out of stock at the time. This, like the colour blindness and the yearning for Joan Price, did me no good. I was a lone walker home – the tram depot, Bowes Road, Claremont Road (O claremont, O loving, O sweet Virgin Mary), Alison Street, Graeme Street, Great Western Street, Raby Street, 21 Princess Road, half a crown's worth of food on the tea table.

We had only one Christmas at 21 Princess Road. I was given fine presents – a conjurer's outfit, the *Chick's Own Annual* (my first book), a magic lantern with slides of jungle animals. I had been regularly patronizing the cinema next door, and there was a regular subsidiary feature called *Wild Life Round the World*. The Wilsons and the two Dwyer daughters, torpid after turkey, were to be shown a still but coloured version of this, and a candle was placed inside the magic lantern and lighted. '*Wild Life Round the World*,' I announced, and shoved in my first slide. Nothing appeared on the wall. The candle was too long. We had to wait till it burned down to lens-level, and Uncle Jimmy said: 'Play us something, Joe, while we're waiting.' So my father hammered out Musetta's song from *La Bohème*. Eventually the candle shortened, and the wild life roved stately on the wall that was a buff-coloured screen. What I cannot understand to this day is why the entire family agreed to wait on the candle's convenience. What was to stop our chopping it down to size? Were we stupid or merely torpid? I put this event or non-event into my early novel *Inside Mr Enderby*. Like T. S. Eliot's gamblers under the vine-crowned lintel or the white horse galloping in the meadow, this has remained as a symbol of something profound but unknowable. The image is accompanied by my stepmother's belching in the corner. She had become a great and loud belcher. 'Let it come up,' she told us. 'That's what the doctor says. You can always say excuse me.' But she never said excuse me.

How did I know it was Musetta's song my father played? He told me. It was the printed title above the music in one volume of many that had appeared in the sitting-room, the total compendium called *The Music Lover's Portfolio*. There was also *Music Masterpieces*, which came out in fortnightly parts. I do not know why there was this sudden incursion of middlebrow music – Boccherini's Minuet, a selection from *Madam Butterfly*, Tchaikovsky's Fifth Symphony in molecular instalments, also chatty articles by Tetrazzini, Percy Pitt and even Ernest Newman. I think that it was a matter of shopkeeper's reciprocity – a heavy-smoking music dealer had to be encouraged to fuel himself at Wilson's, 21 Princess Road.

My father did not now go at once to the Alexandra Hotel, or Big Alec, in contradistinction to the Little Alec on Alexandra Road, at five-thirty when it opened. He played the piano for a while out of *The Music Lover's Portfolio*. He did more. He played a march of his own composition which he had intended for the Royal Flying Corps. Then he complained of pains at the base of his spine which could be alleviated only by standing at a bar and drinking draught Bass. I was partly or wholly responsible for these pains. Working in the shop back room in shirtsleeves and bowler, he had stood to reach over for the daybook on the windoward side of the table. I had pulled his chair away and he sat down heavily on the floor. There was no malice in the act: it was something I had seen in comic papers and comic films. He may, after loud shouts to heaven all round, have interpreted it as a gesture of my desire for more notice than I was getting. He gave me this notice, though not much of it. I was seven now, and hence had arrived at the age of reason: I had to become a rational son of the Church by making my first confession and by taking my first communion. I needed advice about this confession, to be made in a dark box to Father O'Reilly at the Church of the English Martyrs. I had committed sins, I knew, and that removal of my father's chair had been one of them, but I was vaguely aware of a frontier between true peccancy and mere unacceptable social behaviour. For instance, nose-picking and deliberate farting could not be regarded by God the Father and Son (though I could see them going into earnest discussion about it) as acts worthy of hell. But there was a little song that I had been singing to myself, and I felt it was obscene enough to be sinful. What was the song, my father wanted to know. With shame I sang it:

There is a happy land far far away,
Where little piggies run three times a day.
Oh, you should see them run,
With their fingers up their bum,
Oh, you should see them run
Six times a day.

My father was grave about this, and said that I would have to sing to an assembled congregation while the organ played the tune. I did not, frankly, believe him. It struck me that, in the manner of a proddy dog, he was poking fun at a holy sacrament.

I did not have to sing the song. Father O'Reilly accepted the generalized package of dirty words and bad thoughts, and I received my absolution, though with, I thought, a disproportionate penance of five Our Fathers and five Hail Marys. The morning of my first communion should have been the happiest moment of my life. It was, up to that point, the most terrifying. I was given the body and blood of Jesus Christ in the form of a thin wafer that cleaved to the roof of my mouth, and I came away from the altar, hands joined, eyes closed, murmuring 'My Lord and my God.' I could clean Christ from my palate with my tongue, but hellfire awaited if my teeth touched him. If even a morsel of food or a droplet of liquid had preceded his ingestion, then heaven would rage and fresh coal be trundled in against my sudden and unrepentant death. It became, from the moment of being a full communicant, very important to put off death. I made my first communion with Manchester rain beating down. On my way to church I had opened my mouth to receive a few drops. Was that liquid nourishment? From now on, I had to be good. I had qualified for hell. My stepsister Madge was devout and over-scrupulous, far more so than the priests. Father Fitzjames at the Church of the Holy Name had thumped his evening paper (open at the racing page) and told her not to be a little fool. Father Myerscough had told her not to be disturbed at the incursion of some minuscule malice: the old boy, he said, had merely been tickling her with his tail. She was not convinced, and she passed on her fear of hell to me. It was all too easy to sin. Life, indeed, seemed all sin. I bought a twopenny sausage roll at Price's and then remembered it was Friday. I ate it nevertheless. Still chewing, I ran to evening confession. Swallowing the last flake, I began to whimper.

Both my stepsisters were courting, and presumably they permitted kisses but nothing else. The agony of the long courtship, as Graham Greene's whisky priest puts it, before the relief of marriage, the salty pretzels that exacerbate thirst for the cocktail. Agnes's marriage was to come first, and her fiancé was Jack Tollitt. *The Music Lover's Portfolio* was rightly of folio size, with great virgin flyleaves that cried out for ravishment with a pencil, and at the end of Volume One I drew Jack Tollitt. I emphasized his Nipponese buck teeth. He was a small, wiry, toothsucking Mancunian from Chorlton-on-Medlock, a follower of Manchester City football club, whose stadium at Maine Road was not far away from the shop, a Protestant undergoing slow instruction before being received into the Church, a condition of the impending marriage. He was now working in the shop, with the vigour and efficiency of one who foresaw a familial role in its running. My father was pleased to delegate responsibility. He had other interests than sitting bowler-hatted before cash books. He needed a longer lunchtime session in the Alec, where prolonged standing eased the pain at the base of his spine. In summer he liked to watch county cricket at Old Trafford; in winter he patronized the Manchester steeplechase meetings. Jack Tollitt had no time to shut me in a cardboard box, like Harold Smith. Harold Smith had left to emigrate to some corner of the Empire (the Wembley exhibition had, even at a Manchester remove, impressed him), and his successor had not lasted long: he had the habit of adding the date to the pounds, shillings and pence on the invoices. Jack and Agnes Tollitt were to set up their home at 21 Princess Road, which had three storeys and ample room for the breeding of a Catholic family. But residual Protestantism, as well as obstetric difficulties that were to oppress both my stepsisters, promoted an interest in Dr Marie Stopes's *Married Love*, and there was to be no philoprogenitiveness on the Irish pattern.

This proposed setting up of a new ménage at 21 Princess Road clinched the fulfilment of an enterprise that my stepmother had brooded on ever since the revelation that the new business was doing well. She was lonely without the noise, smoke and effluvia of drink and drama that had animated her life at the Golden Eagle. She wanted to be back, as she put it, in the public. A new pub was out of the question: it was unheard of to run one of those and a tobacco business as well. She compromised with a beer, wine and spirits store, an off-licence as it was termed, and there was one available at 261 Moss Lane East, a mere five minutes' walk from Princess Road. So she, who had so recently sold stock and goodwill in one place, now bought it in another. My father would not be concerned with the new venture. He would leave home for work in the morning like any other man, ready bowler-hatted, after his breakfast of a thick slice of pork pie and a pint of draught Bass, conveniently sleeping in its barrel on the premises. He would come home at three o'clock, when the Alec closed, for his lunch of grilled sweetbreads. He would fret in the house on Sundays over the *News of the World*, after the roast and the lemon pudding, his favourite, or only, dessert. The off-licence followed pub hours, and no evening family life was envisaged. Once more I was to see little of my father.

The off-licence was at the corner of Moss Lane East and Lincroft Street, where David Lloyd George had been born. A smaller and more radical politician lived on that street now, a man named Edwards, whose wife and children looked as if they had just served long stretches, for their heads were cropped to the limit. Their furniture was wooden boxes.

Edwards had ambitions to bring communism to the City Corporation, but he was never elected, since he could never put up the deposit. He would get up on a soap box on the rec, or recreation ground, a grim black gritty expanse at the head of Lincroft Street, and rant about the wrongs of the times, with a peroration on polluted Corporation water. Moss Side was a respectable district, and Edwards let down the tone. On the other hand he was all we had in the way of eccentricity and he had to be ambiguously cherished.

Our new shop, which was to end as a Caribbean shebeen, was very well patronized by Moss Siders who preferred to do their drinking at home. Their respectability was sometimes suspect: one old man came every evening with a jug for the supper ale and could be seen going home down an entry, where he would drink off a portion and make up the volume by urinating in the jug. When he was too old for this regular errand, his family complained about a loss of strength in the beer. Prim old ladies would come for a quarter bottle of gin, known in those cheap days as mother's ruin, and complain about the growing presence of black men in the town. These were probably Indians who had come to learn about cotton and ways of undercutting our major industry. 'They ought to be kept in their own country' was the usual judgement. An off-licence madam had to tolerate the prejudices of her customers, just like a pub landlady, and my stepmother had no difficulty there, for she subscribed to all the current bigotries. She would even, for the benefit of trade, agree with anticatholics who blamed the Pope for the coming war with America or alleged that the Eucharist was rank cannibalism. Haters of the Irish, who were many, met no opposition in her. Her Irishry was purely ancestral now, and she hid even that behind an English surname. England, she agreed with my father, was plagued by come-all-ye's and July barbers. A come-all-ye ('Come all ye good Irish and hark to my song / Of the butchers of England who did Ireland wrong') was an Irish immigrant rough, and a July barber was over to cut the harvest.

My stepmother did not improve as a character on the closer acquaintance now granted to me. She had few topics of talk beyond her days as a factory lass, an era of sweated freedom, when she and Katie 'Erbert got stuck in the works elevator or 'oist. This was not an anagram of Otis. She was rigorously consistent in her aitchlessness. When she said, as she regularly did, that she had a 'orrible 'eadache, she did not understand my father's wit when he said all she needed was a couple of aspirates. She picked her teeth with tram tickets and cleaned the wax out of her ears with hair-clips. Her teeth ached, just as her bunions did, and she had jealously stolen from my father his pains in the base of the spine. I would, perversely fascinated, tick off an anatomical manifest – head, nose, neck, chest, stomach, legs – and conclude that she was a symptomologist's gift. It seemed impossible to me that anyone so afflicted should wish to survive, but she maintained a large vigour. Occasionally she would move out of the prison of pain, money and memory to speak of the world at large, which meant the royal family; the Old Queen, the Duke of Clarence who was really Jack the Ripper, King Teddy and the Jersey Lily (who dropped ice cream down King Teddy's back), Queen Mary's enamel maquillage. King Alphonsus and Queen Edna (sic, sic) of Spain once appeared on the margin. She recognized that foreign nations existed, since sherry had an Iberian provenance, and she had a respect for the Italians, of whom the Pope (dying from dropsy, she affirmed) was one. She was friendly with a Mrs Frascati, whose English was as aitchless as hers, and spoke once of seeing a woman in the street so beautiful and dark she had to be Italian. Gipsies frightened her, and she always bought their clothes pegs.

Her cooking remained good if plain, but she recognized no other arts. When we moved into 261 Moss Lane East, she gave Madge a handful of silver and told her to buy some second-hand pictures in the manner of buying oranges (no spotty or overripe ones allowed). So we had *The Light of the World* and *The Lady of Shalott* and *Dignity and Impudence* and even *The Stag at Bay*, as well as a few weeping moral anecdotes with bustles and Elgarian moustaches. In the bedrooms were pictures of the Pope blessing *urbem et orbem* and hagiographs straight from art-loving Dublin – the Sacred Heart, the Mater Dolorosa, St Anthony, St John the Baptist with an anachronistic infant Jesus. There were whatnots around, tenanted by a diminishing sequence of ebony elephants, a ringless ring tree, a ceramic girleen with her skirt wind-raised, a cloisonné dish bought in fear from a wandering Chinaman, a seashell ashtray (souvenir of Cleveleys), empty tortoiseshell spectacle cases, the remains of a doll's tea service, a backscratcher penitentially unemployed: we all wore wool next to the skin. There were no books even as part of the décor. Books were timewasters or worse. When, in my teens, I came home with a 1683 chapbook bought for twopence, she shrieked at it and put it on the fire with the tongs: she had heard of the Great Plague and here was a paper bubonic rodent.

People, even stepmothers, are not to be condemned for lack of art or aitches. I had no claim on her love and only a minimal one on what must be called her duty. She had accepted me as a pale thin adjunct of my father, whom draught Bass was rendering neither pale nor thin, and had to see me fed, clothed and educated up to the age of ten – or fourteen, when she had been apprised of the law. She herself had left school at ten, and this explained her illiteracy. Education did not guarantee success in the world, as witness my father, who had even been given piano lessons and yet spent his working time as an employee of M. Wilson, quondam Dwyer, née Byrne, and his leisure time boozing. Education for the priesthood was a different matter: you needed Latin for the Sunday hocus pocus. She saw from the start that I was not cut out to be a priest, and priests anyway were reserved to the Dwyer dynasty. She was to frown later on my reading of books, but she was tolerant of *Comic Cuts* and *Funny Wonder* and *Film Fun*, which passed harmlessly through the system, did not have too many words, and could be used for lighting the kitchen fire. I had now graduated from the coloured nursery fodder of *Chick's Own* to the black and white vulgarity of Weary Willy and Tired Tim.

My Aunt Annie came sometimes to visit me, bringing on one occasion the gift of a half-crown gramophone which soon overwound. I should have conceived a nostalgia for the days when she seemed to be my first-hand mother, but, with a child's brutality, I rejected her as the president of damp, snakes, and a nightmare gipsy as well as, I now learned, an inadequate cuisine. She faded into her own greyness and died. Elsie and Betty, now called my cousins, occasionally wrote little letters. They were still writing them when I was a university student, and I objected to being addressed as Master Jack Wilson. But one of my fellow students said it sounded fine, like something Elizabethan. Elsie died single but Betty married after a long Lancashire courtship – twenty years, I believe. That was no record in Manchester. A lady named Miss Horrabin kept a newspaper and tobacco kiosk outside the Opera House on Quay Street, and she had been courted by a Mr Whittle for forty years. Of this couple the following was told, a typical Lancashire paring down to bare dialogue: 'Isn't it time we got wed, Jim?' – 'Ay, but who'd have us now?' I wrote to Betty congratulating her on her marriage and got a letter back telling me that, alas, her dear husband died on the wedding night. Excitement lethally exacerbated, said one of my pedantic friends, by excessive deferral. In Lancashire the comic and tragic easily mix.

PENGUIN 60s

ISABEL ALLENDE · *Voices in My Ear*
NICHOLSON BAKER · *Playing Trombone*
LINDSEY BAREHAM · *The Little Book of Big Soups*
KAREN BLIXEN · *From the Ngong Hills*
DIRK BOGARDE · *Coming of Age*
ANTHONY BURGESS · *Childhood*
ANGELA CARTER · *Lizzie Borden*
CARLOS CASTANEDA · *The Sorcerer's Ring of Power*
ELIZABETH DAVID · *Peperonata and Other Italian Dishes*
RICHARD DAWKINS · *The Pocket Watchmaker*
GERALD DURRELL · *The Pageant of Fireflies*
RICHARD ELLMANN · *The Trial of Oscar Wilde*
EPICURUS · *Letter on Happiness*
MARIANNE FAITHFULL · *Year One*
KEITH FLOYD · *Hot and Spicy Floyd*
ALEXANDER FRATER · *Where the Dawn Comes Up Like Thunder*
ESTHER FREUD · *Meeting Bilal*
JOHN KENNETH GALBRAITH · *The Culture of Contentment*
ROB GRANT AND DOUG NAYLOR · *Scenes from the Dwarf*
ROBERT GRAVES · *The Gods of Olympus*
JANE GRIGSON · *Puddings*
SOPHIE GRIGSON · *From Sophie's Table*
KATHARINE HEPBURN · *Little Me*
SUSAN HILL · *The Badness Within Him*
ALAN HOLLINGHURST · *Adventures Underground*
BARRY HUMPHRIES · *Less is More Please*
HOWARD JACOBSON · *Expulsion from Paradise*
P. D. JAMES · *The Girl Who Loved Graveyards*
STEPHEN KING · *Umney's Last Case*
LAO TZU · *Tao Te Ching*
DAVID LEAVITT · *Chips Is Here*

PENGUIN 60s

LAURIE LEE · *To War in Spain*
PATRICK LEIGH FERMOR · *Loose as the Wind*
ELMORE LEONARD · *Trouble at Rindo's Station*
DAVID LODGE · *Surprised by Summer*
BERNARD MAC LAVERTY · *The Miraculous Candidate*
SHENA MACKAY · *Cloud-Cuckoo-Land*
NORMAN MAILER · *The Dressing Room*
PETER MAYLE · *Postcards from Summer*
JAN MORRIS · *Scenes from Havian Life*
BLAKE MORRISON · *Camp Cuba*
VLADIMIR NABOKOV · *Now Remember*
REDMOND O'HANLON · *A River in Borneo*
STEVEN PINKER · *Thinking in Tongues*
CRAIG RAINE · *Private View*
CLAUDIA RODEN · *Ful Medames and Other Vegetarian Dishes*
HELGE RUBINSTEIN · *Chocolate Parfait*
SIMON SCHAMA · *The Taking of the Bastille*
WILL SELF · *The Rock of Crack As Big As the Ritz*
MARK SHAND · *Elephant Tales*
NIGEL SLATER · *30-Minute Suppers*
RICK STEIN · *Fresh from the Sea*
LYTTON STRACHEY · *Florence Nightingale*
PAUL THEROUX · *Slow Trains to Simla*
COLIN THUBRON · *Samarkand*
MARK TULLY · *Beyond Purdah*
LAURENS VAN DER POST · *Merry Christmas, Mr Lawrence*
MARGARET VISSER · *More than Meets the Eye*
GAVIN YOUNG · *Something of Samoa*

and

Thirty Obituaries from Wisden · SELECTED BY MATTHEW ENGEL

READ MORE IN PENGUIN

For complete information about books available from Penguin and how to order them, please write to us at the appropriate address below. Please note that for copyright reasons the selection of books varies from country to country.

IN THE UNITED KINGDOM: Please write to *Dept. EP, Penguin Books Ltd, Bath Road, Harmondsworth, Middlesex UB7 ODA.*

IN THE UNITED STATES: Please write to *Consumer Sales, Penguin USA, P.O. Box 999, Dept. 17109, Bergenfield, New Jersey 07621-0120.* VISA and MasterCard holders call 1-800-253-6476 to order Penguin titles.

IN CANADA: Please write to *Penguin Books Canada Ltd, 10 Alcorn Avenue, Suite 300, Toronto, Ontario M4V 3B2.*

IN AUSTRALIA: Please write to *Penguin Books Australia Ltd, P.O. Box 257, Ringwood, Victoria 3134.*

IN NEW ZEALAND: Please write to *Penguin Books (NZ) Ltd, Private Bag 102902, North Shore Mail Centre, Auckland 10.*

IN INDIA: Please write to *Penguin Books India Pvt Ltd, 706 Eros Apartments, 56 Nehru Place, New Delhi 110 019.*

IN THE NETHERLANDS: Please write to *Penguin Books Netherlands bv, Postbus 3507, NL-1001 AH Amsterdam.*

IN GERMANY: Please write to *Penguin Books Deutschland GmbH, Metzlerstrasse 26, 60594 Frankfurt am Main.*

IN SPAIN: Please write to *Penguin Books S. A., Bravo Murillo 19, 1° B, 28015 Madrid.*

IN ITALY: Please write to *Penguin Italia s.r.l., Via Felice Casati 20, I-20124 Milano.*

IN FRANCE: Please write to *Penguin France S. A., 17 rue Lejeune, F-31000 Toulouse.*

IN JAPAN: Please write to *Penguin Books Japan, Ishikiribashi Building, 2-5-4, Suido, Bunkyo-ku, Tokyo 112.*

IN GREECE: Please write to *Penguin Hellas Ltd, Dimocritou 3, GR-106 71 Athens.*

IN SOUTH AFRICA: Please write to *Longman Penguin Southern Africa (Pty) Ltd, Private Bag X08, Bertsham 2013.*

DIRK BOGARDE

COMING OF AGE

PENGUIN BOOKS

PENGUIN BOOKS

Published by the Penguin Group. Penguin Books Ltd, 27 Wrights Lane, London W8 5TZ, England. Penguin Books USA Inc., 375 Hudson Street, New York, New York 10014, USA. Penguin Books Australia Ltd, Ringwood, Victoria, Australia. Penguin Books Canada Ltd, 10 Alcorn Avenue, Toronto, Ontario, Canada M4V 3B2. Penguin Books (NZ) Ltd, 182–190 Wairau Road, Auckland 10, New Zealand · Penguin Books Ltd, Registered Offices: Harmondsworth, Middlesex, England · This extract is from *Backcloth* by Dirk Bogarde, first published by Viking 1986. Published in Penguin Books 1987. This edition published 1996. · Typeset by Rowland Phototypesetting Ltd, Bury St Edmunds, Suffolk. Printed in England by Clays Ltd, St Ives plc
10 9 8 7 6 5 4 3 2 1

From the early spring of 1944 until the end of the war in Europe in May 1945, Flt/Lt Christopher Greaves and I were joined at the hip as air photographic interpreters attached to 39 Wing of the Canadian Royal Air Force. I really don't remember where we were 'paired off', probably at Odiham airfield, but there we were, an unlikely couple in many ways, but as immutable as Laurel and Hardy, Huntley and Palmer, or Rolls and Royce.

Chris was senior to me by some years, had already had distinguished service in the RAF in Malta, survived the siege, contracted polio, and constantly fell in love with his nurses: he was, later, to marry one and raise a large family. But after Malta, and convalescence, he was stuck with me.

We had a truck which served as our 'office', with a couple of desks and lamps and not much else. In this, plus a jeep, we drove across Europe in the wake of our Forward Recce Squadron who took the photographs.

Being determined young men with great ambitions

the pilots had their airstrip as near the front as they possibly could be, dragging us, in consequence, along with them; for we had to be on hand for every sortie flown, ready to interpret.

I have often wondered, and did at the time, how Chris put up with me for so long. We were stuck together in that truck for hours and hours on end, and even when we did manage to get a break, usually when the weather was too bad for flying, we went off into the shattered countryside contentedly and painted. We never had a dispute or row, and remained together in work and in the snatched moments of leisure. We were a good team.

As I have said, the leisure was pretty nearly always in bad weather, which is why the great majority of my paintings had lowering skies, pouring rain and acres of mud and puddles. I never got to paint a sunny day – I rather doubt if I could have done so even if such a day had presented itself. I preferred 'mournful' light.

Chris was a professional artist; I only had the sparse training which I had gleaned at Chelsea Poly in between bouts of fumbling passion at the Classic cinema. But together we painted almost the entire campaign in Normandy, and were made Unofficial War Artists: our work belonged to the Air Ministry and was only returned to us after the German surrender.

At first, after the landings, there wasn't much time for painting anything. The early weeks were, to say the least of it, bewildering, on occasions unnerving. But as the Allied thrust got under way we started to settle in, knowing that we were there to stay until the end which, I was convinced, had to be in Berlin.

On the fortieth anniversary of D-Day, Chris telephoned from his home in the West Country.

'I don't know if you've been looking at telly today?' he said. 'Have you? Do you get that kind of thing in France?'

'All of it. I tuned in for ten minutes and stayed right through until the end.'

'Amazing, wasn't it? What about Mrs Reagan in that awful coat and NO hat! I mean, can you imagine a woman going to a memorial service without a HAT? Damned discourteous, I thought.'

'Oh well . . . it was all a long time ago, Chris.'

'Seemed just like last week to me, but then I'm getting ancient, I suppose. But you know, Pip, it was damned dangerous, wasn't it? If I'd have known how bloody awful it was going to be I'd never have gone!'

Fortunately for us both we neither of us thought

much of the danger at the time. Perhaps sheer youth takes care of that emotion, I don't know.

And Chris, who did most of the driving while I navigated, did some extremely dangerous things on our 'off days'. Driving along a wide stretch of open road along a ridge above the still-occupied town of Caen, shells fell behind and ahead of us, sending up ugly bursts of smoke and shrapnel.

'They're getting closer each time,' I said.

Chris was bent over the wheel of the jeep like a crouching charioteer, his cap had fallen off, his glasses glittered in the wet light.

'Bracketing us,' he said through clenched teeth.

One shell to the back, another to the front, each time the range was slightly altered. And they came nearer and nearer. It was extremely uncomfortable.

'Playing silly buggers.'

'So are we. Can't we get off this road?'

'You should know, you've got the map. I've got enough to do.'

There was no turn-off, the map shook and flapped, and was impossible to read. I only knew that when the shell behind us and the shell ahead of us landed simultaneously in the one place, we'd be dead centre.

 The spectacle, to the Germans below the ridge,

must have been amusing – although they are not a race noted for their humour.

But a single jeep belting along a dead straight road, silhouetted against the sky, as if the hounds of hell were after it, obviously proved an irresistible target for 'bracketing'.

A hawthorn hedge on the right of the road suddenly, providentially, was there and Chris swung into a field behind its sparse shelter of thorn and torn leaves.

We crawled out; lay flat in the crushed corn.

The Germans went on 'playing silly buggers' for about twenty minutes and then, mercifully, decided to give up. I couldn't help wondering, with each splintering crash, why they bothered to waste so much ammunition on so meagre and unimportant a target. Perhaps they thought we were Churchill? But in any case the German is always a very thorough creature.

Anyway, they stopped.

In the silence which followed the cease-fire, we crouched our way back to the jeep, inching across the trampled corn.

A group of Canadian soldiers suddenly rose as one man from a high-hedged bank, rifles cocked, mouths open in surprise.

'Where did you come from? For Chrissakes that's Jerry territory!'

'An error in map reading,' said Chris.

'I couldn't read the blasted map bucketing along like that with God knows what flying about. I honestly don't see the point in taking unnecessary risks, Chris, we've got quite enough to take without inventing more.'

'Rubbish.' Chris crammed on his cap and restarted the engine. 'A nice little country run. No need to get fidgety, old boy.'

So I shut up. It was all kids' stuff anyway. *Boys' Own Paper* nonsense.

Nothing to it. And we were still all in one piece.

Bigger and better things were ahead.

Two nights later we all stood in the shelter of the trees in the orchard, rocking and stumbling into each other, as wave after wave of giant bombers roared low over our heads and ripped the heart out of Caen.

We held on to each other, or the scaly trunks of trees. Showers of leaves and tiny apples shook around us as the earth rippled beneath our feet with the shock of the bombs which thundered down three kilometres away. The air trembled and rolled with the sound as

 if a thousand drums were beating a gigantic tattoo,

and the night was drenched in noise, drowning speech or even coherent thought.

We stood, heads bowed, eyes screwed up against the onslaught, grabbing about for support, like men drowning.

Ahead, through the trees, the whole skyline north of Caen was ablaze with white light, the clear night sky columned with enormous clouds of smoke and earth which barrelled upwards lit from the fires below, appearing to support a vast canopy of crimson cloud above the blazing town. A monstrous cathedral of flame.

With each shuddering blast, which seemed to suck the air upwards and leave us gasping for breath, the trees, in the light of the explosions, doubled themselves as leaping shadows, zigzagging against the dancing shapes of the tents. In the midst of the fury, a cow, maddened with terror, crashed among us trailing a broken rope at its neck, bellowing with fear, until it tripped in the guy-ropes and crashed to the ground under a sagging canopy of once-taut canvas.

There were no more Germans along the ridge road at Carpiquet to play at 'silly buggers' with a lone jeep: by the next day Caen had fallen and the battle for Normandy was almost over.

It was no time at all, I reckoned, for hermit crabs. All that, with so much else which I had devised for my personal protection, was cautiously set aside. Self-preservation and anonymity were, however, still uppermost in my mind. However, the former now took first place to the latter.

Strangely, I discovered in the first two months of battle that, though I was, indeed, often dry-mouthed with fear (or perhaps fright is a less craven word), at the same time the in-built eye of the observer was as alert as ever: I was curious, anxious to see, to experience, to be aware of the extraordinary things which were taking place about me.

And, in the letters to my father, to whom I wrote every week at least, if not twice a week, I was still 'keeping notes', just as I had done a thousand years ago in the Anthracite Years.

There was plenty of scope.

August that year, according to the letters which he had kept for me, appears to have been like a childhood summer: that is to say, eternal sunshine, cloudless, hot and clear.

The sky was always blue, that strange intense blue of northern France, sea-washed, wind-cleansed, limitless, criss-crossed with lazy scrawls of vapour trails like the idle scribbles of a child in a crayoning-book.

In the orchards the shade lay heavy beneath the trees, spiked here and there with emerald blades of grass and clumps of campion.

But everywhere the land was still. There was no birdsong.

Sometimes a bee would drone up and away, or a grasshopper scissor in the crushed weeds of the chalky soil, and then fall silent as if the effort had been too much, in the still heat, or as if, perhaps, reproved that there was no response in the ominous quiet.

No rabbits scuttled in the hedgerows, the corn stood high, ripe, heavy in the ear, unharvested, and in the meadows cows lay on their sides, stiff-legged, like milking stools, bellies bloated with gas.

Sometimes one of them would explode with a sound like a heavy sigh, dispersing memories of a lost childhood in the sickly stench of decay.

Death was monarch of that summer landscape: only the bee and the grasshopper gave a signal of life, or suggested that it existed. The familiar had become unfamiliar and frightening. A world had stopped and one waited uneasily to see if it would start again: a clock to be rewound in an empty room.

But that comforting tick-tock of normality, of the life pulse, had been provisionally arrested. In some cases it had been stopped for good, for a little further back, towards the beaches, they were burying those who would remain for ever in silence.

There was plenty of noise back there: of gears grinding, engines roaring, tracks rattling, metal groaning.

At the edge of an elm-fringed meadow, I stood against a tree watching, curiously unmoved, the extraordinary ballet between machines and corpses, which proved conclusively that the human body was nothing but a fragile, useless container without the life force.

For some reason it had never fully occurred to me before: I had seen a good number of dead men and had, as a normal reaction, felt a stab of pity, a creep of fear that perhaps it could be me next time, but I had become accustomed to them and got on with my own living.

But that afternoon in the shade of the elms I stood watching the bulldozers (a new toy to us then) shovelling up the piles of dead very much as spoiled fruit is swept into heaps after a market-day, and with as little care. Shuddering, wrenching, jerking, stinking of hot oil in the high sun, they swivelled slowly about with open jaws ripping at the earth to form deep pits, and then, nudging and grabbing at the shreds and pieces, rotting, bloody, unidentifiable, which heavy trucks had let slither from raised tail-boards in tumbled heaps of arms and legs, they tossed them into the pits.

Back and forth they droned and crunched, swinging about with casual ease, manoeuvred by cheerful young men, masked against the stench and flies, arms burned black by the August sun.

'Tidying up,' said someone with me. 'One day they will turn this meadow into a war cemetery. Rows and rows of crosses and neat little walks; perhaps they'll erect a fine granite monument, a flagstaff will carry a proud flag to be lowered at the Last Post, they'll plant those bloody yew trees, and relatives will walk in silence through the toy-town precision and order, looking for their dead.'

I remember what he said, because I wrote it all down later, but I can't remember who he was.

Fairly typical of me, I fear.

The words stayed with me for the simple reason that they moved me more than the things which I was observing. The dead lying there in putrid heaps among the sorrel and buttercups didn't move me at all: they were no more than torn, tattered, bloody bundles. The soul had sped; there could only be regret for those who had loved the individual bodies in this seeping mass: for everyone there had once belonged to someone. That was the sadness.

The absolute anonymity of mass death had dulled grief.

The silence didn't last long – silence in war never does. One gets to discover that very early on.

The ominous stillness which had reproved both grasshopper and bee simply preceded a gigantic storm: Caen fell, the Germans began their terrible retreat to the east. The battle for Normandy was over.

I use the word 'terrible' advisedly, for the retreat, estimated at that time to be composed of at least 300,000 men plus vehicles and arms, crammed the dusty high-hedged roads and lanes, even the cart tracks through fields and orchards, in a desperate attempt to reach the ferries across the river Seine: the Allied armies surrounded them on three sides. We knew that all the main bridges had been blown, so it appeared evident to us that we contained the entire German fighting force in one enormous killing-ground. Tanks and trucks, horse-drawn limbers, staff cars, private cars, farm carts and all kinds of tracked vehicles, anything in fact which could move, inched along the jammed lanes and roads in slow convoys of death.

Unable to turn back, to turn left or right, they had no alternative but to go ahead to the river, providing undefended, easy targets for Allied aircraft which homed down on them as they crawled along and blasted them to destruction: ravening wolves with cornered prey.

By 21 August it was over.

Across the shattered farms, the smouldering cornfields, the smoking ruins in the twisting lanes, smoke drifted lazily in the heat and once again the frightening silence came down over a landscape of shattering carnage.

Those of us in the middle of things really thought that a colossal victory had been achieved. The Germans had been destroyed along with their weapons. There could be nothing left of them to fight, the Russians were about to invade their homeland, surely now victory was ours and the war would finish before the end of the summer?

We were wrong. The people who are in the middle are nearly always wrong. The canvas of war is far too great to comprehend as one single picture. We only knew a very limited part – and even that part was not as it seemed. Gradually we began to realize that the war was not over, that it was still going to go on, that the Germans were still fighting, still highly armed, stubborn and tougher than they had been before. Slowly 'a colossal victory' faded from our minds and we accepted the fact that something must have gone a little bit wrong in our jubilant assessment of an early peace.

It had indeed gone wrong. But it was only some years later, when the generals who had squabbled, quarrelled, and bickered all the way through the campaign began to write their autobiographies, that one learned that, far from a victory, the retreat had been a catastrophe.

By that time it was far too late for thousands of men to worry.

They were laid out in neat rows under white crosses.

What had happened, quite simply, is that the Allied generals, by disagreeing among themselves, had left the back door open to the killing-ground permitting thousands of Germans, and their arms, to escape and live to fight another day.

But we didn't know it, fortunately, at the time.

Standing in the aftermath of violent death is a numbing experience: the air about one feels torn, ripped and stretched. The cries of panic and pain, of

rending metal, though long since dispersed into the

atmosphere, still seem to echo in the stillness which drums in one's ears.

On the main road from Falaise to Trun, one of the main escape routes which we *did* manage to block, among the charred and twisted remains of exploded steel, dead horses indescribably chunked by flying shrapnel, eyes wide in terror, yellow teeth bared in frozen fear, still-smouldering tanks, the torn, bullet-ripped cars and the charred corpses huddled in the burned grass, it was perfectly clear that all that I had been taught in the past about Hell and damnation had been absolutely wrong.

Hell and damnation were not some hell-fire alive with dancing horned devils armed with toasting-forks. Nothing which Sister Veronica or Sister Marie Joseph had told me was true. Clearly they had got it all wrong in those early, happy Twickenham days. Hell and damnation were here, on this once peaceful country road, and I was right in the middle of it all.

My boots were loud on the gravel, oily smoke meandered slowly from smouldering tyres. Blackened bodies, caught when the petrol tanks of the trucks and cars had exploded, grinned up at me from crisped faces with startling white teeth, fists clenched in charcoaled agony.

Down the road in a haze of smoke stood a small boy of about seven; in his hand a tin can with a twisted wire handle.

I walked towards him and he turned quickly, then scrambled up the bank where a woman was bending over a body in the black grass, a hammer and chisel in her hand.

The boy tugged at her skirts, she stood upright, stared at me shading her eyes with the flat of her hand, then she shrugged, cuffed the boy gently, and bent again to her task.

Hammering gold teeth from the grinning dead.

The boy raised the tin for me to see. It was almost a third full of bloody nuggets and bits of bridge-work.

Waste not, want not.

In the ditch below us a staff car lay tilted on its side, the bodywork riddled with bullet holes in a precise line as if a riveter had been at work rather than a machine-gun from a low flying plane.

A woman was slumped in the back seat, a silver fox fur at her feet, her silk dress blood-soaked, a flowered turban drunkenly squint on her red head. A faceless man in the uniform of the SS lay across her thighs.

I kicked one of her shoes lying in the road, a wedge-heeled cork-soled scrap of coloured cloth.

The woman with the hammer shouted down, '*Sale Boche! Eh? Collaboratrice . . . c'est plein de femmes comme ça! Sale Boche!*'

I walked back to my jeep. My driver was sitting in his seat smoking.

'Where do they all come from?'

'Who?'

'Those blokes . . . wandering about having a good old loot. They just go through the pockets, get the wallets, pinch the bits of jewellery. There's a squad of women civilians in all this lot. Gives you a bit of a turn seeing dead women in this sort of set-up.'

Here and there, pulling at the blackened corpses, wrenching open the doors of the bullet-riddled cars, a few elderly peasants clambered about the wreckage collecting anything of value. God knew where they had come from – every building nearby was destroyed, but like the woman on the bank with the boy, they had come to scavenge what they could.

As we drove away the first bulldozers began to arrive to clear the road. I didn't speak: the sight of the dead girl with the red hair had distressed me profoundly.

I was prepared for people to be dead in uniform, but my simple mind would not come to terms with the sight of a dead woman in a silk dress on a battlefield.

That didn't seem to be right. They hadn't warned us about *that* on the assault course in Kent.

We had to pull aside to let a bulldozer grind past; I looked back and saw an old man dancing a little jig. In a fox fur cape.

Chris was kneeling on the grass before a five-gallon petrol can, sleeves rolled to his elbows, kneading a shapeless mass like a baker.

'What on earth are you doing?'

'Don't come near!' he yelled. 'If you light a cigarette we'll be blown to smithereens.'

'I'm not smoking. What are you doing?'

'Cleaning my uniform. Absolutely filthy.'

'So is mine.'

He dredged up a sodden battledress jacket. The smell of petrol was overwhelming.

'Just look at it! Black! Filthy!'

'Is there any particular reason why you want to clean the thing now?'

He looked up at me, dunked the jacket again, did a bit more kneading.

'Thought we might go to Paris,' he said. 'Can't arrive looking like a tramp.'

 'But it's not fallen yet . . . they're still fighting.'

'Well, as soon as it stops. Couple of days' time. Seems fitting.'

'But it's forbidden to the British. Only the Free French and the Yanks.'

'Which is damned unfair, we've got every right to be there too, why not?'

On the morning of 26 August, almost before it was light, we set off in the jeep with the unexpired-portions-of-the-daily-ration, a painted paper Union Jack, which Chris had made and stuck on the windscreen, and a fairly taciturn driver who didn't drink.

'He's essential,' said Chris. 'Teetotaller. We aren't; and liberating Paris should mean a couple of glasses here and there. Got to get back in one piece.'

We liberated Paris: a celebration of the heart in an atmosphere of exploding gaiety and joy.

Driving back to the airstrip, just as evening nudged the edge of nightfall, I realized how wise Chris had been to bring a teetotal driver with us.

We'd never have got back without him.

Teetotal and taciturn he was; indeed he had hardly moved a limb, nor once smiled all day, among the tumultuous crowds of cheering and laughing people. His only comment, which almost brought us to complete sobriety, was: 'These French haven't got no control. Know what I mean? All over you before you can lift a finger to say bugger off – not so much as an "Excuse me". Bloody liberty! Foreigners! What can you expect?'

But he drove safely back through the dark while Chris and I assured each other solemnly that we had spent a really *most* agreeable day. A very agreeable day indeed. Probably the most agreeable day we'd had since the landings. *Certainly* so. A *splendid* day. We decided, after a mumbling silence, that we ought to liberate another city as soon as one became available.

We had our wish granted a week or so later when Brussels fell, and the unexpired-portion-of-the-daily-ration, wrapped in a sheet of the *Daily Mirror*, proved to be a great success in an expensive restaurant on rue Neuve, where our two tins of bully-beef were presented to the room at large on a giant silver salver, sliced as thin as a paper handkerchief, garnished with tomato and cucumber rings, and offered, at our request, to the elderly clientele who accepted with well-fed, but graceful, bows and nods.

The black market, it would appear, didn't run to bully-beef. Yet.

That was early September – ahead lay another city awaiting liberation.

This time we failed disastrously.

There was to be no liberation for Arnhem.

Another catastrophe.

I (seconded to an infantry division) sat in the mud and ice during a long, bitter winter just across the river while the Dutch starved to death on the other side.

This time the catastrophe was obvious. We had no need of the books the generals might later write to explain things. We saw it happen before our eyes, unwilling witnesses to a shattering disaster.

The euphoria of Paris and Brussels drained away. The tough times were back. It was just as well that I was aware of that fact for there was worse to come.

In April, as the last of the snows melted in the larch forests like strips of soiled bandage, we came to Belsen and the first concentration camp: a hideous 'liberation' this time which erased for ever the erroneous idea we had had that 'Jerry is really just the same as us'.

No way was he.

The war ended, for Christopher and me, not as I had somehow always thought it might, triumphantly in Berlin, but while we were sitting on a pile of logs in a pine forest near Lüneberg Heath, drinking coffee in tin mugs.

'Well, old dear,' said Chris. 'That's it. All done; all over.'

I had never felt so useless in my life.

In a letter to my father dated 7 May 1945, I wrote:

. . . It is the strangest feeling imaginable to know that it is over: one just idles about. There are no 'sorties' being flown so no work. And there won't be need of us, *or* our work, from now on. There is a weird vacuum: for so many months now it has been a fourteen or sixteen (sometimes twenty-four) hour day of strain and anxiety. All gone now. The in-built fear that someone somewhere might take a shot at you, or drop a bomb on you, has evaporated. There are still hazards about. Mines, and a band of zealots called Werewolves who are determined to fight on, but, apart from stringing piano wire across the roads thus decapitating one or two unfortunate blokes driving jeeps or motorcycles, they don't amount to much and most of them are kids anyway, about fifteen or so. So we don't worry much.

Jodle apparently capitulated to Ike today in Rheims, and if that is so, that's that. I don't know quite what will happen to me now, it's been a bit sudden in some ways, but I expect I'll be given UK leave and then get shipped off to the Far East. There is still a war there. One sometimes forgets! It'll suit me in a way. I think I'll have a serious try at staying on with the Army: if I survive the next lot of course! I've

 enjoyed the companionship and the unexpected lack of responsibility. The Army, as far as it can, DOES take care of you, and I'm not at all certain now that I would ever be able to settle down among civilians again. I've got my books, a tent, a servant and a jeep. I honestly don't think I could be happier! But time will tell, it's very early days after all, and I *do* need a job to do. Maybe the planning for the fall of Singapore? It's in the air . . .

They swooped low, swung upwards in a spiralling loop, spun down, and scattered into glossy leaves of a banyan tree, screeching and squabbling as they settled to roost. Aunt Kitty's flights of scarlet birds across an opal sky.

These weren't scarlet – just ordinary green parrots – but the sky was opal, the high monsoon clouds were rising against the darkening sky, washed in carmine, orange, blue and green.

Over the verandah of the Mess, which had once been Tagore's house, peacocks planed down as gracefully and silently as hang-gliders to settle on the crumbling dome of a little temple buried in long grasses, marigolds and zinnias. They preened, bobbed, and fluttered their tails like foppish fans. Raindrops from the last heavy fall edged the leaves of the Canna lilies like diamonds.

Somewhere, from the very back of memory, these

sights were somehow familiar. Even to the monkeys who swung through the jacaranda trees baring yellow teeth in hideous grins, defecating in anger.

In the bazaar, across the compound, the sense of texture and scent which she had offered me all those years ago was mine in abundance: silks, cottons, linen, trembling voiles, blazing everywhere in colours far too brilliant for any northern light; and the scents of coriander, mace, clove and nutmeg, of flour and damp hemp, ghee, camel dung and patchouli, swamped the senses.

As the light failed, the wail of flutes and the tapping of drums mixed with the cries of the merchants and beggars, and the high laughter of children trailing kites.

A different world to the one I had left a few months ago, arriving as a Draft of One, to cross India and begin, as I had expected, to join the planning of Operation 'Zipper'.

Only there was no planning because the monsoon had arrived with me; and that meant no flights and no flights meant no sorties and so, workless, one idled through the humid days.

'Difficult to say what they'll do with you,' said Scotty rattling the ice-cubes in his gin-sling. 'No telling really. Once we start off again, after the rains, we might get a clue – you'll probably be sent down to one of the Divisions, I shouldn't wonder. The bloody Japs have got their backs to the wall but they fight like hell.'

'So I have been told.'

'Sub-human, the buggers. For God's sake don't think otherwise. Monstrous people. Don't get taken prisoner. Take your cyanide pill instead.'

Remembering Belsen I said: 'The Germans weren't actually Fairy Twinkle Toes.'

'These are worse. Unfathomable. Savages. Bound four of our chaps with bailing wire into a tidy bundle, head to feet, doused them with petrol and set 'em alight. Alive.'

'Christ!'

'*He* wasn't around at the time; they've no pity, no mercy.' He drained his drink, tipped the melting ice-cubes into a potted palm. 'Should be exterminated like the vermin they are.' He got to his feet, pulled down the skirt of his bush-jacket.

'Want the other half of that?'

I followed him into the Mess.

Three nights later we heard that the bomb had been dropped on Hiroshima.

In the silence which greeted the news in the

crowded, still Mess, someone said: 'God Almighty! Now look what we've done, let the bloody genie out of the bottle, we'll never get it back in, never.'

Just for good measure they dropped another on Nagasaki three days after, and a week later the Japanese capitulated. The war was finally over.

If I had felt absolutely useless when Germany had surrendered, I felt worse now. There wasn't a war to fight and I wanted to stay on in the army: I was deeply thankful that I would not have to face the Japanese in battle - everything I had been told by the old hands had horrified me into incomprehension of so barbaric an enemy – but I consoled myself further by my awareness that there would be much to do in the areas which they had occupied and ravaged and in which they had spread their dreadful gospel of hate and vengeance.

Someday someone would send for me.

But they didn't: I was forgotten for the time being. The army had other things to do apart from worrying about one lone captain who wanted to stay on.

In the atmosphere of euphoria and exotic laziness, among the sights and sounds and scents, I drifted into an affair with a woman some years older than myself.

Nan was no starry-eyed girl. Quite the opposite: she knew very well, instinctively, that I was cautious, evasive, unwilling to be trapped. Afraid of possession.

So she played her cards supremely well, encouraging me to read, to write my dire poems, even (time was so heavy on our hands) to write a play, which she carefully typed out for me in the evenings in the now deserted office. She encouraged, flattered, suggested a brilliant future in civilian life, and almost convinced me that I should not remain with my regiment and stay in the army.

She never once, in all the plans which she laid for my future, included herself. Far too clever for that, she was certain that in a matter of time I would come to depend on her for so much that I should find it impossible to break the bond which she was carefully forging.

And the bond, at that time, was strong: we were inseparable, and she was fun. We danced at the Club almost every evening, spent all our time together, rode mules into Sikkim on a three-week trek which I planned could take us to Tibet because I had a great passion to see Lhasa. We never got to Tibet – that was forbidden territory – but at least we saw Everest and lay hand in hand under the stars and the deodars.

As far as our companions were concerned we were 'paired'. I think that Nan believed so too.

I did not. At nights, lying in the noisy darkness beneath my mosquito net, her body heavy in sleep beside me, the scent of 'Je Reviens' on her throat and shoulders, I felt a wrench of panic that I was entering a maze from which there could, decently, be no escape. My love for her was provisional only. I hadn't the remotest idea how to escape from an intense affair which I had helped create only to ease the tedium of my boredom and idleness, and which was now beginning to overwhelm me.

But the army had not forgotten me.

After three months, I was despatched to Java where, Scotty informed me with some degree of relish, they were 'having a hell of a time with a bloody civil war; the Japs surrendered to the Indonesians and *they* won't give the guns back to the Dutch! You'll have a very jolly time, old boy.'

Nan came down to Kidderpore Docks to see me off on the LST which was to carry me across the Equator.

'It seems very small to cross the Indian Ocean in,' she said. 'A walnut shell.'

'It is.'

'LST 3033. At least I know what you're in and where you are going.'

'Yes . . . keep your ears open; in case the fishes get me.'

'And you'll write? Remember, after the 27th of next month write to my sister's place. Ladbroke Grove. She'll keep them for me.'

'I will. As soon as I'm settled in.'

Somewhere among the jostling, feverish crowds on the quayside, someone shouted: 'Quit India! Quit India!'; others joined in waving clenched fists in the air at no one in particular.

'You'd better get away, they are starting to get restless. Bloody Congress, bloody Gandhi. Don't get stuck, go now.'

'I will. The gharri's there. Ladbroke Grove, remember?'

'After the 27th.'

I watched her walking straight-backed, but with a slight limp – the strap on her sandal had snapped. She carried it in one hand.

I knew that she wouldn't look back, and she did not.

The bond had been broken.

I turned away as the engine started up, a dull throbbing shuddering up through the metal deck. I went below as a Draft of One: for Java.

•

We had crossed the equator in the early hours of the morning; I had set my tin alarm clock for 3.00 a.m. and went up on deck to watch. Some well-meaning idiot at the bar in Raffles Hotel the day before had assured me that there really was a visible line in the sea, and I had laughed, naturally; but none the less set an alarm clock.

To make sure.

And there was. Or so it pleased me to think.

Stars blazed from a jet sky and a half-moon appeared to cast a strange rippling line across the water: it was exactly as if two tides were meeting, riffling together, merging, shimmering in the heavy swell. It satisfied me, leaning over the thin iron rail of the ship.

I liked the idea, even though I knew perfectly well that it could only be an illusion. But then so much of my life in the last two or three years had seemed to be an illusion that one more wasn't going to upset my particular apple-cart. I accepted the line for a 'line', and that was that. I had, after all, *seen* a strange joining of the waters, like the interlocking of fingers, and that is how I would always remember it, and do.

Our snub-nosed LST cut through the phosphorescent waters with an elegant curl of white foam tumbling the wake behind us in folds of gold and silver.

Apart from the throb of engines far below my feet, and the soft creaking of a metal stanchion, there was no other sound except the swish and swirl of the sea against the hull.

I felt strangely alone, exceedingly rich, drenched in these sights and gentle sounds with no one in the world to share them, and no one to shatter the beauty by comment and the banality of human speech. That kind of beauty needs no underlining.

It just is. Perfect, complete, rare, unshareable.

Far away to starboard a tiny light flashed with the regularity of a metronome. A lighthouse on the coast of Sumatra, brighter even than the stars.

We slid across the 'visible' line through the glittering night, with the Southern Cross tilted high above, into equatorial waters.

I had come a long way from Great Meadow and the Cottage, from the mud-scented delights of the river at Twickenham, from the grey conformity of the Anthracite Years which had been, after all, the anvil on which my strength, such as it was, had been forged.

I knew that tomorrow all this glory would be memory, which is probably why I spent so much time on that deck memorizing it for ever, imprinting it on my mind so that wherever I went, whatever became of me, as long as I should be breathing and aware, I could remember and in remembering be enriched once again.

My short stay in Singapore during the last two days had heightened my sense of awareness, re-reminding me that life is at best ephemeral, at worst too easily lost and rubbished into oblivion: tomorrow, I knew, I should land on a strange island, wrenched by strife, anguish, bitterness and blind hatred, to take my part as a 'policeman', nothing else, in the bloody shaping of its future.

It seemed to me at the time a pretty daunting enterprise, and unworkable, which so it proved to be eventually, but I had no sense of fear then, or the remotest apprehension: it was a job which I should enjoy somehow, even though I would be forbidden to fire a shot in anger, even to protect myself.

I knew, of course, that it was almost impossible, indeed it *was* impossible, to try and impose law and order on a country hell-bent in ridding itself of colonial rule. I'd seen a good deal of that already in India with the rioting of the Congress Party. If the wretched island to which I was presently on my way wanted its Dutch rulers out, there was nothing, I knew, that anyone, however well-meaning and however imbued with a sense of order and control, could do to stop the surging masses, hysterical with slogans and blood-lust.

In Calcutta one afternoon I had seen the kind of fury that lay just beneath the surface of apparent orderliness when a Hindu youth of about sixteen jumped a food queue and was, there and then, hacked limb from limb in the busy street. There was no quarter, no mercy, no possibility of law or order, no reasoning.

Nan had grabbed my cap and buried her face, trying at the same time to cover her ears so that the screams could, at least, be muffled.

No one tried to help; but then, no one ever did.

We stood trapped in the seething, screaming crowd.

The youth's trunk lay bloodily in the gutter, head savagely battered, hair matted, eyes staring wide in surprise among an incongruous litter of old confetti and orange peel.

It was a fairly common occurrence in those days; mob violence was only a skin's-depth away, and incidents such as this were just the lid rattling on the boiling pot.

Caught in such a situation, the wisest thing to do was to try to ease oneself away as discreetly and quietly as possible; *never* push or hurry; walk slowly.

Capless, I led a weeping Nan through the shouting crowd; her long hair had fallen about her face and shoulders in an untidy cascade, and this probably helped our departure, for we were unrecognizable as officers of His Majesty's detested services by the jostling, screaming horde with its foam-frilled lips.

In India we knew that the fuse was short, the mechanism ticking, the bomb gigantic. When we left, as leave we knew we must, a tidal wave of hatred, violence and heedless frenzy would sweep the great continent, and Hindu and Muslim would only stop to catch their breaths when the killings were done.

The Indian Christians, and the terrified Eurasians, knew this equally well, and begged constantly for help, to be allowed to leave with us when we went, but no one gave a fig for them frankly; no one even bothered to do anything about them.

When we left we'd lower all the flags and quit, and then, as someone said in the Mess one night: 'We'll let the inmates run the bloody asylum, sort it out among themselves – they won't be able to, of course, but let the buggers try if that's what they want.'

It was a sentiment frequently expressed by a great number of men in the army who had come out from Britain to hold India against a Japanese invasion.

It was a negative approach of course – but then India induces negativity.

Standing on the deck that night, now so long ago, I remember being very glad that I had left the country at last; I knew that the official war was over, that the Japanese had surrendered, and that I had chucked my cyanide pill into the sea long since. *That* fact comforted me very much indeed.

I was sailing to a new job as a 'policeman', and if that was the role I had to play, so be it – it was a great deal better than having to fight the Japs, for I knew that if that had been my fate I could never have survived.

I felt pretty certain (wrongly of course) that it would be a fairly peaceful affair; I'd be there to assist in collecting the lost POWs and the Dutch internees (that had been my briefing in Calcutta) and help get them safely home. Nothing to it really – almost a Red Cross job.

So there I stood against the rail, filled with contentment by the splendour of the night all about me, and a feeling that the worst was over, and that I had survived: so far.

I waited until the first thin thread of scarlet day split the night on the portside horizon, beyond Borneo.

I was linked with my earliest memories; for these were Aunt Kitty's islands and already, in my imagination, they were half familiar.

I thought.

It is true that defeat has an odour.

It meandered through the paint-peeling streets of Singapore like a slowly dispersing marsh gas, lying in pockets here and there, loitering in rooms and corridors, bitter, clinging, sickening.

We docked in Keppel harbour: rusted cranes, a half-sunken steamer, ruined warehouses with hollow, bullet-pocked façades. Military trucks, piles of stores, oil drums, a Union Jack hanging limply from a pole. It was five weeks after the Japanese surrender.

Beyond the wrecked buildings, which lined the dockyard like a row of rotten teeth, the towers, palms and pinnacles of the city struck hard against the intensity of the blue sky; sampans criss-crossed the oily waters like waterboatmen, and birds, strange to me, mewed and cried, swooping low above the churning wake of our LST.

The day was already hot and humid when I set off through the dockyard to go and see the city which had 'died' so ignominiously in the February of 1942.

A whitewashed bastard Tunbridge Wells – with palm trees.

Domed, arched, turreted, pillared, apparently empty.

Miss Havisham's wedding cake crumbling in defeat and cobwebs after three and a half years of Japanese occupation.

On the Singapore River Chinese life, however, went its way in a tidy explosion of activity.

Sampans jammed the muddy waters like the tumble of a thousand dominoes spilled along the winding fringes of the riverbanks.

In Chinatown proper, washing hung from every window and balcony, or from bamboo poles thrust out across the narrow streets; shutters were bleached by years of sun and tropical rains, some had never been opened, others hung like lolling tongues. On the shops, Chinese lettering danced and sprang in scarlet strokes in the brilliant light, and rickshaws and bicycles bounced over the pot-holes in the twisting alleys, tinny bells furiously ringing, weaving through crowds of laughing, playing children, as innocent as butterfly swarms.

Among this cheerful chaos, ramshackle stalls were piled with all kinds of goods, from dried mushrooms and rice to Japanese whisky and scrawny hens bunched alive, hanging by their legs looking anxious. Everywhere there was the cloying smell of frying oil and dried fish, heavy on the morning air, but above all there was activity and life.

The European quarter was different.

A deserted Sunday afternoon lethargy. Some military personnel here and there, jeeps and trucks revving up, turning, tail-boards clattering noisily in the almost deserted streets, Robinsons Department Store (the Harrods of the East, they said) had been struck by bombs and stared in sullen shock across the silent street with empty eyes: sockets in a scabbed, decaying face.

The city smelled of drains, damp and desolation. The mustiness of a long-closed room. My booted footsteps cracked back in echo in the stillness.

In Raffles Place there was a small parked Austin car with rusted chrome and a flat tyre, and two Chinese men in flip-flops carrying a bamboo ladder.

Far above, in the dazzle of the morning sky, kites planed and swung, coasting in the currents of higher air.

Beyond the cricket club grounds, rutted and worn,

St Andrew's Cathedral crouched in abandoned grace

surrounded by a filigree of jacaranda and flame trees, as alien and out of place as a swan on the Ganges, and all around the pompous pillared buildings, heavy with swagged stone urns and porticos, stood silent, vacant, blind – their Colonial grandeur humbled as if they too, like the occupants who had been forced to leave them, had also 'lost face'.

I hitched a lift on a truck to Tanglin Barracks and the Club; we drove through wincingly genteel suburbs, past gable-beamed and pebbledashed houses with names like 'Fairholm' and 'The Paddocks', buried now in bougainvillaea and flame trees, the jungle already weaving lianas through shattered verandahs, and thrusting bamboo thickets across long-forgotten lawns and rose gardens.

Some had been used as desperate, hopeless strong-points in a lost battle. Blackened shells, incongruous chimney stacks striking up through charred beams, latticed windows swinging urgently in the stiff breeze which rustled the sword-like spikes of the palms. Some stood in an almost pristine state of suburban elegance, and these, my companions told me, had been used as Happy Homes for the Japanese rank and file; but the sounds of feminine laughter and the whisper of silken kimonos had dispersed into the air as surely as the 'thwack!' and 'thwock!' of tennis balls on the overgrown courts of the 'unconquerable' memsahibs.

In the almost empty bar of the Tanglin Club a friendly Australian ex-POW came over and offered to 'buy you a round, okeydoke?'

Ronnie had a long face and no teeth. 'Rifle butt; I answered back.' His skin was drum-taut over angular bones, his joints, elbows and knees were swollen like melons on arms and legs as thick as drinking-straws, his new jungle green uniform hung on his tall, bony frame like a tent.

'Been here since '42. We arrived just as the bloody place folded up. Great bit of timing. Shoved us up into the rubber and said: "Dig defences", but there weren't any shovels and the English bastard who owned the plantation said we'd be fined if we so much as laid a finger on one of his fuckin' trees. I ask you! The bloody Japs were up the road. Fined! Christ! This was the island that *no one* could touch. It was impregnable. Took me a day to work out what that word meant and by the time I had it didn't bloody matter anymore, it didn't apply. The Empire the sun never sets on they all said. Trouble was they didn't know a fuckin' sunset when they saw one.'

 'I thought you had all been repatriated?'

'Yah, we've nearly all gone. I go Wednesday and I tell you one thing, cobber, I won't be coming back, never want to see this sodding country ever again. I just survived, by the grace of God, and next time they can stuff their bleeding Empire.'

'I think they have.'

'I think so too. Good on 'em. When did you land?'

I told him and signalled for the unsmiling Malayan boy in his white jacket and ordered another round.

'Timed it really nice. All over bar the shouting, right? You know there's one thing saved our bacon: those bombs. If you lot had tried an invasion, know what the Japs were going to do? Kill all their prisoners – men, women, kids . . . mind you, they'd been doing their best to do it for nearly four years, but that's what we heard. Wipe us all out. The day they dropped that bomb was the best day that I can remember.'

He spoke quietly, in a tired level voice; there was no anger left in him. 'Only thing is,' he said, pushing his empty glass round in circles on the table, 'only thing I say is, they should have dropped twenty more, wiped the bastards off the face of the earth, because you know why? One day they'll try it again; betcha. All jammed on to those fuckin' little islands. Breeding like rats, they'll be falling off the edges soon, and then what? Plenty of room in Australia, it's dead *empty*. Get me?'

I got him. I was unshocked. The quietness of his voice and the authority with which he spoke of terrible things defused argument.

'Well, not for a while,' I said.

The boy came back with two bottles of Tiger beer and set them on the table. Ronnie began to refill his glass, his hands shook slightly.

'Maybe. Not for a while,' he said. 'If I'm talkin' funny it's because of no teeth, sorry, mate. You stuck here long? Singapore?'

'Leave for Java, day after tomorrow.'

'Good on you. No place to stay: they're all so bloody ashamed here. Lost face you see, and the Malays and Chinks *know* it. Doesn't do to "lose face", it isn't forgotten. Never in front of the natives.'

He sipped his beer for a moment in silence. Put his glass down. 'The men are all right, not too bad, the civvies, I mean. It's the bloody women, they are the worst, they ran this place. They didn't come here with smiling faces, they came here as bloody rulers. Do this! Get that! Rule Britannia! Christ!'

A small boy with a rubber inner-tube round his middle clambered out of the swimming-pool beside us and came across to the table, his wet hair dripping. He wiped his nose on the back of his hand, pointed to a small dish of rice-cookies.

'Can I have those?'

I pushed the dish towards him and he took a handful, without thanks.

A pale, blonde woman, at the far end of the pool, lying on a Lilo, suddenly sat up in her bathing costume, one arm across her breasts. She wasn't bad, long hair, a drawn face, thin, looking angry and embarrassed all at the same time.

'Jeremy!' she called. 'Jeremy! Come here, I told you not to. They're *soldiers*, come back at once.' A voice as harsh as a cane striking steel: meant for us to hear.

The boy swivelled slowly on his heels and went back to her pushing cookies into his mouth. She said something to him, slapped the cookies out of his hand, lay back.

Ronnie shrugged, sipped his beer. 'See what I mean? Really got a complex, all of them.'

Not all of them however: Mrs McCrombie hadn't any complexes whatsoever, at least as far as I could see. If she had, then she hid them quite admirably.

She was sitting on the lawns of Raffles Hotel in a

Lloyd Loom chair, wearing a man's khaki shirt and khaki slacks, a red ribbon tied about her short, iron-grey hair, face as wrinkled as a winter apple, eyes as sharp and blue as sapphires, and she smiled a lot.

She was, I suppose, then, about sixty-five or so (old in my youthful opinion). Her husband, David, who had survived the ordeal of Changi Jail, had gone up-country to see what, if anything, remained of the rubber plantations of which he was once the manager, and she had settled for a readjustment to life with friends in a small flat in the city after four years in Syme Road Camp.

'Frankly,' she said, 'I hope he *doesn't* find anything worth saving up there. He's most terribly conscientious of course, but I really have a *terrific* hankering for home – home's in Dorset. Near Corfe, do y'know it?'

'Very well. My father used to paint there a lot.'

'Artist, was he? Oh, we had masses of them. I expect you knew the Greyhound pub then?'

'Lord, yes! Smiths crisps and ice cream soda; shandy when I got bigger.'

'The crisps,' she said, 'with those little twists of salt in blue paper.'

For a moment I realized that I had lost her, she had drifted away, her eyes looking beyond the staff cars and manoeuvring trucks on the carriage drive of the hotel.

Unseeing; a tiny smile trembling.

Suddenly she rubbed her forehead nervously, almost with irritation, adjusted the red ribbon, smiled back at me.

'Sorry. I went off somewhere. It was all such a dreadful muddle here, you know. People *do* behave in the oddest ways in times of trouble. I mean to say, here in this place, they were dancing and playing tennis just as if nothing was happening! The Japs had crossed the Causeway, and we'd pulled out of the naval base leaving it quite undamaged! David saw it. Everything intact. It was madness.'

'Did they really come across on bicycles, the Japs?'

'Oh yes! That's quite, quite true. Hundreds of the blighters spinning along on those dreadful little Japanese bikes. Can you imagine? *We* couldn't. No one here did – we never thought of that, naturally. Bikes! They are, of course, the *most* ingenious people – quite caught us on the hop.' She laughed suddenly, like a dry cough. 'Hop!' she said. 'That's what they did, and that's what we were doing, or they were doing. Dancing. Tennis.

Funny. Do you know a dance tune, something called, was it "Deep Purple"?'

'Oh yes. Yes I know that.'

'I hate it,' she said.

A stiff breeze from the sea wrestled with the traveller's trees stuck along the edges of the lawn, snapped the Union Jack on its pole above the façade.

She looked up at it.

'Nice to see it back again.' She folded her arms on the table top. 'We had to kill the dogs. I think that was almost the worst thing really.'

'The dogs?'

'Well, when we realized that it was the end, David and I knew what we had to do; he got the Humber out and we took the dogs to the vet.' She leant forward, her hands cupping her face.

'They thought they were going for "walkies". You know? They adored the car an' all. But of course everyone else had the same idea at the same time. There was a queue of cars simply miles long; people walking too; weeping. So many dogs. All kinds. Tongues hanging out, pulling at their leashes, some being dragged. They were anxious, aware of our grief. Dogs are; did you know? They sense one's anxiety, one's fear, one's

 distress. Of course you got the odd Jack Russell behaving badly, snarling and jumping at everyone. Terror I imagine – most of them knew what was happening. I know that mine did. Barney was trembling from head to foot, and Rollo, he was David's dog, just stayed close to him, his head jammed tight against his master. He never moved from him. Never.'

She cleared her throat, placed her arms on the table top again. 'Poor people. The vets were dead with exhaustion. Collies, spaniels, Airedales, pekes, all kinds . . . so many – but we simply had to do it; had to.' She sat back in the Lloyd Loom chair and when she spoke again her voice was firm and brisk.

'*You* don't want to hear all these awful things! Too depressing – all in the past now anyway. Gosh!' she said, her eyes sparkling. 'We *were* glad that you all got here when you did! I don't think that we could have managed for very much longer really, things were getting pretty grim. We *were* glad! Oh goodness yes!'

'I'm afraid I wasn't here for the Liberation. I'm on my way down to Java, I only got in yesterday.'

'Well. You know what I mean, don't you? All of you, so young and fresh, so strong; we really never thought it possible towards the very end. There *was* a rumour that they would kill us all. Too many mouths to feed and what to do with us if you had invaded, you know? And then that bomb was dropped; after that it was different. But before, in the dreadful days, goodness what muddles! No one knew what to do, and when the *Repulse* and the poor *Prince of Wales* went down, that was pretty well that. No navy, no air force to speak of, and the Japs were so *much* stronger than we were, thousands of them swarming all over the place. We hadn't a chance. Just caved in, I'm afraid.'

She laughed shortly. Pushed the ribbon about on her forehead. 'Not *really* the sort of thing to tell one's grandchildren, is it?'

Long, long after the disaster of the Falaise Gap in Normandy, we learned just what had happened there; and long after my meeting with Mrs McCrombie, and long after I had stood miserably in the fog on Guildford station, I discovered what had actually happened in Singapore, and why the British were so deeply shamed and, as Ronnie had told me, 'lost face'.

Lieutenant General Yamashita, commanding the Japanese forces at that time, was outnumbered by three to one, short of supplies and exhausted. If he had had to hold on and face a counter-attack, he admitted later, he would have lost, and the greatest military disaster in history, as it has since been called, would never have occurred.

But no one knew at the time. And there was no thought of a counter-attack.

Hindsight is a woeful word.

So, as in Normandy, as in Malaya. Those in the middle of things didn't know. Bickering, squabbling, incompetence, absurd snobbery and idiotic arrogance caused the deaths of thousands of men and lost the British their Empire – perhaps not immediately, but the chocks had been kicked away and the ship of state, so to speak, was on the move down the slipway to disaster.

I have always thought that it would have been comforting to think that Mrs McCrombie, and others like her, would never learn the true facts; but if she survived I suppose that, inevitably, she did.

But thousands upon thousands would never know – would never realize that it had all been in vain finally. There are no learned revelations for the dead.

Near the District Commissioner's tennis court in Kohima there is a modest memorial to all those who died in that campaign. It carries a simple message, four lines long:

When you go home
Tell them of us and say
For your tomorrow
We gave our today.

Who goes now to Kohima?

After I had done my stint as a 'policeman' in Java, I returned once again to Singapore and Tanglin Barracks, waiting for a berth back to England and repatriation.

Many changes had taken place since my first visit. The streets were busy again; Orchard Road was jammed with trucks, cars and rickshaws; ENSA was installed; there were scores of tatty little restaurants 'In Bounds to HM Forces'; people were dancing again at The Happy World; Raffles Hotel stated, on a discreet card, that 'If you are wearing HM Uniform you are not welcome'; and there was a subtle, understated, segregation of Singapore civilians and military personnel in the Tanglin Club, part of which had been commandeered as an Officers' Club, where the dough-kneed newcomers (with one Defence Medal up) sat about in their over-starched shorts drinking Tiger beer and gin-slings, talking too loudly; and in the city, Kelly and Walshe's splendid bookshop had opened up again with new deliveries of books from America and Britain.

It was there that I went to find something to read on the long seven-week voyage home. I found just what I needed: a copy of *Gone With the Wind*. As I put out my hand to take it, a neatly gloved woman's hand reached towards it at the same moment.

I instantly withdrew mine, and offered her the book politely.

She was a middle-aged woman, straight-backed, grey-haired, in a blue tussore suit and a blue straw hat, a handbag in the crook of her elbow.

I can see her in this room now – at this very moment.

She turned abruptly away from me, and calling down the entire length of the shop, to a startled assistant, she said: 'Boy! Tell this officer that if he wishes to address me, to do so through you.'

Not everything had changed in Singapore.

Major-General Douglas Hawthorn, DSO, was not standing with open arms to greet me as we docked at Tandjoeng Priok. To be perfectly fair he had no idea that I was coming to join his Division.

No one else had either, for that matter.

The place was swarming with people of all kinds and colours, with tanks and trucks, with perspiring coolies, with running Japanese in little squads, naked save for their boots, peaked caps and flapping loincloths, with jeeps jolting over the rubbled concrete, with turbaned Indians and tall, bony British military police in crisp green uniforms and gleaming white lanyards. A bewildering crowd scene overwhelmed by the acrid stink of burning rubber and the more subtle, and far harder to identify individually, scent of spices.

With my tin trunk, portable typewriter and a canvas suitcase I stood abandoned in the midst of carnival. Unwanted, unplaced, unexpected.

A military policeman, with a ginger moustache and the disdain of a llama, led me to the office where, he said, with no degree of certainty: 'Someone will sort it out for you.'

The office was sweltering, even at this early hour, and a pallid corporal, with skin as translucent and as pale as a potato shoot, wearily looked up from some files.

'Any idea where they are? Your people?'

'None. I was sent down from Calcutta; told to report to 23 Indian Div. HQ.'

'Could be anywhere. I'm new myself. Calcutta, did you say?'

'Yes.'

'Long way, sir.'

'Long enough.'

'You come in on 3033, did you?'

'I did. She's unloading over there.'

'Dicey trip.'

'Oh. Why dicey?'

'Submarines, sir.' He was rustling papers. 'They say that there are Jap subs all over the place and that some of them don't know, or won't believe, there's been a surrender. Could have been nasty, if you see what I mean.'

'Very. I can't swim.'

He looked up sharply, a paper in his hand. 'Not much point in swimming. That sea is stiff with sharks.' He went to his telephone. 'Got some "gen" here, we won't be long now.'

Two hours later I was still sitting on my tin trunk, wreathed in the fumes of rubber smoke and spices; but any thoughts of Aunt Kitty's magical islands in the Indian Ocean had long been dispersed.

The subaltern who finally arrived helped me load my gear, and started off through the swarming crowds. He was disinclined to talk, but offered the excuse that he had been on night duty, was bushed, and that no one knew I was coming.

As if I hadn't realized this with blinding clarity some hours before.

The sky grew darker as we got nearer the City, the sun floated, an aluminium disc, behind the heavy pall of smoke which hung above the distant buildings like a wavering canopy.

The traffic was intense, the subaltern's driving alarming, the roads pot-holed, swarming with dogs and children, rickshaws and bicycles, sagging electric light cables and heavy trucks pushing through heedlessly; he suggested that I hold on tight.

'Extremists,' he said suddenly, indicating the billowing cloud of smoke under which we now were weaving an intricate, and near-suicidal, path. 'They hit a rubberstore last night, got the oil depot the night before, hacked thirty internees to bits near Bekassi, and you'd better watch out for landmines – *and* grenades. They chuck them about like ping-pong balls, all in the name of freedom. It's not like Margate.'

I wondered why on earth he would have thought I might think it was. But said nothing. I was dispirited enough without this generous information.

A small villa in a suburban street, standing in a long-abandoned quarter-acre was where I finally landed. This was 'A' Mess. It said so on a piece of cardboard nailed to a pole in the front garden.

In a prim, almost empty little room, with sun-rotted lace curtains at the bay window, a picture of a windmill and a canal on one wall, and a rusty tin garden table against another, a silent, but grinning, Gurkha with an embarrassment of gold teeth unpacked my kit, erected my camp bed and mosquito net, and indicated that his name was Goa.

As far as I could comprehend, for we had no common tongue, and it was only by his pointing to himself with his finger and repeating an incomprehensible string of words that I was able to isolate, phonetically, an assumed name, Goa.

Goa he remained for the rest of my tour of duty, and I came to love him dearly. When the time arrived, eventually, for me to leave Java, Goa smuggled himself, and his kit, into my transport to the docks and pleaded to be allowed to come with me to England. He was splendidly smart, his brasses gleamed, his belt was blanco'd, his boots shone, his tears streamed down his cheeks.

By this time, a year later, we had invented a strange form of language which we used together. Anyone listening to us would not have understood a word, but we did. Which is, after all, what mattered.

'No, Goa. No – *Sahib go*. Not possible Goa go.'

For a moment he looked at me in stubborn silence.

'Goa stay along Pip-sahib. Stay along.'

'Pip-sahib go along Britain. *Tikh hai?*'

He suddenly fumbled in the pocket of his battledress jacket and brought out a worn and tattered piece of card. Stuck on it was a photograph of King George and Queen Elizabeth cut from a magazine.

He held it out to me, then turned it towards himself at arm's length, drew himself to attention, and saluted.

'Goa, go. Look-see burra sahib. Burra, burra sahib Brit-inn. Okay?'

'*Not*-okay. Not good. Goa not go. Goa rest along Division. Is *duty*. *Tikh hai?*'

He looked at me with such bewildered pain and distress that I felt a lump rise in my throat as large as a fist.

Our 'language' was far too limited to explain why he could not come with me to see his King.

He stood perfectly still, then replaced the piece of card, never once taking his eyes from mine, rebuttoned his pocket, moved one pace back, slammed to attention in his brilliantly polished boots, saluted, turned on his heel, hoisted his kitbag over one shoulder, and was lost in the jostling crowd pushing about at the foot of the gang-plank.

He'd gone. And I never saw him again.

He had been 'allotted' to me temporarily, at first,

because he was considered to be hot-tempered, difficult, stubborn – and he was all these things, but we grew fond of each other and respected each other. In some strange way we made a pattern of life together which worked well: he retained his pride at all times while serving as my batman-driver, which must have been difficult for him because he was a fierce, brave fighting man, and it was never his wish to be a servant.

No one else was anxious to have him for the simple reason that he had removed the head of his last officer, neatly, with a single swipe of his *kukri* while the man was asleep. Apparently there was good reason for this extravagant act, for the officer had, in some way which was never fully explained to me, insulted Goa, his bravery, his religion and his race. The whole ugly affair had been hushed up and dealt with discreetly within the Division, for it was well known that Goa was a fair and fearless man, and had shown incredible bravery and courage in battle from Imphal onwards.

The story may, indeed, have been apocryphal, but I accepted it as true. It was far more interesting.

He was proud, funny, devoted to the Division, kind and at all times passionately loyal to his King. He was, I imagine, in his early forties and had a wife and three sons in the hills of Nepal and I can only hope that he got back to them safely in the end.

And forgave me for leaving him behind.

There is a profound difference between being 'alone' and 'lonely'.

I was both for the first few days after my arrival in the Division, stuck in one or other of the three bleak little villas which constituted 'A' Mess. My brother officers were perfectly civil at all times, but there was a clear feeling that I was an outsider among a group of people who had fought together, and suffered heavy casualties doing so, in bitter and costly battles up on the Assam–Burma border, which they had secured against the Japanese.

I knew nothing of their war, they knew nothing of mine in Europe. I spoke English only, no Urdu or Malayan. We had absolutely nothing in common. The problems which they found in Java were not what they had expected at all. It was by no means (as *I* had cheerfully thought on my LST) simply a matter of being a 'policeman' and shunting POWs and Dutch internees back to Singapore and doing, as I had been told earlier, a simple Red Cross job.

 It was far graver than that.

PENGUIN 60s

ISABEL ALLENDE · *Voices in My Ear*
NICHOLSON BAKER · *Playing Trombone*
LINDSEY BAREHAM · *The Little Book of Big Soups*
KAREN BLIXEN · *From the Ngong Hills*
DIRK BOGARDE · *Coming of Age*
ANTHONY BURGESS · *Childhood*
ANGELA CARTER · *Lizzie Borden*
CARLOS CASTANEDA · *The Sorcerer's Ring of Power*
ELIZABETH DAVID · *Peperonata and Other Italian Dishes*
RICHARD DAWKINS · *The Pocket Watchmaker*
GERALD DURRELL · *The Pageant of Fireflies*
RICHARD ELLMANN · *The Trial of Oscar Wilde*
EPICURUS · *Letter on Happiness*
MARIANNE FAITHFULL · *Year One*
KEITH FLOYD · *Hot and Spicy Floyd*
ALEXANDER FRATER · *Where the Dawn Comes Up Like Thunder*
ESTHER FREUD · *Meeting Bilal*
JOHN KENNETH GALBRAITH · *The Culture of Contentment*
ROB GRANT AND DOUG NAYLOR · *Scenes from the Dwarf*
ROBERT GRAVES · *The Gods of Olympus*
JANE GRIGSON · *Puddings*
SOPHIE GRIGSON · *From Sophie's Table*
KATHARINE HEPBURN · *Little Me*
SUSAN HILL · *The Badness Within Him*
ALAN HOLLINGHURST · *Adventures Underground*
BARRY HUMPHRIES · *Less is More Please*
HOWARD JACOBSON · *Expulsion from Paradise*
P. D. JAMES · *The Girl Who Loved Graveyards*
STEPHEN KING · *Umney's Last Case*
LAO TZU · *Tao Te Ching*
DAVID LEAVITT · *Chips Is Here*

PENGUIN 60s

LAURIE LEE · *To War in Spain*
PATRICK LEIGH FERMOR · *Loose as the Wind*
ELMORE LEONARD · *Trouble at Rindo's Station*
DAVID LODGE · *Surprised by Summer*
BERNARD MAC LAVERTY · *The Miraculous Candidate*
SHENA MACKAY · *Cloud-Cuckoo-Land*
NORMAN MAILER · *The Dressing Room*
PETER MAYLE · *Postcards from Summer*
JAN MORRIS · *Scenes from Havian Life*
BLAKE MORRISON · *Camp Cuba*
VLADIMIR NABOKOV · *Now Remember*
REDMOND O'HANLON · *A River in Borneo*
STEVEN PINKER · *Thinking in Tongues*
CRAIG RAINE · *Private View*
CLAUDIA RODEN · *Ful Medames and Other Vegetarian Dishes*
HELGE RUBINSTEIN · *Chocolate Parfait*
SIMON SCHAMA · *The Taking of the Bastille*
WILL SELF · *The Rock of Crack As Big As the Ritz*
MARK SHAND · *Elephant Tales*
NIGEL SLATER · *30-Minute Suppers*
RICK STEIN · *Fresh from the Sea*
LYTTON STRACHEY · *Florence Nightingale*
PAUL THEROUX · *Slow Trains to Simla*
COLIN THUBRON · *Samarkand*
MARK TULLY · *Beyond Purdah*
LAURENS VAN DER POST · *Merry Christmas, Mr Lawrence*
MARGARET VISSER · *More than Meets the Eye*
GAVIN YOUNG · *Something of Samoa*

and

Thirty Obituaries from Wisden · SELECTED BY MATTHEW ENGEL

READ MORE IN PENGUIN

For complete information about books available from Penguin and how to order them, please write to us at the appropriate address below. Please note that for copyright reasons the selection of books varies from country to country.

IN THE UNITED KINGDOM: Please write to *Dept. EP, Penguin Books Ltd, Bath Road, Harmondsworth, Middlesex UB7 0DA.*

IN THE UNITED STATES: Please write to *Consumer Sales, Penguin USA, P.O. Box 999, Dept. 17109, Bergenfield, New Jersey 07621-0120.* VISA and MasterCard holders call 1-800-253-6476 to order Penguin titles.

IN CANADA: Please write to *Penguin Books Canada Ltd, 10 Alcorn Avenue, Suite 300, Toronto, Ontario M4V 3B2.*

IN AUSTRALIA: Please write to *Penguin Books Australia Ltd, P.O. Box 257, Ringwood, Victoria 3134.*

IN NEW ZEALAND: Please write to *Penguin Books (NZ) Ltd, Private Bag 102902, North Shore Mail Centre, Auckland 10.*

IN INDIA: Please write to *Penguin Books India Pvt Ltd, 706 Eros Apartments, 56 Nehru Place, New Delhi 110 019.*

IN THE NETHERLANDS: Please write to *Penguin Books Netherlands bv, Postbus 3507, NL-1001 AH Amsterdam.*

IN GERMANY: Please write to *Penguin Books Deutschland GmbH, Metzlerstrasse 26, 60594 Frankfurt am Main.*

IN SPAIN: Please write to *Penguin Books S. A., Bravo Murillo 19, 1° B, 28015 Madrid.*

IN ITALY: Please write to *Penguin Italia s.r.l., Via Felice Casati 20, I–20124 Milano.*

IN FRANCE: Please write to *Penguin France S. A., 17 rue Lejeune, F–31000 Toulouse.*

IN JAPAN: Please write to *Penguin Books Japan, Ishikiribashi Building, 2–5–4, Suido, Bunkyo-ku, Tokyo 112.*

IN GREECE: Please write to *Penguin Hellas Ltd, Dimocritou 3, GR–106 71 Athens.*

IN SOUTH AFRICA: Please write to *Longman Penguin Southern Africa (Pty) Ltd, Private Bag X08, Bertsham 2013.*

RICHARD

ELLMANN

THE TRIAL OF OSCAR WILDE

PENGUIN BOOKS

PENGUIN BOOKS

Published by the Penguin Group. Penguin Books Ltd, 27 Wrights Lane, London W8 5TZ, England. Penguin Books USA Inc., 375 Hudson Street, New York, New York 10014, USA. Penguin Books Australia Ltd, Ringwood, Victoria, Australia. Penguin Books Canada Ltd, 10 Alcorn Avenue, Toronto, Ontario, Canada M4V 3B2. Penguin Books (NZ) Ltd, 182–190 Wairau Road, Auckland 10, New Zealand · Penguin Books Ltd, Registered Offices: Harmondsworth, Middlesex, England · This extract is from *Oscar Wilde*, by Richard Ellmann, first published by Hamish Hamilton 1987. Published in Penguin Books 1988. This edition published 1996. · Typeset by Rowland Phototypesetting Ltd, Bury St Edmunds, Suffolk. Printed in England by Clays Ltd, St Ives plc · ·
10 9 8 7 6 5 4 3 2 1

'I Am the Prosecutor in This Case'

It often happens that the real tragedies of life occur in such an inarticulate manner that they hurt one by their crude violence, their absolute incoherence, their absurd want of meaning, their entire lack of style.

MOUNTING PRESSURE

'All trials are trials for one's life,' Wilde would declare after his trials were over and his destruction by them was complete. Still, it was a paradox after his own manner that the first trial should not be his own but the one he forced upon Queensberry, whose life was in no such jeopardy. John Sholto Douglas, the ninth Marquess, was a very rich man. He could have lost a dozen libel cases without flinching, and no doubt would have persisted in hounding Wilde whatever happened in court. This was so plain that Wilde's litigiousness gave proof of a distraught mind rather than an indignant one. The trial ended the two years of provocation. From Queensberry's point of view, of course, he was the victim not the aggressor. Wilde and Douglas had tauntingly continued to appear with each other in spite of his repeated threats to go to Scotland Yard. From Wilde's point of view, it was intolerable that a boor and bully should dictate his conduct. Moreover, his life with Douglas, including the publicity of their romantic passion, reflected his intention to oblige a hypocritical age to take him as he was.

Verbal abuse was something to which Wilde was accustomed, and few of the attacks he had suffered during his forty years had drawn blood. He had weathered the mockery of the American and British press over his aesthetic renaissance. Once Whistler had accused him of the purely literary crime of plagiarism, but he had outlived the charge and vindicated himself as an original genius. Much of the gossip about his homosexual tendencies had disappeared with his marriage, but, courting disfavor as he was prone to do, he had roused more gossip by *The Picture of Dorian Gray* and 'The Portrait of Mr W.H.' Even Lillie Langtry talked against him at this time. There had been literary attacks upon him in 1881, from *The Colonel* and *Patience*; 1892, from *The Poet and the Puppets*; and 1894, from *The Green Carnation*. If he was accused of being precious, plumed and effeminate, he had checked his accusers by intellect and grace. After all, even Queensberry had submitted for an hour or two to his charm.

Wilde seems to have overlooked his vulnerability. He was confident of the devotion of his many friends in the political and literary world. With some of them he did not trouble to be circumspect. So he said to the actress Aimée Lowther, 'Aimée, if you were only a boy I could adore you.' Ellen Terry said innocently, 'Oscar, you really didn't mean it?' An embarrassed silence fell, and Henry Irving had to explain to her later. His attitude to sexual transactions was the conventional one of his class. He did not think of his behavior with boys as of any consequence. Except for Shelley, they were prostitutes, to be bought or sold. The boys knew Wilde had treated them well, but tried to make him treat them better still. As for Douglas, Wilde had a right to feel virtuous rather than not. Having long since given up sexual relations with him, he might think of their attachment as an approximation of the Greek ideal. Wilde had made some effort to check Douglas's excesses, and had rescued him from a number of scrapes. If anyone had ruined Bosie, in Wilde's view, it was his parents. Queensberry had treated Bosie even in infancy with contempt for his physical weakness, and Lady Queensberry, in reaction to the paternal bullying, had spoiled him. Queensberry was unruly though he loved rules.

That Wilde anticipated the result of his actions is unlikely, though his sense of doom had been present since childhood. He believed in his unlucky star as much as in his lucky one. The exfoliation of his nature licensed recklessness and promoted foreboding. His first success, 'Ravenna', had described a city fallen from greatness. That he might lose 'a soul's inheritance' is foreshadowed in his prefatory poem, 'Hélas!' Tragic themes had come to him earlier than comic ones. For a man who condemned sacrifice, his plays were full of it. Vera dies to save the Czar, Guido attempts to die to save the Duchess only to have her die as well. Mrs Erlynne sacrifices herself for her daughter as Mrs Arbuthnot has sacrificed herself for her son. The Happy Prince sacrifices himself to help the poor: sacrifice is close to suicide. In *Dorian Gray* both the hero and Sibyl Vane kill themselves, though Dorian does it with more ambiguity. Wilde needed less Greek than he had to know that overreaching would attract Nemesis.

4 His prosecution of Queensberry for criminal libel

was the end not the beginning of a long series of legal maneuvers. He had consulted Humphreys about a prosecution in May 1894 and again in July. Queensberry had also taken advice. In the summer of 1894 some passionate letters of Wilde to his son fell into his hands, in particular the Hyacinth letter (either the original or a copy), and a letter of March 1893 which said, 'You are the divine thing I want, the thing of grace and beauty.' Wilde had bought back others, but not these. Queensberry's solicitor advised that the letters alone would not sustain a charge of sodomy against Wilde, so he had adopted the allegation that Wilde was a posing sodomite, which did not necessarily entail commission of the offense. His plea of privilege as a father could be invoked. If Queensberry was not a father in feeling, he was one in fact, and fully exploited this role. His blood was up and he was determined to make Wilde pay for what he appeared to be doing. He would protect his son from similar charges by his influence with the authorities. Queensberry's memories of the death of his son and heir, and of the nullification of his marriage, were still fresh. By bringing down an established reputation like Wilde's he could remake his own, as Prince Hal said he would do by conquering Hotspur. 5

Wilde and Douglas talked over the situation during the weeks that followed their separate returns from Algiers. Up to now they had told the other members of the family, including Bosie's brother Percy (Lord Douglas of Hawick), now the eldest son, that Queensberry was a victim of delusions. Wilde urged Douglas to tell his brother the truth, but Douglas, though reckless, was not brave, and refused. He proposed to go on just as in the past. By now Wilde was living entirely away from home. On 28 January Constance had to approach Ross to ask Wilde for some money for her when he came home from Algiers, as she was going to Torquay for a month. On 12 March she still did not know her husband's address. Three days later she thanked Ross for sending it. The reason for her ignorance of his whereabouts was that he was avoiding her.

During this time he took rooms at the Avondale Hotel in Piccadilly. Douglas came to stay with him, and ran up a lavish bill at once. Wilde was distinctly uneasy. Queensberry had been denied entrance to the opening night of *The Importance of Being Earnest*, and forced to content himself with leaving a bouquet of vegetables at the stage door instead of making the public

 denunciation which he had planned. Humphreys, consulted again, wrote on 28 February that he could do nothing because neither Alexander nor his staff would give evidence. When Douglas proposed to keep a young man in the hotel at Wilde's expense, Wilde refused. Douglas left the Avondale in a pet, and moved to another hotel with the friend. There followed a series of letters accusing Wilde of cowardice.

THE BOOBY TRAP

> In your war of hate with your father I was at once shield and weapon to each of you.

The first of the letters came on Thursday morning, 28 February 1895, before Wilde set out for the Albemarle Club, not far from his hotel. The club was to prove no refuge from the father any more than the hotel had proved a refuge from the son. The hall porter, Sidney Wright, immediately handed him the card left by the Marquess of Queensberry ten days before. Wright had not deciphered the words – no one was to do so accurately – but he understood that an insult was intended and had written on the back the details of its receipt, 4.30 on 18 February. Wilde probably made out the words as 'To Oscar Wilde, ponce and Somdomite'. He did not smile at Queensberry's aristocratic misspelling, but took it as a written and public repetition of the charge Queensberry had made in Tite Street. What Queensberry actually wrote was 'To Oscar Wilde posing Somdomite', but in court he said that the words were 'posing as a Somdomite', an easier accusation to defend. What he had wanted, from leaving the card, was an interview. Wilde was goaded beyond that.

For Wilde the significance of the card was that Queensberry, having failed to invade his theatre, was invading his club. There was no hope of confining the matter to private correspondence, or to the knowledge of a small circle. Understandably Wilde felt sorry for himself, on receiving from the father a message as vitriolic as that he had received an hour earlier from the son. 'I felt I stood between Caliban and Sporus,' he wrote to Alfred Douglas later. He went back to the hotel with the idea of bolting to Paris, as he had once before. But the manager, hearing of his intention, said that he must first pay his bill, and that until he did his luggage would be impounded. Wilde did not have the money, and felt trapped.

He was more vexed than despairing. Queensberry must be stopped from making these wanton attacks.

He wrote to Douglas asking him to call early on Friday morning, but to Robert Ross he wrote more fully:

Dearest Bobbie, Since I saw you something has happened. Bosie's father has left a card at my club with hideous words on it. I don't see anything now but a criminal prosecution. My whole life seems ruined by this man. The tower of ivory is assailed by the foul thing. On the sand is my life spilt. I don't know what to do. If you could come here at 11.30 please do so tonight. I mar your life by trespassing ever on your love and kindness. I have asked Bosie to come tomorrow.

Ever yours
Oscar

He wrote to George Lewis to ask his advice, but Lewis reminded him that he had already been engaged by Queensberry. Afterwards Lewis was to say that, if he had been free to advise Wilde, he would have told him to tear up Queensberry's card and forget about it.

When Ross came round that night, he urged Wilde to take no action, but when Wilde persisted suggested he consult Humphreys again. Wilde agreed, and in the morning took Douglas with him to the solicitor's chambers. Douglas was triumphant: his father had put down his charge in writing and could now be prosecuted. Before his friend's eagerness Wilde began to have doubts, but there was no resisting Douglas's

fierceness. 'It is what we fear that happens to us,' he said. Humphreys displayed a combination of opportunism and naïveté. He scented a spectacular case, saw a celebrity eager to take on another celebrity in court, and urged prosecution. He cannot easily be absolved of blame, since he must have known that Ross, who had sent Wilde to him, was homosexual, and he had the evidence of great intimacy between Douglas and Wilde before him. He chose to suspect nothing, though he asked the routine questions and received decorous answers. As Wilde afterwards remarked, 'What is loathsome to me is the memory of interminable visits paid by me to the solicitor Humphreys in your company, when in the ghastly glare of a bleak room you and I would sit with serious faces telling serious lies to a bald man, till I really groaned and yawned with *ennui*.' Later he would dismiss Humphreys as one 'who would bluster, and threaten, and lie,' but the lying was not all on Humphreys' side. Ross offered to tell the truth to Humphreys and Lord Douglas of Hawick, who was sympathetic: Wilde and Douglas absolutely refused. On the assumption of his client's innocence, Humphreys announced that a prosecution of Queensberry was bound to succeed. He
10 was a hopeful man. By this time Wilde had lost his

initial impetus, and played a last card which he expected to be decisive: he had no money. Bosie, determined to keep him up to the mark, announced that his brother Lord Douglas and Lady Queensberry would be delighted to pay costs. Goaded by the whole Queensberry clan, Wilde had no opportunity to withdraw. Humphreys and Douglas escorted him, a white flower in his buttonhole, to a four-wheeler, which took them to Marlborough Street police station on 1 March. He swore out a warrant for the arrest of Queensberry, which took place shortly afterwards. The Marquess was brought to Marlborough police court on the charge of publishing a libel against Wilde.

To some extent Wilde was the prey of his own consciousness as well as of Queensberry father and son. His inclination to betray himself, such as he attributed to mankind in general in 'Humanitad', was not thoroughgoing. He thought of self-betrayal as proceeding in surges, after which there would be recoveries. The role of victim – Sebastian or Marsyas – was only one among several, including the dandy and the apostle of joy, through which he could see himself passing. In his flirtation with Catholicism, he spoke of going to see Newman 'to burn my fingers a little more.' He half invited obloquy, half lost his nerve in the process, meaning or almost meaning to pull back at the last. But the age in which he lived was unexpectedly eager (like most ages), and the right to choose left him before he had time to exercise it. So he emulated his father's disgrace – also over the implications of a libel suit, exceeded it even, and fulfilled his own half wish to kill the success he loved. It would be wrong to assume that this urge to destroy the beloved object, himself or another, came to him after his fall. In *The Ballad of Reading Gaol* the act of killing what we love is made largely deliberate, as it is also in *Salome*, but in other works Wilde, like Lord Arthur Savile, blamed fate not will. We are by nature our own enemies, 'the lips betraying and the lips betrayed.' We seek the events that unconsciously befit us, which consciously we fear. Flaunting and fleeing, Wilde could not embrace a single course of action.

THE LIBEL SUIT

Blindly I staggered as an ox into the shambles.

The proceedings were launched. Humphreys appeared for Wilde, and Sir George Lewis made his first and only appearance for Queensberry, saying that the Marquess would plead justification. Wilde was asked, 'Are you a dramatist and an author?' He replied airily, 'I believe I am well known in that capacity.' 'Only answer the questions, please,' the magistrate admonished him. It was an untoward beginning. Queensberry, questioned by the magistrate as to whether he had anything to say, replied, 'I have simply, your worship, to say this. I wrote that card simply with the intention of bringing matters to a head, having been unable to meet Mr Wilde otherwise, and to save my son, and I abide by what I wrote.' On this he was committed for trial.

The case was adjourned for eight days. On 7 March Wilde, accompanied by his wife and Douglas, attended *The Importance of Being Earnest*. Mrs Wilde had tears in her eyes. At the hearing on 9 March, Lewis having kept his word and withdrawn from the case out of friendship for Wilde, a barrister appeared instead. This was Edward Carson, a fellow-student of Wilde's from Trinity College, Dublin, and a man of great forensic power. Carson had been admitted to the English bar only a year before, but was beginning to be known. When Wilde learned that it would be Carson against him, he said at first, according to Carson's biographer, 'I'm going to be cross-examined by old Ned

Carson,' as if he now had nothing to fear. But Travers Humphreys, who was C.O. Humphreys' son, remembered Wilde saying to him, 'No doubt he will perform his task with the added bitterness of an old friend.' It was like Isaac Butt with Jane Wilde in the Mary Travers case years before. There is nothing like the courtroom to obliterate fellow-feeling.

Carson, to give him his due, had not entered the case at once. Queensberry's new solicitor, Charles Russell, invited him to accept the brief, but for a while Carson protested that Wilde was a fellow-Irishman from the same university. He had, however, offered another reason when one was enough, the second being that the case against Wilde was too weak. Russell took the hint and set himself to strengthen the case, meanwhile not approaching any other barrister. Help came from an unexpected quarter. Charles Brookfield and Charles Hawtrey, both of whom had profited from Wilde's career by acting in his plays and by writing their parody, *The Poet and the Puppets*, furnished information about his young friends. At the same time private detectives were looking about London, and one, a man named Littlejohn, happened to visit a shop in the West End which the police had under observation. A woman prostitute, asked how business was, said it was very bad because of competition for male clients from boys under the influence of Oscar Wilde. The detective asked eagerly for further information, and was told, 'All you have to do is break into the top flat at 13 Little College Street, and you will find all the evidence you require.' He went there, and pushed past the caretaker, an old woman, who tried to prevent his entry. He had come to the lodgings of Alfred Taylor. In the flat was a kind of post-box, containing the names and addresses of boys with whom Wilde consorted. On this information, he found William Allen and Robert Clibborn, who were hiding in Broadstairs, and soon Wood, Walter Grainger, Alfonso Harold Conway, and others. According to George Ives, these young men were sequestered in a house and terrified into giving evidence against Wilde.

With this new information, and some other leads as well, Russell returned to Carson to ask him to take the brief. Carson deliberated: the details were revolting and abundant enough, and he could see himself triumphant. College loyalty faded before Protestant morality. As a final step he consulted Lord Hailsbury, the previous Lord Chancellor, who urged him to take the case. Finally he agreed. Wilde and Douglas were fairly confident, having no inkling of the new evidence that had been turned up. Douglas was even able to persuade Wilde to take him to Monte Carlo, where, though he said Wilde had cured him of gambling, he gave himself up to the gaming tables, while Wilde sat alone and disquieted. They were away from 13 March for a week or more. An article in the *Observer* said that they were expelled from their hotel in Monte Carlo at the request of other guests. On their return they discussed the case with Humphreys, who advised them to find a reputable witness who would testify that *Dorian Gray* was not an immoral book. Wilde thereupon went, probably on Saturday 23 March, to see Frank Harris. Harris proved himself a true friend: he would give the evidence Wilde wanted. But he asked Wilde about the case, and Wilde explained that Queensberry would not only bring up his formal literary works, but also had got hold of some letters from Wilde to Douglas, in spite of Wilde's effort to pay blackmail and get them back. Harris needed to hear no more. He advised Wilde that the case was sure to go against him even if he were in the right. No jury would convict a father for protecting his son, and the letters would show that Douglas needed protecting. 'You are sure to lose it,' he warned, 'you haven't a dog's chance, and the English despise the beaten – *vae victis!* Don't commit suicide.'

His words frightened Wilde enough to make him agree to meet Harris for a further talk on Sunday night. During the day Harris sampled the opinion of various people, including someone in the office of the Director of Public Prosecutions. The sentiment against Wilde was overwhelming: Queensberry's charges were generally regarded as true. The letters to Douglas and the fact that Wilde had paid blackmail would count heavily. Harris urged that Wilde, as a leading man of letters, had not the right to set the clock back fifty years by rousing full enforcement of the law.

It was agreed to meet again next day at the Café Royal, where Harris had already arranged to have lunch with contributors to the *Saturday Review*, including Bernard Shaw. Wilde asked if he might bring Douglas along, and Harris offered no objection. When he came, however, he was alone. Shaw and Harris were still sitting over their lunch. Shaw offered to leave, but Wilde told him to stay. Wilde asked Harris to testify to the high artistic character of *Dorian Gray*. Harris put the request aside as irrelevant. Instead of answering he now gave an accurate prediction of what was to come. If Wilde would not drop the case, he would certainly lose it. If he dropped it, he could go at once to Paris, and he must take his wife with him.

There could be no staying on in London, since Queensberry would not relent. From Paris he could write to *The Times* in his best style, saying he despaired of receiving justice because Queensberry was pretending to be the good father. After Harris had finished, Shaw registered agreement, and Wilde was swaying that way. Just then Douglas came up to their table. He listened with mounting impatience as Harris reiterated his arguments, and then, as Harris described it, 'cried with his little white venomous, distorted face, "Such advice shows you are no friend of Oscar's."' 'What do you mean?' asked Harris, but Douglas had already turned on his heel to leave the restaurant. To Harris's astonishment, this exit overcame Wilde. He too rose: 'It is not friendly of you Frank, it really is not friendly,' he said. 'Don't be absurd,' cried Harris, but Wilde said, with forced anger, 'No, it is not friendly.' Leonine Wilde sheepishly followed Douglas out.

Wilde had prepared himself to defend his writings, including the letters to Douglas. There was, however, one more legal step. English law requires that the defendant in a libel action must enter his Plea of Justification, with particulars, before the trial begins. This was done by Queensberry on 30 March. Humphreys

 brought Wilde and Douglas to see it on the 1st or 2nd

of April, and they could only find it appalling. In fifteen separate counts, it accused Wilde of soliciting more than twelve boys, of whom ten were named, to commit sodomy:

1. Edward Shelley, between February and May 1892.
2. Sidney Mavor, in October 1892. (Mavor testified that Wilde had done nothing wrong.)
3. Freddie Atkins, on 20 November 1892, in Paris. (His evidence was thrown out.)
4. Maurice Schwabe, on 22 November 1892. (Did not testify.)
5. Certain (unnamed) young men, between 25 January and 5 February 1892, in Paris.
6. Alfred Wood, in January 1893.
7. A certain young man, about 7 March 1893, in the Savoy Hotel.
8. Another young man, on or about 20 March 1893, in the Savoy Hotel.
9. Charles Parker, in March and April 1893.
10. Ernest Scarfe, between October 1893 and April 1894. (Did not testify.)
11. Herbert Tankard, in March 1893 at Savoy Hotel. (Did not testify.)

12. Walter Grainger, in June 1893 in Oxford and in June, July and August at Goring.
13. Alfonso Harold Conway, in August–September 1894 at Worthing and about 27 September in Brighton.

The last two counts spoke of the immorality of *Dorian Gray* and of the maxims Wilde had published in the *Chameleon* in December 1894. These two counts were the ones with which Carson chose to begin.

Although Frank Harris, and other friends, urged Wilde to drop the case, Wilde was constantly being urged by Douglas not to play the coward. 'I can't, I can't,' he told Harris, 'you only distress me by predicting disaster.' Toulouse-Lautrec, in London at the time, found Wilde still outwardly confident and contemptuous of the British public. The strain showed, however, in his tirades and complaints. (He refused to sit for a drawing.) That he accepted the idea of being a martyr may be true, but must be reconciled with his obvious preference for not being one. He was rushed along, by solicitor, lover, barrister, into a situation from which there could be no retreat except voluntary exile, something he detested. Confronted by this choice, better to suffer in Athens than glory in

Thebes. If nothing else, he would put on a good show.

The trial opened on 3 April 1895 at the Old Bailey, before Mr Justice R. Henn Collins. There was the sense that a great legal battle was to be fought, and a crowd watched the arrival of the principals. Wilde drove to court in a brougham with two horses and liveried servants. He entered without smiles. The Marquess of Queensberry, sporting a Cambridge-blue hunting stock instead of a collar and tie, was already in court. Collins arrived ten minutes late, and the trial began. Sir Edward Clarke made the opening speech for the prosecution. He had, as Harris noted, the bleak face and severe side whiskers that went with a nonconformist parson of some time back, but his manner was 'quiet and conversational'. It was not a good performance. Most of it had been composed before he saw the Plea of Justification, and he merely inserted a reference to that at the beginning of his speech. It was no longer simply a matter of injured reputation:

By the plea which the defendant has brought before the Court a much graver issue has been raised. The defendant has said that the statement is true and that it is for the public benefit that the statement was made, and he has given particulars in the plea of matters which he has alleged show that the statement is true in regard to Mr Oscar Wilde. The plea has not been read to you, gentlemen. There is no allegation in the plea that Mr Oscar Wilde has been guilty of the offence of which I have spoken, but there is a series of accusations in it mentioning the names of persons, and it is said with regard to these persons that Mr Wilde solicited them to commit with him the grave offence, and that he has been guilty with each and all of them of indecent practices. It is for those who have taken the responsibility of putting into the plea those serious allegations to satisfy you, gentlemen, if they can, by credible witnesses, or evidence which they think worthy of consideration and entitled to belief, that these allegations are true. I can understand how it is that these statements have been put in the form in which they are found, for these people, who may be called upon to sustain these charges, are people who will necessarily have to admit in cross-examination that they themselves have been guilty of the gravest offences.

The rest was a defence of Wilde's letters to Douglas, which Clarke determined to quote before Carson had a chance to do so, and of his epigrams in the *Chameleon* and his novel *Dorian Gray*. (There was a certain naïveté on Clarke's part in not realizing that he would be dealing with worse stains than those made by ink.) It was an attempt to show that Wilde was orotund but not vicious, that his verbal flowers were not weeds. But the main interest attached to Wilde's testimony.

When he took the stand, he said, 'I am the prosecutor in this case', though it was already clear that by this time matters had been turned round. 'I am thirty-nine years of age,' he said. Carson, a forty-one-year-old Trinity classmate, took note of this computation. The account Wilde now gave of his blackmail by Wood, Allen, and Clibborn was as adroit as it could have been:

WILDE: . . . From November 3rd, 1892, till March, 1894, I did not see the defendant, but in 1893 I heard that some letters which I had addressed to Lord Alfred Douglas had come into the hands of certain persons.

CLARKE: Did anyone say that he had found letters of yours?

WILDE: Yes. A man named Wood saw me at the rooms of Mr Alfred Taylor and told me that he had found some letters in a suit of clothes which Lord Alfred Douglas had been good enough to give him . . .

CLARKE: What happened?

WILDE: When he entered the room, he said, 'I suppose you will think very badly of me.' I replied, 'I hear that you have letters of mine to Lord Alfred Douglas which you certainly ought to have given back.' He handed me three or four letters, and said they had been stolen from him 'the day before yesterday' by a man named Allen, and that he (Wood) had had to employ a detective to get them back. I read the letters, and said that I did not think them of any importance. He said, 'I am very much afraid of staying in London, as this man and other men are threatening me. I want money to go to America.' I asked what better opening as a clerk he could have in America than in England, and he replied that he was anxious to get out of London in order to escape from the man who had taken the letters from him. He made a very strong appeal to me. He said that he could find nothing to do in London. I paid him £15. The letters remained in my hand all the time.

CLARKE: Did some man shortly afterwards come with another letter?

WILDE: A man called and told me that the letter, a copy of which had been sent to Mr Beerbohm Tree, was not in his possession. His name was Allen.

CLARKE: What happened at that interview?

WILDE: I felt that this was the man who wanted money from me. I said, 'I suppose you have come about my beautiful letter to Lord Alfred Douglas. If you had not been so foolish as to send a copy of it to Mr Beerbohm Tree, I would gladly have paid you a very large sum of money for the letter, as I consider it to be a work of art.' He said, 'A very curious construction can be put on that letter.' I said in reply, 'Art is rarely intelligible to the criminal classes.' He said, 'A man has offered me £60 for it.' I said to him, 'If you take my advice you will go to that man and sell my letter to him for £60. I myself have never received so large a sum for any prose work of that length; but I am glad to find that there is someone in England who considers a letter of mine worth £60.' He was somewhat taken aback by my manner, perhaps, and said, 'The man is out of town.' I replied, 'He is sure to come back,' and I advised him to get the £60. He then changed his manner a little, saying that he had not a single penny, and that he had been on many occasions trying to find me. I said that I could not guarantee his cab expenses, but that I would gladly give him half a sovereign. He took the money and went away.

CLARKE: Was anything said about a sonnet?

WILDE: Yes, I said, 'The letter, which is a prose poem, will shortly be published in sonnet form in a delightful magazine, and I will send you a copy of it.'

CLARKE: As a matter of fact, the letter was the basis of a French poem that was published in the *Spirit Lamp*?

WILDE: Yes.

CLARKE: It is signed 'Pierre Louÿs.' Is that the *nom de plume* of a friend of yours?

WILDE: Yes, a young French poet of great distinction, a friend of mine who has lived in England.

CLARKE: Did Allen then go away?

WILDE: Yes, and in about five minutes Clibborn came to the house. I went out to him and said, 'I cannot bother any more about this matter.' He produced the letter out of his pocket, saying, 'Allen has asked me to give it back to you.' I did not take it immediately, but asked: 'Why does Allen give me back this letter?' He said, 'Well, he says that you were kind to him, and that there is no use trying to "rent" you as you only laugh at us.' I took the letter and said, 'I will accept it back, and you can thank Allen from me for all the anxiety he has shown about it.' I looked at the letter, and saw that it was extremely soiled. I said to him, 'I think it is quite unpardonable that better care was not taken of this original manuscript of mine' (Laughter). He said he was very sorry, but it had been in so many hands. I gave him half a sovereign for his trouble, and then said, 'I am afraid you are leading a wonderfully wicked life.' He said, 'There is good and bad in every one of us.' I told him he was a born philosopher, and he then left.

Although Wilde had obviously paid at least £15 blackmail, the episode was too funny to take seriously. In his more heroic mode, Wilde then described the meeting with Lord Queensberry:

WILDE: . . . At the end of June, 1894, there was an interview between Lord Queensberry and myself in my house. He called upon me, not by appointment, about four o'clock in the afternoon, accompanied by a gentleman with whom I was not acquainted. The interview took place in my library. Lord Queensberry was standing by the window. I walked over to the fireplace, and he said to me, 'Sit down.' I said to him, 'I do not allow anyone to talk like that to me in my house or anywhere else. I suppose you have come to apologise for the statements you made about my wife and myself in letters you wrote to your son. I should have the right any day I chose to prosecute you for writing such a letter.' He said, 'The letter was privileged, as it was written to my son.' I said, 'How dare you say such things to me about your son and me?' He said, 'You were both kicked out of the Savoy Hotel at a moment's notice for your disgusting conduct.' I said, 'That is a lie.' He said, 'You have taken furnished rooms for him in Piccadilly.' I said, 'Somebody has been telling you an absurd set of lies about your son and me. I have not done anything of the kind.' He said, 'I hear you were thoroughly well blackmailed for a disgusting letter you wrote to my son.' I said, 'The letter was a beautiful letter, and I never write except for publication.' Then I asked: 'Lord Queensberry, do you seriously accuse your son and me of improper conduct?' He said, 'I do not say that you are it, but you look it' (Laughter).

MR JUSTICE COLLINS: I shall have the court cleared if I hear the slightest disturbance again.

WILDE: (continuing Lord Queensberry's remarks) 'But you look it, and you pose at it, which is just as bad. If I catch you and my son together again in any public restaurant I will thrash you.' I said, 'I do not know what Queensberry rules are, but the Oscar Wilde rule is to shoot at sight.'

I then told Lord Queensberry to leave my house. He said he would not do so. I told him that I would have him put out by the police. He said, 'It is a disgusting scandal.' I said, 'If it be so, you are the author of the scandal, and no one else.' I then went into the hall and pointed him out to my servant. I said, 'This is the Marquess of Queensberry, the most infamous brute in London. You are never to allow him to enter my house again.'

THE CROSS-EXAMINATION

The sins of another were being placed to my account.

Carson rose to cross-examine. His performance has been very much praised. Professionals are impressed by proficiency, and unperturbed by disloyalty. Carson had so much evidence, and of such a kind, that he only needed to be persistent, not clever. Even if he failed to worst Wilde on literary matters, he would impugn the witness's reliability and prepare for unliterary accusations. He began well by forcing Wilde to admit that he was neither thirty-eight years of age, as Sir Edward Clarke had said, nor thirty-nine, as he had said himself, but forty. The purpose of this was not just to catch Wilde out, but also to emphasize the disparity in age between him and Alfred Douglas, who was twenty-four. Carson took up the subject of the *Chameleon*, his questions being intended to suggest that the magazine was a homosexual one. It contained Douglas's poem, 'Two Loves', one heterosexual and one homosexual. 'Did you think that made any improper suggestion?' 'None whatever,' Wilde replied, and called it a beautiful poem. Carson went on to the story, 'The Priest and the Acolyte', and presumed that Wilde had sanctioned the story and approved of its contents. Wilde denied both allegations.

As the cross-examination proceeded, it became clear that Wilde was retorting cavalierly to Carson's questions. Instead of expounding his theory of art as an enhancement and expansion of life, he presented himself as amoral artist and scorned the moral mob. Early in the prosecution case, as Ralph Hodgson recalled, Carson read a passage from *Dorian Gray*, and demanded, 'Did you write that?' Wilde said he had the honor to be the author. Carson laid down the book with a sneer and turned over some papers. Wilde was lost in thought. Presently Carson read aloud a piece of verse from one of Wilde's articles, 'And I suppose you wrote that also, Mr Wilde?' Wilde waited till you could hear a pin drop and then said, very quietly, 'Ah no, Mr Carson, Shakespeare wrote that.' Carson went scarlet. He turned pages again and read another piece of verse and said, 'And I suppose Shakespeare wrote that also, Mr Wilde?' 'Not as you read it, Mr Carson,' Oscar said. The judge said he would clear the court if there was more noise. Wilde deliberately turned his back, folded his arms, and looked far away through the ceiling in rapt concentration. It was effectively done. Carson thundered at him to conduct himself properly: and he appealed to the judge, 'M'lud, M'lud.' Wilde stared deeper into the void for a full minute. Suddenly he swung round as if he heard Carson for the first time and said, assuming a most apologetic tone, 'I beg your pardon, Mr Carson; I do beg your pardon.' When Carson suggested that *Dorian Gray* was perverted, Wilde replied, 'That could only be to brutes and illiterates. The views of Philistines on art are incalculably stupid.' This élitism could scarcely have favored his cause, and Carson drove it home:

CARSON: The affection and love of the artist of Dorian Gray might lead an ordinary individual to believe that it might have a certain tendency?

WILDE: I have no knowledge of the views of ordinary individuals.

CARSON: Have you ever adored a young man madly?

WILDE: No, not madly. I prefer love – that is a higher form.

CARSON: Never mind about that. Let us keep down to the level we are at now.

WILDE: I have never given adoration to anybody except myself. (Loud laughter)

CARSON: I suppose you think that a very smart thing?

WILDE: Not at all.

CARSON: Then you have never had that feeling?

WILDE: No. The whole idea was borrowed from Shakespeare, I regret to say – yes, from Shakespeare's sonnets.

CARSON: I believe you have written an article to show that Shakespeare's sonnets were suggestive of unnatural vice.

WILDE: On the contrary I have written an article to show that they are not. I objected to such a perversion being put upon Shakespeare.

Carson was not capable of cornering Wilde through literary criticism. At last he began on the young men. Wilde had said in direct examination that he denied all the charges in the Plea of Justification which had to do with sodomy. But the mustering of a considerable list by Carson, the multifarious details, the constant (as it wrongly seemed) association with homeless and shiftless boys, as Carson persisted in calling them, had its effect. The defense had done its work well, and Carson had instance after instance to adduce. There were Wood, Allen, and Clibborn to begin with, whose association with Wilde had not been limited to blackmailing him. Wilde liked to talk of the pleasure of feasting with panthers, but these panthers had all been defanged by Queensberry's men, and were ready to say anything to stay free. If they often mixed up what they had done with Wilde with what they had done with Douglas, so much the better.

As Carson began to sink his teeth into Wilde, Clarke realized he must do something. Up to now he had withheld Queensberry's letters to his son and ex-wife, but he now read them out as evidence. They proved that Queensberry was beside himself, but they also reasserted the wholesome fatherliness of his motives. On 1 April 1894 Queensberry had admonished his son for doing nothing, and for being intimate with Wilde. In the second letter, in answer to Douglas's telegram 'What a funny little man you are', Queensberry threatened to thrash Douglas, and to create a public scandal if he caught him again with Wilde. On 6 July he wrote his father-in-law, Alfred Montgomery, complaining of his ex-wife's support of Alfred Douglas. 'Your daughter must be mad by the way she is behaving . . . I am now fully convinced that the Rosebery-Gladstone-Royal insult that came to me through my other son, that she worked that . . .' On 21 August 1894, in reply to a vicious postcard from his son, he said in part, 'You reptile. You are no son of mine and I never thought you were.' And on 28 August he wrote to 'You miserable creature . . . If you are my son, it is only confirming proof to me, if I needed any, how right I was to face every horror and misery I have done rather than run the risk of bringing more creatures into the world like yourself, and that was the entire and only reason of my breaking with your mother as a wife, so intensely was I dissatisfied with her as the mother of you children, and particularly yourself, whom, when quite a baby I cried over you the bitterest tears a man ever shed, that I had brought such a creature into the world, and unwittingly committed such a crime. If you are not my son, and in the Christian country with these hypocrites 'tis a wise father who knows his own child, and no wonder on the principles they intermarry on . . . You must be demented; there is madness on your mother's side.'

The effect of these letters was not what Clarke intended. According to Marjoribanks, who must have got it from Carson, the introduction of the names of

Rosebery and Gladstone, which at once appeared in the continental press, made it inevitable that Wilde should be tried when the Queensberry case was over, in case it looked as if these men had favored him out of a need to protect themselves.

In any case the letters did not stop the merciless march of Carson through Wilde's liaisons. There were Charley Parker and his brother, one a valet, the other a groom, whom Wilde had met through Taylor. Asked if he knew their occupations, Wilde replied, 'I did not know it, but if I had I should not have cared. I didn't care twopence what they were. I liked them. I have a passion to civilise the community.' This was the opposite of his condemnation of the general reading public, and Carson was quick to fasten upon 'the valet and the groom' as strange companions for an artist. Then there was Fred Atkins, whom Wilde had taken with him to Paris. There was Ernest Scarfe, whom he had met through Taylor. There was Sidney Mavor, who stayed at the Albemarle Hotel with Wilde one night. Carson came at last to Walter Grainger, a servant at a house in the High Street, Oxford, where Douglas had rooms. 'Did you ever kiss him?' 'Oh, dear no. He was a peculiarly plain boy. He was, unfortunately, extremely ugly. I pitied him for it.'

CARSON: Was that the reason why you did not kiss him?

WILDE: Oh, Mr Carson, you are pertinently insolent.

CARSON: Why, sir, did you mention that this boy was extremely ugly?

WILDE: For this reason. If I were asked why I did not kiss a door-mat, I should say because I do not like to kiss door-mats. I do not know why I mentioned that he was ugly, except that I was stung by the insolent question you put to me and the way you have insulted me through this hearing. Am I to be cross-examined because I do not like it?

Carson persisted, and at last Wilde answered, 'You sting me and insult me and try to unnerve me; and at times one says things flippantly when one ought to speak more seriously. I admit it.' Carson went on to the Savoy, and asked whether an incident involving buggery had occurred. Wilde denied it absolutely. Carson returned to Atkins and Charley Parker, and took up various presents made to them and other boys. He then turned to Edward Shelley. Wilde denied any wrongdoing, and in rebuttal Clarke read letters written by Shelley asking Wilde for help and expressing admiration for his writings. Carson then ended with some questions about Conway and Wood. The exchange of letters between Humphreys and

Queensberry in 1894 was read, and Carson also made clear that the 'exalted personages' – that is, Rosebery, Gladstone, and the Queen, were not mentioned in relation to the question of Wilde's sodomy. It was then time for Carson's opening speech. He said that Queensberry had been animated from the beginning to end 'by one hope alone – that of saving his son.' Wilde, on the other hand, was consorting with 'some of the most immoral characters in London,' such as Taylor, 'a most notorious character – as the police will tell the court.' He vividly contrasted Wilde's artistic élitism with his democratic taste for common boys. On the literary works of Wilde alone, Queensberry's charge would have been justified. But there was also his payment of blackmail to Wood, who was no longer out of the country, but was here and would testify. Carson did not allege any misconduct between Wilde and Douglas. 'God forbid! But everything shows that the young man was in a dangerous position in that he acquiesced in the domination of Mr Wilde, a man of great ability and attainments.' (Queensberry had succeeded in protecting his son.) He was now going to bring forward the young men, who would testify to 'shocking acts' with Wilde. Conway, for example, would testify to Wilde's having dressed him up in good clothes, so as to make him appear a fit companion.

At this point Sir Edward Clarke plucked Carson by the gown and with the judge's permission went aside to confer with him. There had been a discussion that morning with Wilde, who was not in court. His solicitor Matthews said that he and Clarke would keep the trial going if Wilde wished so he would have time to get to France. The defense would be allowed to call its witnesses, as a delaying tactic. Otherwise Clarke would have to abandon the prosecution at once. 'I'll stay,' said Wilde. Clarke hoped that Carson would accept a verdict of not guilty, '"not guilty" having reference to the word "posing"' and to *Dorian Gray* and the epigrams in the *Chameleon*. Nothing would then be conceded about Wilde's acts of sodomy as itemized in the Plea of Justification. Wilde agreed, but in the event Carson insisted, and Clarke had to consent, that the whole plea must be allowed, that is, Queensberry was justified in calling Wilde a sodomite in the public interest. The judge instructed the jury so to rule. Queensberry was applauded, and Mr Justice Collins, as Frank Harris noted, made no attempt to stop the cheering, but simply folded up his papers and left. He sent a message to Carson,

Dear Carson
I never heard a more powerful speech nor a more searching crossXam. I congratulate you on having escaped the rest of the filth.

Yrs ever
R. Henn Collins

What made Carson unmade Wilde.

Doom Deferred

GUIDO: Guilty? – Let those
Who know not what a thing temptation is,
Let those who have not walked as we have done,
In the red fire of passion, those whose lives
Are dull and colourless, in a word let those,
If any such there be, who have not loved,
Cast stones against you.

ON FORTUNE'S WHEEL

The quarry was about to fall. If Queensberry had not brought Wilde down, someone else might well have done so. The easy and half acknowledged indulgence which he practiced with Alfred Douglas's ardent complicity involved a succession of young men, many of them Douglas's castoffs, any one of whom might have toppled Wilde. It was, as Henri de Régnier said, 'a chronological error.' If he had lived in the days of the Greeks, no one would have minded. That summer of 1893, when Douglas, having gone down from Oxford without a degree, joined Wilde at Goring, may stand for many instances of their common imprudence.

In *De Profundis* Wilde brings up the subject of Goring, so as to upbraid Douglas for making him spend the staggering sum of £1,340 in less than a summer. But he says nothing of their riskier joint enterprise, the Philip Danney case. Of it Oscar Browning commented, disingenuously, 'This was the first time I ever heard Oscar was given to those proceedings.'

Wilde had to pick his way among blackmailing boys and furious fathers. He ran a risk with the father of Edward Shelley, John Lane's office employee, who was as indignant as Queensberry, and with the father of a public school boy, Sidney Mavor, just as earlier he had roused the indignation of Frank Miles's father. He was circling nearer to some kind of legal confrontation. Only self-assurance, and the thoughtless flurry of his activities, made him trust to his luck.

Still, the furious fathers mostly stayed in the background, while the blackmailing boys were always about, ready to sell themselves or Wilde. The £35

 (probably not £15) he had given to Wood in 1893, in

the hope that the young man would go to America and stay there, was not likely to be enough. From America Wood had ominously written, 'Tell Oscar he can send me a draft for an Easter egg.' The gang – for Wood, Allen, Clibborn and others constituted a gang – had obviously marked Wilde for prolonged milking. It was as tricky a game for them as for him, since there were heavier penalties for blackmail than for indecency. Their running such risks fascinated Wilde. Clibborn and Allen, in particular, he admired for waging 'an infamous war against life.' Clibborn liked to tell Wilde of his adventures, and one, with Lord Euston – prominent in the Cleveland Street scandal – required such avaricious tenacity on Clibborn's part as to entitle him, Wilde said, to the Victoria Cross.

Clibborn continued to confide in Wilde as the trial drew near. One day he was telling him, as George Ives recounts, 'the plots that were being planned by threats and money and all kind of means, to bring about his [Wilde's] ruin.' Wilde paid little heed, but suddenly looked up and asked a question that had evidently been long in his mind: 'Bob, what I want to know is, did you ever *love* any boy for his own sake?' Clibborn replied, 'No, Oscar, I can't say I ever did!' For Ives this was an instance of Wilde's mystical search for the truth of things even on the verge of his own collapse. His curiosity was less mystical when he suggested bringing together 'the panther,' as he often called Clibborn, with Ives, who prided himself on being a 'cold disciplined Hellenist,' to see what would happen. But that meeting never took place.

It must be said for Wilde that the risk was impossible to estimate. Society put up with a great deal that was illegal, and sometimes did so knowingly. Countenancing illegality did not amount to sanctioning it, however, and the atmosphere could change at any time. Wilde was dimly aware from the beginning that his genius gave him only a limited immunity. But the way of life which Alfred Douglas had opened up was necessarily reckless. There was something fascinating in being the rival, the accomplice, and the object of each other's love. Shared indiscretion cemented them romantically together. Prudence would have been a form of betrayal.

Events had taken him beyond erotic fantasy and indulgence. After Queensberry's exoneration Wilde was indecisive when others were decisive. Clarke's concession that Wilde's being called a sodomite was in the public interest made prosecution almost certain.
 To be quite sure, Charles Russell, within minutes

of Queensberry's acquittal, addressed a letter to Hamilton Cuffe, Director of Prosecutions,

Dear Sir,

In order that there may be no miscarriage of justice I think it my duty at once to send you a copy of all our witnesses' statements together with a copy of the shorthand notes of the trial.

Queensberry, for his part, informed Wilde, 'I will not prevent your flight, but if you take my son with you, I will shoot you like a dog.' He added, to the French press, 'But I don't think he'll be allowed to go. This case has cost me 30,000 francs, but I don't regret anything, since I know all I have done is for the good of my sons, the honour of my family, and the public benefit.' He said later he had been misquoted; he had said that he would shoot Wilde like a dog, if he had a mind to do so and if it seemed worthwhile. It was probably Queensberry's detectives, rather than Scotland Yard's, who were instructed to stay on Wilde's trail.

That trail led Wilde first to his solicitor Humphreys, then to Sir George Lewis, who threw up his hands and said, 'What is the good of coming to me now?' Then to the Holborn Viaduct Hotel. Douglas, his brother Percy, and Robert Ross accompanied Wilde, and in the hotel he wrote a letter to the editor of the *Evening News*:

It would have been impossible for me to have proved my case without putting Lord Alfred Douglas in the witness-box against his father. Lord Alfred Douglas was extremely anxious to go into the box, but I would not let him do so. Rather than put him in so painful a position I determined to retire from the case, and to bear on my own shoulders whatever ignominy and shame might result from my prosecuting Lord Queensberry.

Oscar Wilde

The letter reads as if Wilde thought the matter might end there. After lunch he gave Ross a cheque to cash for £200 and went on to the Cadogan Hotel, where he was joined by Reggie Turner. Douglas had been staying there for five weeks. Ross and Turner urged Wilde to take a train for Dover and a boat for France, but he seemed incapable of decision. He said 'The train is gone. It is too late.' In fact he still had a chance, but seemed disinclined to take it. Douglas was off trying to see his cousin, the M.P. George Wyndham, and stir up influential friends. Wilde asked Ross to see Constance Wilde and inform her what had happened. She wept and said, 'I hope Oscar is going away abroad.' George Wyndham arrived at four o'clock and asked to see Wilde, but Wilde, fearing recriminations, had Ross talk with him. Wyndham began to scold Ross for allowing Wilde and Douglas to be together, but Ross disarmed him by saying that he and all Wilde's friends had been trying to separate them for years. Wyndham changed his tack and asked Ross to persuade Wilde to leave the country at once. They were still talking when Douglas rushed in, and took Wyndham off to see someone who might help.

At five o'clock a sympathetic reporter from the *Star* arrived and told Ross that the warrant for Wilde's arrest had been issued. In fact, Charles Russell had busily gone round to see Sir John Bridge at Bow Street in the early afternoon and persuaded him that Wilde should be arrested. Ross told Wilde, who 'went very grey in the face.' Up to now he had not let Ross give him the money from the bank, but he now asked for it, and Ross thought he must have decided upon flight. Instead Wilde settled down in his chair and said, 'I shall stay and do my sentence whatever it is.'

A half-packed suitcase lay on the bed, emblem of contradictory impulses. He was tired of action. Like Hamlet, as he understood that hero, he wished to distance himself from his plight, to be the spectator of his own tragedy. His stubbornness, his courage, and his gallantry also kept him there. He had always met adversity head on, to face hostile journalists, moralistic reviewers, and canting, ranting fathers. A man so concerned with his image disdained to think of himself as a fugitive, skulking in dark corners instead of lording it in the limelight. He preferred to be a great figure, doomed by fate and the unjust laws of a foreign country. Suffering was more becoming than embarrassment. Writers, after all, had been prisoners before him. Cunninghame Graham and Blunt came to mind. His mind would survive, superior to any indignities his inferiors could heap upon him. If he was to be immolated, so must be his age. Reveal him as pederast, reveal his society as hypocrite. So he waited, defiant. At ten past six came the expected knock at the door. A waiter entered, followed by two detectives. They said, 'We have a warrant here, Mr Wilde, for your arrest on a charge of committing indecent acts.' Wilde asked if he would be given bail and the detectives were doubtful. As he rose and groped unsteadily for his overcoat and for a book with a yellow cover, it was suddenly evident that he had been drinking heavily. He asked Ross to get him a change of clothes and bring it to him. 'Where shall I be taken?' he asked. 'To Bow

Street,' was the reply. The cab drove off, and the Wilde epoch came to an end.

DESPAIR AND ITS ANODYNES

Every great love has its tragedy, and now ours has too.

Ross went as directed to Tite Street. Mrs Wilde had locked the bedroom door and library and gone out. Wilde's servant, Arthur, was there, and helped Ross to break into the bedroom and pack a bag. At Bow Street he was refused admission, either to see Wilde or to leave the clothing. He realized that Wilde's papers were in danger from Queensberry's men or the police, and hurried back to Tite Street. Again with Arthur's help, he broke open the library door, and removed some of Wilde's letters and manuscripts. He noted grimly that the two most recent writings, *A Florentine Tragedy* and an enlarged version of 'The Portrait of Mr W.H.,' which had been returned to Wilde a few days before, were not to be found. (Both survived.) After all this, Ross drove to his mother's house and collapsed.

Ross was named in the newspapers as having been

with Wilde at the time of the arrest and had to resign from some of his clubs. Mrs Ross was understandably alarmed for her son and insisted that he go abroad. He demurred on the grounds that he would be abandoning his friend, and she offered £500 to help in Wilde's defense if he would leave at once. He allowed himself to be persuaded, and took himself off to the Terminus Hotel at Calais and a week later to Rouen. Reggie Turner and Maurice Schwabe also decamped. Henry Harland wrote to Edmund Gosse that six hundred gentlemen had crossed from Dover to Calais on a night when normally only sixty would have done so. Douglas, however, elected to stay on, though he appeared to be in greater danger than the others. In fact, his father had evidently resolved to protect him, probably by having Russell arrange matters with the Director of Prosecutions. Robert Sherard and Ada and Ernest Leverson were the other friends of Wilde who remained conspicuously loyal and helpful. But dozens fell away.

Wilde left a message for Douglas that he would be at Bow Street Police Station that night, and asked him to try to get his brother Percy, and George Alexander and Lewis Waller (from the theatres where Wilde's plays were running), to attend next morning to give bail. Only Percy was willing. Wilde also asked Douglas to secure Humphreys' services for the hearings. Douglas went round to Bow Street in the evening in the hope of seeing Wilde, but like Ross he was refused. He resolved, however, to see him every day. For his part, Wilde ate a bit of cold chicken, drank some coffee, was refused permission to smoke, and spent a wretched night.

'With what a crash this fell!' Wilde wrote to the Leversons on 9 April. It was like the history of Timon of Athens, or of Wilde's old admiration, *Agamemnon*, yet meaner. Wilde's name was removed from the hoardings of the two theatres where *An Ideal Husband* and *The Importance of Being Earnest* were playing to large audiences, and soon, with public feeling running high, the plays were taken off. The same thing happened in New York, and the actress Rose Coghlan, who was about to take *A Woman of No Importance* on tour in the United States, cancelled it. Not only did Wilde's friends in England drop away; so did most of his friends in France. On 13 April 1895 Jules Huret, in his '*Petite chronique des lettres*' in *Le Figaro littéraire*, named three French writers as Wilde's intimates: Catulle Mendès, Marcel Schwob, and Jean Lorrain. A furore resulted. Schwob sent his seconds to meet

Huret's seconds, and was angry when they accepted Huret's explanation. Lorrain had Huret publish a letter from him denying intimacy, and forgot having dedicated his story, 'Lanterne magique', to Wilde in *L'Echo de Paris* of 14 December 1891. Catulle Mendès was not so easily fobbed off. He and Huret had a duel with épées in the 'premières feuilles' of the forest of St Germain, on 17 April at 3 p.m. Blood was shed, but as a commentator remarked, in droplets only. Colette's husband, Willy, registered his amusement in *L'Echo de Paris* for 17 April at Wilde's behavior and England's embarrassment over it; but on 20 April Henry Bauer mocked Willy for pretending that homosexuality was only an English vice. 'I will not disavow now having known and visited him,' he said. Wilde's heteroclite tastes were not his affair. Nor had Wilde done any harm: 'Young Douglas was old enough to go out without his governess, and without his father's permission.' Octave Mirbeau also wrote sympathetically of Wilde in an article, '*A Propos du* "Hard Labour."' As for Sarah Bernhardt, when Sherard asked her to buy the rights to *Salome* for $1,500 to $2,000 to cover court costs, she expressed sympathy, dithered, and did nothing.

50 If Wilde hoped that the hearings that began on 6

April would soon be over, he was mistaken. They dragged on and on, with intervals of several days between each. Meanwhile he was in Bow Street in physical pain, never saying a word to the other prisoners, making subdued groans as he changed his standing position from time to time. He was then transferred to Holloway Prison except when recalled for another hearing. He hoped for bail, and the magistrate had it in his power to grant it. But Sir John Bridge was revolted by the crime of sodomy. As the French newspapers commented with some bewilderment, in England sodomy ranked only one step below murder. Though Humphreys pointed out that Wilde could have run away if he had wanted to, Bridge insisted that the gravity of the charge made bail unthinkable.

Wilde's second hearing took place on 11 April, the third on 18 April. The Grand Jury found true bills against Wilde and Alfred Taylor, whose case was linked with Wilde's very much against Wilde's interest, on 23 April. The charges were indecency and sodomy. Meanwhile various incidents added to the tensions. On 11 April a stationer tried to sell photographs of Wilde; the resulting fracas made the police intervene and stop the sale. On 24 April, a bankruptcy sale of Wilde's effects was forced by Queensberry, who demanded payment of his £600 costs, and by other creditors who followed his lead. Douglas had promised that his family would pay the costs of the trial; they did not. Wilde was rendered miserable by the sale not only of his manuscripts and his own books, but of presentation volumes from Hugo, Whitman, Swinburne, Mallarmé, Morris, and Verlaine, his Burne-Jones and Whistler drawings, paintings by Monticelli and Simeon Solomon, expensive china, Thomas Carlyle's writing desk and a hundred other things. A few were bought by friends. There was still not enough money to pay off the debts, so the estate remained in receivership until Ross eventually rescued it, long after Wilde's death.

At the dismal proceedings Wilde was represented by young Travers Humphreys and later by Sir Edward Clarke, who offered to represent him without fee. The prosecutor was Charles Gill, like Carson a Trinity College, Dublin man, and equally prejudiced against Wilde. There was some effort by the prosecution to persuade Taylor to turn state's evidence and so get off, but, perhaps because Wilde had talked to him before the trial, Taylor refused to betray his friend in any way. A long array of witnesses was produced, headed by the infamous Parker brothers, who claimed they had been recruited by Taylor to minister to Wilde's wishes. At first Charles Parker pretended to be nineteen; under cross-examination he proved to be twenty-one. In fact, none of the young men was under the statutory age of seventeen. There was testimony from Taylor's fellow-tenants and landladies about his peculiarly curtained and perfumed rooms, and the young men who came to tea there. Alfred Wood the blackmailer was there to testify about receiving £35 from Wilde in exchange for the letters Wilde had sent to Douglas, who had failed to remove them from his clothes before giving them to Wood. Sidney (better known as Jenny) Mavor had been threatened into testifying, but Douglas managed to collar him before his appearance and to remind him that he was a public school boy with a sense of honor, counselling him to deny having anything to do with Wilde. So this young man, asked what had happened the time he spent a night in Wilde's bed, replied, 'Nothing.'

The Savoy Hotel was represented by its 'professor of massage', Antonio Migge, who testified to having seen a young man sleeping in Wilde's bed while Wilde was dressing. The chambermaid Jane Cotter also claimed to have seen a boy there. A former housekeeper at the hotel, Mrs Perkins, testified that there had been fecal stains on the bedsheets. As for Taylor, there was testimony that he had gone through a form of marriage, dressed as a woman. The more Sir John Bridge heard of this testimony, the more he bristled, and when asked again for bail he said that 'no worse crime than this' existed, and bail could not be allowed. After the Grand Jury presented its charge, Wilde's lawyers asked that the case be postponed until the May Sessions, to give the defense time to prepare and to allow public opinion to die down. The prosecutor, Gill, objected, and Mr Justice Charles, who was to hear the case, agreed to an immediate trial, beginning on 26 April, promising it would be a fair one.

Douglas on 19 April sent a letter to the *Star*, complaining that Wilde was being judged before his trial, not at it. What was only too clear about this and subsequent letters from him to the press was that he was thinking more about himself than about his friend, and Wilde in *De Profundis* was severe on the subject: 'they [the letters] were simply to say that you hated your father. Nobody cared if you did or not.'

No doubt such thoughts glanced off his mind at the time. Mostly he was conscious only of Douglas's love for him, and his for Douglas. The almost daily visits meant a great deal. They were limited to about fifteen minutes, and there was so much noise that Wilde, who was rather deaf in one ear, could hardly hear. Wilde informed the Leversons on 9 April, 'I write to you from prison, where your kind words have reached me and given me comfort, though they have made me cry, in my loneliness. Not that I am really alone. A slim thing, goldhaired like an angel, stands always at my side. His presence overshadows me. He moves in the gloom like a white flower . . . I thought but to defend him from his father: I thought of nothing else, and now –.' To Ross and his close friend More Adey (translator of Ibsen's *Brand* and an art expert), both at Calais, he wrote on 9 April, 'Bosie is so wonderful. I think of nothing else. I saw him yesterday.' To Ada Leverson he wrote on 17 April, 'As for me, the wings of great love encompass me: holy ground.' As his trial approached, he wrote to her, 'I care less when I think that he is thinking of me. I think of nothing else.' In the meantime he sent Douglas a number of passionate letters.

But Sir Edward Clarke felt that Douglas's presence at the trial would be prejudicial to Wilde's interests, as stirring up recollections of the supposed corruption of the young man by him. Douglas would not go without Wilde's express request, and insisted upon having it in writing. At the last meeting, Douglas recalled, Wilde 'kissed the end of my finger through an iron grating at Newgate, and he begged me to let nothing in the world alter my attitude and my conduct towards him.' The young man joined Ross and Turner at the Hôtel Terminus in Calais, then went on to Rouen and Paris. He told the press that he had gone because of his mother's illness in Italy, but this pretext was quickly exploded. To a reporter for *Le Journal*, on 25 May 1895, he said that there had been danger of his being called as a witness, presumably by the prosecution, which he did not want. But in his *Autobiography*, Douglas said that on the third day of the trial he telegraphed certain information to Sir Edward Clarke, though it was prejudicial to himself, and again offered to give evidence. Presumably he took responsibility for the incidents of buggery, since Wilde did not practice this. The solicitors replied that his telegram was very improper, and that he should not make Clarke's task more difficult than it was already. Wilde wrote to him on the last day of the trial, 29 April:

My dearest boy, This is to assure you of my immortal, my eternal love for you. Tomorrow all will be over. If prison and dishonour be my destiny, think that my love for you and this idea, this still more divine belief, that you love me in return will sustain me in my unhappiness and will make me capable, I hope, of bearing my grief most patiently. Since the hope, nay rather the certainty, of meeting you again in some world is the goal and the encouragement of my present life, ah! I must continue to live in this world because of that . . . If one day, at Corfu or in some enchanted isle, there were a little house where we could live together, oh! life would be sweeter than it has ever been. Your love has broad wings and is strong, your love comes to me through my prison bars and comforts me, your love is the light of all my hours. Those who know not what love is will write, I know, if fate is against us, that I have had a bad influence upon your life. If they do that, you shall write, you shall say in your turn, that it is not so. Our love was always beautiful and noble, and if I have been the butt of a terrible tragedy, it is because the nature of that love has not been understood. In your letter this morning you say something which gives me courage. I must remember it. You write that it is my duty to you and to myself to live in spite of everything. I think that is true. I shall try and I shall do it . . . I stretch out my hands towards you, Oh! may I live to touch your hair and your hands.

WILDE'S FIRST TRIAL

The form of government that is most suitable to the artist is no government at all.

The trial, which opened on 26 April 1895, went over the same ground as the Queensberry trial and the three hearings at Bow Street, and perhaps never in the Nineties was so much unsavory evidence given so much publicity. The prosecutor insisted upon a speedy trial, in which the cases of Taylor and Wilde would be joined because Taylor had procured young men to commit acts of indecency with Wilde. So some charges related to conspiracy. Mr Justice Sir Arthur Charles agreed, over Clarke's protest, but eventually the conspiracy charges were dropped voluntarily by the prosecution, and the judge then said he had never felt that they were properly joined to the other charges. Taylor, a bad witness (as Beerbohm says), and badly represented by J. T. Grein, was simply an additional weight on Wilde's head. In other respects the case was conducted by the Treasury with considerable hypocrisy. Not only was homosexuality common in the English public schools which most of the legal personages present had attended. Also there had evidently been an agreement between Gill and Charles Russell, Queensberry's solicitor, that Douglas's name would be kept out of the case as far as possible in return for Queensberry's detailed evidence against Wilde. Who it was who introduced Atkins and Mavor to Wilde remained a mystery, though clearly a soluble one. As to why none of the important people whom George Wyndham approached saw fit to prevent the trial, there was a reluctance to interfere with the course of justice, and a lack of appetite to take on Queensberry as an adversary. There was also the old difficulty that Rosebery's name had been mentioned in one of Queensberry's letters. George Ives heard, nonetheless, that Rosebery had considered doing something to help Wilde until Balfour told him, 'If you do, you will lose the election.' (In the event, he lost the election anyway.) Everyone seemed to have a reason for leaning over backwards to avoid any suggestion of going easy on Wilde. As for Lockwood, the Solicitor-General, Carson is said to have suggested that he leave Wilde alone, as having suffered enough, but Lockwood said he had no alternative but to continue what Carson had initiated.

Wilde looked thin; his hair had been cut shorter than

usual. He was, said the *New York Times*, 'careworn and anxious.' His cross-examination had few surprises to offer. He admitted that he knew the boys who had testified, but not that he had had indecent relations with them. The serious addition to the charges had to do with one young man who was not a prostitute, Edward Shelley. His testimony, given with extreme discomfort, was somewhat vitiated by his admission that he had at times been out of his mind, and also by the fact that he had pursued Wilde's friendship and asked his help long after he had supposedly been corrupted by him.

In cross-examining Wilde, Gill tried to follow Carson's lead and besmirch him by association with the *Chameleon*, not so much with 'The Priest and the Acolyte' as with two homosexual poems by Douglas in it. 'What is the "Love that dare not speak its name"?' he asked. After all his lies, denials, and shifts, Wilde suddenly found a voice:

> The 'Love that dare not speak its name' in this century is such a great affection of an elder for a younger man as there was between David and Jonathan, such as Plato made the very basis of his philosophy, and such as you find in the sonnets of Michaelangelo and Shakespeare. It is that deep, spiritual affection that is as pure as it is perfect. It dictates

and pervades great works of art like those of Shakespeare and Michaelangelo, and those two letters of mine, such as they are. It is in this century misunderstood, so much misunderstood that it may be described as the 'Love that dare not speak its name,' and on account of it I am placed where I am now. It is beautiful, it is fine, it is the noblest form of affection. There is nothing unnatural about it. It is intellectual, and it repeatedly exists between an elder and a younger man, when the elder man has intellect, and the younger man has all the joy, hope and glamour of life before him. That it should be so the world does not understand. The world mocks at it and sometimes puts one in the pillory for it.

This *cri de coeur* had its effect, though it could not, as the prosecutor noted, apply to the male prostitutes in the case, and Wilde himself said it could only happen once in a lifetime. For once Wilde spoke not wittily but well. As Max Beerbohm wrote to Reggie Turner after attending the trial, 'Oscar has been quite superb. His speech about the Love that dares not tell his name was simply wonderful and carried the whole court right away, quite a tremendous burst of applause. Here was this man, who had been for a month in prison and loaded with insults and crushed and buffeted, perfectly self-possessed, dominating the Old Bailey with his fine presence and musical voice. He has never had so great a triumph, I am sure, as when the gallery burst into applause – I am sure it affected the jury.'

The rest of the cross-examination went less favorably. Wilde had again to defend his letters to Douglas. As for the evidence of the hotel servants, Wilde said, 'It is entirely untrue. Can I answer for what hotel servants say years after I have left the hotel?' He denied all Shelley's evidence of impropriety, as well as the Parkers', Atkins's, and Wood's.

Why did you take up with these youths? – I am a lover of youth. (Laughter)

You exalt youth as a sort of god? – I like to study the young in everything. There is something fascinating in youthfulness.

So you would prefer puppies to dogs and kittens to cats? – I think so. I should enjoy, for instance, the society of a beardless, briefless barrister quite as much as that of the most accomplished Q.C. (Laughter)

This time Sir Edward Clarke was better prepared. He persuasively denied that *Dorian Gray* or 'Phrases and Philosophies for the Use of the Young' was in any sense corrupting or corrupted. He pointed out that Wilde, instead of shrinking like a guilty man from
 public exposure, had sought publicity by prosecuting

Lord Queensberry. As to the hotel evidence against Wilde, it was extraordinary that the prosecution had been able to find such a paucity of it, when Wilde had stayed in hotel after hotel for years. The evidence of the Parkers, of Wood, and of Atkins obviously superimposed on what was true much that was false, as the best lies do. Wilde was undoubtedly taken in by them, which was evidence of imprudence not crime. They were blackmailers whose evidence could not be trusted. Atkins had been proved on the stand to have perjured himself. 'I ask the jury,' Clarke said, 'to clear from this frightful imputation one of our most renowned and accomplished men of letters of today, and in clearing him, to clear society from a stain.' Grein then made a weak defense of Taylor. Gill, for the prosecution, insisted that the letters to Douglas 'breathe an unholy passion,' and that Wilde's admitted presents to these many boys were proof of his gratitude. As Ives commented in his journal, Wilde suffered because of his generosity, which was not confined to young men. Granted that some of the boys were not of the highest type, there was still the case of Shelley, whose testimony was not tainted by blackmail charges. Finally, Gill gave up the charges of conspiracy. The case now went to the judge.

Mr Justice Charles agreed to omit the conspiracy charges, and to direct a verdict of acquittal upon them. On the literary question he proved enlightened. He was inclined to agree with Clarke that Wilde was not culpable for having written *Dorian Gray* or for the *Chameleon* pieces which he had not written. As to the letters to Douglas, he was not inclined to accept Gill's statement that these proved anything. He acknowledged that Shelley was unstable. He found the stories of the maids and other functionaries at the Savoy Hotel difficult to credit. As to the fecal stains, he pointed out that these might have an innocent explanation. The judge did not however reject the testimony of the witnesses about Wilde's and Taylor's behavior. He put four questions to the jury:

1) Do you think that Wilde committed indecent acts with Edward Shelley and Alfred Wood and with a person or persons unknown at the Savoy Hotel or with Charles Parker?
2) Did Taylor procure or attempt to procure the commission of these acts or of any of them?
3) Did Wilde and Taylor or either of them attempt to get Atkins to commit indecencies?
4) Did Taylor commit indecent acts with Charles Parker or with William Parker?

The jury was out from 1.35 to 5.15 p.m. They then reported that they could agree only on the question about Atkins, where their verdict was not guilty. One newspaper, *L'Echo de Paris* of 4 May, said that the vote to convict Wilde had been ten to two, as revealed by an indiscreet juror in a Pall Mall club, while Max Beerbohm heard that it was eleven to one, and Alfred Douglas agreed that only one juror voted for acquittal. Beerbohm reported to More Adey, 'Hoscar stood very upright when he was brought up to hear the verdict and looked most leonine and sphinx-like. I pitied poor little Alfred Taylor – nobody remembered his existence . . . Hoscar is thinner and in consequence finer to look at. Willie [Wilde] has been extracting fivers from Humphreys. It was horrible leaving the court day after day and having to pass through a knot of renters (the younger Parker wearing Her Majesty's uniform, another form of female attire) who were allowed to hang around after giving their evidence and to wink at likely persons.'

Owing to the jury's failure to reach a verdict, a new trial was ordered. The judge again refused bail, but Clarke announced he would seek it from another judge in chambers. Clarke proposed that the next trial be postponed, but Gill said it would be the usual course to hold it in the next sessions, and the judge agreed. Many people urged that harm 'would be done to the public morals' if the case were renewed. T. M. Healy begged Lockwood not to put Wilde on trial again. Lockwood said, 'I would not but for the abominable rumours against Rosebery.' So the long drawn-out farce went into its third and last act.

BETWEEN TRIALS

What are called criminals nowadays are not
criminals at all.

Bereft of the company of his lover Douglas, and his friends Ross and Turner – all three fugitive in the Hôtel de la Poste in Rouen – and unsought by most of his other friends, Wilde could feel the shades of the prison house drawing round him figuratively as well as literally. He had twenty-five days to go before his second trial ended. The first five were spent in Holloway Prison. There was now no reason to deny him bail, but Mr Justice Charles perhaps wished to indicate that he had no sympathy for pederasts, even

 those who might be innocent. Yet only a misdemeanor,

not a felony, was involved, so bail could not long be refused. Two days later, on 3 May, Charles Matthews applied again on Wilde's behalf, this time to Mr Baron Pollock in chambers, for bail until the new trial should begin. He proposed two sureties of £1,000 each.

On 4 May Pollock set bail at £5,000, of which £2,500 would be allowed to Wilde on his own recognizance. It took two days to round up sureties for the remaining £2,500. Frank Harris says he volunteered, but was ruled ineligible because he was not a householder. Bosie's brother Percy had no money in hand, but out of loyalty to Bosie scraped together half of what was required in defiance of his father. The other half was harder. It may have been Ernest Leverson who, being himself debarred by the terms of his business partnership from going bail for anyone, approached first Selwyn Image, who did not have the money, and then the Reverend Stewart Headlam, who did. Headlam – whom Wilde had privately dubbed 'the heresiarch' – was scarcely acquainted with him, having met him only twice, but he was a man of conviction, and strongly supported the view that Wilde was entitled not to be prejudged. Being a socialist and an unorthodox Christian, he knew that he would suffer notoriety for his kind of action, and worse, be thought to have sought it. His maid left his service, some of his friends defected, and an enemy accused him of wading in Gomorrah on his way to building Jerusalem. At least there would be no financial loss if Wilde jumped bail; so Leverson had promised, and Wilde gave his word not to flee. With Headlam's £1,225 and Percy Douglas's in hand, all impediments to bail were removed. The bail hearing at Bow Street Police Station on 7 May concluded with Wilde's release.

Where to go was not so easily decided. Two rooms had been engaged for him at the Midland Hotel at St Pancras, far from his usual haunts, but just as he was sitting down to a late dinner, the manager entered. 'You are Oscar Wilde, I believe.' Wilde did not disavow it. 'You must leave the hotel at once.' Some of Queensberry's pugilistic roughnecks, egged on by the Marquess himself, had threatened the manager with reprisals for receiving Wilde, and they followed him as he drove across town to another hotel. There too, after a few minutes, the manager apologized, but said that some men had threatened to sack the hotel and raise the street against Wilde if he did not leave at once. By now it was near midnight. In the end Wilde had no alternative but to go to the house where his brother Willie was living with his second wife, Lily

Lees, and Lady Wilde, 146 Oakley Street. It was not pleasant to have to plead with his brother, to whom he had not spoken for a year and a half, 'Willie, give me shelter or I shall die in the streets.' As Willie described the scene later, 'He came tapping with his beak against the window-pane, and fell down on my threshold like a wounded stag.' For the moment magnanimity was in order.

Willie gave his brother a room with a small camp-bed in a corner between the fireplace and the wall, and here for some days Oscar was physically ill. His friends in France heard about it and asked Robert Sherard to go over and see him. Sherard did so. He found Wilde's face 'flushed and swollen.' 'Oh, why have you brought me no poison from Paris?' he asked alliteratively in a broken voice. Sherard offered to take him to the country to recover his health, but he did not want to move. Sherard managed to rouse him by proposing they read some Wordsworth; in one sonnet Wordsworth was caught out rhyming 'love' with 'shove,' and Wilde feigned outrage and said severely to the hapless descendant, 'Robert, what does this mean?'

It soon became apparent that the family setting in Oakley Street would prove anything but easy. Willie was setting up as a moralist: 'At least my vices were decent,' he muttered in his cups. He told Oscar that he was defending him all over London, at which Oscar commented to a friend, 'My poor, dear brother, he would compromise a steam engine.' 'Willie makes such a merit of giving me shelter,' he told Harris, and confided that, as Beerbohm had said, his brother had sold old letters to Humphreys in what amounted to blackmail. For his part, Willie had his own rhythmical explanations of his brother's fall: 'It is his vanity that has brought all this disgrace upon him; they swung incense before him, they swung it before his heart.' Both Willie and Lady Wilde were determined that Oscar should stay and stand trial; Willie would assure visitors, 'Oscar is an Irish gentleman, and he will face the music.' As for Lady Wilde, she declaimed to Oscar in her grand manner, 'If you stay, even if you go to prison, you will always be my son. It will make no difference to my affection. But if you go, I will never speak to you again.' Wilde promised her that he would stay.

But as he approached martyrdom his friends wished to deny him it. Percy, though one of his guarantors, declared, 'It will practically ruin me if I lose all that money at the present moment, but if there is a chance even of conviction, in God's name let him go.' Sherard urged Wilde to leave, and Frank Harris brought matters to a head. Harris insisted upon taking Wilde out to lunch, against Willie's wishes, and proposed the Café Royal, scene of so many meals in the past. Oscar did not feel it would be seemly, so Harris brought him instead to a restaurant in Great Portland Street, where they had a private room. Harris wanted to stiffen Wilde's resistance. He proposed that Wilde should say he liked the company of young men because he liked writing about them. Wilde did not respond, and never adopted this tactic. Harris described the testimony as a pack of lies, and Wilde said that the testimony of the chambermaids at the Savoy Hotel was based on their mixing up his room with Douglas's. Harris offered to make a plan of the rooms and get the maids to admit their error, but Wilde did not want Douglas to be implicated. At any rate, he said, Shelley's testimony remained, and the judge had said that this was unimpugnable. Harris declared that Shelley was an accomplice, and therefore could not be believed without corroboration, of which there was none. At this Wilde broke out, and said, 'You talk with passion and conviction, as if I were innocent.' 'But you are innocent,' said Harris, 'aren't you?' 'No,' said Wilde. 'I thought you knew that all along.' Harris said, 'I did not believe it for a moment.' 'This will make a great difference to you?' asked Wilde, but Harris assured him it would not.

He now developed his fallback plan, that Wilde should escape. A Jewish businessman of his acquaintance happened to mention owning a yacht, and Harris asked him if he would rent it for a month. The man was willing, and asked what Harris planned to do. On impulse Harris told him exactly what he wanted it for, and the yachtsman then said, 'In that case you can have it for nothing.' He too wanted Wilde to escape. Harris now made his proposal to Wilde. The yacht was at Erith, he said, and they could leave at once. Much scepticism has been shown about this yacht, yet both Yeats and Ada Leverson knew of the plan, and it seems to have been available even if it was not waiting at Erith with steam up, as Harris dramatically pictured it. Wilde, however, refused to go.

It was while he was still in Oakley Street that the Leversons invited Wilde to dinner, and discovered how unhappy he was, living with his brother. They bravely invited him to stay with them, and he accepted. Before he arrived with his belongings, they called the servants together and offered them a month's wages

 if they wished to leave rather than be in the house

with this notorious man. All chose to stay with 'poor Mr Wilde,' as one called him, and Mrs Leverson drove over to Oakley Street to fetch him, on about 18 May. The address was kept secret to ward Queensberry off. The Leversons' son was in the country, so Wilde was shown up to the nursery, which consisted of two large rooms and a bathroom. 'Shall I remove the toys?' she asked, but he replied, 'Please leave them.' So among the rocking horses and doll's houses he received his solicitors and friends, gathering the threads of destitution and disgrace. To avoid embarrassing his hosts he took his meals upstairs and did not come down until six o'clock. Then he appeared in dinner clothes, flower in buttonhole, and made a point of talking to Mrs Leverson about everything but his main concerns. His old hairdresser came to shave him and wave his hair every day.

Later Mrs Leverson would remember some of his conversation. He had romantic ideas about absinthe, and described its effect to her: 'After the first glass, you see things as you wish they were. After the second, you see things as they are not. Finally you see things as they really are, and that is the most horrible thing in the world.' 'How do you mean?' 'I mean disassociated. Take a top-hat! You think you see it as it really is. But you don't, because you associate it with other things and ideas. If you had never heard of one before, and suddenly saw it alone, you'd be frightened, or laugh. That is the effect absinthe has, and that is why it drives men mad.' He went on, 'Three nights I sat up all night drinking absinthe, and thinking that I was singularly clearheaded and sane. The waiter came in and began watering the sawdust. The most wonderful flowers, tulips, lilies, and roses sprang up and made a garden of the café. "Don't you see them?" I said to him. "*Mais, non, monsieur, il n'y a rien.*"' There was no drug to make the world flower now. He turned to other subjects, especially books. Dickens was an old phobia, and it was to amuse her he made his classic remark, 'One must have a heart of stone to read the death of Little Nell without laughing.' Or he made up unChristian parables in the manner of *Lives of the Saints*. He liked one or another of these well enough to ask for something to write it down, but Mrs Leverson could not put her hand on anything. 'You have all the equipment of a writer, my dear Sphinx,' he said to her, 'except pens, ink and paper.'

While Oscar Wilde was with the Leversons, Yeats came on 19 May to Oakley Street in search of him. Yeats's father had told him he owed it to Wilde to offer to testify for him, or do some service, and Yeats brought along a packet of letters he had collected from Irish men of letters, including George Russell, to encourage his friend. (Only Professor Edward Dowden refused.) He was met, however, by Willie, who said, 'Before I give him this, you must tell me what is in it. Are you telling him to run away? All his friends are telling him that, and we have made up our minds that he must go to prison if necessary.' Yeats replied, 'No, I certainly would not advise him to run away.' Which was true: to Yeats it seemed a great moment for Wilde to show his mettle. He wrote to Dowden about his visit:

I went to try and see Wilde today and to tell him how much I sympathised with him in his trouble. He has left Oakley Street but they told me this much about his movements. A yacht and a very large sum of money was placed at his disposal and all settled for his flight but he refused to go. He says he will stand it out and face the worst and no matter how it turns out work on. He will not go down, they said, or drink, or take poison. I mentioned how I had found some of our Dublin literary men sympathetic to him and my words were received with most pathetic gentleness and I promised to tell them about his plans. I write to suggest that you either write direct to him, some sympathetic words,

Morris has already written, or write some answer to this which I can get shown to him.

Others were keener than Yeats and Willie to save him from prison, however it might spoil the drama. Constance Wilde came to see her husband at the Leversons' and spent two hours with him. She brought an earnest message from her lawyer, imploring him to go away before his next trial, which would undoubtedly be calamitous. She left in tears, and Ada Leverson saw on his face 'a look of immovable obstinacy.' Mrs Leverson herself had the temerity to send up a note asking him to do what his wife urged. There was no reply until he came down to dinner, when he handed her back her note, only remarking, 'That is not like you, Sphinx,' before he changed the subject.

Wilde had made a decision, and intended to stick to it. Mrs Leverson thought him too involved in a fantasy of success to believe that anything bad could happen to him, but Wilde's life had offered no such cycle of triumphs as she supposed. There had been his broken engagement to Florence Balcombe, his removal from Frank Miles's house, the failure of his early plays, his troubled American lecture tour, years of not having enough money, and the chaotic affair with Douglas. As he was to declare later, his works had always had a telltale undercurrent of sorrow. And he knew what running away would be like, whether he did it in the boisterous company of Frank Harris or by himself. There would be no dignity in that. He might well be stopped, or if not stopped, he would have to slink about the Continent as a fugitive from British justice. As his trip to Florence had shown, slinking was not Wilde's style. Ostracism (a subject about which he had quarreled with Jebb years before) was not for him. What he wrote to Douglas just before the trial ended was what he felt all along: 'I decided that it was nobler and more beautiful to stay . . . I did not want to be called a coward or a deserter. A false name, a disguise, a hunted life, all that is not for me.' He chose to be convicted, knowing that people would wrongly say that he chose out of weakness or megalomania – yet neither obliged his choice. Could he really have preferred picking oakum to ruling a dinner table? He recognized that of the ignominious alternatives available to him, this was the least unheroic. (It was also the most modest.) Yeats was delighted when an old enemy of Wilde, perhaps Henley, met him in the street, and said with admiration of Wilde, 'He has made of infamy a new Thermopylae.' As for Yeats himself, he wrote later, 'I have never doubted, even for an instant, that he made the right decision, and that he owes to that decision half of his renown.' He submitted to the society he had criticized, and so earned the right to criticize it further.

Heroics were not the daily fare at the Leversons' house. Wilde did not claim heroism, nor do any more than resist pleas that he run away, without giving any grounds in particular, least of all grandiloquent ones. As the day of the trial approached, he showed something like resignation. He told Sherard that he thought he could bear a year's imprisonment, but Sherard warned him that he might well get the maximum sentence of two years. Wilde fell back for comfort on his love of Douglas, and wrote him letters of the most fervent kind: 'Now, in anguish and pain, in grief and humiliation, I feel that my love for you, your love for me, are the two signs of my life, the divine sentiments which make all bitterness bearable.' Douglas had admitted his own blame (he would deny it later) but Wilde said 'Let destiny, Nemesis, or the unjust gods alone receive the blame for everything that has happened.' And again, 'My sweet rose, my delicate flower,

 my lily of lilies, it is perhaps in prison that I am going

to test the power of love. I am going to see if I cannot make the bitter waters sweet by the intensity of the love I bear you.' These letters were of a different kind from those produced in court, which had been very nearly the formal literary productions that Wilde claimed. He was still prodigal of phrases: 'None of God's created beings, and you are the Morning Star to me, have been so wildly worshipped, so madly adored.' Beneath the purple alliteration was real feeling. Douglas wryly commented long afterwards in his *Autobiography*: 'The emotion of the great crisis fanned the waning fires of our devotion to each other.' He replied to Wilde with less eloquence, though with comparable emotion. He also wrote to his brother, begging him to make Wilde leave England while it was still possible. Percy replied that he hoped he would. In Paris Bosie took heart and wrote to Wilde, 'It seems too dreadful to be here without you, but I hope you will join me next week. Do keep up your spirits, my dearest darling. I continue to think of you day and night, and send you all my love. I am always your own loving and devoted boy Bosie.'

Douglas's state of mind in this period was exceedingly disturbed. He sent a series of letters to the press, of varying degrees of indiscretion. On 19 April he had written to the *Star* to complain of Wilde's being prejudged, and of Sir John Bridge's obvious bias against him. But the principal part of the letter read:

I feel, therefore, that I am taking my life in my hands in daring to raise my voice against the chorus of the pack of those who are now hounding Mr Oscar Wilde to his ruin; the more so as I feel assured that the public has made up its mind to accept them as it has accepted everybody and everything connected with this case, at Mr Carson's valuation. I, of course, am the undutiful son who, in his arrogance and folly, has kicked against his kind and affectionate father, and who has further aggravated his offence by not running away and hiding his face after the discomfiture of his friend.

Wilde understandably felt even at the time, though he did not tell Douglas till later, that this was a commonplace production; it was worse, indeed, because Douglas saw himself as the center of interest. He followed this up five days later with a letter saying he had received thousands of letters in support of his stand for Wilde. By 25 May the French press had caught up with him and Georges Docquois published an interview with him on that date. Douglas had claimed that he left England (on the second day of Wilde's trial, according to Raffalovich) because of the illness of his mother in Italy, but the press had found out she was in fact well. He now admitted that he had left because Wilde's lawyers had warned him he might be called as a witness, which he did not want. He had arrived in Paris on 15 May, but dodged the press for eight days. Asked about his letter to *Le Temps*, he explained, 'You do not know what an absolutely abominable man the Marquess of Queensberry is . . . Until I was twelve, I saw him at most twenty times, and I didn't feel at all sure from the way he treated me that I was his son.' The reporter inquired delicately about his relationship with Wilde, but Douglas insisted it was extraterrestrial, a communion together in the symbol rather than something seedy ('*louche*'). He knew no joy greater than to dine with Wilde when the latter was in 'good form.' They had once been joined by a dilettantish pleasure, now they were joined by persecution. To another French journalist he wrote on 30 May that he knew a hundred overt homosexuals in the best English society.

Lady Queensberry had some inkling of how Bosie was behaving, and she encouraged her son Percy to go to Rouen to see him at the end of May. She also consulted an old friend, the Reverend Sebastian Bowden, and asked him to find some trustworthy person to stay with Bosie and prevent his behaving foolishly out of loyalty to the fallen Wilde. Bowden asked More Adey to do this; Adey replied that his first duty was to Robert Ross, but that he would deal with Douglas as soon as he had calmed Ross down. Ross's family meanwhile forbade his remaining with Douglas, and Douglas, as Adey informed Bowden, planned a trip to Florence to see Lord Henry Somerset, almost as scandalous a character as Wilde.

A NEW THERMOPYLAE

How steep the stairs within kings' houses are.

Meanwhile Wilde was faced with the reality of his last trial. On its eve, 21 May, he serenely bade his friends farewell, and informed each of a little present from the few possessions left to him which would be a souvenir in case he did not return. When he was going to his room he asked Ada Leverson to leave a sleeping draught for him on the mantelpiece, not that he would take it, but that its presence would have a magical effect. Next day, before leaving with More Adey to join Stewart Headlam, he said to her, 'If the worst comes to the worst, Sphinx, you'll write to me?' During the next six days he was met in the morning and escorted back at night by Headlam, sometimes by Percy Douglas as well. At the Old Bailey all the seats were taken, so Queensberry, wearing a white cravat and a flower, had to stand, listening attentively, small and ferocious. Sir Edward Clarke was determined to try to secure some advantage for Wilde, and moved that Wilde and Taylor should be tried separately. Sir Frank Lockwood as Solicitor-General opposed the motion, on the grounds that the cases were intertwined. But Mr Justice Sir Alfred Wills ruled in Clarke's favor. Lockwood then proposed to take Taylor's case first, and Clarke again protested, for Taylor really had no defense at all, was well known to the police, and certain to be convicted. Over Clarke's protest the judge agreed. He said that Taylor had been in prison for seven weeks already, without bail, and that his trial should be delayed no longer.

This decision, which seemed minor, was very much to Wilde's detriment. The testimony in the Taylor case would involve him as well, and if Taylor were convicted, Wilde could scarcely be acquitted by the same jury without evident injustice. The Taylor case was quickly heard and quickly decided. The prosecutor had decided to reduce the charge from sodomy to indecency, as being easier to prove, and to secure a conviction. Taylor was found guilty on two counts of indecency with the Parker brothers, but not guilty of procuring Wood for Wilde, since, as the judge pointed out, he had not introduced the two men to each other. One of the Parker brothers had been promised immunity by ex-Inspector Littlefield if he would turn state's evidence against Wilde, but he nobly refused. Mr Justice Wills deferred sentence. Queensberry sent a telegram to his son Percy's wife: 'To Lady Douglas – must congratulate on verdict. Cannot on Percy appearance. Looked like a dug-up corpse. Fear too much madness in kissing. Taylor guilty. Wilde's turn to-morrow. Queensberry.' He also, on the mistaken notion that Wilde was staying with Percy and her, went to their house that night, knocked on the door, and made a disturbance. To Percy's wife he sent an illustration from a popular weekly of an iguanodon, with a childish note, 'Perhaps an ancestor of Oscar Wilde.' The following morning in Bond Street, in front of Scott's the hatters, Percy caught sight of his father and asked him if he were going to continue to annoy his wife with his communications. A street fight broke out, with Lord Douglas getting a black eye. They were both arrested and bound over next day on their own sureties of £500 to keep the peace for six months.

In this atmosphere of near-hysteria, the second trial of Oscar Wilde was to take place. The press had been discussing Wilde for weeks, with condemnation general except for *Reynolds's News*, which had private information about the extraordinary zeal with which Wilde was being prosecuted. Most of the newspapers considered that Queensberry had rightly brought down the 'High Priest of the Decadents,' as the *National Observer* saw fit to label Wilde.

The trial had few surprises. It became clear that two of the most important witnesses, the brothers Parker, were being maintained at Chiswick under the care of a Crown detective. It did not become clear, though it was apparently true, that all the witnesses had been receiving £5 a week from the beginning of Wilde's prosecution of Queensberry until his conviction. The star witness, Charles Parker, had received a new suit of clothes at Crown expense, ostensibly because he could not appear in court in a soldier's uniform. (He was to be cashiered.) This time the prosecution began not with him, however, but with Shelley, who made his usual blubbering denunciation of Wilde's sexual advances. This was again countered by the now familiar letters which he addressed to Wilde after the alleged offenses, asking for financial help. For a moment or two the case veered in Wilde's favor as the judge ruled that Shelley was, as Harris had claimed, an accomplice, and therefore not credible unless corroborated. This eliminated the prosecution's trump card, since Shelley alone of the important witnesses was neither male prostitute nor blackmailer. The next day Sir Frank Lockwood, once Wilde's friend, tried to persuade the judge to change his view, but the judge stood firm. Lockwood was heard to murmur outside, 'The old fool!' Testimony disclosed that the person who introduced Taylor to Wilde was Lockwood's nephew by marriage, Maurice Schwabe, a point upon which Lockwood was careful not to dilate.

Clarke did his best. He pointed out that, as anyone could see who had been at the other trials, Wilde was a broken man. It was inconceivable that he would have subjected himself to possible prosecution, by charging Queensberry with libel, if he had himself been so vulnerable. 'This trial seems to be operating as an act of indemnity for all the blackmailers in London,' he said, and it was obvious that the witnesses could better have been the accused rather than the accusers. They had nothing on Wilde, for otherwise they would have blackmailed him relentlessly. Charles Parker was an uncorroborated witness, and a peculiarly unstable one. The testimony of the chambermaids did not prove that Wilde had committed any improper acts. 'If on an examination of the evidence you, therefore, feel it your duty to say that the charges against the prisoner have not been proved, then I am sure that you will be glad that the brilliant promise which has been clouded by these accusations, and the bright reputation which was so nearly quenched in the torrent of prejudice which a few weeks ago was sweeping through the press, have been saved by your verdict from absolute ruin; and that it leaves him, a distinguished man of letters and a brilliant Irishman, to live among us a life of honour and repute, and to give in the maturity of his genius gifts to our literature, of which he has given only the promise in his early youth.'

The last day of the trial, 25 May, was the Queen's birthday. In the midst of patriotic fervor Lockwood made his final speech for the prosecution. He raked Wilde over; he dealt with the suspect letters to Douglas, the payment of blackmail to Wood, the relations with Taylor, Wood, Parker, Conway, which he insisted corroborated each other. If the evidence of the chambermaids was false, why had not Lord Alfred

Douglas been called to deny it? As Wilde listened to 'Lockwood's appalling denunciation,' which sounded, he said later, 'like a thing out of Tacitus, like a passage in Dante, like one of Savonarola's indictments of the Popes at Rome,' he felt 'sickened with horror at what I heard. Suddenly it occurred to me, "*How splendid it would be, if I was saying all this about myself!*" I saw then at once that what is said of a man is nothing. The point is, who says it.' As he wrote to Ross later, 'the idea of "The Ballad of Reading Gaol" came to me while I was in the dock.' He was not cowed, his imagination was secretly triumphing over the proceedings.

Then came the summing-up. Mr Justice Wills was too prosaic to accept the affectation of Wilde's letters to Douglas as anything but indecent, and he spoke of them in unpleasant terms as Mr Justice Charles had not. As he went on he became more vehement, as if the heinousness of the offense was being borne in upon him the more he talked of it. 'It is the worst case I have ever tried,' he declared. He agreed that the fecal stains on the Savoy sheets might have been due to diarrhoea, but did not encourage this supposition. He impressed upon the jury the importance of maintaining the highest moral tone. The jury retired at half past three, and returned at twenty-five minutes to six with a question about some minor evidence. Lockwood, conscious that the rejection of Shelley's testimony meant that only the testimony of accomplices was left, said to Clarke, 'You'll dine your man in Paris tomorrow.' But Clarke said, 'No, no, no.' The jury retired again but returned a few minutes later to find the defendant guilty on all counts except that relating to Edward Shelley. Clarke asked the judge not to pass sentence until the next session, so as to consider a legal technicality. But the Solicitor-General opposed the motion, and the judge rejected it. He then turned to the prisoners:

Oscar Wilde and Alfred Taylor, the crime of which you have been convicted is so bad that one has to put stern restraint upon one's self to prevent one's self from describing, in language which I would rather not use, the sentiments which must rise to the breast of every man of honour who has heard the details of these two terrible trials. That the jury have arrived at a correct verdict in this case I cannot persuade myself to entertain the shadow of a doubt; and I hope, at all events that those who sometimes imagine that a judge is half-hearted in the cause of decency and morality because he takes care no prejudice shall enter into the case, may see that that is consistent at least with the common sense of indignation at the horrible charges brought home to both of you.

It is no use for me to address you. People who can do these things must be dead to all sense of shame, and one cannot hope to produce any effect upon them. It is the worst case I have ever tried. That you, Taylor, kept a kind of male brothel it is impossible to doubt. And that you, Wilde, have been the centre of a circle of extensive corruption of the most hideous kind among young men, it is equally impossible to doubt.

I shall, under such circumstances, be expected to pass the severest sentence that the law allows. In my judgement it is totally inadequate for such a case as this. The sentence of the Court is that each of you be imprisoned and kept to hard labour for two years.

A cry of 'Shame' was heard in the court. Wilde blanched and his discomposed face worked with pain. 'My God, my God!' he said. He struggled to speak, and may have managed to say (though witnesses differ), 'And I? May I say nothing, my lord?' But the judge merely waved his hand to the warders, who took hold of Wilde just as he swayed and seemed about to fall to the ground. Taylor followed him, indifferent, as if conscious of having no place in the drama. But he had shielded Wilde, as Wilde had shielded Douglas. (After serving his sentence Taylor emigrated to America and oblivion.) Outside, Yeats said, the harlots danced on the pavement. They were delighted to have this rival removed. Lord Queensberry, too, was triumphant, and that night he and Charles Brookfield and Charles Hawtrey held a victory dinner in celebration.

PENGUIN 60S

ISABEL ALLENDE · *Voices in My Ear*
NICHOLSON BAKER · *Playing Trombone*
LINDSEY BAREHAM · *The Little Book of Big Soups*
KAREN BLIXEN · *From the Ngong Hills*
DIRK BOGARDE · *Coming of Age*
ANTHONY BURGESS · *Childhood*
ANGELA CARTER · *Lizzie Borden*
CARLOS CASTANEDA · *The Sorcerer's Ring of Power*
ELIZABETH DAVID · *Peperonata and Other Italian Dishes*
RICHARD DAWKINS · *The Pocket Watchmaker*
GERALD DURRELL · *The Pageant of Fireflies*
RICHARD ELLMANN · *The Trial of Oscar Wilde*
EPICURUS · *Letter on Happiness*
MARIANNE FAITHFULL · *Year One*
KEITH FLOYD · *Hot and Spicy Floyd*
ALEXANDER FRATER · *Where the Dawn Comes Up Like Thunder*
ESTHER FREUD · *Meeting Bilal*
JOHN KENNETH GALBRAITH · *The Culture of Contentment*
ROB GRANT AND DOUG NAYLOR · *Scenes from the Dwarf*
ROBERT GRAVES · *The Gods of Olympus*
JANE GRIGSON · *Puddings*
SOPHIE GRIGSON · *From Sophie's Table*
KATHARINE HEPBURN · *Little Me*
SUSAN HILL · *The Badness Within Him*
ALAN HOLLINGHURST · *Adventures Underground*
BARRY HUMPHRIES · *Less is More Please*
HOWARD JACOBSON · *Expulsion from Paradise*
P. D. JAMES · *The Girl Who Loved Graveyards*
STEPHEN KING · *Umney's Last Case*
LAO TZU · *Tao Te Ching*
DAVID LEAVITT · *Chips Is Here*

PENGUIN 60S

LAURIE LEE · *To War in Spain*
PATRICK LEIGH FERMOR · *Loose as the Wind*
ELMORE LEONARD · *Trouble at Rindo's Station*
DAVID LODGE · *Surprised by Summer*
BERNARD MAC LAVERTY · *The Miraculous Candidate*
SHENA MACKAY · *Cloud-Cuckoo-Land*
NORMAN MAILER · *The Dressing Room*
PETER MAYLE · *Postcards from Summer*
JAN MORRIS · *Scenes from Havian Life*
BLAKE MORRISON · *Camp Cuba*
VLADIMIR NABOKOV · *Now Remember*
REDMOND O'HANLON · *A River in Borneo*
STEVEN PINKER · *Thinking in Tongues*
CRAIG RAINE · *Private View*
CLAUDIA RODEN · *Ful Medames and Other Vegetarian Dishes*
HELGE RUBINSTEIN · *Chocolate Parfait*
SIMON SCHAMA · *The Taking of the Bastille*
WILL SELF · *The Rock of Crack As Big As the Ritz*
MARK SHAND · *Elephant Tales*
NIGEL SLATER · *30-Minute Suppers*
RICK STEIN · *Fresh from the Sea*
LYTTON STRACHEY · *Florence Nightingale*
PAUL THEROUX · *Slow Trains to Simla*
COLIN THUBRON · *Samarkand*
MARK TULLY · *Beyond Purdah*
LAURENS VAN DER POST · *Merry Christmas, Mr Lawrence*
MARGARET VISSER · *More than Meets the Eye*
GAVIN YOUNG · *Something of Samoa*

and

Thirty Obituaries from Wisden · SELECTED BY MATTHEW ENGEL

READ MORE IN PENGUIN

For complete information about books available from Penguin and how to order them, please write to us at the appropriate address below. Please note that for copyright reasons the selection of books varies from country to country.

IN THE UNITED KINGDOM: Please write to *Dept. EP, Penguin Books Ltd, Bath Road, Harmondsworth, Middlesex UB7 0DA.*

IN THE UNITED STATES: Please write to *Consumer Sales, Penguin USA, P.O. Box 999, Dept. 17109, Bergenfield, New Jersey 07621-0120.* VISA and MasterCard holders call 1-800-253-6476 to order Penguin titles.

IN CANADA: Please write to *Penguin Books Canada Ltd, 10 Alcorn Avenue, Suite 300, Toronto, Ontario M4V 3B2.*

IN AUSTRALIA: Please write to *Penguin Books Australia Ltd, P.O. Box 257, Ringwood, Victoria 3134.*

IN NEW ZEALAND: Please write to *Penguin Books (NZ) Ltd, Private Bag 102902, North Shore Mail Centre, Auckland 10.*

IN INDIA: Please write to *Penguin Books India Pvt Ltd, 706 Eros Apartments, 56 Nehru Place, New Delhi 110 019.*

IN THE NETHERLANDS: Please write to *Penguin Books Netherlands bv, Postbus 3507, NL-1001 AH Amsterdam.*

IN GERMANY: Please write to *Penguin Books Deutschland GmbH, Metzlerstrasse 26, 60594 Frankfurt am Main.*

IN SPAIN: Please write to *Penguin Books S. A., Bravo Murillo 19, 1° B, 28015 Madrid.*

IN ITALY: Please write to *Penguin Italia s.r.l., Via Felice Casati 20, I–20124 Milano.*

IN FRANCE: Please write to *Penguin France S. A., 17 rue Lejeune, F–31000 Toulouse.*

IN JAPAN: Please write to *Penguin Books Japan, Ishikiribashi Building, 2–5–4, Suido, Bunkyo-ku, Tokyo 112.*

IN GREECE: Please write to *Penguin Hellas Ltd, Dimocritou 3, GR–106 71 Athens.*

IN SOUTH AFRICA: Please write to *Longman Penguin Southern Africa (Pty) Ltd, Private Bag X08, Bertsham 2013.*

LYTTON

STRACHEY

FLORENCE NIGHTINGALE

PENGUIN BOOKS

PENGUIN BOOKS

Published by the Penguin Group. Penguin Books Ltd, 27 Wrights Lane, London W8 5TZ, England. Penguin Books USA Inc., 375 Hudson Street, New York, New York 10014, USA. Penguin Books Australia Ltd, Ringwood, Victoria, Australia. Penguin Books Canada Ltd, 10 Alcorn Avenue, Toronto, Ontario, Canada M4V 3B2. Penguin Books (NZ) Ltd, 182–190 Wairau Road, Auckland 10, New Zealand · Penguin Books Ltd, Registered Offices: Harmondsworth, Middlesex, England · This extract is from *Eminent Victorians*, by Lytton Strachey, first published by Chatto & Windus 1918. Published in Penguin Books 1948. This edition published 1996 ·

Typeset by Rowland Phototypesetting Ltd, Bury St Edmunds, Suffolk. Printed in England by Clays Ltd, St Ives plc ·

10 9 8 7 6 5 4 3 2 1

I

Every one knows the popular conception of Florence Nightingale. The saintly, self-sacrificing woman, the delicate maiden of high degree who threw aside the pleasures of a life of ease to succour the afflicted, the Lady with the Lamp, gliding through the horrors of the hospital at Scutari, and consecrating with the radiance of her goodness the dying soldier's couch – the vision is familiar to all. But the truth was different. The Miss Nightingale of fact was not as facile fancy painted her. She worked in another fashion, and towards another end; she moved under the stress of an impetus which finds no place in the popular imagination. A Demon possessed her. Now demons, whatever else they may be, are full of interest. And so it happens that in the real Miss Nightingale there was more that was interesting than in the legendary one; there was also less that was agreeable.

Her family was extremely well-to-do, and connected by marriage with a spreading circle of other well-to-do families. There was a large country house in

Derbyshire; there was another in the New Forest; there were Mayfair rooms for the London season and all its finest parties; there were tours on the Continent with even more than the usual number of Italian operas and of glimpses at the celebrities of Paris. Brought up among such advantages, it was only natural to suppose that Florence would show a proper appreciation of them by doing her duty in that state of life unto which it had pleased God to call her – in other words, by marrying, after a fitting number of dances and dinner-parties, an eligible gentleman, and living happily ever afterwards. Her sister, her cousins, all the young ladies of her acquaintance, were either getting ready to do this or had already done it. It was inconceivable that Florence should dream of anything else; yet dream she did. Ah! To do her duty in that state of life unto which it had pleased God to call her! Assuredly she would not be behindhand in doing her duty; but unto what state of life *had* it pleased God to call her? That was the question. God's calls are many, and they are strange. Unto what state of life had it pleased Him to call Charlotte Corday, or Elizabeth of Hungary? What was that secret voice in her ear, if it was not a call? Why had she felt, from her earliest years, those mysterious promptings towards . . . she hardly knew what, but certainly towards something very different from anything around her? Why, as a child in the nursery, when her sister had shown a healthy pleasure in tearing her dolls to pieces, had *she* shown an almost morbid one in sewing them up again? Why was she driven now to minister to the poor in the cottages, to watch by sick-beds, to put her dog's wounded paw into elaborate splints as if it was a human being? Why was her head filled with queer imaginations of the country house at Embley turned, by some enchantment, into a hospital, with herself as matron moving about among the beds? Why was even her vision of heaven itself filled with suffering patients to whom she was being useful? So she dreamed and wondered, and, taking out her diary, she poured into it the agitations of her soul. And then the bell rang, and it was time to go and dress for dinner.

As the years passed, a restlessness began to grow upon her. She was unhappy, and at last she knew it. Mrs Nightingale, too, began to notice that there was something wrong. It was very odd; what could be the matter with dear Flo? Mr Nightingale suggested that a husband might be advisable; but the curious thing was that she seemed to take no interest in husbands. And with her attractions, and her accomplishments, too! There was nothing in the world to prevent her making a really brilliant match. But no! She would think of nothing but how to satisfy that singular craving of hers to be *doing* something. As if there was not plenty to do in any case, in the ordinary way, at home. There was the china to look after, and there was her father to be read to after dinner. Mrs Nightingale could not understand it; and then one day her perplexity was changed to consternation and alarm. Florence announced an extreme desire to go to Salisbury Hospital for several months as a nurse; and she confessed to some visionary plan of eventually setting up in a house of her own in a neighbouring village, and there founding 'something like a Protestant Sisterhood, without vows, for women of educated feelings'. The whole scheme was summarily brushed aside as preposterous; and Mrs Nightingale, after the first shock of terror, was able to settle down again more or less comfortably to her embroidery. But Florence, who was now twenty-five and felt that the dream of her life had been shattered, came near to desperation.

And, indeed, the difficulties in her path were great. For not only was it an almost unimaginable thing in those days for a woman of means to make her own way in the world and to live in independence, but the particular profession for which Florence was clearly marked out both by her instincts and her capacities was at that time a peculiarly disreputable one. A 'nurse' meant then a coarse old woman, always ignorant, usually dirty, often brutal, a Mrs Gamp, in bunched-up sordid garments, tippling at the brandy bottle or indulging in worse irregularities. The nurses in the hospital were especially notorious for immoral conduct; sobriety was almost unknown among them; and they could hardly be trusted to carry out the simplest medical duties. Certainly, things have changed since those days; and that they *have* changed is due, far more than to any other human being, to Miss Nightingale herself. It is not to be wondered at that her parents should have shuddered at the notion of their daughter devoting her life to such an occupation. 'It was as if,' she herself said afterwards, 'I had wanted to be a kitchen-maid.' Yet the want, absurd, impracticable as it was, not only remained fixed immovably in her heart, but grew in intensity day by day. Her wretchedness deepened into a morbid melancholy. Everything about her was vile, and she herself, it was clear, to have deserved such misery, was even viler than her surroundings. Yes, she had sinned – 'standing before God's judgement seat'. 'No one,' she declared, 'has so grieved the Holy Spirit'; of that she was quite certain. It was in vain that she prayed to be delivered from vanity and hypocrisy, and she could not bear to smile or to be gay, 'because she hated God to hear her laugh, as if she had not repented her sin'.

A weaker spirit would have been overwhelmed by the load of such distresses – would have yielded or snapped. But this extraordinary young woman held firm, and fought her way to victory. With an amazing persistency, during the eight years that followed her rebuff over Salisbury Hospital, she struggled and worked and planned. While superficially she was carrying on the life of a brilliant girl in high society, while internally she was a prey to the tortures of regret and of remorse, she yet possessed the energy to collect the knowledge and to undergo the experience which alone could enable her to do what she had determined she would do in the end. In secret she devoured the reports of medical commissions, the pamphlets of sanitary authorities, the histories of hospitals and homes. She spent the intervals of the London season in ragged schools and workhouses. When she went abroad with her family, she used her spare time so well that there was hardly a great hospital in Europe with which she was not acquainted, hardly a great city whose slums she had not passed through. She managed to spend some days in a convent school in Rome, and some weeks as a '*Soeur de Charité*' in Paris. Then, while her mother and sister were taking the waters at Carlsbad, she succeeded in slipping off to a nursing institution at Kaiserswerth, where she remained for more than three months. This was the critical event of her life. The experience which she gained as a nurse at Kaiserswerth formed the foundation of all her future action and finally fixed her in her career.

But one other trial awaited her. The allurements of the world she had brushed aside with disdain and loathing; she had resisted the subtler temptation which, in her weariness, had sometimes come upon her, of devoting her baffled energies to art or literature; the last ordeal appeared in the shape of a desirable young man. Hitherto, her lovers had been nothing to her but an added burden and a mockery; but now – for a moment, she wavered. A new feeling swept over her – a feeling which she had never known before, which she was never to know again. The most powerful and the profoundest of all the instincts of humanity laid claim upon her. But it rose before her, that instinct, arrayed – how could it be otherwise? – in the inevitable habiliments of a Victorian marriage; and she had the strength to stamp it underfoot. 'I have an intellectual nature which requires satisfaction,' she noted, 'and that would find it in him. I have a passional nature which requires satisfaction, and that would find it in him. I have a moral, an active nature which requires satisfaction, and that would not find it in his life. Sometimes I think that I will satisfy my passional nature at all events . . .' But no, she knew in her heart that it could not be. 'To be nailed to a continuation and exaggeration of my present life . . . to put it out of my power ever to be able to seize the chance of forming for myself a true and rich life' – that would be a suicide. She made her choice, and refused what was at least a certain happiness for a visionary good which might never come to her at all. And so she returned to her old life of waiting and bitterness. 'The thoughts and feelings that I have now,' she wrote, 'I can remember since I was six years old. A profession, a trade, a necessary occupation, something to fill and employ all my faculties, I have always felt essential to me, I have always longed for. The first thought I can remember, and the last, was nursing work; and in the absence of this, education work, but more the education of the bad than of the young . . . Everything has been tried, foreign travel, kind friends, everything.

My God! What is to become of me?' A desirable young man? Dust and ashes! What was there desirable in such a thing as that? 'In my thirty-first year,' she noted in her diary, 'I see nothing desirable but death.'

Three more years passed, and then at last the pressure of time told; her family seemed to realize that she was old enough and strong enough to have her way; and she became the superintendent of a charitable nursing home in Harley Street. She had gained her independence, though it was in a meagre sphere enough; and her mother was still not quite resigned: surely Florence might at least spend the summer in the country. At times, indeed, among her intimates, Mrs Nightingale almost wept. 'We are ducks,' she said with tears in her eyes, 'who have hatched a wild swan.' But the poor lady was wrong; it was not a swan that they had hatched, it was an eagle.

2

Miss Nightingale had been a year in her nursing home in Harley Street, when Fate knocked at the door. The Crimean War broke out; the battle of the Alma was fought; and the terrible condition of our military hospitals at Scutari began to be known in England. It sometimes happens that the plans of Providence are a little difficult to follow, but on this occasion all was plain; there was a perfect coordination of events. For years Miss Nightingale had been getting ready; at last she was prepared – experienced, free, mature, yet still young – she was thirty-four – desirous to serve, accustomed to command: at that precise moment the desperate need of a great nation came, and she was there to satisfy it. If the war had fallen a few years earlier, she would have lacked the knowledge, perhaps even the power, for such a work; a few years later and she would, no doubt, have been fixed in the routine of some absorbing task, and moreover, she would have been growing old. Nor was it only the coincidence of Time that was remarkable. It so fell out that Sidney

Herbert was at the War Office and in the Cabinet; and Sidney Herbert was an intimate friend of Miss Nightingale's, convinced, from personal experience in charitable work, of her supreme capacity. After such premises, it seems hardly more than a matter of course that her letter, in which she offered her services for the East, and Sidney Herbert's letter, in which he asked for them, should actually have crossed in the post. Thus it all happened, without a hitch. The appointment was made, and even Mrs Nightingale, overawed by the magnitude of the venture, could only approve. A pair of faithful friends offered themselves as personal attendants; thirty-eight nurses were collected; and within a week of the crossing of the letters Miss Nightingale, amid a great burst of popular enthusiasm, left for Constantinople.

Among the numerous letters which she received on her departure was one from Dr Manning, who at that time was working in comparative obscurity as a Catholic priest in Bayswater. 'God will keep you,' he wrote, 'and my prayer for you will be that your one object of Worship, Pattern of Imitation, and source of consolation and strength may be the Sacred Heart of our Divine Lord.'

To what extent Dr Manning's prayer was answered

must remain a matter of doubt; but this much is certain, that, if ever a prayer was needed, it was needed then for Florence Nightingale. For dark as had been the picture of the state of affairs at Scutari, revealed to the English public in the dispatches of *The Times* correspondent and in a multitude of private letters, yet the reality turned out to be darker still. What had occurred was, in brief, the complete breakdown of our medical arrangements at the seat of war. The origins of this awful failure were complex and manifold; they stretched back through long years of peace and carelessness in England; they could be traced through endless ramifications of administrative incapacity – from the inherent faults of confused systems to the petty bunglings of minor officials, from the inevitable ignorance of Cabinet Ministers to the fatal exactitudes of narrow routine. In the inquiries which followed it was clearly shown that the evil was in reality that worst of all evils – one which has been caused by nothing in particular and for which no one in particular is to blame. The whole organization of the war machine was incompetent and out of date. The old Duke had sat for a generation at the Horse Guards repressing innovations with an iron hand. There was an extraordinary overlapping of authorities, an almost incredible shifting of responsibilities to and fro. As for such a notion as the creation and the maintenance of a really adequate medical service for the army – in that atmosphere of aged chaos, how could it have entered anybody's head? Before the war, the easygoing officials at Westminster were naturally persuaded that all was well – or at least as well as could be expected; when someone, for instance, actually had the temerity to suggest the formation of a corps of Army nurses, he was at once laughed out of court. When the war had begun, the gallant British officers in control of affairs had other things to think about than the petty details of medical organization. Who had bothered with such trifles in the Peninsula? And surely, on that occasion, we had done pretty well. Thus the most obvious precautions were neglected, the most necessary preparations put off from day to day. The principal medical officer of the Army, Dr Hall, was summoned from India at a moment's notice, and was unable to visit England before taking up his duties at the front. And it was not until after the battle of the Alma, when we had been at war for many months, that we acquired hospital accommodation at Scutari for more than a thousand men. Errors, follies, and vices on the part of individuals there doubtless were; but, in the general reckoning, they were of small account – insignificant symptoms of the deep disease of the body politic – the enormous calamity of administrative collapse.

Miss Nightingale arrived at Scutari – a suburb of Constantinople, on the Asiatic side of the Bosphorus – on 4 November 1854; it was ten days after the battle of Balaclava, and the day before the battle of Inkerman. The organization of the hospitals, which had already given way under the stress of the battle of the Alma, was now to be subjected to the further pressure which these two desperate and bloody engagements implied. Great detachments of wounded were already beginning to pour in. The men, after receiving such summary treatment as could be given them at the smaller hospitals in the Crimea itself, were forthwith shipped in batches of two hundred across the Black Sea to Scutari. This voyage was in normal times one of four days and a half; but the times were no longer normal, and now the transit often lasted for a fortnight or three weeks. It received, not without reason, the name of the 'middle passage'. Between, and sometimes on the decks, the wounded, the sick, and the dying were crowded – men who had just undergone the amputation of limbs, men in the clutches of fever or of frostbite, men in the last stages of dysentery and cholera

– without beds, sometimes without blankets, often hardly clothed. The one or two surgeons on board did what they could; but medical stores were lacking, and the only form of nursing available was that provided by a handful of invalid soldiers, who were usually themselves prostrate by the end of the voyage. There was no other food beside the ordinary salt rations of ship diet; and even the water was sometimes so stored that it was out of reach of the weak. For many months, the average of deaths during these voyages was seventy-four in the thousand; the corpses were shot out into the waters; and who shall say that they were the most unfortunate? At Scutari, the landing-stage, constructed with all the perverseness of Oriental ingenuity, could only be approached with great difficulty, and, in rough weather, not at all. When it was reached, what remained of the men in the ships had first to be disembarked, and then conveyed up a steep slope of a quarter of a mile to the nearest of the hospitals. The most serious cases might be put upon stretchers – for there were far too few for all; the rest were carried or dragged up the hill by such convalescent soldiers as could be got together, who were not too obviously infirm for the work. At last the journey was accomplished; slowly, one by one, living or dying, the wounded were carried up into the hospital. And in the hospital what did they find?

Lasciate ogni speranza, voi ch'entrate: the delusive doors bore no such inscription; and yet behind them Hell yawned. Want, neglect, confusion, misery – in every shape and in every degree of intensity – filled the endless corridors and the vast apartments of the gigantic barrack-house, which, without forethought or preparation, had been hurriedly set aside as the chief shelter for the victims of the war. The very building itself was radically defective. Huge sewers underlay it, and cesspools loaded with filth wafted their poison into the upper rooms. The floors were in so rotten a condition that many of them could not be scrubbed; the walls were thick with dirt; incredible multitudes of vermin swarmed everywhere. And, enormous as the building was, it was yet too small. It contained four miles of beds, crushed together, so close that there was but just room to pass between them. Under such conditions, the most elaborate system of ventilation might well have been at fault; but here there was no ventilation. The stench was indescribable. 'I have been well acquainted,' said Miss Nightingale, 'with the dwellings of the worst parts of most of the great cities

 in Europe, but have never been in any atmosphere

which I could compare with that of the Barrack Hospital at night.' The structural defects were equalled by the deficiencies in the commonest objects of hospital use. There were not enough bedsteads; the sheets were of canvas, and so coarse that the wounded men recoiled from them, begging to be left in their blankets; there was no bedroom furniture of any kind, and empty beer bottles were used for candlesticks. There were no basins, no towels, no soap, no brooms, no mops, no trays, no plates; there were neither slippers nor scissors, neither shoe-brushes nor blacking; there were no knives or forks or spoons. The supply of fuel was constantly deficient. The cooking arrangements were preposterously inadequate, and the laundry was a farce. As for purely medical materials, the tale was no better. Stretchers, splints, bandages – all were lacking; and so were the most ordinary drugs.

To replace such wants, to struggle against such difficulties, there was a handful of men overburdened by the strain of ceaseless work, bound down by the traditions of official routine, and enfeebled either by old age or inexperience or sheer incompetence. They had proved utterly unequal to their task. The principal doctor was lost in the imbecilities of a senile optimism. The wretched official whose business it was to provide for the wants of the hospital was tied fast hand and foot by red tape. A few of the younger doctors struggled valiantly, but what could they do? Unprepared, disorganized, with such help only as they could find among the miserable band of convalescent soldiers drafted off to tend their sick comrades, they were faced with disease, mutilation, and death in all their most appalling forms, crowded multitudinously about them in an ever-increasing mass. They were like men in a shipwreck, fighting, not for safety, but for the next moment's bare existence – to gain, by yet another frenzied effort, some brief respite from the waters of destruction.

In these surroundings, those who had been long inured to scenes of human suffering – surgeons with a world-wide knowledge of agonies, soldiers familiar with fields of carnage, missionaries with remembrances of famine and of plague – yet found a depth of horror which they had never known before. There were moments, there were places, in the Barrack Hospital at Scutari, where the strongest hand was struck with trembling, and the boldest eye would turn away its gaze.

Miss Nightingale came, and she, at any rate, in that
 inferno, did not abandon hope. For one thing, she

brought material succour. Before she left London she had consulted Dr Andrew Smith, the head of the Army Medical Board, as to whether it would be useful to take out stores of any kind to Scutari; and Dr Andrew Smith had told her that 'nothing was needed'. Even Sidney Herbert had given her similar assurances; possibly, owing to an oversight, there might have been some delay in the delivery of the medical stores, which, he said, had been sent out from England 'in profusion', but 'four days would have remedied this'. She preferred to trust her own instincts, and at Marseilles purchased a large quantity of miscellaneous provisions, which were of the utmost use at Scutari. She came, too, amply provided with money – in all, during her stay in the East, about £7,000 reached her from private sources; and, in addition, she was able to avail herself of another valuable means of help. At the same time as herself, Mr Macdonald, of *The Times*, had arrived at Scutari, charged with the duty of administering the large sums of money collected through the agency of that newspaper in aid of the sick and wounded; and Mr Macdonald had the sense to see that the best use he could make of *The Times* Fund was to put it at the disposal of Miss Nightingale. 'I cannot conceive,' wrote an eye-witness, 'as I now calmly look back on the first three weeks after the arrival of the wounded from Inkerman, how it could have been possible to have avoided a state of things too disastrous to contemplate, had not Miss Nightingale been there, with the means placed at her disposal by Mr Macdonald.' But the official view was different. What! Was the public service to admit, by accepting outside charity, that it was unable to discharge its own duties without the assistance of private and irregular benevolence? Never! And accordingly when Lord Stratford de Redcliffe, our ambassador at Constantinople, was asked by Mr Macdonald to indicate how *The Times* Fund could best be employed, he answered that there was indeed one object to which it might very well be devoted – the building of an English Protestant Church at Pera.

Mr Macdonald did not waste further time with Lord Stratford, and immediately joined forces with Miss Nightingale. But, with such a frame of mind in the highest quarters, it is easy to imagine the kind of disgust and alarm with which the sudden intrusion of a band of amateurs and females must have filled the minds of the ordinary officer and the ordinary military surgeon. They could not understand it; what had women to do with war? Honest Colonels relieved their spleen by the cracking of heavy jokes about 'the Bird';

while poor Dr Hall, a rough terrier of a man, who had worried his way to the top of his profession, was struck speechless with astonishment, and at last observed that Miss Nightingale's appointment was extremely droll.

Her position was, indeed, an official one, but it was hardly the easier for that. In the hospitals it was her duty to provide the services of herself and her nurses when they were asked for by the doctors, and not until then. At first some of the surgeons would have nothing to say to her, and, though she was welcomed by others, the majority were hostile and suspicious. But gradually she gained ground. Her good will could not be denied, and her capacity could not be disregarded. With consummate tact, with all the gentleness of supreme strength, she managed at last to impose her personality upon the susceptible, overwrought, discouraged, and helpless group of men in authority who surrounded her. She stood firm; she was a rock in the angry ocean; with her alone was safety, comfort, life. And so it was that hope dawned at Scutari. The reign of chaos and old night began to dwindle; order came upon the scene, and common sense, and forethought, and decision, radiating out from the little room off the great gallery in the Barrack Hospital where, day and night, the Lady Superintendent was at her task. Progress might be

slow, but it was sure. The first sign of a great change came with the appearance of some of those necessary objects with which the hospitals had been unprovided for months. The sick men began to enjoy the use of towels and soap, knives and forks, combs and tooth-brushes. Dr Hall might snort when he heard of it, asking, with a growl, what a soldier wanted with a tooth-brush; but the good work went on. Eventually the whole business of purveying to the hospitals was, in effect, carried out by Miss Nightingale. She alone, it seemed, whatever the contingency, knew where to lay her hands on what was wanted; she alone could dispense her stores with readiness; above all she alone possessed the art of circumventing the pernicious influences of official etiquette. This was her greatest enemy, and sometimes even she was baffled by it. On one occasion 27,000 shirts, sent out at her instance by the Home Government, arrived, were landed, and were only waiting to be unpacked. But the official 'Purveyor' intervened; he could not unpack them, he said, 'without a Board'. Miss Nightingale pleaded in vain; the sick and wounded lay half-naked shivering for want of clothing; and three weeks elapsed before the Board released the shirts. A little later, however,
 on a similar occasion, Miss Nightingale felt that she

could assert her own authority. She ordered a Government consignment to be forcibly opened, while the miserable 'Purveyor' stood by, wringing his hands in departmental agony.

Vast quantities of valuable stores sent from England lay, she found, engulfed in the bottomless abyss of the Turkish Customs House. Other ship-loads, buried beneath munitions of war destined for Balaclava, passed Scutari without a sign, and thus hospital materials were sometimes carried to and fro three times over the Black Sea, before they reached their destination. The whole system was clearly at fault, and Miss Nightingale suggested to the home authorities that a Government Store House should be instituted at Scutari for the reception and distribution of the consignments. Six months after her arrival this was done.

In the meantime she had reorganized the kitchens and the laundries in the hospitals. The ill-cooked hunks of meat, vilely served at irregular intervals, which had hitherto been the only diet for the sick men, were replaced by punctual meals, well-prepared and appetizing, while strengthening extra foods – soups and wines and jellies ('preposterous luxuries', snarled Dr Hall) – were distributed to those who needed them.

One thing, however, she could not effect. The separation of the bones from the meat was no part of official cookery: the rule was that the food must be divided into equal portions, and if some of the portions were all bone – well, every man must take his chance. The rule, perhaps, was not a very good one; but there it was. 'It would require a new Regulation of the Service,' she was told, 'to bone the meat.' As for the washing arrangements, they were revolutionized. Up to the time of Miss Nightingale's arrival the number of shirts the authorities had succeeded in washing was seven. The hospital bedding, she found, was 'washed' in cold water. She took a Turkish house, had boilers installed, and employed soldiers' wives to do the laundry work. The expenses were defrayed from her own funds and that of *The Times*; and henceforward the sick and wounded had the comfort of clean linen.

Then she turned her attention to their clothing. Owing to military exigencies the greater number of the men had abandoned their kit; their knapsacks were lost for ever; they possessed nothing but what was on their persons, and that was usually only fit for speedy destruction. The 'Purveyor', of course, pointed out that, according to the regulations, all soldiers should bring with them into hospital adequate supply of clothing, and he declared that it was no business of his to make good their deficiencies. Apparently, it was the business of Miss Nightingale. She procured socks, boots, and shirts in enormous quantities; she had trousers made, she rigged up dressing-gowns. 'The fact is,' she told Sidney Herbert, 'I am now clothing the British Army.'

All at once, word came from the Crimea that a great new contingent of sick and wounded might shortly be expected. Where were they to go? Every available inch in the wards was occupied; the affair was serious and pressing, and the authorities stood aghast. There were some dilapidated rooms in the Barrack Hospital, unfit for human habitation, but Miss Nightingale believed that if measures were promptly taken they might be made capable of accommodating several hundred beds. One of the doctors agreed with her; the rest of the officials were irresolute: it would be a very expensive job, they said; it would involve building; and who could take the responsibility? The proper course was that a representation should be made to the Director-General of the Army Medical Department in London; then the Director-General would apply to the Horse Guards, the Horse Guards would move the Ordnance, the Ordnance would lay the matter before the

Treasury, and, if the Treasury gave its consent, the work might be correctly carried through, several months after the necessity for it had disappeared. Miss Nightingale, however, had made up her mind, and she persuaded Lord Stratford – or thought she had persuaded him – to give his sanction to the required expenditure. One hundred and twenty-five workmen were immediately engaged, and the work was begun. The workmen struck; whereupon Lord Stratford washed his hands of the whole business. Miss Nightingale engaged two hundred other workmen on her own authority, and paid the bill out of her own resources. The wards were ready by the required date; five hundred sick men were received in them; and all the utensils, including knives, forks, spoons, cans and towels, were supplied by Miss Nightingale.

This remarkable woman was in truth performing the function of an administrative chief. How had this come about? Was she not in reality merely a nurse? Was it not her duty simply to tend the sick? And indeed, was it not as a ministering angel, a gentle 'lady with a lamp', that she actually impressed the minds of her contemporaries? No doubt that was so; and yet it is no less certain that, as she herself said, the specific

 business of nursing was 'the least important of the

functions into which she had been forced'. It was clear that in the state of disorganization into which the hospitals at Scutari had fallen, the most pressing, the really vital need was for something more than nursing; it was for the necessary elements of civilized life – the commonest material objects, the most ordinary cleanliness, the rudimentary habits of order and authority. 'Oh, dear Miss Nightingale,' said one of her party as they were approaching Constantinople, 'when we land, let there be no delays, let us get straight to nursing the poor fellows!' 'The strongest will be wanted at the wash-tub,' was Miss Nightingale's answer. And it was upon the wash-tub, and all that the wash-tub stood for, that she expended her greatest energies. Yet to say that is perhaps to say too much. For to those who watched her at work among the sick, moving day and night from bed to bed, with that unflinching courage, with that indefatigable vigilance, it seemed as if the concentrated force of an undivided and unparalleled devotion could hardly suffice for that portion of her task alone. Wherever, in those vast wards, suffering was at its worst and the need for help was greatest, there, as if by magic, was Miss Nightingale. Her superhuman equanimity would, at the moment of some ghastly operation, nerve the victim to endure and almost to hope. Her sympathy would assuage the pangs of dying and bring back to those still living something of the forgotten charm of life. Over and over again her untiring efforts rescued those whom the surgeons had abandoned as beyond the possibility of cure. Her mere presence brought with it a strange influence. A passionate idolatry spread among the men: they kissed her shadow as it passed. They did more. 'Before she came,' said a soldier, 'there was cussin' and swearin', but after that it was as 'oly as a church.' The most cherished privilege of the fighting man was abandoned for the sake of Miss Nightingale. In those 'lowest sinks of human misery', as she herself put it, she never heard the use of one expression 'which could distress a gentlewoman'.

She was heroic; and these were the humble tributes paid by those of grosser mould to that high quality. Certainly, she was heroic. Yet her heroism was not of that simple sort so dear to the readers of novels and the compilers of hagiologies – the romantic sentimental heroism with which mankind loves to invest its chosen darlings: it was made of sterner stuff. To the wounded soldier on his couch of agony she might well appear in the guise of a gracious angel of mercy; but the

 military surgeons, and the orderlies, and her own

nurses, and the 'Purveyor', and Dr Hall, and even Lord Stratford himself could tell a different story. It was not by gentle sweetness and womanly self-abnegation that she had brought order out of chaos in the Scutari hospitals, that, from her own resources, she had clothed the British Army, that she had spread her dominion over the serried and reluctant powers of the official world; it was by strict method, by stern discipline, by rigid attention to detail, by ceaseless labour, by the fixed determination of an indomitable will. Beneath her cool and calm demeanour lurked fierce and passionate fires. As she passed through the wards in her plain dress, so quiet, so unassuming, she struck the casual observer simply as the pattern of a perfect lady; but the keener eye perceived something more than that – the serenity of high deliberation in the scope of the capacious brow, the sign of power in the dominating curve of the thin nose, and the traces of a harsh and dangerous temper – something peevish, something mocking, and yet something precise – in the small and delicate mouth. There was humour in the face; but the curious watcher might wonder whether it was humour of a very pleasant kind; might ask himself, even as he heard the laughter and marked the jokes with which she cheered the spirits of her patients, what sort of sardonic merriment this same lady might not give vent to, in the privacy of her chamber. As for her voice, it was true of it, even more than of her countenance, that it 'had that in it one must fain call master'. Those clear tones were in no need of emphasis: 'I never heard her raise her voice,' said one of her companions. Only, when she had spoken, it seemed as if nothing could follow but obedience. Once, when she had given some direction, a doctor ventured to remark that the thing could not be done. 'But it must be done,' said Miss Nightingale. A chance bystander, who heard the words, never forgot through all his life the irresistible authority of them. And they were spoken quietly – very quietly indeed.

Late at night, when the long miles of beds lay wrapped in darkness, Miss Nightingale would sit at work in her little room, over her correspondence. It was one of the most formidable of all her duties. There were hundreds of letters to be written to the friends and relations of soldiers; there was the enormous mass of official documents to be dealt with; there were her own private letters to be answered; and, most important of all, there was the composition of her long and confidential reports to Sidney Herbert. These were by no means official communications. Her soul, pent up all day in the restraint and reserve of a vast responsibility, now at last poured itself out in these letters with all its natural vehemence, like a swollen torrent through an open sluice. Here, at least, she did not mince matters. Here she painted in her darkest colours the hideous scenes which surrounded her; here she tore away remorselessly the last veils still shrouding the abominable truth. Then she would fill pages with recommendations and suggestions, with criticisms of the minutest details of organization, with elaborate calculations of contingencies, with exhaustive analyses and statistical statements piled up in breathless eagerness one on top of the other. And then her pen, in the virulence of its volubility, would rush on to the discussion of individuals, to the denunciation of an incompetent surgeon or the ridicule of a self-sufficient nurse. Her sarcasm searched the ranks of the officials with the deadly and unsparing precision of a machine-gun. Her nicknames were terrible. She respected no one: Lord Stratford, Lord Raglan, Lady Stratford, Dr Andrew Smith, Dr Hall, the Commissary-General, the Purveyor – she fulminated against them all. The intolerable futility of mankind obsessed her like a nightmare, and she gnashed her teeth against it. 'I do well to be angry,' was the burden of her cry. How many just men were there at Scutari? How many who cared at all for the sick, or had done anything for their relief? Were there ten? Were there five? Was there even one? She could not be sure.

At one time, during several weeks, her vituperations descended upon the head of Sidney Herbert himself. He had misinterpreted her wishes, he had traversed her positive instructions, and it was not until he had admitted his error and apologized in abject terms that he was allowed again into favour. While this misunderstanding was at its height an aristocratic young gentleman arrived at Scutari with a recommendation from the Minister. He had come out from England filled with a romantic desire to render homage to the angelic heroine of his dreams. He had, he said, cast aside his life of ease and luxury; he would devote his days and nights to the service of that gentle lady; he would perform the most menial offices, he would 'fag' for her, he would be her footman – and feel requited by a single smile. A single smile, indeed, he had, but it was of an unexpected kind. Miss Nightingale at first refused to see him, and then, when she consented, believing that he was an emissary sent by Sidney Herbert to put her in the wrong over their dispute,

 she took notes of her conversation with him, and

insisted on his signing them at the end of it. The young gentleman returned to England by the next ship.

This quarrel with Sidney Herbert was, however, an exceptional incident. Alike by him, and by Lord Panmure, his successor at the War Office, she was firmly supported; and the fact that during the whole of her stay at Scutari she had the Home Government at her back, was her trump card in her dealings with the hospital authorities. Nor was it only the Government that was behind her: public opinion in England early recognized the high importance of her mission, and its enthusiastic appreciation of her work soon reached an extraordinary height. The Queen herself was deeply moved. She made repeated inquiries as to the welfare of Miss Nightingale; she asked to see her accounts of the wounded, and made her the intermediary between the throne and the troops. 'Let Mrs Herbert know,' she wrote to the War Minister, 'that I wish Miss Nightingale and the ladies would tell these poor noble, wounded, and sick men that *no one* takes a warmer interest or feels *more* for their sufferings or admires their courage and heroism *more* than their Queen. Day and night she thinks of her beloved troops. So does the Prince. Beg Mrs Herbert to communicate these my words to those ladies, as I know that *our* sympathy is much valued by these noble fellows.' The letter was read aloud in the wards by the Chaplain. 'It is a very feeling letter,' said the men.

And so the months passed, and that fell winter which had begun with Inkerman and had dragged itself out through the long agony of the investment of Sebastopol, at last was over. In May 1855, after six months of labour, Miss Nightingale could look with something like satisfaction at the condition of the Scutari hospitals. Had they done nothing more than survive the terrible strain which had been put upon them, it would have been a matter for congratulation; but they had done much more than that; they had marvellously improved. The confusion and the pressure in the wards had come to an end; order reigned in them, and cleanliness; the supplies were bountiful and prompt; important sanitary works had been carried out. One simple comparison of figures was enough to reveal the extraordinary change: the rate of mortality among the cases treated had fallen from forty-two per cent to twenty-two per thousand. But still the indefatigable lady was not satisfied. The main problem had been solved – the physical needs of the men had been provided for; their mental and spiritual needs remained. She set up and furnished reading-rooms and recreation-rooms. She started classes and lectures. Officers were amazed to see her treating their men as if they were human beings, and assured her that she would only end by 'spoiling the brutes'. But that was not Miss Nightingale's opinion, and she was justified. The private soldier began to drink less, and even – though that seemed impossible – to save his pay. Miss Nightingale became a banker for the Army, receiving and sending home large sums of money every month. At last, reluctantly, the Government followed suit, and established machinery of its own for the remission of money. Lord Panmure, however, remained sceptical; 'it will do no good,' he pronounced; 'the British soldier is not a remitting animal.' But, in fact, during the next six months, £71,000 was sent home.

Amid all these activities, Miss Nightingale took up the further task of inspecting the hospitals in the Crimea itself. The labour was extreme, and the conditions of life were almost intolerable. She spent whole days in the saddle, or was driven over those bleak and rocky heights in a baggage cart. Sometimes she stood for hours in the heavily falling snow, and would only reach her hut at dead of night after walking for miles through perilous ravines. Her powers of resistance seemed incredible, but at last they were exhausted.

She was attacked by fever, and for a moment came very near to death. Yet she worked on; if she could not move, she could at least write; and write she did until her mind had left her; and after it had left her, in what seemed the delirious trance of death itself, she still wrote. When, after many weeks, she was strong enough to travel, she was implored to return to England, but she utterly refused. She would not go back, she said, before the last of the soldiers had left Scutari.

This happy moment had almost arrived, when suddenly the smouldering hostilities of the medical authorities burst out into a flame. Dr Hall's labours had been rewarded by a KCB – letters which, as Miss Nightingale told Sidney Herbert, she could only suppose to mean 'Knight of the Crimean Burial-grounds' – and the honour had turned his head. He was Sir John, and he would be thwarted no longer. Disputes had lately arisen between Miss Nightingale and some of the nurses in the Crimean hospitals. The situation had been embittered by rumours of religious dissensions, for, while the Crimean nurses were Roman Catholics, many of those at Scutari were suspected of a regrettable propensity towards the tenets of Dr Pusey. Miss Nightingale was by no means disturbed by these sectarian differences, but any suggestion that her supreme authority over all the nurses with the Army was in doubt was enough to rouse her to fury; and it appeared that Mrs Bridgeman, the Reverend Mother in the Crimea, had ventured to call that authority in question. Sir John Hall thought that his opportunity had come, and strongly supported Mrs Bridgeman – or, as Miss Nightingale preferred to call her, the 'Reverend Brickbat'. There was a violent struggle; Miss Nightingale's rage was terrible. Dr Hall, she declared, was doing his best to 'root her out of the Crimea'. She would bear it no longer; the War Office was playing her false; there was only one thing to be done – Sidney Herbert must move for the production of papers in the House of Commons, so that the public might be able to judge between her and her enemies. Sidney Herbert with great difficulty calmed her down. Orders were immediately dispatched putting her supremacy beyond doubt, and the Reverend Brickbat withdrew from the scene. Sir John, however, was more tenacious. A few weeks later, Miss Nightingale and her nurses visited the Crimea for the last time, and the brilliant idea occurred to him that he could crush her by a very simple expedient – he would starve her into submission; and he actually ordered that no rations of any kind should be supplied to her. He had already tried this plan with great effect upon an unfortunate medical man whose presence in the Crimea he had considered an intrusion; but he was now to learn that such tricks were thrown away upon Miss Nightingale. With extraordinary foresight, she had brought with her a great supply of food; she succeeded in obtaining more at her own expense and by her own exertions; and thus for ten days, in that inhospitable country, she was able to feed herself and twenty-four nurses. Eventually the military authorities intervened in her favour, and Sir John had to confess that he was beaten.

It was not until July 1856 – four months after the Declaration of Peace – that Miss Nightingale left Scutari for England. Her reputation was now enormous, and the enthusiasm of the public was unbounded. The royal approbation was expressed by the gift of a brooch, accompanied by a private letter. 'You are, I know, well aware,' wrote Her Majesty,

> of the high sense I entertain of the Christian devotion which you have displayed during this great and bloody war, and I need hardly repeat to you how warm my admiration is for your services, which are fully equal to those of my dear and brave soldiers, whose sufferings you have had the *privilege* of alleviating in so merciful a manner. I am, however,

anxious of marking my feelings in a manner which I trust will be agreeable to you, and therefore send you with this letter a brooch, the form and emblems of which commemorate your great and blessed work, and which I hope you will wear as a mark of the high approbation of your Sovereign!

'It will be a very great satisfaction to me,' Her Majesty added, 'to make the acquaintance of one who has set so bright an example to our sex.'

The brooch, which was designed by the Prince Consort, bore a St George's cross in red enamel, and the Royal cipher surmounted by diamonds. The whole was encircled by the inscription 'Blessed are the Merciful'.

3

The name of Florence Nightingale lives in the memory of the world by virtue of the lurid and heroic adventure of the Crimea. Had she died – as she nearly did – upon her return to England, her reputation would hardly have been different; her legend would have come down to us almost as we know it today – that gentle vision of female virtue which first took shape before the adoring eyes of the sick soldiers at Scutari. Yet, as a matter of fact, she lived for more than half a century after the Crimean War; and during the greater part of that long period all the energy and all the devotion of her extraordinary nature were working at their highest pitch. What she accomplished in those years of unknown labour could, indeed, hardly have been more glorious than her Crimean triumphs; but it was certainly more important. The true history was far stranger even than the myth. In Miss Nightingale's own eyes the adventure of the Crimea was a mere incident – scarcely more than a useful stepping-stone in her career. It was the fulcrum with which she hoped to move the world; but it was only the fulcrum. For more than a generation she was to sit in secret, working her lever: and her real life began at the very moment when, in the popular imagination, it had ended.

She arrived in England in a shattered state of health. The hardships and the ceaseless effort of the last two years had undermined her nervous system; her heart was pronounced to be affected; she suffered constantly from fainting-fits and terrible attacks of utter physical prostration. The doctors declared that one thing alone would save her – a complete and prolonged rest. But that was also the one thing with which she would have nothing to do. She had never been in the habit of resting; why should she begin now? Now, when her opportunity had come at last; now, when the iron was hot, and it was time to strike? No; she had work to do; and, come what might, she would do it. The doctors protested in vain; in vain her family lamented and entreated, in vain her friends pointed out to her the madness of such a course. Madness? Mad – possessed – perhaps she was. A demoniac frenzy had seized upon her. As she lay upon her sofa, gasping, she devoured blue-books, dictated letters, and, in the intervals of her palpitations, cracked her febrile jokes. For months at a stretch she never left her bed. For years she was in daily expectation of death. But she would not rest. At this rate, the doctors assured her, even if she did not die, she would become an invalid for life. She could not help that; there was the work to be done; and, as for rest, very likely she might rest . . . when she had done it.

Wherever she went, to London or in the country, in the hills of Derbyshire, or among the rhododendrons at Embley, she was haunted by a ghost. It was the spectre of Scutari – the hideous vision of the organization of a military hospital. She would lay that phantom, or she would perish. The whole system of the Army Medical Department, the education of the Medical Officer, the regulations of hospital procedure . . . *rest*? How could she rest while these things were as they were, while, if the like necessity were to arise again, the like results would follow? And, even in peace and at home, what was the sanitary condition of the Army? The mortality in the barracks, was, she found, nearly double the mortality in civil life. 'You might as well take 1,100 men every year out upon Salisbury Plain and shoot them,' she said. After inspecting the hospitals at Chatham, she smiled grimly. 'Yes, this is one more symptom of the system which, in the Crimea, put to death 16,000 men.' Scutari had given her knowledge; and it had given her power too: her enormous reputation was at her back – an incalculable force. Other work, other duties, might lie before her; but the most urgent, the most obvious, of all was to look to the health of the Army.

One of her very first steps was to take advantage of the invitation which Queen Victoria had sent her to the Crimea, together with the commemorative brooch. Within a few weeks of her return she visited Balmoral, and had several interviews with both the Queen and the Prince Consort. 'She put before us,' wrote the Prince in his diary, 'all the defects of our present military hospital system, and the reforms that are needed.' She related 'the whole story' of her experiences in the East; and, in addition, she managed to have some long and confidential talks with His Royal Highness on metaphysics and religion. The impression which she created was excellent. '*Sie gefällt uns sehr*,' noted the Prince, '*ist sehr bescheiden*.' Her Majesty's comment was different – 'Such a *head*! I wish we had her at the War Office.'

But Miss Nightingale was not at the War Office, and for a very simple reason: she was a woman. Lord Panmure, however, *was* (though indeed the reason for that was not quite so simple); and it was upon Lord

Panmure that the issue of Miss Nightingale's efforts for reform must primarily depend. That burly Scottish nobleman had not, in spite of his most earnest endeavours, had a very easy time of it as Secretary of State for War. He had come into office in the middle of the Sebastopol Campaign, and he felt himself very well fitted for the position, since he had acquired in former days an inside knowledge of the Army – as a Captain of Hussars. It was this inside knowledge which had enabled him to inform Miss Nightingale with such authority that 'the British soldier is not a remitting animal'. And perhaps it was this same consciousness of a command of his subject which had impelled him to write a dispatch to Lord Raglan blandly informing the Commander-in-Chief in the Field just how he was neglecting his duties, and pointing out to him that if he would only try he really might do a little better next time. Lord Raglan's reply, calculated as it was to make its recipient sink into the earth, did not quite have that effect upon Lord Panmure, who, whatever might have been his faults, had never been accused of being supersensitive. However, he allowed the matter to drop; and a little later Lord Raglan died – worn out, some people said, by work and anxiety. He was succeeded by an excellent red-nosed old gentleman,

General Simpson, whom nobody has ever heard of, and who took Sebastopol. But Lord Panmure's relations with him were hardly more satisfactory than his relations with Lord Raglan; for, while Lord Raglan had been too independent, poor General Simpson erred in the opposite direction, perpetually asked advice, suffered from lumbago, doubted, his nose growing daily redder and redder, whether he was fit for his post, and, by alternate mails, sent in and withdrew his resignation. Then, too, both the General and the Minister suffered acutely from that distressingly useful new invention, the electric telegraph. On one occasion General Simpson felt obliged actually to expostulate. 'I think, my Lord,' he wrote, 'that some telegraphic messages reach us that cannot be sent under due authority, and are perhaps unknown to you, although under the protection of your Lordship's name. For instance, I was called up last night, a dragoon having come express with a telegraphic message in these words, "Lord Panmure to General Simpson – Captain Jarvis has been bitten by a centipede. How is he now?"' General Simpson might have put up with this, though to be sure it did seem 'rather too trifling an affair to call for a dragoon to ride a couple of miles in the dark that he may knock up the Commander of the Army out of the very small allowance of sleep permitted him'; but what was really more than he could bear was to find 'upon sending in the morning another mounted dragoon to inquire after Captain Jarvis, four miles off, that he never has been bitten at all, but has had a boil, from which he is fast recovering'. But Lord Panmure had troubles of his own. His favourite nephew, Captain Dowbiggin, was at the front, and to one of his telegrams to the Commander-in-Chief the Minister had taken occasion to append the following carefully qualified sentence – 'I recommend Dowbiggin to your notice, should you have a vacancy, and if he is fit.' Unfortunately, in those early days, it was left to the discretion of the telegraphist to compress the messages which passed through his hands; so that the result was that Lord Panmure's delicate appeal reached its destination in the laconic form of 'Look after Dowb.' The Headquarters Staff were at first extremely puzzled; they were at last extremely amused. The story spread; and 'Look after Dowb' remained for many years the familiar formula for describing official hints in favour of deserving nephews.

And now that all this was over, now that Sebastopol
 had been, somehow or another, taken, now that peace

was, somehow or another, made, now that the troubles of office might surely be expected to be at an end at last – here was Miss Nightingale breaking in upon the scene, with her talk about the state of the hospitals and the necessity for sanitary reform. It was most irksome; and Lord Panmure almost began to wish that he was engaged upon some more congenial occupation – discussing, perhaps, the constitution of the Free Church of Scotland – a question in which he was profoundly interested. But no; duty was paramount; and he set himself, with a sigh of resignation, to the task of doing as little of it as he possibly could.

'The Bison' his friends called him; and the name fitted both his physical demeanour and his habit of mind. That large low head seemed to have been created for butting rather than for anything else. There he stood, four-square and menacing, in the doorway of reform; and it remained to be seen whether the bulky mass, upon whose solid hide even the barbed arrows of Lord Raglan's scorn had made no mark, would prove amenable to the pressure of Miss Nightingale. Nor was he alone in the doorway. There loomed behind him the whole phalanx of professional conservatism, the stubborn supporters of the out-of-date, the worshippers and the victims of War Office routine.

Among these it was only natural that Dr Andrew Smith, the head of the Army Medical Department, should have been pre-eminent – Dr Andrew Smith, who had assured Miss Nightingale, before she left England, that 'nothing was wanted at Scutari'. Such were her opponents; but she too was not without allies. She had gained the ear of Royalty – which was something; at any moment that she pleased she could gain the ear of the public – which was a great deal. She had a host of admirers and friends; and – to say nothing of her personal qualities – her knowledge, her tenacity, her tact – she possessed, too, one advantage which then, far more even than now, carried an immense weight – she belonged to the highest circle of society. She moved naturally among Peers and Cabinet Ministers – she was one of their own set; and in those days their set was a very narrow one. What kind of attention would such persons have paid to some middle-class woman with whom they were not acquainted, who possessed great experience of Army nursing and had decided views upon hospital reform? They would have politely ignored her; but it was impossible to ignore Flo Nightingale. When she spoke, they were obliged to listen; and, when they had once begun to do that – what might not follow? She knew her power, and she used it. She supported her weightiest minutes with familiar witty little notes. The Bison began to look grave. It might be difficult – it might be damned difficult – to put down one's head against the white hand of a lady.

Of Miss Nightingale's friends, the most important was Sidney Herbert. He was a man upon whom the good fairies seemed to have showered, as he lay in his cradle, all their most enviable goods. Well born, handsome, rich, the master of Wilton – one of those great country-houses, clothed with the glamour of a historic past, which are the peculiar glory of England – he possessed, besides all these advantages, so charming, so lively, so gentle a disposition that no one who had once come near him could ever be his enemy. He was, in fact, a man of whom it was difficult not to say that he was a perfect English gentleman. For his virtues were equal even to his good fortune. He was religious – deeply religious: 'I am more and more convinced every day,' he wrote, when he had been for some years a Cabinet Minister, 'that in politics, as in everything else, nothing can be right which is not in accordance with the spirit of the Gospel.' No one was more unselfish; he was charitable and benevolent to a remarkable degree; and he devoted the whole of his life with an unwavering conscientiousness to the public service. With such a character, with such opportunities, what high hopes must have danced before him, what radiant visions of accomplished duties, of ever-increasing usefulness, of beneficent power, of the consciousness of disinterested success! Some of those hopes and visions were, indeed, realized; but, in the end, the career of Sidney Herbert seemed to show that, with all their generosity, there was some gift or other – what was it? – some essential gift – which the good fairies had withheld, and that even the qualities of a perfect English gentleman may be no safeguard against anguish, humiliation, and defeat.

That career would certainly have been very different if he had never known Miss Nightingale. The alliance between them which had begun with her appointment to Scutari, which had grown closer and closer while the war lasted, developed, after her return, into one of the most extraordinary of friendships. It was the friendship of a man and a woman intimately bound together by their devotion to a public cause; mutual affection, of course, played a part in it, but it was an incidental part; the whole soul of the relationship was a community of work. Perhaps out of England such an intimacy could hardly have existed – an intimacy so utterly untinctured not only by passion itself but by the suspicion of it. For years Sidney Herbert saw Miss Nightingale almost daily, for long hours together, corresponding with her incessantly when they were apart; and the tongue of scandal was silent; and one of the most devoted of her admirers was his wife. But what made the connection still more remarkable was the way in which the parts that were played in it were divided between the two. The man who acts, decides, and achieves; the woman who encourages, applauds, and – from a distance – inspires: the combination is common enough; but Miss Nightingale was neither an Aspasia nor an Egeria. In her case it is almost true to say that the roles were reversed; the qualities of pliancy and sympathy fell to the man, those of command and initiative to the woman. There was one thing only which Miss Nightingale lacked in her equipment for public life; she had not – she never could have – the public power and authority which belong to the successful politician. That power and authority Sidney Herbert possessed; that fact was obvious, and the conclusions no less so: it was through the man that the woman must work her will She took hold of him, taught him, shaped him, absorbed him, dominated him through and through. He did not resist – he did not wish to resist, his natural inclination lay along the same path as hers; only that terrific personality swept him forward at her own fierce pace and with her own relentless stride. Swept him – where to? Ah! Why had he ever known Miss Nightingale? If Lord Panmure was a bison, Sir Herbert, no doubt, was a stag – a comely, gallant creature springing through the forest; but the forest is a dangerous place. One has the image of those wide eyes fascinated suddenly by something feline, something strong; there is a pause; and then the tigress has her claws in the quivering haunches; and then . . .!

Besides Sidney Herbert, she had other friends who, in a more restricted sphere, were hardly less essential to her. If, in her condition of bodily collapse, she were to accomplish what she was determined that she should accomplish, the attentions and the services of others would be absolutely indispensable. Helpers and servers she must have; and accordingly there was soon formed about her a little group of devoted disciples upon whose affections and energies she could implicitly rely. Devoted, indeed, these disciples were, in no ordinary sense of the term; for certainly she was no light task-mistress, and he who set out to be of use to Miss Nightingale was apt to find, before he had gone very far, that he was in truth being made use of in good earnest – to the very limit of his endurance and his capacity. Perhaps, even beyond those limits; why not? Was she asking of others more than she was giving herself? Let them look at her lying there pale and breathless on the couch; could it be said that she spared herself? Why, then, should she spare others? And it was not for her own sake that she made these claims. For her own sake, indeed! No! They all knew it! It was for the sake of the work. And so the little band, bound body and soul in that strange servitude, laboured on ungrudgingly. Among the most faithful was her 'Aunt Mai', her father's sister, who from the earliest days had stood beside her, who had helped her to escape from the thraldom of family life, who had been with her at Scutari, and who now acted almost the part of a mother to her, watching over her with infinite care in all the movements and uncertainties which her state of health involved. Another constant attendant was her brother-in-law, Sir Harry Verney, whom she found particularly valuable in parliamentary affairs. Arthur Clough, the poet, also a connection by marriage, she used in other ways. Ever since he had lost his faith at the time of the Oxford Movement, Clough had passed his life in a condition of considerable uneasiness, which was increased rather than diminished by the practice of poetry. Unable to decide upon the purpose of an existence whose savour had fled together with his belief in the Resurrection, his spirits lowered still further by ill-health, and his income not all that it should be, he had determined to seek the solution of his difficulties in the United States of America. But, even there the solution was not forthcoming; and when, a little later, he was offered a post in a government department at home, he accepted it, came to live in London, and immediately fell under the influence of Miss Nightingale. Though the purpose of existence might still be uncertain and its nature still unsavoury, here, at any rate, under the eye of this inspired woman, was something real, something earnest: his only doubt was – could he be of any use? Certainly he could. There were a great number of miscellaneous little jobs which there was nobody handy to do. For instance, when Miss Nightingale was travelling, there were the railway-tickets to be taken; and there were proof-sheets to be corrected; and then there were parcels to be done up in brown paper, and carried to the post. Certainly he could be useful. And so, upon such occupations as these, Arthur Clough was set to work. 'This that I see, is not all,' he comforted himself by reflecting, 'and this that I do is but little; nevertheless it is good, though there is better than it.'

As time went on, her 'Cabinet', as she called it, grew larger. Officials with whom her work brought her into touch and who sympathized with her objects, were pressed into her service; and old friends of the Crimean days gathered round her when they returned to England. Among these the most indefatigable was Dr Sutherland, a sanitary expert, who for more than thirty years acted as her confidential private secretary, and surrendered to her purposes literally the whole of his life. Thus sustained and assisted, thus slaved for and adored, she prepared to beard the Bison.

Two facts soon emerged, and all that followed turned upon them. It became clear, in the first place, that that imposing mass was not immovable, and, in the second, that its movement, when it did move, would be exceeding slow. The Bison was no match for the Lady. It was in vain that he put down his head and planted his feet in the earth; he could not withstand her; the white hand forced him back. But the process was an extraordinarily gradual one. Dr Andrew Smith and all his War Office phalanx stood behind, blocking the way; the poor Bison groaned inwardly, and cast a wistful eye towards the happy pastures of the Free Church of Scotland; then slowly, with infinite reluctance, step by step, he retreated, disputing every inch of the ground.

The first great measure, which, supported as it was by the Queen, the Cabinet, and the united opinion of the country, it was impossible to resist, was the appointment of a Royal Commission to report upon the health of the Army. The question of the composition of the Commission then immediately arose; and it was over this matter that the first hand-to-hand encounter between Lord Panmure and Miss Nightingale took place. They met, and Miss Nightingale was victorious; Sidney Herbert was appointed Chairman; and, in the end, the only member of the Commission opposed to her views was Dr Andrew Smith. During the interview, Miss Nightingale made an important discovery: she found that 'the Bison was bullyable' – the hide was the hide of a Mexican buffalo, but the spirit was the spirit of an Alderney calf. And there was one thing above all others which the huge creature dreaded – an appeal to public opinion. The faintest hint of such a terrible eventuality made his heart dissolve within him; he would agree to anything – he would cut short his grouse-shooting – he would make a speech in the

House of Lords – he would even overrule Dr Andrew Smith – rather than that. Miss Nightingale held the fearful threat in reserve – she would speak out what she knew; she would publish the truth to the whole world, and let the whole world judge between them. With supreme skill, she kept this sword of Damocles poised above the Bison's head, and more than once she was actually on the point of really dropping it. For his recalcitrancy grew and grew. The personnel of the Commission once determined upon, there was a struggle, which lasted for six months, over the nature of its powers. Was it to be an efficient body, armed with the right of full inquiry and wide examination, or was it to be a polite official contrivance for exonerating Dr Andrew Smith? The War Office phalanx closed its ranks, and fought tooth and nail; but it was defeated: the Bison was bullyable. 'Three months from this day,' Miss Nightingale had written at last, 'I publish my experience of the Crimean Campaign, and my suggestions for improvement, unless there has been a fair and tangible pledge by that time for reform.' Who could face that?

And, if the need came, she meant to be as good as her word. For she had now determined, whatever might be the fate of the Commission, to draw up her own report upon the questions at issue. The labour involved was enormous; her health was almost desperate; but she did not flinch, and after six months of incredible industry she had put together and written with her own hand her *Notes affecting the Health, Efficiency, and Hospital Administration of the British Army*. This extraordinary composition, filling more than eight hundred closely printed pages, laying down vast principles of far-reaching reform, discussing the minutest details of a multitude of controversial subjects, containing an enormous mass of information of the most varied kinds – military, statistical, sanitary, architectural – was never given to the public, for the need never came; but it formed the basis of the Report of the Royal Commission; and it remains to this day the leading authority on the medical administration of armies.

Before it had been completed the struggle over the powers of the Commission had been brought to a victorious close. Lord Panmure had given way once more; he had immediately hurried to the Queen to obtain her consent; and only then, when Her Majesty's initials had been irrevocably affixed to the fatal document, did he dare to tell Dr Andrew Smith what he had done. The Commission met, and another immense load fell
 upon Miss Nightingale's shoulders. Today she would,

of course, have been one of the Commission herself; but at that time the idea of a woman appearing in such a capacity was unheard of; and no one even suggested the possibility of Miss Nightingale's doing so. The result was that she was obliged to remain behind the scenes throughout, to coach Sidney Herbert in private at every important juncture, and to convey to him and to her other friends upon the Commission the vast funds of her expert knowledge – so essential in the examination of witnesses – by means of innumerable consultations, letters, and memoranda. It was even doubtful whether the proprieties would admit of her giving evidence; and at last, as a compromise, her modesty only allowed her to do so in the form of written answers to written questions. At length the grand affair was finished. The Commission's Report, embodying almost word for word the suggestions of Miss Nightingale, was drawn up by Sidney Herbert. Only one question remained to be answered – would anything, after all, be done? Or would the Royal Commission, like so many other Royal Commissions before and since, turn out to have achieved nothing but the concoction of a very fat blue-book on a very high shelf?

And so the last and the deadliest struggle with the Bison began. Six months had been spent in coercing him into granting the Commission effective powers; six more months were occupied by the work of the Commission; and now yet another six were to pass in extorting from him the means whereby the recommendations of the Commission might be actually carried out. But, in the end, the thing was done. Miss Nightingale seemed, indeed, during these months, to be upon the very brink of death. Accompanied by the faithful Aunt Mai, she moved from place to place – to Hampstead, to Highgate, to Derbyshire, to Malvern – in what appeared to be a last desperate effort to find health somewhere; but she carried that with her which made health impossible. Her desire for work could now scarcely be distinguished from mania. At one moment she was writing a 'last letter' to Sidney Herbert; at the next she was offering to go out to India to nurse the sufferers in the Mutiny. When Dr Sutherland wrote, imploring her to take a holiday, she raved. Rest! –

I am lying without my head, without my claws, and you all peck at me. It is *de rigueur*, *d'obligation*, like the saying something to one's hat, when one goes into church, to say to me all that has been said to me 110 times a day during the last three months. It is the *obbligato* on the violin, and
 the twelve violins all practise it together, like the clocks

striking twelve o'clock at night all over London, till I say like Xavier de Maistre, *Assez, je le sais, je ne le sais que trop.* I am not a penitent; but you are like the R.C. confessor, who says what is *de rigueur* . . .

Her wits began to turn, and there was no holding her. She worked like a slave in a mine. She began to believe, as she had begun to believe at Scutari, that none of her fellow-workers had their hearts in the business; if they had, why did they not work as she did? She could only see slackness and stupidity around her. Dr Sutherland, of course, was grotesquely muddle-headed; and Arthur Clough incurably lazy. Even Sidney Herbert . . . oh yes, he had simplicity and candour and quickness of perception, no doubt; but he was an eclectic; and what could one hope for from a man who went away to fish in Ireland just when the Bison most needed bullying? As for the Bison himself he had fled to Scotland, where he remained buried for many months. The fate of the vital recommendation in the Commission's Report – the appointment of four Sub-Commissions charged with the duty of determining upon the details of the proposed reforms and of putting them into execution – still hung in the balance. The Bison consented to everything; and then, on a flying visit to London, withdrew his consent and hastily returned to Scotland. Then for many weeks all business was suspended; he had gout – gout in the hands, so that he could not write. 'His gout was always handy,' remarked Miss Nightingale. But eventually it was clear even to the Bison that the game was up, and the inevitable surrender came.

There was, however, one point in which he triumphed over Miss Nightingale. The building of Netley Hospital had been begun, under his orders, before her return to England. Soon after her arrival she examined the plans, and found that they reproduced all the worst faults of an out-of-date and mischievous system of hospital construction. She therefore urged that the matter should be reconsidered, and in the meantime the building stopped. But the Bison was obdurate; it would be very expensive, and in any case it was too late. Unable to make any impression on him, and convinced of the extreme importance of the question, she determined to appeal to a higher authority. Lord Palmerston was Prime Minister; she had known him from her childhood; he was a near neighbour of her father's in the New Forest. She went down to the New Forest, armed with the plans of the proposed hospital and all the relevant information, stayed the night at Lord Palmerston's house, and convinced him of the necessity of rebuilding Netley. 'It seems to me,' Lord Palmerston wrote to Lord Panmure, 'that at Netley all consideration of what would best tend to the comfort and recovery of the patients has been sacrificed to the vanity of the architect, whose sole object has been to make a building which should cut a dash when looked at from the Southampton river . . . Pray, therefore, stop all further progress in the work until the matter can be duly considered.' But the Bison was not to be moved by one peremptory letter, even if it was from the Prime Minister. He put forth all his powers of procrastination, Lord Palmerston lost interest in the subject, and so the chief military hospital in England was triumphantly completed on insanitary principles, with unventilated rooms, and with all the patients' windows facing north-east.

But now the time had come when the Bison was to trouble and to be troubled no more. A vote in the House of Commons brought about the fall of Lord Palmerston's Government, and Lord Panmure found himself at liberty to devote the rest of his life to the Free Church of Scotland. After a brief interval, Sidney Herbert became Secretary of State for War. Great was the jubilation in the Nightingale Cabinet: the day of achievement had dawned at last. The next two and a half years (1859–61) saw the introduction of the whole system of reforms for which Miss Nightingale had been struggling so fiercely – reforms which make Sidney Herbert's tenure of power at the War Office an important epoch in the history of the British Army. The four Sub-Commissions, firmly established under the immediate control of the Minister, and urged forward by the relentless perseverance of Miss Nightingale, set to work with a will. The barracks and the hospitals were remodelled; they were properly ventilated and warmed and lighted for the first time; they were given a water supply which actually supplied water, and kitchens where, strange to say, it was possible to cook. Then the great question of the Purveyor – that portentous functionary whose powers and whose lack of powers had weighed like a nightmare upon Scutari – was taken in hand, and new regulations were laid down, accurately defining his responsibilities and his duties. One Sub-Commission reorganized the medical statistics of the Army. Another established – in spite of the last convulsive efforts of the Department – an Army Medical School. Finally the Army Medical Department itself was completely reorganized; an administrative code was drawn up; and the great and novel principle was established that it was as much a part of the duty of the authorities to look after the soldier's health as to look after his sickness. Besides this, it was at last officially admitted that he had a moral and intellectual side. Coffee-rooms and reading-rooms, gymnasiums and workshops were instituted. A new era did in truth appear to have begun. Already by 1861 the mortality in the Army had decreased by one-half since the days of the Crimea. It was no wonder that even vaster possibilities began now to open out before Miss Nightingale. One thing was still needed to complete and to assure her triumphs. The Army Medical Department was indeed reorganized; but the great central machine was still untouched. The War Office itself – ! – If she could remould *that* nearer to her heart's desire – there indeed would be a victory! And until that final act was accomplished, how could she be certain that all the rest of her achievements might not, by some capricious turn of Fortune's wheel – a change of Ministry, perhaps replacing Sidney Herbert by some puppet of the permanent official gang – be swept to limbo in a moment?

Meanwhile, still ravenous for more and yet more work, her activities had branched out into new directions. The Army in India claimed her attention. A Sanitary Commission, appointed at her suggestion, and working under her auspices, did for our troops there what the four Sub-Commissions were doing for those at home. At the same time, these very years which saw her laying the foundations of the whole modern system of medical work in the Army, saw her also beginning to bring her knowledge, her influence, and her activity into the service of the country at large. Her *Notes on Hospitals* (1859) revolutionized the theory of hospital construction and hospital management. She was immediately recognized as the leading expert upon all the questions involved; her advice flowed unceasingly and in all directions, so that there is no great hospital today which does not bear upon it the impress of her mind. Nor was this all. With the opening of the Nightingale Training School for Nurses at St Thomas's Hospital (1860), she became the founder of modern nursing.

But a terrible crisis was now fast approaching. Sidney Herbert had consented to undertake the root and branch reform of the War Office. He had sallied forth into that tropical jungle of festooned obstructiveness, of intertwisted irresponsibilities, of crouching prejudices, of abuses grown stiff and rigid with antiquity, which for so many years to come was destined to lure reforming Ministers to their doom.

'The War Office,' said Miss Nightingale, 'is a very slow office, an enormously expensive office, and one in which the Minister's intentions can be entirely negatived by all his sub-departments, and those of each of the sub-departments by every other.' It was true; and, of course, at the first rumour of a change, the old phalanx of reaction was bristling with its accustomed spears. At its head stood no longer Dr Andrew Smith, who, some time since, had followed the Bison into outer darkness, but a yet more formidable figure, the Permanent Under-Secretary himself, Sir Benjamin Hawes – Ben Hawes the Nightingale Cabinet irreverently dubbed him – a man remarkable even among civil servants for adroitness in baffling inconvenient inquiries, resource in raising false issues, and, in short, a consummate command of all the arts of officially sticking in the mud. 'Our scheme will probably result in Ben Hawes's resignation,' Miss Nightingale said; 'and that is another of its advantages.' Ben Hawes himself, however, did not quite see it in that light. He set himself to resist the wishes of the Minister by every means in his power. The struggle was long and desperate; and, as it proceeded, it gradually became evident to Miss Nightingale that something was the matter with Sidney Herbert. What was it? His health, never very strong, was, he said, in danger of collapsing under the strain of his work. But, after all, what is illness, when there is a War Office to be reorganized? Then he began to talk of retiring altogether from public life. The doctors were consulted, and declared that, above all things, what was necessary was rest. Rest! She grew seriously alarmed. Was it possible that, at the last moment, the crowning wreath of victory was to be snatched from her grasp? She was not to be put aside by doctors; they were talking nonsense; the necessary thing was not rest but the reform of the War Office; and, besides, she knew very well from her own case what one could do even when one was on the point of death. She expostulated vehemently, passionately; the goal was so near, so very near; he could not turn back now! At any rate, he could not resist Miss Nightingale. A compromise was arranged. Very reluctantly, he exchanged the turmoil of the House of Commons for the dignity of the House of Lords, and he remained at the War Office. She was delighted. 'One fight more, the best and the last,' she said.

For several more months the fight did indeed go on. But the strain upon him was greater even than she perhaps could realize. Besides the intestine war in his

 office, he had to face a constant battle in the Cabinet

with Mr Gladstone – a more redoubtable antagonist even than Ben Hawes – over the estimates. His health grew worse and worse. He was attacked by fainting-fits; and there were some days when he could only just keep himself going by gulps of brandy. Miss Nightingale spurred him forward with her encouragements and her admonitions, her zeal and her example. But at last his spirit began to sink as well as his body. He could no longer hope; he could no longer desire; it was useless, all useless; it was utterly impossible. He had failed. The dreadful moment came when the truth was forced upon him: he would never be able to reform the War Office. But a yet more dreadful moment lay behind; he must go to Miss Nightingale and tell her that he was a failure, a beaten man.

'Blessed are the Merciful!' What strange ironic prescience had led Prince Albert, in the simplicity of his heart, to choose that motto for the Crimean brooch? The words hold a double lesson; and, alas! When she brought herself to realize at length what was indeed the fact and what there was no helping, it was not in mercy that she turned upon her old friend. 'Beaten!' she exclaimed. 'Can't you see that you've simply thrown away the game? And with all the winning cards in your hands! And so noble a game! Sidney Herbert beaten! And beaten by Ben Hawes! It is a worse disgrace . . .', her full rage burst out at last, '. . . a worse disgrace than the hospitals at Scutari.'

He dragged himself away from her, dragged himself to Spa, hoping vainly for a return to health, and then, despairing, back again to England, to Wilton, to the majestic house standing there resplendent in the summer sunshine, among the great cedars which had lent their shade to Sir Philip Sidney, and all those familiar, darling haunts of beauty which he loved, each one of them, 'as if they were persons'; and at Wilton he died. After having received the Eucharist, he had become perfectly calm; then, almost unconscious, his lips were seen to be moving. Those about him bent down. 'Poor Florence! Poor Florence!' they just caught. '. . . Our joint work . . . unfinished . . . tried to do . . .' and they could hear no more.

When the onward rush of a powerful spirit sweeps a weaker one to its destruction, the commonplaces of the moral judgement are better left unmade. If Miss Nightingale had been less ruthless, Sidney Herbert would not have perished; but then, she would not have been Miss Nightingale. The force that created was the force that destroyed. It was her Demon that was responsible. When the fatal news reached her, she was overcome by agony. In the revulsion of her feelings, she made a worship of the dead man's memory; and the facile instrument which had broken in her hand she spoke of for ever after as her 'Master'. Then, almost at the same moment, another blow fell on her. Arthur Clough, worn out by labours very different from those of Sidney Herbert, died too: never more would he tie up her parcels. And yet a third disaster followed. The faithful Aunt Mai did not, to be sure, die; no, she did something almost worse: she left Miss Nightingale. She was growing old, and she felt that she had closer and more imperative duties with her own family. Her niece could hardly forgive her. She poured out, in one of her enormous letters, a passionate diatribe upon the faithlessness, the lack of sympathy, the stupidity, the ineptitude of women. Her doctrines had taken no hold among them; she had never known one who had *appris à apprendre*; she could not even get a woman secretary; 'they don't know the names of the Cabinet Ministers – they don't know which of the Church has Bishops and which not.' As for the spirit of self-sacrifice, well – Sidney Herbert and Arthur Clough were men, and they indeed had shown their devotion; but women . . .! She would mount three widow's caps 'for a sign'. The first two would be for

Clough and for her Master; but the third – 'the biggest widow's cap of all' – would be for Aunt Mai. She did well to be angry; she was deserted in her hour of need; and, after all, could she be sure that even the male sex was so impeccable? There was Dr Sutherland, bungling as usual. Perhaps even he intended to go off, one of these days, too? She gave him a look, and he shivered in his shoes. No! – she grinned sardonically; she would always have Dr Sutherland. And then she reflected that there was one thing more that she would always have – her work.

4

Sidney Herbert's death finally put an end to Miss Nightingale's dream of a reformed War Office. For a moment, indeed, in the first agony of her disappointment, she had wildly clutched at a straw; she had written to Mr Gladstone to beg him to take up the burden of Sidney Herbert's work. And Mr Gladstone had replied with a sympathetic account of the funeral.

Succeeding Secretaries of State managed between them to undo a good deal of what had been accomplished, but they could not undo it all; and for ten years more (1862–72) Miss Nightingale remained a potent influence at the War Office. After that, her direct connection with the Army came to an end, and her energies began to turn more and more completely towards more general objects. Her work upon hospital reform assumed enormous proportions; she was able to improve the conditions in infirmaries and workhouses; and one of her most remarkable papers forestalls the recommendations of the Poor Law Commission of 1909. Her training school for nurses, with all that it involved in initiative, control, responsibility, and combat, would have been enough in itself to have absorbed the whole efforts of at least two lives of ordinary vigour. And at the same time her work in connection with India, which had begun with the Sanitary Commission on the Indian army, spread and ramified in a multitude of directions. Her tentacles reached the India Office and succeeded in establishing a hold even upon those slippery high places. For many years it was *de rigueur* for the newly appointed Viceroy, before he left England, to pay a visit to Miss Nightingale.

After much hesitation, she had settled down in a small house in South Street, where she remained for the rest of her life. That life was a very long one; the dying woman reached her ninety-first year. Her ill health gradually diminished; the crises of extreme danger became less frequent, and at last altogether ceased; she remained an invalid, but an invalid of a curious character – an invalid who was too weak to walk downstairs and who worked harder than most Cabinet Ministers. Her illness, whatever it may have been, was certainly not inconvenient. It involved seclusion; and an extraordinary, an unparalleled seclusion was, it might almost have been said, the mainspring of Miss Nightingale's life. Lying on her sofa in the little upper room in South Street, she combined the intense vitality of a dominating woman of the world with the mysterious and romantic quality of a myth. She was a legend in her lifetime, and she knew it. She tasted the joys of power, like those Eastern Emperors whose autocratic rule was based upon invisibility, with the mingled satisfactions of obscurity and fame. And she found the machinery of illness hardly less effective as a barrier against the eyes of men than the ceremonial of a palace. Great statesmen and renowned generals were obliged to beg for audiences; admiring princesses from foreign countries found that they must see her at her own time, or not at all; and the ordinary mortal had no hope of ever getting beyond the downstairs sitting-room and Dr Sutherland. For that indefatigable disciple did, indeed, never desert her. He might be impatient, he might be restless, but he remained. His 'incurable looseness of thought', for so she termed it, continued at her service to the end. Once, it is true, he had actually ventured to take a holiday; but he was recalled, and he did not repeat the experiment. He was wanted downstairs. There he sat, transacting business, answering correspondence, interviewing callers, and exchanging innumerable notes with the unseen power above. Sometimes word came down that Miss

Nightingale was just well enough to see one of her visitors. The fortunate man was led up, was ushered, trembling, into the shaded chamber, and, of course, could never afterwards forget the interview. Very rarely, indeed, once or twice a year, perhaps, but nobody could be quite certain, in deadly secrecy, Miss Nightingale went out for a drive in the Park. Unrecognized, the living legend flitted for a moment before the common gaze. And the precaution was necessary; for there were times when, at some public function, the rumour of her presence was spread abroad; and ladies, mistaken by the crowd for Miss Nightingale, were followed, pressed upon, and vehemently supplicated – 'Let me touch your shawl'; 'Let me stroke your arm'; such was the strange adoration in the hearts of the people. That vast reserve of force lay there behind her; she could use it, if she would. But she preferred never to use it. On occasions, she might hint or threaten; she might balance the sword of Damocles over the head of the Bison; she might, by a word, by a glance, remind some refractory Minister, some unpersuadable Viceroy, sitting in audience with her in the little upper room, that she was something more than a mere sick woman, that she had only, so to speak, to go to the window and wave her handkerchief, for

. . . dreadful things to follow. But that was enough; they understood; the myth was there – obvious, portentous, impalpable; and so it remained to the last.

With statesmen and governors at her beck and call, with her hands on a hundred strings, with mighty provinces at her feet, with foreign governments agog for her counsel, building hospitals, training nurses – she still felt that she had not enough to do. She sighed for more worlds to conquer – more, and yet more. She looked about her – what was there left? Of course! Philosophy! After the world of action, the world of thought. Having set right the health of the British Army, she would now do the same good service for the religious convictions of mankind. She had long noticed – with regret – the growing tendency towards free-thinking among artisans. With regret, but not altogether with surprise: the current teaching of Christianity was sadly to seek; nay, Christianity itself was not without its defects. She would rectify these errors. She would correct the mistakes of the Churches; she would point out just where Christianity was wrong; and she would explain to the artisans what the facts of the case really were. Before her departure for the Crimea, she had begun this work; and now, in the intervals of her other labours, she completed it. Her

Suggestions for Thought to the Searchers after Truth among the Artisans of England (1860), unravels, in the course of three portly volumes, the difficulties – hitherto, curiously enough, unsolved – connected with such matters as Belief in God, the Plan of Creation, the Origin of Evil, the Future Life, Necessity and Free Will, Law, and the Nature of Morality. The Origin of Evil, in particular, held no perplexities for Miss Nightingale. 'We cannot conceive,' she remarks, 'that Omnipotent Righteousness would find satisfaction in *solitary existence*.' This being so, the only question remaining to be asked is, 'What beings should we then conceive that God would create?' Now, He cannot create perfect beings, 'since, essentially, perfection is one'; if He did so, He would only be adding to Himself. Thus the conclusion is obvious: He *must* create *im*perfect ones. Omnipotent Righteousness, faced by the intolerable *impasse* of a solitary existence, finds itself bound, by the very nature of the case, to create the hospitals at Scutari. Whether this argument would have satisfied the artisans, was never discovered, for only a very few copies of the book were printed for private circulation. One copy was sent to Mr Mill, who acknowledged it in an extremely polite letter. He felt himself obliged, however, to confess that he had not been altogether convinced by Miss Nightingale's proof of the existence of God. Miss Nightingale was surprised and mortified; she had thought better of Mr Mill; for surely her proof of the existence of God could hardly be improved upon. 'A law,' she had pointed out, 'implies a lawgiver.' Now the Universe is full of laws – the law of gravitation, the law of excluded middle, and many others; hence it follows that the Universe has a lawgiver – and what would Mr Mill be satisfied with, if he was not satisfied with that?

Perhaps Mr Mill might have asked why the argument had not been pushed to its logical conclusion. Clearly, if we are to trust the analogy of human institutions, we must remember that laws are, as a matter of fact, not dispensed by lawgivers, but passed by Act of Parliament. Miss Nightingale, however, with all her experience of public life, never stopped to consider the question whether God might not be a Limited Monarchy.

Yet her conception of God was certainly not orthodox. She felt towards Him as she might have felt towards a glorified sanitary engineer; and in some of her speculations she seems hardly to distinguish between the Deity and Drains. As one turns over these singular pages, one has the impression that Miss

Nightingale has got the Almighty too into her clutches, and that, if He is not careful, she will kill Him with overwork.

Then, suddenly, in the very midst of the ramifying generalities of her metaphysical disquisitions there is an unexpected turn, and the reader is plunged all at once into something particular, something personal, something impregnated with intense experience – a virulent invective upon the position of women in the upper ranks of society. Forgetful alike of her high argument and of the artisans, the bitter creature rails through a hundred pages of close print at the falsities of family life, the ineptitudes of marriage, the emptiness of convention, in the spirit of an Ibsen or a Samuel Butler. Her fierce pen, shaking with intimate anger, depicts in biting sentences the fearful fate of an unmarried girl in a wealthy household. It is a *cri du coeur*; and then, as suddenly, she returns once more to instruct the artisans upon the nature of Omnipotent Righteousness.

Her mind was, indeed, better qualified to dissect the concrete and distasteful fruits of actual life than to construct a coherent system of abstract philosophy. In spite of her respect for Law, she was never at home with a generalization. Thus, though the great achievement of her life lay in the immense impetus which she gave to the scientific treatment of sickness, a true comprehension of the scientific method itself was alien to her spirit. Like most great men of action – perhaps like all – she was simply an empiricist. She believed in what she saw, and she acted accordingly; beyond that she would not go. She had found in Scutari that fresh air and light played an effective part in the prevention of the maladies with which she had to deal; and that was enough for her; she would not inquire further; what were the general principles underlying that fact – or even whether there were any – she refused to consider. Years after the discoveries of Pasteur and Lister, she laughed at what she called the 'germ-fetish'. There was no such thing as 'infection'; she had never seen it, therefore it did not exist. But she *had* seen the good effects of fresh air; therefore there could be no doubt about them; and therefore it was essential that the bedrooms of patients should be well ventilated. Such was her doctrine; and in those days of hermetically sealed windows it was a very valuable one. But it was a purely empirical doctrine, and thus it led to some unfortunate results. When, for instance, her influence in India was at its height, she issued orders that all hospital windows should be invariably kept open. The authorities, who knew what an open window in the hot weather meant, protested, but in vain; Miss Nightingale was incredulous. She knew nothing of the hot weather, but she did know the value of fresh air – from personal experience; the authorities were talking nonsense; and the windows must be kept open all the year round. There was a great outcry from all the doctors in India, but she was firm; and for a moment it seemed possible that her terrible commands would have to be put into execution. Lord Lawrence, however, was Viceroy, and he was able to intimate to Miss Nightingale, with sufficient authority, that he himself had decided upon the question, and that his decision must stand, even against her own. Upon that, she gave way, but reluctantly and quite unconvinced; she was only puzzled by the unexpected weakness of Lord Lawrence. No doubt, if she had lived today, and if her experience had lain not among cholera cases at Scutari, but among yellow-fever cases in Panama, she would have declared fresh air a fetish, and would have maintained to her dying day that the only really effective way of dealing with disease was by the destruction of mosquitoes.

Yet her mind, so positive, so realistic, so ultra-
 practical, had its singular revulsions, its mysterious

moods of mysticism and of doubt. At times, lying sleepless in the early hours, she fell into long, strange, agonized meditations, and then, seizing a pencil, she would commit to paper the confessions of her soul. The morbid longings of her pre-Crimean days came over her once more; she filled page after page with self-examination, self-criticism, self-surrender. 'O Father,' she wrote, 'I submit, I resign myself, I accept with all my heart this stretching out of Thy hand to save me . . . O how vain it is, the vanity of vanities, to live in men's thoughts instead of God's!' She was lonely, she was miserable. 'Thou knowest that through all these horrible twenty years, I have been supported by the belief that I was working with Thee who wert bringing every one, even our poor nurses, to perfection' – and yet, after all, what was the result? Had not even she been an unprofitable servant? One night, waking suddenly, she saw, in the dim light of the night-lamp, tenebrous shapes upon the wall. The past rushed back upon her. 'Am I she who once stood on that Crimean height?' she wildly asked – ' "The Lady with a lamp shall stand . . ." The lamp shows me only my utter shipwreck.'

She sought consolation in the writings of the Mystics and in a correspondence with Mr Jowett. For many years the Master of Balliol acted as her spiritual adviser. He discussed with her in a series of enormous letters the problems of religion and philosophy; he criticized her writings on those subjects with the tactful sympathy of a cleric who was also a man of the world; and he even ventured to attempt at times to instil into her rebellious nature some of his own peculiar suavity. 'I sometimes think,' he told her, 'that you ought seriously to consider how your work may be carried on, not with less energy, but in a calmer spirit. I am not blaming the past . . . But I want the peace of God to settle on the future.' He recommended her to spend her time no longer in 'conflicts with Government offices', and to take up some literary work. He urged her to 'work out her notion of Divine Perfection', in a series of essays for *Frazer's Magazine*. She did so; and the result was submitted to Mr Froude, who pronounced the second essay to be 'even more pregnant than the first. I cannot tell,' he said, 'how sanitary, with disordered intellects, the effects of such papers will be.' Mr Carlyle, indeed, used different language, and some remarks of his about a lost lamb bleating on the mountains having been unfortunately repeated to Miss Nightingale, all Mr Jowett's suavity was required to keep the peace. In a letter of fourteen sheets, he turned her attention from this painful topic towards a discussion of Quietism. 'I don't see why,' said the Master of Balliol, 'active life might not become a sort of passive life too.' And then, he added, 'I sometimes fancy there are possibilities of human character much greater than have been realized.' She found such sentiments helpful, underlining them in blue pencil; and, in return, she assisted her friend with a long series of elaborate comments upon the Dialogues of Plato, most of which he embodied in the second edition of his translation. Gradually her interest became more personal; she told him never to work again after midnight, and he obeyed her. Then she helped him to draw up a special form of daily service for the College Chapel, with selections from the Psalms under the heads of 'God the Lord, God the Judge, God the Father, and God the friend' – though, indeed, this project was never realized; for the Bishop of Oxford disallowed the alterations, exercising his legal powers, on the advice of Sir Travers Twiss.

Their relations became intimate. 'The spirit of the Twenty-third Psalm and the spirit of the Nineteenth Psalm should be united in our lives,' Mr Jowett said. Eventually, she asked him to do her a singular favour. Would he, knowing what he did of her religious views, come to London and administer to her the Holy Sacrament? He did not hesitate, and afterwards declared that he would always regard the occasion as a solemn event in his life. He was devoted to her; though the precise nature of his feelings towards her never quite transpired. Her feelings towards him were more mixed. At first, he was 'that great and good man' – 'that true saint, Mr Jowett'; but, as time went on, some gall was mingled with the balm; the acrimony of her nature asserted itself. She felt that she gave more sympathy than she received; she was exhausted, she was annoyed, by his conversation. Her tongue, one day, could not refrain from shooting out at him. 'He comes to me, and he talks to me,' she said, 'as if I were someone else.'

5

At one time she had almost decided to end her life in retirement, as a patient of St Thomas's Hospital. But partly owing to the persuasions of Mr Jowett, she changed her mind; for forty-five years she remained in South Street; and in South Street she died. As old age approached, though her influence with the official world gradually diminished, her activities seemed to remain as intense and widespread as before. When hospitals were to be built, when schemes of sanitary reform were in agitation, when wars broke out, she was still the adviser of all Europe. Still, with a characteristic self-assurance, she watched from her Mayfair bedroom over the welfare of India. Still, with an indefatigable enthusiasm, she pushed forward the work, which perhaps, was nearer to her heart, more completely her own, than all the rest – the training of nurses. In her moments of deepest depression, when her greatest achievements seemed to lose their lustre, she thought of her nurses, and was comforted. The ways of God, she found, were strange indeed. 'How inefficient I was in the Crimea,' she noted. 'Yet He has raised up from it trained nursing.'

At other times she was better satisfied. Looking back, she was amazed by the enormous change which, since her early days, had come over the whole treatment of illness, the whole conception of public and domestic health – a change in which, she knew, she had played her part. One of her Indian admirers, the Aga Khan, came to visit her. She expatiated on the marvellous advances she had lived to see in the management of hospitals, in drainage, in ventilation, in sanitary work of every kind. There was a pause; and then, 'Do you think you are improving?' asked the Aga Khan. She was a little taken aback, and said, 'What do you mean by "improving"?' He replied, 'Believing more in God.' She saw that he had a view of God which was different from hers. 'A most interesting man,' she noted after the interview; 'but you could never teach him sanitation.'

When old age actually came, something curious happened. Destiny, having waited very patiently, played a queer trick on Miss Nightingale. The benevolence and public spirit of that long life had only been equalled by its acerbity. Her virtue had dwelt in hardness, and she had poured forth her unstinted usefulness with a bitter smile upon her lips. And now the sarcastic years brought the proud woman her punishment. She was not to die as she had lived. The sting was to be taken out of her: she was to be made soft; she was to be reduced to compliance and complacency. The change came gradually, but at last it was unmistakable. The terrible commander who had driven Sidney Herbert to his death, to whom Mr Jowett had applied the words of Homer, ἄμοτον μεμανῖα – raging insatiably – now accepted small compliments with gratitude, and indulged in sentimental friendships with young girls. The author of *Notes on Nursing* – that classical compendium of the besetting sins of the sisterhood, drawn up with the detailed acrimony, the vindictive relish, of a Swift – now spent long hours in composing sympathetic Addresses to Probationers, whom she petted and wept over in turn. And, at the same time, there appeared a corresponding alteration in her physical mould. The thin, angular woman, with her haughty eye and her acrid mouth, had vanished; and in her place was the rounded, bulky form of a fat old lady, smiling all day long. Then something else became visible. The brain which had been steeled at Scutari was indeed, literally, growing soft. Senility – an even more and more amiable senility – descended. Towards the end, consciousness itself grew lost in a roseate haze, and melted into nothingness. It was just then, three years before her death, when she was eighty-seven years old (1907), that those in authority bethought them that the opportune moment had come for bestowing a public honour on Florence Nightingale. She was offered the Order of Merit. That Order, whose roll contains, among other distinguished names, those of Sir Lawrence Alma Tadema and Sir Edward Elgar, is remarkable chiefly for the fact that, as its title indicates, it is bestowed because its recipient deserves it, and for no other reason. Miss Nightingale's representatives accepted the honour, and her name, after a lapse of many years, once more appeared in the Press. Congratulations from all sides came pouring in. There was a universal burst of enthusiasm – a final revivification of the ancient myth. Among her other admirers, the German Emperor took his opportunity of expressing his feelings towards her. 'His Majesty,' wrote the German Ambassador, 'having just brought to a close a most enjoyable stay in the beautiful neighbourhood of your old home near Romsey, has commanded me to present you with some flowers as a token of his esteem.' Then, by Royal command, the Order of Merit was brought to South Street, and there was a little ceremony of presentation. Sir Douglas Dawson, after a short speech, stepped forward, and handed the insignia of the Order to Miss Nightingale. Propped up by pillows, she dimly recognized that some compliment was being paid her. 'Too kind – too kind,' she murmured; and she was not ironical.

PENGUIN 60S

ISABEL ALLENDE · *Voices in My Ear*
NICHOLSON BAKER · *Playing Trombone*
LINDSEY BAREHAM · *The Little Book of Big Soups*
KAREN BLIXEN · *From the Ngong Hills*
DIRK BOGARDE · *Coming of Age*
ANTHONY BURGESS · *Childhood*
ANGELA CARTER · *Lizzie Borden*
CARLOS CASTANEDA · *The Sorcerer's Ring of Power*
ELIZABETH DAVID · *Peperonata and Other Italian Dishes*
RICHARD DAWKINS · *The Pocket Watchmaker*
GERALD DURRELL · *The Pageant of Fireflies*
RICHARD ELLMANN · *The Trial of Oscar Wilde*
EPICURUS · *Letter on Happiness*
MARIANNE FAITHFULL · *Year One*
KEITH FLOYD · *Hot and Spicy Floyd*
ALEXANDER FRATER · *Where the Dawn Comes Up Like Thunder*
ESTHER FREUD · *Meeting Bilal*
JOHN KENNETH GALBRAITH · *The Culture of Contentment*
ROB GRANT AND DOUG NAYLOR · *Scenes from the Dwarf*
ROBERT GRAVES · *The Gods of Olympus*
JANE GRIGSON · *Puddings*
SOPHIE GRIGSON · *From Sophie's Table*
KATHARINE HEPBURN · *Little Me*
SUSAN HILL · *The Badness Within Him*
ALAN HOLLINGHURST · *Adventures Underground*
BARRY HUMPHRIES · *Less is More Please*
HOWARD JACOBSON · *Expulsion from Paradise*
P. D. JAMES · *The Girl Who Loved Graveyards*
STEPHEN KING · *Umney's Last Case*
LAO TZU · *Tao Te Ching*
DAVID LEAVITT · *Chips Is Here*

PENGUIN 60s

LAURIE LEE · *To War in Spain*
PATRICK LEIGH FERMOR · *Loose as the Wind*
ELMORE LEONARD · *Trouble at Rindo's Station*
DAVID LODGE · *Surprised by Summer*
BERNARD MAC LAVERTY · *The Miraculous Candidate*
SHENA MACKAY · *Cloud-Cuckoo-Land*
NORMAN MAILER · *The Dressing Room*
PETER MAYLE · *Postcards from Summer*
JAN MORRIS · *Scenes from Havian Life*
BLAKE MORRISON · *Camp Cuba*
VLADIMIR NABOKOV · *Now Remember*
REDMOND O'HANLON · *A River in Borneo*
STEVEN PINKER · *Thinking in Tongues*
CRAIG RAINE · *Private View*
CLAUDIA RODEN · *Ful Medames and Other Vegetarian Dishes*
HELGE RUBINSTEIN · *Chocolate Parfait*
SIMON SCHAMA · *The Taking of the Bastille*
WILL SELF · *The Rock of Crack As Big As the Ritz*
MARK SHAND · *Elephant Tales*
NIGEL SLATER · *30-Minute Suppers*
RICK STEIN · *Fresh from the Sea*
LYTTON STRACHEY · *Florence Nightingale*
PAUL THEROUX · *Slow Trains to Simla*
COLIN THUBRON · *Samarkand*
MARK TULLY · *Beyond Purdah*
LAURENS VAN DER POST · *Merry Christmas, Mr Lawrence*
MARGARET VISSER · *More than Meets the Eye*
GAVIN YOUNG · *Something of Samoa*

and

Thirty Obituaries from Wisden · SELECTED BY MATTHEW ENGEL

READ MORE IN PENGUIN

For complete information about books available from Penguin and how to order them, please write to us at the appropriate address below. Please note that for copyright reasons the selection of books varies from country to country.

IN THE UNITED KINGDOM: Please write to *Dept. EP, Penguin Books Ltd, Bath Road, Harmondsworth, Middlesex UB7 ODA.*

IN THE UNITED STATES: Please write to *Consumer Sales, Penguin USA, P.O. Box 999, Dept. 17109, Bergenfield, New Jersey 07621-0120.* VISA and MasterCard holders call 1-800-253-6476 to order Penguin titles.

IN CANADA: Please write to *Penguin Books Canada Ltd, 10 Alcorn Avenue, Suite 300, Toronto, Ontario M4V 3B2.*

IN AUSTRALIA: Please write to *Penguin Books Australia Ltd, P.O. Box 257, Ringwood, Victoria 3134.*

IN NEW ZEALAND: Please write to *Penguin Books (NZ) Ltd, Private Bag 102902, North Shore Mail Centre, Auckland 10.*

IN INDIA: Please write to *Penguin Books India Pvt Ltd, 706 Eros Apartments, 56 Nehru Place, New Delhi 110 019.*

IN THE NETHERLANDS: Please write to *Penguin Books Netherlands bv, Postbus 3507, NL-1001 AH Amsterdam.*

IN GERMANY: Please write to *Penguin Books Deutschland GmbH, Metzlerstrasse 26, 60594 Frankfurt am Main.*

IN SPAIN: Please write to *Penguin Books S. A., Bravo Murillo 19, 1° B, 28015 Madrid.*

IN ITALY: Please write to *Penguin Italia s.r.l., Via Felice Casati 20, I–20124 Milano.*

IN FRANCE: Please write to *Penguin France S. A., 17 rue Lejeune, F–31000 Toulouse.*

IN JAPAN: Please write to *Penguin Books Japan, Ishikiribashi Building, 2–5–4, Suido, Bunkyo-ku, Tokyo 112.*

IN GREECE: Please write to *Penguin Hellas Ltd, Dimocritou 3, GR–106 71 Athens.*

IN SOUTH AFRICA: Please write to *Longman Penguin Southern Africa (Pty) Ltd, Private Bag X08, Bertsham 2013.*

VLADIMIR NABOKOV

NOW REMEMBER

PENGUIN BOOKS

PENGUIN BOOKS

Published by the Penguin Group. Penguin Books Ltd, 27 Wrights Lane, London W8 5TZ, England. Penguin Books USA Inc., 375 Hudson Street, New York, New York 10014, USA. Penguin Books Australia Ltd, Ringwood, Victoria, Australia. Penguin Books Canada Ltd, 10 Alcorn Avenue, Toronto, Ontario, Canada M4V 3B2. Penguin Books (NZ) Ltd, 182–190 Wairau Road, Auckland 10, New Zealand · Penguin Books Ltd, Registered Offices: Harmondsworth, Middlesex, England · These extracts are from *Speak, Memory* by Vladimir Nabokov, revised and expanded edition published by Weidenfeld & Nicolson 1967. Published in Penguin Books 1969. This edition published 1996. · Typeset by Rowland Phototypesetting Ltd, Bury St Edmunds, Suffolk. Printed in England by Clays Ltd, St Ives plc · · 10 9 8 7 6 5 4 3 2 1

I

As far back as I remember myself (with interest, with amusement, seldom with admiration or disgust), I have been subject to mild hallucinations. Some are aural, others are optical, and by none have I profited much. The fatidic accents that restrained Socrates or egged on Joaneta Darc have degenerated with me to the level of something one happens to hear between lifting and clapping down the receiver of a busy party-line telephone. Just before falling asleep, I often become aware of a kind of one-sided conversation going on in an adjacent section of my mind, quite independently from the actual trend of my thoughts. It is a neutral, detached, anonymous voice, which I catch saying words of no importance to me whatever – an English or a Russian sentence, not even addressed to me, and so trivial that I hardly dare give samples, lest the flatness I wish to convey be marred by a molehill of sense. This silly phenomenon seems to be the auditory counterpart of certain praedormitary visions, which I also know well. What I mean is not the bright mental image (as, for instance, the face of a beloved parent long dead) conjured up by a wing-stroke of the will; *that* is one of the bravest movements a human spirit can make. Nor am I alluding to the so-called *muscae volitantes* – shadows cast upon the retinal rods by motes in the vitreous humor, which are seen as transparent threads drifting across the visual field. Perhaps nearer to the hypnagogic mirages I am thinking of is the colored spot, the stab of an afterimage, with which the lamp one had just turned off wounds the palpebral night. However, a shock of this sort is not really a necessary starting point for the slow, steady development of the visions that pass before my closed eyes. They come and go, without the drowsy observer's participation, but are essentially different from dream pictures for he is still master of his senses. They are often grotesque. I am pestered by roguish profiles, by some coarse-featured and florid dwarf with a swelling nostril or ear. At times, however, my photisms take on a rather soothing *flou* quality, and then I see – projected, as it were, upon the inside of the eyelid – gray figures walking between beehives, or small black parrots gradually vanishing among mountain snows, or a mauve remoteness melting beyond moving masts.

On top of all this I present a fine case of colored hearing. Perhaps 'hearing' is not quite accurate, since the color sensation seems to be produced by the very act of my orally forming a given letter while I imagine its outline. The long *a* of the English alphabet (and it is this alphabet I have in mind farther on unless otherwise stated) has for me the tint of weathered wood, but a French *a* evokes polished ebony. This black group also includes hard *g* (vulcanized rubber) and *r* (a sooty rag being ripped). Oatmeal *n*, noodle-limp *l*, and the ivory-backed hand mirror of *o* take care of the whites. I am puzzled by my French *on* which I see as the brimming tension-surface of alcohol in a small glass. Passing on to the blue group, there is steely *x*, thundercloud *z*, and huckleberry *k*. Since a subtle interaction exists between sound and shape, I see *q* as browner than *k*, while *s* is not the light blue of *c*, but a curious mixture of azure and mother-of-pearl. Adjacent tints do not merge, and diphthongs do not have special colors of their own, unless represented by a single character in some other language (thus the fluffy-gray, three-stemmed Russian letter that stands for *sh*, a letter as old as the rushes of the Nile, influences its English representation).

I hasten to complete my list before I am interrupted. In the green group, there are alder-leaf *f*, the unripe apple of *p*, and pistachio *t*. Dull green, combined somehow with violet, is the best I can do for *w*. The yellows comprise various *e*'s and *i*'s, creamy *d*, bright-golden *y*, and *u* whose alphabetical value I can express only by 'brassy with an olive sheen.' In the brown group, there are the rich rubbery tone of soft *g*, paler *j*, and the drab shoelace of *h*. Finally, among the reds, *b* has the tone called burnt sienna by painters, *m* is a fold of pink flannel, and today I have at last perfectly matched *v* with 'Rose Quartz' in Maerz and Paul's *Dictionary of Color*. The word for rainbow, a primary, but decidedly muddy, rainbow, is in my private language the hardly pronounceable: *kzspygv*. The first author to discuss *audition colorée* was, as far as I know, an albino physician in 1812, in Erlangen.

The confessions of a synesthete must sound tedious and pretentious to those who are protected from such leakings and drafts by more solid walls than mine are. To my mother, though, this all seemed quite normal. The matter came up, one day in my seventh year, as I was using a heap of old alphabet blocks to build a tower. I casually remarked to her that their colors were all wrong. We discovered then that some of her letters had the same tint as mine and that, besides, she was optically affected by musical notes. These evoked no chromatisms in me whatsoever. Music, I regret to say, affects me merely as an arbitrary succession of more or less irritating sounds. Under certain emotional circumstances I can stand the spasms of a rich violin, but the concert piano and all wind instruments bore me in small doses and flay me in larger ones. Despite the number of operas I was exposed to every winter (I must have attended *Ruslan* and *Pikovaya Dama* at least a dozen times in the course of half as many years), my weak responsiveness to music was completely overrun by the visual torment of not being able to read over Pimen's shoulder or of trying in vain to imagine the hawkmoths in the dim bloom of Juliet's garden.

My mother did everything to encourage the general sensitiveness I had to visual stimulation. How many were the aquarelles she painted for me; what a revelation it was when she showed me the lilac tree that grows out of mixed blue and red! Sometimes, in our St Petersburg house, from a secret compartment in the wall of her dressing room (and my birth room), she would produce a mass of jewelry for my bedtime amusement. I was very small then, and those flashing tiaras and chokers and rings seemed to me hardly inferior in mystery and enchantment to the illumination in the city during imperial fêtes, when, in the padded stillness of a frosty night, giant monograms, crowns, and other armorial designs, made of colored electric bulbs – sapphire, emerald, ruby – glowed with a kind of charmed constraint above snow-lined cornices on housefronts along residential streets.

2

My numerous childhood illnesses brought my mother and me still closer together. As a little boy, I showed an abnormal aptitude for mathematics, which I completely lost in my singularly talentless youth. This gift played a horrible part in tussles with quinsy or scarlet fever, when I felt enormous spheres and huge numbers swell relentlessly in my aching brain. A foolish tutor had explained logarithms to me much too early, and I had read (in a British publication, the *Boy's Own Paper*, I believe) about a certain Hindu calculator who in exactly two seconds could find the seventeenth root of, say, 3529471145760275132301897342055866171392 (I am not sure I have got this right; anyway the root was 212). Such were the monsters that thrived on my delirium, and the only way to prevent them from crowding me out of myself was to kill them by extracting their hearts. But they were far too strong, and I would sit up and laboriously form garbled sentences as I tried to explain things to my mother. Beneath my delirium, she recognized sensations she had known herself, and her understanding would bring my expanding universe back to a Newtonian norm.

The future specialist in such dull literary lore as autoplagiarism will like to collate a protagonist's experience in my novel *The Gift* with the original event. One day, after a long illness, as I lay in bed still very weak, I found myself basking in an unusual euphoria of lightness and repose. I knew my mother had gone to buy me the daily present that made those convalescences so delightful. What it would be this time I could not guess, but through the crystal of my strangely translucent state 5

I vividly visualized her driving away down Morskaya Street toward Nevski Avenue. I distinguished the light sleigh drawn by a chestnut courser. I heard his snorting breath, the rhythmic clacking of his scrotum, and the lumps of frozen earth and snow thudding against the front of the sleigh. Before my eyes and before those of my mother loomed the hind part of the coachman, in his heavily padded blue robe, and the leather-encased watch (twenty minutes past two) strapped to the back of his belt, from under which curved the pumpkin-like folds of his huge stuffed rump. I saw my mother's seal furs and, as the icy speed increased, the muff she raised to her face – that graceful, winter-ride gesture of a St Petersburg lady. Two corners of the voluminous spread of bearskin that covered her up to the waist were attached by loops to the two side knobs of the low back of her seat. And behind her, holding on to these knobs, a footman in a cockaded hat stood on his narrow support above the rear extremities of the runners.

Still watching the sleigh, I saw it stop at Treumann's (writing implements, bronze baubles, playing cards). Presently, my mother came out of this shop followed by the footman. He carried her purchase, which looked to me like a pencil. I was astonished that she did not carry so small an object herself, and this disagreeable question of dimensions caused a faint renewal, fortunately very brief, of the 'mind dilation effect' which I hoped had gone with the fever. As she was being tucked up again in the sleigh, I watched the vapor exhaled by all, horse included. I watched, too, the familiar pouting movement she made to distend the network of her close-fitting veil drawn too tight over her face, and as I write this, the touch

 of reticulated tenderness that my lips used to feel when I kissed her veiled cheek comes back to me – *flies* back to me with a shout of joy out of the snow-blue, blue-windowed (the curtains are not yet drawn) past.

A few minutes later, she entered my room. In her arms she held a big parcel. It had been, in my vision, greatly reduced in size – perhaps, because I subliminally corrected what logic warned me might still be the dreaded remnants of delirium's dilating world. Now the object proved to be a giant polygonal Faber pencil, four feet long and correspondingly thick. It had been hanging as a showpiece in the shop's window, and she presumed I had coveted it, as I coveted all things that were not quite purchasable. The shopman had been obliged to ring up an agent, a 'Doctor' Libner (as if the transaction possessed indeed some pathological import). For an awful moment, I wondered whether the point was made of real graphite. It was. And some years later I satisfied myself, by drilling a hole in the side, that the lead went right through the whole length – a perfect case of art for art's sake on the part of Faber and Dr Libner since the pencil was far too big for use and, indeed, was not meant to be used.

'Oh yes,' she would say as I mentioned this or that unusual sensation. 'Yes, I know all that,' and with a somewhat eerie ingenuousness she would discuss such things as double sight, and little raps in the woodwork of tripod tables, and premonitions, and the feeling of the *déjà vu*. A streak of sectarianism ran through her direct ancestry. She went to church only at Lent and Easter. The schismatic mood revealed itself in her healthy distaste for the ritual of the Greek Catholic Church and for its priests. She found a deep appeal in the moral and poetical side of the Gospels, but felt no need in the support of any dogma. The appalling insecurity of an afterlife and its lack of privacy did not enter her thoughts. Her intense and pure religiousness took the form of her having equal faith in the existence of another world and in the impossibility of comprehending it in terms of earthly life. All one could do was to glimpse, amid the haze and the chimeras, something real ahead, just as persons endowed with an unusual persistence of diurnal cerebration are able to perceive in their deepest sleep, somewhere beyond the throes of an entangled and inept nightmare, the ordered reality of the waking hour.

3

To love with all one's soul and leave the rest to fate, was the simple rule she heeded. '*Vot zapomni* [now remember],' she would say in conspiratorial tones as she drew my attention to this or that loved thing in Vyra – a lark ascending the curds-and-whey sky of a dull spring day, heat lightning taking pictures of a distant line of trees in the night, the palette of maple leaves on brown sand, a small bird's cuneate footprints on new snow. As if feeling that in a few years the tangible part of her world would perish, she cultivated an extraordinary consciousness of the various time marks distributed throughout our country place. She cherished her own past with the same retrospective fervor that I now do her image and my past. Thus, in a way, I inherited an exquisite simulacrum – the beauty of intangible property, unreal estate – and this proved a splendid training for the endurance of later losses. Her special tags and imprints became as dear and as sacred to me as they were to her. There was the room which in the past had been reserved for her mother's pet hobby, a chemical laboratory; there was the linden tree marking the spot, by the side of the road that sloped up toward the village of Gryazno (accented on the ultima), at the steepest bit where one preferred to take one's 'bike by the horns' (*bïka za roga*) as my father, a dedicated cyclist, liked to say, and where he had proposed; and there was, in the so-called 'old' park, the obsolete tennis court, now a region of moss, mole-heaps, and mushrooms, which had been the scene of gay rallies in the eighties and nineties (even her grim father would shed his coat and give the heaviest racket an appraisive shake) but which, by the time I was ten, nature had effaced with the thoroughness of a felt eraser wiping out a geometrical problem.

By then, an excellent modern court had been built at the end of the 'new' part of the park by skilled workmen imported from Poland for that purpose. The wire mesh of an ample enclosure separated it from the flowery meadow that framed its clay. After a damp night the surface acquired a brownish gloss and the white lines would be repainted with liquid chalk from a green pail by Dmitri, the smallest and oldest of our gardeners, a meek, black-booted, red-shirted dwarf slowly retreating, all hunched up, as his paintbrush went down the line. A pea-tree hedge (the 'yellow acacia' of northern Russia), with a midway opening, corresponding to the court's screen door, ran parallel to the enclosure and to a path dubbed *tropinka Sfinksov* ('path of the Sphingids') because of the hawkmoths visiting at dusk the fluffy lilacs along the border that faced the hedge and likewise broke in the middle. This path formed the bar of a great T whose vertical was the alley of slender oaks, my mother's coevals, that traversed (as already said) the new park through its entire length. Looking down that avenue from the base of the T near the drive one could make out quite distinctly the bright little gap five hundred yards away - or fifty years away from where I am now. Our current tutor or my father, when he stayed with us in the country, invariably had my brother for partner in our temperamental family doubles. 'Play!' my mother would cry in the old manner as she put her little foot forward and bent her white-hatted head to ladle out an assiduous but feeble serve. I got easily cross with her, and she, with the ballboys, two barefooted peasant lads (Dmitri's pug-nosed grandson and the twin brother of pretty Polenka, the head coachman's daughter). The northern summer became tropical around harvest time. Scarlet Sergey would stick his racket between his knees and laboriously wipe his glasses. I see my butterfly net propped against the enclosure – just in case. Wallis Myers' book on lawn tennis lies open on a bench, and after every exchange my father (a first-rate player, with a cannonball service of the Frank Riseley type and a beautiful 'lifting drive') pedantically inquires of my brother and me whether the 'follow-through,' that state of grace, has descended upon us. And sometimes a prodigious cloudburst would cause us to huddle under a shelter at the corner of the court while old Dmitri would be sent to fetch umbrellas and raincoats from the house. A quarter of an hour later he would reappear under a mountain of clothing in the vista of the long avenue which as he advanced would regain its leopard spots with the sun blazing anew and his huge burden unneeded.

She loved all games of skill and gambling. Under her expert

 hands, the thousand bits of a jigsaw puzzle gradually formed an English hunting scene; what had seemed to be the limb of a horse would turn out to belong to an elm and the hitherto unplaceable piece would snugly fill up a gap in the mottled background, affording one the delicate thrill of an abstract and yet tactile satisfaction. At one time, she was very fond of poker, which had reached St Petersburg society via diplomatic circles, so that some of the combinations came with pretty French names – *brelan* for 'three of a kind,' *couleur* for 'flush,' and so on. The game in use was the regular 'draw poker,' with, occasionally, the additional tingle of jackpots and an omnivicarious joker. In town, she often played poker at the houses of friends until three in the morning, a society recreation in the last years before World War One; and later, in exile, she used to imagine (with the same wonder and dismay with which she recalled old Dmitri) the chauffeur Pirogov who still seemed to be waiting for her in the relentless frost of an unending night, although, in his case, rum-laced tea in a hospitable kitchen must have gone a long way to assuage those vigils.

One of the greatest pleasures in summer was the very Russian sport of *hodit' po gribï* (looking for mushrooms). Fried in butter and thickened with sour cream, her delicious finds appeared regularly on the dinner table. Not that the gustatory moment mattered much. Her main delight was in the quest, and this quest had its rules. Thus, no agarics were taken; all she picked were species belonging to the edible section of the genus *Boletus* (tawny *edulis*, brown *scaber*, red *aurantiacus*, and a few close allies), called 'tube mushrooms' by some and coldly defined by mycologists as 'terrestrial, fleshy, putrescent, centrally stipitate fungi.' Their compact pilei – tight-fitting in infant plants, robust and appetizingly domed in ripe ones – have a smooth (not lamellate) under-surface and a neat, strong stem. In classical simplicity of form, boletes differ considerably from the 'true mushroom,' with its preposterous gills and effete stipal ring. It is, however, to the latter, to the lowly and ugly agarics, that nations with timorous taste buds limit their knowledge and appetite, so that to the Anglo-American lay mind the aristocratic boletes are, at best, reformed toadstools.

Rainy weather would bring out these beautiful plants in profusion under the firs, birches and aspens in our park, especially in its older part, east of the carriage road that divided the park in two. Its shady recesses would then harbor that special boletic reek which makes a Russian's nostrils dilate – a dark, dank, satisfying blend of damp moss, rich earth, rotting leaves. But one had to poke and peer for a goodish while among the wet underwood before something really nice, such as a family of bonneted baby *edulis* or the marbled variety of *scaber*, could be discovered and carefully teased out of the soil.

On overcast afternoons, all alone in the drizzle, my mother, carrying a basket (stained blue on the inside by somebody's whortleberries), would set out on a long collecting tour. Toward dinnertime, she could be seen emerging from the nebulous depths of a park alley, her small figure cloaked and hooded in greenish-brown wool, on which countless droplets of moisture made a kind of mist all around her. As she came nearer from under the dripping trees and caught sight of me, her face would show an odd, cheerless expression, which might have spelled poor luck, but which I knew was the tense, jealously contained beatitude of the successful hunter. Just before reaching me, with an abrupt, drooping movement of the arm and shoulder and a 'Pouf!' of magnified exhaustion, she would let her basket sag, in order to stress its weight, its fabulous fullness.

Near a white garden bench, on a round garden table of iron, she would lay out her boletes in concentric circles to count and sort them. Old ones, with spongy, dingy flesh, would be eliminated, leaving the young and the crisp. For a moment, before they were bundled away by a servant to a place she knew nothing about, to a doom that did not interest her, she would stand there admiring them, in a glow of quiet contentment. As often happened at the end of a rainy day, the sun might cast a lurid gleam just before setting, and there, on the damp round table, her mushrooms would lie, very colorful, some bearing traces of extraneous vegetation – a grass blade sticking to a viscid fawn cap, or moss still clothing the bulbous base of a dark-stippled stem. And a tiny looper caterpillar would be there, too, measuring, like a child's finger and thumb, the rim of the table, and every now and then stretching upward to grope, in vain, for the shrub from which it had been dislodged.

4

Not only were the kitchen and the servants' hall never visited by my mother, but they stood as far removed from her consciousness as if they were the corresponding quarters in a hotel. My father had no inclination, either, to run the house. But he did order the meals. With a little sigh, he would open a kind of album laid by the butler on the dinner table after dessert and in his elegant, flowing hand write down the menu for the following day. He had a peculiar habit of letting his pencil or fountain pen vibrate just above the paper while he pondered the next ripple of words. My mother nodded a vague consent to his suggestions or made a wry face. Nominally, the housekeeping was in the hands of her former nurse, at that time a bleary, incredibly wrinkled old woman (born a slave around 1830) with the small face of a melancholy tortoise and big shuffling feet. She wore a nunnish brown dress and gave off a slight but unforgettable smell of coffee and decay. Her dreaded congratulation on our birthdays and namedays was the serfage kiss on the shoulder. Age had developed in her a pathological stinginess, especially in regard to sugar and preserves, so that by degrees, and with the sanction of my parents, other domestic arrangements, kept secret from her, had quietly come into force. Without knowing it (the knowledge would have broken her heart), she remained dangling as it were, from her own key ring, while my mother did her best to allay with soothing words the suspicions that now and then flitted across the old woman's weakening mind. Sole mistress of her moldy and remote little kingdom, which she thought was the real one (we would have starved had it been so), she was followed by the mocking glances of lackeys and maids as she steadily plodded through long corridors to store away half an apple or a couple of broken Petit-Beurre biscuits she had found on a plate.

Meanwhile, with a permanent staff of about fifty servants and no questions asked, our city household and country place were the scenes of a fantastic merry-go-round of theft. In this, according to nosy old aunts, whom nobody heeded but who proved to be right after all, the chief cook Nikolay Andreevich and the head gardener Egor, both staid-looking, bespectacled men with the hoary temples of trusty retainers, were the two masterminds. When confronted with stupendous and incomprehensible bills, or a sudden extinction of garden strawberries and hothouse peaches, my father, a jurist and a statesman, felt professionally vexed at not being able to cope with the economics of his own home; but every time a complicated case of larceny came to light, some legal doubt or scruple prevented him from doing anything about it. When common sense required the firing of a rascally servant, the man's little son would as likely as not fall desperately ill, and the resolution to get the best doctors in town for him would cancel all other considerations. So, with one thing and another, my father preferred to leave the whole housekeeping situation in a state of precarious equilibrium (not devoid of a certain quiet humor), with my mother deriving considerable comfort from the hope that her old nurse's illusory world would not be shattered.

My mother knew well how hurtful a broken illusion could be. The most trifling disappointment took on for her the dimensions of a major disaster. One Christmas Eve, in Vyra, not long before her fourth baby was to be born, she happened to be laid up with a slight ailment and made my brother and me (aged, respectively, five and six) promise not to look into the Christmas stockings that we would find hanging from our bedposts on the following morning but to bring them over to her room and investigate them there, so that she could watch and enjoy our pleasure. Upon awakening, I held a furtive conference with my brother, after which, with eager hands, each felt his delightfully crackling stocking, stuffed with small presents; these we cautiously fished out one by one, undid the ribbons, loosened the tissue paper, inspected everything by the weak light that came through a chink in the shutters, wrapped up the little things again, and crammed them back where they had been. I next recall our sitting on our mother's bed, holding those lumpy stockings and doing our best to give the performance she had wanted to see; but we had so messed up the wrappings, so amateurish were our renderings of enthusiastic surprise (I can see my brother casting his eyes upward and exclaiming, in imitation of our new French governess, '*Ah, que c'est beau!*'), that, after observing us for a moment, our audience burst into tears. A decade passed. World War One started. A crowd of patriots and my uncle Ruka stoned the German Embassy. *Peterburg* was sunk to *Petrograd* against all rules of nomenclatorial priority. Beethoven turned out to be Dutch. The newsreels showed photogenic explosions, the spasm of a cannon, Poincaré in his leathern leggings, bleak puddles, the poor little Tsarevich in Circassian uniform with dagger and cartridges, his tall sisters so dowdily dressed, long railway trains crammed with troops. My mother set up a private hospital for wounded soldiers. I remember her, in the fashionable nurse's gray-and-white uniform she abhorred, denouncing with the same childish tears the impenetrable meekness of those crippled peasants and the ineffectiveness of part-time compassion. And, still later, when in exile, reviewing the past, she would often accuse herself (unjustly as I see it now) of having been less affected by the misery of man than by the emotional load man dumps upon innocent nature – old trees, old horses, old dogs.

Her particular fondness for brown dachshunds puzzled my critical aunts. In the family albums illustrating her young years, there was hardly a group that did not include one such animal – usually with some part of its flexible body blurred and always with the strange, paranoiac eyes dachshunds have in snapshots.

A couple of obese old-timers, Box I and Loulou, still lolled in the sunshine on the porch when I was a child. Sometime in 1904 my father bought at a dog show in Munich a pup which grew into the bad-tempered but wonderfully handsome Trainy (as I named him because of his being as long and as brown as a sleeping car). One of the musical themes of my childhood is Trainy's hysterical tongue, on the trail of the hare he never got, in the depths of our Vyra park, whence he would return at dusk (after my anxious mother had stood whistling for a long time in the oak avenue) with the old corpse of a mole in his jaws and burs in his ears. Around 1915, his hind legs became paralyzed, and until he was chloroformed, he would dismally drag himself over long, glossy stretches of parquet floor like a *cul de jatte*. Then somebody gave us another pup, Box II, whose grandparents had been Dr Anton Chekhov's Quina and Brom. This final dachshund followed us into exile, and as late as 1930, in a suburb of Prague (where my widowed mother spent her last years, on a small pension provided by the Czech government), he could be still seen going for reluctant walks with his mistress, waddling far behind in a huff, tremendously old and furious with his long Czech muzzle of wire – an émigré dog in a patched and ill-fitting coat.

During our last two Cambridge years, my brother and I used to spend vacations in Berlin, where our parents with the two girls and ten-year-old Kirill occupied one of those large, gloomy, eminently bourgeois apartments that I have let to so many émigré families in my novels and short stories. On the night of 28 March 1922, around ten o'clock, in the living room where as usual my mother was reclining on the red-plush corner couch, I happened to be reading to her Blok's verse on

Italy – had just got to the end of the little poem about Florence, which Blok compares to the delicate, smoky bloom of an iris, and she was saying over her knitting, 'Yes, yes, Florence does look like a *dïmnïy iris*, how true! I remember –' when the telephone rang.

After 1923, when she moved to Prague, and I lived in Germany and France, I was unable to visit her frequently; nor was I with her at her death, which occurred on the eve of World War Two. Whenever I did manage to go to Prague, there was always that initial pang one feels just before time, caught unawares, again dons its familiar mask. In the pitiable lodgings she shared with her dearest companion, Evgeniya Konstantinovna Hofeld (1884–1957), who had replaced, in 1914, Miss Greenwood (who, in her turn, had replaced Miss Lavington) as governess of my two sisters (Olga, born 5 January 1903, and Elena, born 31 March 1906), albums, in which, during the last years, she had copied out her favorite poems, from Maykov to Mayakovski, lay around her on odds and ends of decrepit, secondhand furniture. A cast of my father's hand and a watercolor picture of his grave in the Greek-Catholic cemetery of Tegel, now in East Berlin, shared a shelf with émigré writers' books, so prone to disintegration in their cheap paper covers. A soapbox covered with green cloth supported the dim little photographs in crumbling frames she liked to have near her couch. She did not really need them, for nothing had been lost. As a company of traveling players carry with them everywhere, while they still remember their lines, a windy heath, a misty castle, an enchanted island, so she had with her all that her soul had stored. With great clarity, I can see her sitting at a table and serenely considering the laid-out cards of a game of solitaire: she leans on her left elbow and presses to her cheek the free thumb of her left hand, in which, close to her mouth, she holds a cigarette, while her right hand stretches toward the next card. The double gleam on her fourth finger is two marriage rings – her own and my father's, which, being too large for her, is fastened to hers by a bit of black thread.

Whenever in my dreams I see the dead, they always appear silent, bothered, strangely depressed, quite unlike their dear, bright selves. I am aware of them, without any astonishment, in surroundings they never visited during their earthly existence, in the house of some friend of mine they never knew. They sit apart, frowning at the floor, as if death were a dark taint, a shameful family secret. It is certainly not then – not in dreams – but when one is wide awake, at moments of robust joy and achievement, on the highest terrace of consciousness, that mortality has a chance to peer beyond its own limits, from the mast, from the past and its castle tower. And although nothing much can be seen through the mist, there is somehow the blissful feeling that one is looking in the right direction.

I

The kind of Russian family to which I belonged – a kind now extinct – had, among other virtues, a traditional leaning toward the comfortable products of Anglo-Saxon civilization. Pears' Soap, tar-black when dry, topaz-like when held to the light between wet fingers, took care of one's morning bath. Pleasant was the decreasing weight of the English collapsible tub when it was made to protrude a rubber underlip and disgorge its frothy contents into the slop pail. 'We could not improve the cream, so we improved the tube,' said the English toothpaste. At breakfast, Golden Syrup imported from London would entwist with its glowing coils the revolving spoon from which enough of it had slithered onto a piece of Russian bread and butter. All sorts of snug, mellow things came in a steady procession from the English Shop on Nevski Avenue: fruitcakes, smelling salts, playing cards, picture puzzles, striped blazers, talcum-white tennis balls.

I learned to read English before I could read Russian. My first English friends were four simple souls in my grammar – Ben, Dan, Sam and Ned. There used to be a great deal of fuss about their identities and whereabouts – 'Who is Ben?' 'He is Dan.' 'Sam is in bed,' and so on. Although it all remained rather stiff and patchy (the compiler was handicapped by having to employ – for the initial lessons, at least – words of not more than three letters), my imagination somehow managed to obtain the necessary data. Wan-faced, big-limbed, silent nitwits, proud in the possession of certain tools ('Ben has an axe'), they now drift with a slow-motioned slouch across the remotest backdrop of memory; and, akin to the mad alphabet of an optician's chart, the grammar-book lettering looms again before me.

The schoolroom was drenched with sunlight. In a sweating glass jar, several spiny caterpillars were feeding on nettle leaves (and ejecting interesting, barrel-shaped pellets of olive-green frass). The oilcloth that covered the round table smelled of glue. Miss Clayton smelled of Miss Clayton. Fantastically, gloriously, the blood-colored alcohol of the outside thermometer had risen to 24° Réaumur (86° Fahrenheit) in the shade. Through the window one could see kerchiefed peasant girls weeding a garden path on their hands and knees or gently raking the sun-mottled sand. (The happy days when they would be cleaning streets and digging canals for the State were still beyond the horizon.) Golden orioles in the greenery emitted their four brilliant notes: dee-del-dee-O!

Ned lumbered past the window in a fair impersonation of the gardener's mate Ivan (who was to become in 1918 a member of the local Soviet). On later pages longer words appeared; and at the very end of the brown, inkstained volume, a real, sensible story unfolded its adult sentences ('One day Ted said to Ann: Let us –'), the little reader's ultimate triumph and reward. I was thrilled by the thought that some day I might attain such proficiency. The magic has endured, and whenever a grammar book comes my way, I instantly turn to the last page to enjoy a forbidden glimpse of the laborious student's future, of that promised land where, at last, words are meant to mean what they mean.

2

Summer *soomerki* – the lovely Russian word for dusk. Time: a dim point in the first decade of this unpopular century. Place: latitude 59° north from your equator, longitude 100° east from my writing hand. The day would take hours to fade, and everything – sky, tall flowers, still water – would be kept in a state of infinite vesperal suspense, deepened rather than resolved by the doleful moo of a cow in a distant meadow or by the still more moving cry that came from some bird beyond the lower course of the river, where the vast expanse of a misty-blue sphagnum bog, because of its mystery and remoteness, the Rukavishnikov children had baptized America.

In the drawing room of our country house, before going to bed, I would often be read to in English by my mother. As she came to a particularly dramatic passage, where the hero was about to encounter some strange, perhaps fatal danger, her voice would slow down, her words would be spaced portentously, and before turning the pages she would place upon it her hand, with its familiar pigeon-blood ruby and diamond ring (within the limpid facets of which, had I been a better crystal-gazer, I might have seen a room, people, lights, trees in the rain – a whole period of émigré life for which that ring was to pay).

There were tales about knights whose terrific but wonderfully aseptic wounds were bathed by damsels in grottoes. From a windswept clifftop, a medieval maiden with flying hair and a youth in hose gazed at the round Isles of the Blessed. In 'Misunderstood,' the fate of Humphrey used to bring a more specialized lump to one's throat than anything in Dickens or

Daudet (great devisers of lumps), while a shamelessly allegorical story, 'Beyond the Blue Mountains,' dealing with two pairs of little travelers – good Clover and Cowslip, bad Buttercup and Daisy – contained enough exciting details to make one forget its 'message.'

There were also those large, flat, glossy picture books. I particularly liked the blue-coated, red-trousered, coal-black Golliwogg, with underclothes buttons for eyes, and his meager harem of five wooden dolls. By the illegal method of cutting themselves frocks out of the American flag (Peg taking the motherly stripes, Sarah Jane the pretty stars) two of the dolls acquired a certain soft femininity, once their neutral articulations had been clothed. The Twins (Meg and Weg) and the Midget remained stark naked and, consequently, sexless.

We see them in the dead of night stealing out of doors to sling snowballs at one another until the chimes of a remote clock ('But Hark!' comments the rhymed text) send them back to their toybox in the nursery. A rude jack-in-the-box shoots out, frightening my lovely Sarah, and that picture I heartily disliked because it reminded me of children's parties at which this or that graceful little girl, who had bewitched me, happened to pinch her finger or hurt her knee, and would forthwith expand into a purple-faced goblin, all wrinkles and bawling mouth. Another time they went on a bicycle journey and were captured by cannibals; our unsuspecting travelers had been quenching their thirst at a palm-fringed pool when the tom-toms sounded. Over the shoulder of my past I admire again the crucial picture: the Golliwogg, still on his knees by the pool but no longer drinking; his hair stands on end and the normal black of his face has changed to a weird ashen hue.

There was also the motorcar book (Sarah Jane, always my favorite, sporting a long green veil), with the usual sequel – crutches and bandaged heads.

And, yes – the airship. Yards and yards of yellow silk went to make it, and an additional tiny balloon was provided for the sole use of the fortunate Midget. At the immense altitude to which the ship reached, the aeronauts huddled together for warmth while the lost little soloist, still the object of my intense envy notwithstanding his plight, drifted into an abyss of frost and stars – alone.

3

I next see my mother leading me bedward through the enormous hall, where a central flight of stairs swept up and up, with nothing but hothouse-like panes of glass between the upper landing and the light green evening sky. One would lag back and shuffle and slide a little on the smooth stone floor of the hall, causing the gentle hand at the small of one's back to propel one's reluctant frame by means of indulgent pushes. Upon reaching the stairway, my custom was to get to the steps by squirming under the handrail between the newel post and the first banister. With every new summer, the process of squeezing through became more difficult; nowadays, even my ghost would get stuck.

Another part of the ritual was to ascend with closed eyes. 'Step, step, step,' came my mother's voice as she led me up – and sure enough, the surface of the next tread would receive the blind child's confident foot; all one had to do was lift it a little higher than usual, so as to avoid stubbing one's toe against the riser. This slow, somewhat somnambulistic ascension in self-engendered darkness held obvious delights. The keenest of them was not knowing when the last step would come. At the top of the stairs, one's foot would be automatically lifted to the deceptive call of 'Step,' and then, with a momentary sense of exquisite panic, with a wild contraction of muscles, would sink into the phantasm of a step, padded, as it were, with the infinitely elastic stuff of its own nonexistence.

It is surprising what method there was in my bedtime dawdling. True, the whole going-up-the-stairs business now reveals certain transcendental values. Actually, however, I was merely playing for time by extending every second to its utmost. This would still go on when my mother turned me over, to be undressed, to Miss Clayton or Mademoiselle.

There were five bathrooms in our country house, and a medley of venerable washstands (one of these I would seek out in its dark nook whenever I had been crying, so as to feel on my swollen face which I was ashamed to show, the healing touch of its groping jet while I stepped on the rusty pedal). Regular baths were taken in the evening. For morning ablutions, the round, rubber English tubs were used. Mine was about four feet in diameter, with a knee-high rim. Upon the lathered back of the squatting child, a jugful of water was carefully poured by an aproned servant. Its temperature varied with the hydrotherapeutic notions of successive mentors. There was that bleak period of dawning puberty, when an icy deluge was decreed by our current tutor, who happened to be a medical student. On the other hand, the temperature of one's evening bath remained pleasantly constant at 28° Réaumur (95°

Fahrenheit) as measured by a large kindly thermometer whose wooden sheathing (with a bit of damp string in the eye of the handle) allowed it to share in the buoyancy of celluloid goldfishes and little swans.

The toilets were separate from the bathrooms, and the oldest among them was a rather sumptuous but gloomy affair with some fine panelwork and a tasseled rope of red velvet, which, when pulled, produced a beautifully modulated, discreetly muffled gurgle and gulp. From that corner of the house, one could see Hesperus and hear the nightingales, and it was there that, later, I used to compose my youthful verse, dedicated to unembraced beauties, and morosely survey, in a dimly illuminated mirror, the immediate erection of a strange castle in an unknown Spain. As a small child, however, I was assigned a more modest arrangement, rather casually situated in a narrow recess between a wicker hamper and the door leading to the nursery bathroom. This door I liked to keep ajar; through it I drowsily looked at the shimmer of steam above the mahogany bath, at the fantastic flotilla of swans and skiffs, at myself with a harp in one of the boats, at a furry moth pinging against the reflector of the kerosene lamp, at the stained-glass window beyond, at its two halberdiers consisting of colored rectangles. Bending from my warm seat, I liked to press the middle of my brow, its ophryon to be precise, against the smooth comfortable edge of the door and then roll my head a little, so that the door would move to and fro while its edge remained all the time in soothing contact with my forehead. A dreamy rhythm would permeate my being. The recent 'Step, step, step,' would be taken up by a dripping faucet. And, fruitfully combining rhythmic pattern with rhythmic sound, I would unravel the labyrinthian frets on the linoleum, and find faces where a crack or a shadow afforded a *point de repère* for the eye. I appeal to parents: never, never say, 'Hurry up,' to a child.

The final stage in the course of my vague navigation would come when I reached the island of my bed. From the veranda or drawing room, where life was going on without me, my mother would come up for the warm murmur of her good-night kiss. Closed inside shutters, a lighted candle, Gentle Jesus, meek and mild, something-something little child, the child kneeling on the pillow that presently would engulf his humming head. English prayers and the little icon featuring a suntanned Greek Catholic saint formed an innocent association upon which I look back with pleasure; and above the icon, high up on the wall, where the shadow of something (of the bamboo screen between bed and door?) undulated in the warm candlelight, a framed aquarelle showed a dusky path winding through one of those eerily dense European beechwoods, where the only undergrowth is bindweed and the only sound one's thumping heart. In an English fairy tale my mother had once read to me, a small boy stepped out of his bed into a picture and rode his hobbyhorse along a painted path between silent trees. While I knelt on my pillow in a mist of drowsiness and talc-powdered well-being, half sitting on my calves and rapidly going through my prayer, I imagined the motion of climbing into the picture above my bed and plunging into that enchanted beechwood – which I did visit in due time.

4

A bewildering sequence of English nurses and governesses, some of them wringing their hands, others smiling at me enigmatically, come out to meet me as I re-enter my past.

There was dim Miss Rachel, whom I remember mainly in terms of Huntley and Palmer biscuits (the nice almond rocks at the top of the blue-papered tin box, the insipid cracknels at the bottom) which she unlawfully shared with me after my teeth had been brushed. There was Miss Clayton, who, when I slumped in my chair, would poke me in the middle vertebrae and then smilingly throw back her own shoulders to show what she wanted of me: she told me a nephew of hers at my age (four) used to breed caterpillars, but those she collected for me in an open jar with nettles all walked away one morning, and the gardener said they had hanged themselves. There was lovely, black-haired, aquamarine-eyed Miss Norcott, who lost a white kid glove at Nice or Beaulieu, where I vainly looked for it on the shingly beach among the colored pebbles and the glaucous lumps of sea-changed bottle glass. Lovely Miss Norcott was asked to leave at once, one night at Abbazia. She embraced me in the morning twilight of the nursery, pale-mackintoshed and weeping like a Babylonian willow, and that day I remained inconsolable, despite the hot chocolate that the Petersons' old Nanny had made especially for me and the special bread and butter, on the smooth surface of which my aunt Nata, adroitly capturing my attention, drew a daisy, then a cat, and then the little mermaid whom I had just been reading about with Miss Norcott and crying over, too, so I started to cry again. There was myopic little Miss Hunt, whose short stay with us in

Wiesbaden came to an end the day my brother and I – aged four and five, respectively – managed to evade her nervous vigilance by boarding a steamer that took us quite a way down the Rhine before recapture. There was pink-nosed Miss Robinson. There was Miss Clayton again. There was one awful person who read to me Marie Corelli's *The Mighty Atom*. There were still others. At a certain point they faded out of my life. French and Russian took over; and what little time remained for the speaking of English was devoted to occasional sessions with two gentlemen, Mr Burness and Mr Cummings, neither of whom dwelt with us. They are associated in my mind with winters in St Petersburg, where we had a house on the Morskaya Street.

Mr Burness was a large Scotsman with a florid face, light-blue eyes and lank, straw-colored hair. He spent his mornings teaching at a language school and then crammed into the afternoon more private lessons than the day could well hold. Traveling, as he did, from one part of the town to another and having to depend on the torpid trot of dejected *izvozchik* (cab) horses to get him to his pupils, he would be, with luck, only a quarter of an hour late for his two o'clock lesson (wherever that was), but would arrive after five for his four o'clock one. The tension of waiting for him and hoping that, for once, his superhuman doggedness might balk before the gray wall of some special snowstorm was the kind of feeling that one trusts never to meet with in mature life (but that I did experience again when circumstances forced me, in my turn, to give lessons and when, in my furnished rooms in Berlin, I awaited a certain stone-faced pupil, who would *always* turn up despite the obstacles I mentally piled in his way).

The very darkness that was gathering outside seemed a waste product of Mr Burness' efforts to reach our house. Presently the valet would come to drop the blue voluminous blinds and draw the flowered window draperies. The tick-tock of the grandfather's clock in the schoolroom gradually assumed a dreary, nagging intonation. The tightness of my shorts in the groin and the rough touch of ribbed black stockings rubbing against the tender inside of my bent legs would mingle with the dull pressure of a humble need, the satisfaction of which I kept postponing. Nearly an hour would pass and there would be no sign of Mr Burness. My brother would go to his room and play some practice piece on the piano and then plunge and replunge into some of the melodies that I loathed – the instruction to the artificial flowers in *Faust* (. . . *dites-lui qu'elle est belle* . . .) or Vladimir Lenski's wail (. . . *Koo-dah, koo-dah, koo-dah vï udalilis'*). I would leave the upper floor, where we children dwelt, and slowly slide along the balustrade down to the second story, where my parents' rooms were situated. As often as not, they used to be out at that time, and in the gathering dusk the place acted upon my young senses in a curiously teleological way, as if this accumulation of familiar things in the dark were doing its utmost to form the definite and permanent image that repeated exposure did finally leave in my mind.

The sepia gloom of an arctic afternoon in midwinter invaded the rooms and was deepening to an oppressive black. A bronze angle, a surface of glass or polished mahogany here and there in the darkness, reflected the odds and ends of light from the street, where the globes of tall street lamps along its middle line were already diffusing their lunar glow. Gauzy shadows moved on the ceiling. In the stillness, the dry sound of a chrysanthemum petal falling upon the marble of a table made one's nerves twang.

My mother's boudoir had a convenient oriel for looking out on the Morskaya in the direction of the Maria Square. With lips pressed against the thin fabric that veiled the windowpane I would gradually taste the cold of the glass through the gauze. From that oriel, some years later, at the outbreak of the Revolution, I watched various engagements and saw my first dead man: he was being carried away on a stretcher, and from one dangling leg an ill-shod comrade kept trying to pull off the boot despite pushes and punches from the stretchermen – all this at a goodish trot. But in the days of Mr Burness' lessons there was nothing to watch save the dark, muffled street and its receding line of loftily suspended lamps, around which the snowflakes passed and repassed with a graceful, almost deliberately slackened motion, as if to show how the trick was done and how simple it was. From another angle, one might see a more generous stream of snow in a brighter, violet-tinged nimbus of gaslight, and then the jutting enclosure where I stood would seem to drift slowly up and up, like a balloon. At last one of the phantom sleighs gliding along the street would come to a stop, and with gawky haste Mr Burness in his fox-furred *shapka* would make for our door.

From the schoolroom, whither I had preceded him, I would hear his vigorous footsteps crashing nearer and nearer, and, no matter how cold the day was, his good, ruddy face would be sweating abundantly as he strode in. I remember the terrific energy with which he pressed on the spluttering pen as he wrote down, in the roundest of round hands, the tasks to be prepared for the next day. Usually at the end of the lesson a certain limerick was asked for and granted, the point of the performance being that the word 'screamed' in it was to be involuntarily enacted by oneself every time Mr Burness gave a formidable squeeze to the hand he held in his beefy paw as he recited the lines:

There was a young lady from Russia
Who (squeeze) whenever you'd crush her.
She (squeeze) and she (squeeze) . . .

by which time the pain would have become so excruciating that we never got any farther.

5

The quiet, bearded gentleman with a stoop, old-fashioned Mr Cummings, who taught me, in 1907 or 1908, to draw, had been my mother's drawing master also. He had come to Russia in the early nineties as foreign correspondent and illustrator for the London *Graphic*. Marital misfortunes were rumored to obscure his life. A melancholy sweetness of manner made up for the meagerness of his talent. He wore an ulster unless the weather was very mild, when he would switch to the kind of greenish-brown woolen cloak called a *loden*.

I was captivated by his use of the special eraser he kept in his waistcoat pocket, by the manner in which he held the page taut, and afterwards flicked off, with the back of his fingers, the 'gutticles of the percha' (as he said). Silently, sadly, he illustrated for me the marble laws of perspective: long, straight strokes of his elegantly held, incredibly sharp pencil caused the lines of the room he created out of nothing (abstract walls, receding ceiling and floor) to come together in one remote hypothetical point with tantalizing and sterile accuracy. Tantalizing, because it made me think of railway tracks, symmetrically and trickily converging before the bloodshot eyes of my favorite mask, a grimy engine driver; sterile, because that room remained unfurnished and quite empty, being devoid even of the neutral statues one finds in the uninteresting first hall of a museum.

The rest of the picture gallery made up for its gaunt vestibule. Mr Cummings was a master of the sunset. His little watercolors, purchased at different times for five or ten roubles apiece by members of our household, led a somewhat precarious existence, shifting, as they did, to more and more obscure nooks and finally getting completely eclipsed by some sleek porcelain beast or a newly framed photograph. After I had learned not only to draw cubes and cones but to shade properly with smooth, merging slants such parts of them as had to be made to turn away forever, the kind old gentleman contented himself with painting under my enchanted gaze his own wet little paradises, variations of one landscape: a summer evening with an orange sky, a pasture ending in the black fringe of a distant forest, and a luminous river, repeating the sky and winding away and away.

Later on, from around 1910 to 1912, the well-known 'impressionist' (a term of the period) Yaremich took over; a humorless and formless person, he advocated a 'bold' style, blotches of dull color, smears of sepia and olive-brown, by means of which I had to reproduce on huge sheets of gray paper, humanoid shapes that we modeled of plasticine and placed in 'dramatic' positions against a backcloth of velvet with all kinds of folds and shadow effects. It was a depressing combination of at least three different arts, all approximate, and finally I rebelled.

He was replaced by the celebrated Dobuzhinski who liked to give me his lessons on the *piano nobile* of our house, in one of its pretty reception rooms downstairs, which he entered in a particularly noiseless way as if afraid to startle me from my verse-making stupor. He made me depict from memory, in the greatest possible detail, objects I had certainly seen thousands of times without visualizing them properly: a street lamp, a postbox, the tulip design on the stained glass of our own front door. He tried to teach me to find the geometrical coordinations between the slender twigs of a leafless boulevard tree, a system of visual give-and-takes, requiring a precision of linear expression, which I failed to achieve in my youth, but applied gratefully, in my adult instar, not only to the drawing of butterfly genitalia during my seven years at the Harvard Museum of Comparative Zoology, when immersing myself in the bright wellhole of a microscope to record in India ink this or that new structure; but also, perhaps, to certain camera-lucida needs of literary composition. Emotionally, however, I am still more indebted to the earlier color treats given me by my mother and her former teacher. How readily Mr Cummings would sit down on a stool, part behind with both hands his – what? was he wearing a frock coat? I see only the gesture – and proceed to open the black tin paintbox. I loved the nimble way he had of soaking his paintbrush in multiple color to the accompaniment of a rapid clatter produced by the enamel containers wherein the rich reds and yellows that the brush dimpled were appetizingly cupped; and having thus collected its honey, it would cease to hover and poke, and, by two or three sweeps of its lush tip, would drench the 'Vatmanski' paper with an even spread of orange sky, across which, while that sky was still dampish, a long purple-black cloud would be laid. 'And that's all, dearie,' he would say. 'That's all there is to it.'

On one occasion, I had him draw an express train for me. I watched his pencil ably evolve the cowcatcher and elaborate headlights of a locomotive that looked as if it had been acquired secondhand for the Trans-Siberian line after it had done duty at Promontory Point, Utah, in the sixties. Then came five disappointingly plain carriages. When he had quite finished them, he carefully shaded the ample smoke coming from the huge funnel, cocked his head, and, after a moment of pleased contemplation, handed me the drawing. I tried to look pleased, too. He had forgotten the tender.

A quarter of a century later, I learned two things: that Burness, by then dead, had been well known in Edinburgh as a scholarly translator of the Russian romantic poems that had been the altar and frenzy of my boyhood; and that my humble drawing master, whose age I used to synchronize with that of granduncles and old family servants, had married a young Estonian girl about the time I myself married. When I learned these later developments, I experienced a queer shock; it was as if life had impinged upon my creative rights by wriggling on beyond the subjective limits so elegantly and economically set by childhood memories that I thought I had signed and sealed.

'And what about Yaremich?' I asked M. V. Dobuzhinski,

one summer afternoon in the nineteen-forties, as we strolled through a beech forest in Vermont. 'Is he remembered?'

'Indeed, he is,' replied Mstislav Valerianovich. 'He was exceptionally gifted. I don't know what kind of teacher he was, but I do know that *you* were the most hopeless pupil I ever had.'

I

On a summer morning, in the legendary Russia of my boyhood, my first glance upon awakening was for the chink between the white inner shutters. If it disclosed a watery pallor, one had better not open them at all, and so be spared the sight of a sullen day sitting for its picture in a puddle. How resentfully one would deduce, from a line of dull light, the leaden sky, the sodden sand, the gruel-like mess of broken brown blossoms under the lilacs – and that flat, fallow leaf (the first casualty of the season) pasted upon a wet garden bench!

But if the chink was a long glint of dewy brilliancy, then I made haste to have the window yield its treasure. With one blow, the room would be cleft into light and shade. The foliage of birches moving in the sun had the translucent green tone of grapes, and in contrast to this there was the dark velvet of fir trees against a blue of extraordinary intensity, the like of which I rediscovered only many years later, in the montane zone of Colorado.

From the age of seven, everything I felt in connexion with a rectangle of framed sunlight was dominated by a single passion. If my first glance of the morning was for the sun, my first thought was for the butterflies it would engender. The original event had been banal enough. On the honeysuckle, overhanging the carved back of a bench just opposite the main entrance, my guiding angel (whose wings, except for the absence of a Florentine limbus, resemble those of Fra Angelico's Gabriel) pointed out to me a rare visitor, a splendid, pale-yellow creature with black blotches, blue crenels, and a cinnabar eyespot above each chrome-rimmed black tail. As it probed the inclined flower from which it hung, its powdery body slightly bent, it kept restlessly jerking its great wings, and my desire for it was one of the most intense I have ever experienced. Agile Ustin, our town-house janitor, who for a comic reason (explained elsewhere) happened to be that summer in the country with us, somehow managed to catch it in my cap, after which it was transferred, cap and all, to a wardrobe, where domestic naphthalene was fondly expected by Mademoiselle to kill it overnight. On the following morning, however, when she unlocked the wardrobe to take something out, my Swallowtail, with a mighty rustle, flew into her face, then made for the open window, and presently was but a golden fleck dipping and dodging and soaring eastward, over timber and tundra, to Vologda, Viatka and Perm, and beyond the gaunt Ural range to Yakutsk and Verkhne Kolymsk, and from Verkhne Kolymsk, where it lost a tail, to the fair Island of St Lawrence, and across Alaska to Dawson, and southward along the Rocky Mountains – to be finally overtaken and captured, after a forty-year race, on an immigrant dandelion under an endemic aspen near Boulder. In a letter from Mr Brune to Mr Rawlins, 14 June 1735, in the Bodleian collection, he states that one Mr Vernon followed a butterfly nine miles before he could catch him (*The Recreative Review or Eccentricities of Literature and Life*, Vol. 1, p. 144, London, 1821).

Soon after the wardrobe affair I found a spectacular moth, marooned in a corner of a vestibule window, and my mother dispatched it with ether. In later years, I used many killing agents, but the least contact with the initial stuff would always cause the porch of the past to light up and attract that blundering beauty. Once, as a grown man, I was under ether during appendectomy, and with the vividness of a decalcomania picture I saw my own self in a sailor suit mounting a freshly emerged Emperor moth under the guidance of a Chinese lady who I knew was my mother. It was all there, brilliantly reproduced in my dream, while my own vitals were being exposed: the soaking, ice-cold absorbent cotton pressed to the insect's lemurian head; the subsiding spasms of its body; the satisfying crackle produced by the pin penetrating the hard crust of its thorax; the careful insertion of the point of the pin in the cork-bottomed groove of the spreading board; the symmetrical adjustment of the thick, strong-veined wings under neatly affixed strips of semitransparent paper.

2

I must have been eight when, in a storeroom of our country house, among all kinds of dusty objects, I discovered some wonderful books acquired in the days when my mother's mother had been interested in natural science and had had a famous university professor of zoology (Shimkevich) give private lessons to her daughter. Some of these books were mere curios, such as the four huge brown folios of Albertus Seba's work (*Locupletissimi Rerum Naturalium Thesauri Accurata Descriptio . . .*), printed in Amsterdam around 1750. On their coarse-grained pages I found woodcuts of serpents and butterflies and embryos. The fetus of an Ethiopian female child hanging by the neck in a glass jar used to give me a nasty shock every time I came across it; nor did I much care for the stuffed hydra on plate CII, with its seven lion-toothed turtleheads on seven serpentine necks and its strange, bloated body which bore buttonlike tubercules along the sides and ended in a knotted tail.

Other books I found in that attic, among herbariums full of alpine columbines, and blue palemoniums, and Jove's campions, and orange-red lilies, and other Davos flowers, came closer to my subject. I took in my arms and carried downstairs glorious loads of fantastically attractive volumes: Maria Sibylla Merian's (1647–1717) lovely plates of Surinam insects, and Esper's noble *Die Schmetterlinge* (Erlangen, 1777), and Boisduval's *Icones Historiques de Lépidoptères Nouveaux ou Peu Connus* (Paris, begun in 1832). Still more exciting were the products of the latter half of the century – Newman's *Natural History of British Butterflies and Moths*, Hofmann's *Die Gross-Schmetterlinge Europas*, the Grand Duke Nikolay Mihailovich's *Mémoires* on Asiatic lepidoptera (with incomparably beautiful figures painted by Kavrigin, Rybakov, Lang), Scudder's stupendous work on the *Butterflies of New England*.

Retrospectively, the summer of 1905, though quite vivid in many ways, is not animated yet by a single bit of quick flutter or colored fluff around or across the walks with the village schoolmaster: the Swallowtail of June 1906 was still in the larval stage on a roadside umbellifer; but in the course of that month I became acquainted with a score or so of common things, and Mademoiselle was already referring to a certain forest road that culminated in a marshy meadow full of Small Pearl-bordered Fritillaries (thus called in my first unforgettable and unfadingly magical little manual, Richard South's *The Butterflies of the British Isles*, which had just come out at that time) as *le chemin des papillons bruns*. The following year I became aware that many of our butterflies and moths did not occur in England or Central Europe, and more complete atlases helped me to determine them. A severe illness (pneumonia, with fever up to 41° centigrade), in the beginning of 1907, mysteriously abolished the rather monstrous gift of numbers that had made of me a child prodigy during a few months (today I cannot multiply 13 by 17 without pencil and paper; I can add them up, though, in a trice, the teeth of the three fitting in neatly); but the butterflies survived. My mother accumulated a library and a museum around my bed, and the longing to describe a new species completely replaced that of discovering a new prime number. A trip to Biarritz, in August 1907, added new wonders (though not as lucid and numerous as they were to be in 1909). By 1908, I had gained absolute control over the European lepidoptera as known to Hofmann. By 1910, I had dreamed my way through the first volumes of Seitz's prodigious picture book *Die Gross-Schmetterlinge der Erde*, had purchased a number of rarities recently described, and was voraciously reading entomological periodicals, especially English and Russian ones. Great upheavals were taking place in the development of systematics. Since the middle of the century, Continental lepidopterology had been, on the whole, a simple and stable affair, smoothly run by the Germans. Its high priest, Dr Staudinger, was also the head of the largest firm of insect dealers. Even now, half a century after his death, German lepidopterists have not quite managed to shake off the hypnotic spell occasioned by his authority. He was still alive when his school began to lose ground as a scientific force in the world. While he and his followers stuck to specific and generic names sanctioned by long usage and were content to classify butterflies by characters visible to the naked eye, English-speaking authors were introducing nomenclatorial changes as a result of a strict application of the law of priority and taxonomic changes based on the microscopic study of organs. The Germans did their best to ignore the new trends and continued to cherish the philately-like side of entomology. Their solicitude for the 'average collector who should not be made to dissect' is comparable to the way nervous publishers of popular novels pamper the 'average reader' – who should not be made to think.

There was another more general change, which coincided with my ardent adolescent interest in butterflies and moths. The Victorian and Staudingerian kind of species, hermetic and homogeneous, with sundry (alpine, polar, insular, etc.) 'varieties' affixed to it from the outside, as it were, like incidental appendages, was replaced by a new, multiform and fluid kind of species, organically *consisting* of geographical races or subspecies. The evolutional aspects of the case were thus brought out more clearly, by means of more flexible methods of classification, and further links between butterflies and the central problems of nature were provided by biological investigations.

The mysteries of mimicry had a special attraction for me. Its phenomena showed an artistic perfection usually associated with man-wrought things. Consider the imitation of oozing poison by bubblelike macules on a wing (complete with pseudo-refraction) or by glossy yellow knobs on a chrysalis ('Don't eat me – I have already been squashed, sampled and rejected').

Consider the tricks of an acrobatic caterpillar (of the Lobster Moth) which in infancy looks like bird's dung, but after molting develops scrabbly hymenopteroid appendages and baroque characteristics, allowing the extraordinary fellow to play two parts at once (like the actor in Oriental shows who *becomes* a pair of intertwisted wrestlers): that of a writhing larva and that of a big ant seemingly harrowing it. When a certain moth resembles a certain wasp in shape and color, it also walks and moves its antennae in a waspish, unmothlike manner. When a butterfly has to look like a leaf, not only are all the details of a leaf beautifully rendered but markings mimicking grub-bored holes are generously thrown in. 'Natural selection,' in the Darwinian sense, could not explain the miraculous coincidence of imitative aspect and imitative behavior, nor could one appeal to the theory of 'the struggle for life' when a protective device was carried to a point of mimetic subtlety, exuberance, and luxury far in excess of a predator's power of appreciation. I discovered in nature the nonutilitarian delights that I sought in art. Both were a form of magic, both were a game of intricate enchantment and deception.

3

I have hunted butterflies in various climes and disguises: as a pretty boy in knickerbockers and sailor cap; as a lanky cosmopolitan expatriate in flannel bags and beret; as a fat hatless old man in shorts. Most of my cabinets have shared the fate of our Vyra house. Those in our town house and the small addendum I left in the Yalta Museum have been destroyed, no doubt, by carpet beetles and other pests. A collection of South European stuff that I started in exile vanished in Paris during World War Two. All my American captures from 1940 to 1960 (several thousands of specimens including great rarities and types) are in the Mus. of Comp. Zoology, the Am. Nat. Hist. Mus., and the Cornell Univ. Mus. of Entomology, where they are safer than they would be in Tomsk or Atomsk. Incredibly happy memories, quite comparable, in fact, to those of my Russian boyhood, are associated with my research work at the MCZ, Cambridge, Mass. (1941–8). No less happy have been the many collecting trips taken almost every summer, during twenty years, through most of the states of my adopted country.

In Jackson Hole and in the Grand Canyon, on the mountain slopes above Telluride, Colo., and on a celebrated pine barren near Albany, N.Y., dwell, and will dwell, in generations more numerous than editions, the butterflies I have described as new. Several of my finds have been dealt with by other workers; some have been named after me. One of these, Nabokov's Pug (*Eupithecia nabokovi* McDunnough), which I boxed one night in 1943 on a picture window of James Laughlin's Alta Lodge in Utah, fits most philosophically into the thematic spiral that began in a wood on the Oredezh around 1910 – or perhaps even earlier, on that Nova Zemblan river a century and a half ago.

Few things indeed have I known in the way of emotion or appetite, ambition or achievement, that could surpass in richness and strength the excitement of entomological exploration. From the very first it had a great many interwinkling facets. One of them was the acute desire to be alone, since any companion, no matter how quiet, interfered with the concentrated enjoyment of my mania. Its gratification admitted of no compromise or exception. Already when I was ten, tutors and governesses knew that the morning was mine and cautiously kept away.

In this connexion, I remember the visit of a schoolmate, a boy of whom I was very fond and with whom I had excellent fun. He arrived one summer night – in 1913, I think – from a town some twenty-five miles away. His father had recently perished in an accident, the family was ruined and the stout-hearted lad, not being able to afford the price of a railway ticket, had bicycled all those miles to spend a few days with me.

On the morning following his arrival, I did everything I could to get out of the house for my morning hike without his knowing where I had gone. Breakfastless, with hysterical haste, I gathered my net, pill boxes, killing jar, and escaped through the window. Once in the forest, I was safe; but still I walked on, my calves quaking, my eyes full of scalding tears, the whole of me twitching with shame and self-disgust, as I visualized my poor friend, with his long pale face and black tie, moping in the hot garden – patting the panting dogs for want of something better to do, and trying hard to justify my absence to himself.

Let me look at my demon objectively. With the exception of my parents, no one really understood my obsession, and it was many years before I met a fellow sufferer. One of the first things I learned was not to depend on others for the growth of my collection. One summer afternoon, in 1911, Mademoiselle came into my room, book in hand, started to say she wanted to show me how wittily Rousseau denounced zoology (in favour of botany), and by then was too far gone in the gravitational process of lowering her bulk into an armchair to be stopped by my howl of anguish: on that seat I had happened to leave a glass-lidded cabinet tray with long, lovely series of the Large White. Her first reaction was one of stung vanity: her weight, surely, could not be accused of damaging what in fact it had demolished; her second was to console me: *Allons donc, ce ne sont que des papillons de potager!* – which only made matters worse. A Sicilian pair recently purchased from Staudinger had been crushed and bruised. A huge Biarritz example was utterly mangled. Smashed, too, were some of my choicest local captures. Of these, an aberration resembling the Canarian race of the species might have been mended with a few drops of glue; but a precious gynandromorph, left side male, right side female, whose abdomen could not be traced and whose wings had come off, was lost forever: one might reattach the wings but one could not prove that all four belonged to that headless thorax on its bent pin. Next morning, with an air of great mystery, poor Mademoiselle set off for St Petersburg and came back in the evening bringing me ('something better than your cabbage butterflies') a banal Urania moth mounted on plaster. 'How you hugged me, how you danced with joy!' she exclaimed ten years later in the course of inventing a brand-new past.

Our country doctor, with whom I had left the pupae of a rare moth when I went on a journey abroad, wrote me that everything had hatched finely; but in reality a mouse had got at the precious pupae, and upon my return the deceitful old man produced some common Tortoiseshell butterflies, which, I presume, he had hurriedly caught in his garden and popped into the breeding cage as plausible substitutes (so *he* thought).

 Better than he, was an enthusiastic kitchen boy who would

sometimes borrow my equipment and come back two hours later in triumph with a bagful of seething invertebrate life and several additional items. Loosening the mouth of the net which he had tied up with a string, he would pour out his cornucopian spoil – a mass of grasshoppers, some sand, the two parts of a mushroom he had thriftily plucked on the way home, more grasshoppers, more sand, and one battered Small White.

In the works of major Russian poets I can discover only two lepidopteral images of genuinely sensuous quality: Bunin's impeccable evocation of what is certainly a Tortoiseshell:

> And there will fly into the room
> A colored butterfly in silk
> To flutter, rustle and pit-pat
> On the blue ceiling . . .

and Fet's 'Butterfly' soliloquizing:

> Whence have I come and whither am I hasting
> Do not inquire;
> Now on a graceful flower I have settled
> And now respire.

In French poetry one is struck by Musset's well-known lines (in *Le Saule*):

> *Le phalène doré dans sa course légère*
> *Traverse les prés embaumés*

which is an absolutely exact description of the crepuscular flight of the male of the geometrid called in England the Orange moth; and there is Fargue's fascinatingly apt phrase (in *Les Quatres Journées*) about a garden which, at nightfall, *se glace de bleu comme l'aile du grand Sylvain* (the Poplar Admirable).

And among the very few genuine lepidopterological images in English poetry, my favorite is Browning's

> On our other side is the straight-up rock;
> And a path is kept 'twixt the gorge and it
> By boulder-stones where lichens mock
> The marks on a moth, and small ferns fit
> Their teeth to the polished block.
>
> *('By the Fire-side')*

It is astounding how little the ordinary person notices butterflies. 'None,' calmly replied that sturdy Swiss hiker with Camus in his rucksack when purposely asked by me for the benefit of my incredulous companion if he had seen any butterflies while descending the trail where, a moment before, you and I had been delighting in swarms of them. It is also true that when I call up the image of a particular path remembered in minute detail but pertaining to a summer before that of 1906, preceding, that is, the date of my first locality label, and never revisited, I fail to make out one wing, one wingbeat, one azure flash, one moth-gemmed flower, as if an evil spell had been cast on the Adriatic coast making all its 'leps' (as the slangier among us say) invisible. Exactly thus an entomologist may feel some day when plodding beside a jubilant, and already helmetless botanist amid the hideous flora of a parallel planet, with not a single insect in sight; and thus (in odd proof of the odd fact that whenever possible the scenery of our infancy is used by an economically minded producer as a ready-made setting for our adult dreams) the seaside hilltop of a certain recurrent nightmare of mine, whereinto I smuggle a collapsible net from my waking state, is gay with thyme and melilot, but incomprehensibly devoid of all the butterflies that should be there.

I also found out very soon that a 'lepist' indulging in his quiet quest was apt to provoke strange reactions in other creatures. How often, when a picnic had been arranged, and I would be self-consciously trying to get my humble implements unnoticed into the tar-smelling charabanc (a tar preparation was used to keep flies away from the horses) or the tea-smelling Opel convertible (benzine forty years ago smelled that way), some cousin or aunt of mine would remark: 'Must you *really* take that net with you? Can't you enjoy yourself like a normal boy? Don't you think you are spoiling everybody's pleasure?' Near a sign NACH BODENLAUBE, at Bad Kissingen, Bavaria, just as I was about to join for a long walk my father and majestic old Muromtsev (who, four years before, in 1906, had been President of the first Russian Parliament), the latter turned his marble head toward me, a vulnerable boy of eleven, and said with his famous solemnity: 'Come with us by all means, but do not chase butterflies, child. It spoils the rhythm of the walk.' On a path above the Black Sea, in the Crimea, among shrubs in waxy bloom, in March 1918, a bow-legged Bolshevik sentry attempted to arrest me for signaling (with my net, he said) to a British warship. In the summer of 1929, every time I walked through a village in the Eastern Pyrenees, and happened to look back, I would see in my wake the villagers frozen in the various attitudes my passage had caught them in, as if I were Sodom and they Lot's wife. A decade later, in the Maritime Alps, I once noticed the grass undulate in a serpentine way behind me because a fat rural policeman was wriggling after me on his belly to find out if I were not trapping songbirds.

America has shown even more of this morbid interest in my retiary activities than other countries have – perhaps because I was in my forties when I came there to live, and the older the man, the queerer he looks with a butterfly net in his hand. Stern farmers have drawn my attention to NO FISHING signs; from cars passing me on the highway have come wild howls of derision; sleepy dogs, though unmindful of the worst bum, have perked up and come at me, snarling; tiny tots have pointed me out to their puzzled mamas; broad-minded vacationists have asked me whether I was catching bugs for bait; and one morning on a wasteland, lit by tall yuccas in bloom, near Santa Fe, a big black mare followed me for more than a mile.

4

When, having shaken off all pursuers, I took the rough, red road that ran from our Vyra house toward field and forest, the animation and luster of the day seemed like a tremor of sympathy around me.

Very fresh, very dark Arran Browns, which emerged only every second year (conveniently, retrospection has fallen here into line), flitted among the firs or revealed their red markings and checkered fringes as they sunned themselves on the roadside bracken. Hopping above the grass, a diminutive Ringlet called Hero dodged my net. Several moths, too, were flying – gaudy sun lovers that sail from flower to flower like painted flies, or male insomniacs in search of hidden females, such as that rust-colored Oak Eggar hurtling across the shrubbery. I noticed (one of the major mysteries of my childhood) a soft pale green wing caught in a spider's web (by then I knew what it was: part of a Large Emerald). The tremendous larva of the Goat Moth, ostentatiously segmented, flat-headed, flesh-colored and glossily flushed, a strange creature 'as naked as a worm' to use a French comparison, crossed my path in frantic search for a place to pupate (the awful pressure of metamorphosis, the aura of a disgraceful fit in a public place). On the bark of that birch tree, the stout one near the park wicket, I had found last spring a dark aberration of Sievers' Carmelite (just another gray moth to the reader). In the ditch, under the bridgelet, a bright-yellow Silvius Skipper hobnobbed with a dragonfly (just a blue libellula to me). From a flower head two male Coppers rose to a tremendous height, fighting all the way up – and then, after a while, came the downward flash of one of them returning to his thistle. These were familiar insects, but at any moment something better might cause me to stop with a quick intake of breath. I remember one day when I warily brought my net closer and closer to an uncommon Hairstreak that had daintily settled on a sprig. I could clearly see the white W on its chocolate-brown underside. Its wings were closed and the inferior ones were rubbing against each other in a curious circular motion – possibly producing some small, blithe crepitation pitched too high for a human ear to catch. I had long wanted that particular species, and, when near enough, I struck. You have heard champion tennis players moan after muffing an easy shot. You may have seen the face of the world-famous grandmaster Wilhelm Edmundson when, during a simultaneous display in a Minsk café, he lost his rook, by an absurd oversight, to the local amateur and pediatrician, Dr Schach, who eventually won. But that day nobody (except my older self) could see me shake out a piece of twig from an otherwise empty net and stare at a hole in the tarlatan.

5

Near the intersection of two carriage roads (one, well-kept, running north-south in between our 'old' and 'new' parks, and the other, muddy and rutty, leading, if you turned west, to Batovo) at a spot where aspens crowded on both sides of a dip, I would be sure to find in the third week of June great blue-black nymphalids striped with pure white, gliding and wheeling low above the rich clay which matched the tint of their undersides when they settled and closed their wings. Those were the dung-loving males of what the old Aurelians used to call the Poplar Admirable, or, more exactly, they belonged to its Bucovinan subspecies. As a boy of nine, not knowing that race, I noticed how much our North Russian specimens differed from the Central European form figured in Hofmann, and rashly wrote to Kuznetsov, one of the greatest Russian, or indeed world, lepidopterists of all time, naming my new subspecies '*Limenitis populi rossica*.' A long month later he returned my description and aquarelle of '*rossica* Nabokov' with only two words scribbled on the back of my letter: '*bucovinensis* Hormuzaki.' How I hated Hormuzaki! And how hurt I was when in one of Kuznetsov's later papers I found a gruff reference to 'schoolboys who keep naming minute varieties of the Poplar Nymph!' Undaunted, however, by the *populi* flop, I 'discovered' the following year a 'new' moth. That summer I had been collecting assiduously on moonless nights, in a glade of the park, by spreading a bedsheet over the grass and its annoyed glow-worms, and casting upon it the light of an acetylene lamp (which, six years later, was to shine on Tamara). Into that arena of radiance, moths would come drifting out of the solid blackness around me, and it was in that manner, upon that magic sheet, that I took a beautiful *Plusia* (now *Phytometra*) which, as I saw at once, differed from its closest ally by its mauve-and-maroon (instead of golden-brown) forewings, and narrower bractea mark and was not recognizably figured in any of my books. I sent its description and picture to Richard South, for publication in *The Entomologist*. He did not know it either, but with the utmost kindness checked it in the British Museum collection – and found it had been described long ago as *Plusia excelsa* by Kretschmar. I received the sad news, which was most sympathetically worded ('. . . should be congratulated for obtaining . . . very rare Volgan thing . . . admirable figure . . .') with the utmost stoicism; but many years later, by a pretty fluke (I know I should not point out these plums to people), I got even with the first discoverer of *my* moth by giving his own name to a blind man in a novel.

Let me also evoke the hawkmoths, the jets of my boyhood! Colors would die a long death on June evenings. The lilac shrubs in full bloom before which I stood, net in hand, displayed clusters of a fluffy gray in the dusk – the ghost of purple. A moist young moon hung above the mist of a neighboring meadow. In many a garden have I stood thus in later years – in Athens, Antibes, Atlanta – but never have I waited with such a keen desire as before those darkening lilacs. And suddenly it would come, the low buzz passing from flower to flower, the vibrational halo around the streamlined body of an olive and pink Hummingbird moth poised in the air above the corolla into which it had dipped its long tongue. Its handsome black larva (resembling a diminutive cobra when it puffed out its ocellated front segments) could be found on dank willow herb two months later. Thus every hour and season had its delights. And, finally, on cold, or even frosty, autumn nights, one could sugar for moths by painting tree trunks with a mixture of molasses, beer, and rum. Through the gusty blackness, one's lantern would illumine the stickily glistening furrows of the bark and two or three large moths upon it imbibing the sweets, their nervous wings half open butterfly fashion, the lower ones exhibiting their incredible crimson silk from beneath the lichen-gray primaries. '*Catocala adultera!*' I would triumphantly shriek in the direction of the lighted windows of the house as I stumbled home to show my captures to my father.

6

The 'English' park that separated our house from the hayfields was an extensive and elaborate affair with labyrinthine paths, Turgenevian benches, and imported oaks among the endemic firs and birches. The struggle that had gone on since my grandfather's time to keep the park from reverting to the wild state always fell short of complete success. No gardener could cope with the hillocks of frizzly black earth that the pink hands of moles kept heaping on the tidy sand of the main walk. Weeds and fungi, and ridgelike tree roots crossed and recrossed the sun-flecked trials. Bears had been eliminated in the eighties, but an occasional moose still visited the grounds. On a picturesque boulder, a little mountain ash and a still smaller aspen had climbed, holding hands, like two clumsy, shy children. Other, more elusive trespassers – lost picnickers or merry villagers – would drive our hoary gamekeeper Ivan crazy by scrawling ribald words on the benches and gates. The disintegrating process continues still, in a different sense, for when, nowadays, I attempt to follow in memory the winding paths from one given point to another, I notice with alarm that there are many gaps, due to oblivion or ignorance, akin to the terra-incognita blanks map makers of old used to call 'sleeping beauties.'

Beyond the park, there were fields, with a continuous shimmer of butterfly wings over a shimmer of flowers – daisies, bluebells, scabious, and others – which now rapidly pass by me in a kind of colored haze like those lovely, lush meadows, never to be explored, that one sees from the diner on a transcontinental journey. At the end of this grassy wonderland, the forest rose like a wall. There I roamed, scanning the tree trunks (the enchanted, the silent part of a tree) for certain tiny moths, called Pugs in England – delicate little creatures that cling in the daytime to speckled surfaces, with which their flat wings and turned-up abdomens blend. There, at the bottom of that sea of sunshot greenery, I slowly spun round the great boles. Nothing in the world would have seemed sweeter to me than to be able to add, by a stroke of luck, some remarkable new species to the long list of Pugs already named by others. And my pied imagination, ostensibly, and almost grotesquely, groveling to my desire (but all the time, in ghostly conspiracies behind the scenes, coolly planning the most distant events of my destiny), kept providing me with hallucinatory samples of small print: '. . . the only specimen so far known . . .' '. . . the only specimen known of *Eupithecia petropolitanata* was taken by a Russian schoolboy . . .' '. . . by a young Russian collector . . .' '. . . by myself in the Government of St Petersburg, Tsarskoe Selo District, in 1910 . . . 1911 . . . 1912 . . . 1913 . . .' And then, thirty years later, that blessed black night in the Wasatch Range.

At first – when I was, say, eight or nine – I seldom roamed farther than the fields and woods between Vyra and Batovo. Later, when aiming at a particular spot half-a-dozen miles or more distant, I would use a bicycle to get there with my net strapped to the frame; but not many forest paths were passable on wheels; it was possible to ride there on horseback, of course, but, because of our ferocious Russian tabanids, one could not leave a horse haltered in a wood for any length of time: my spirited bay almost climbed up the tree it was tied to one day trying to elude them: big fellows with watered-silk eyes and tiger bodies, and gray little runts with an even more painful proboscis, but much more sluggish: to dispatch two or three of these dingy tipplers with one crush of the gloved hand as they glued themselves to the neck of my mount afforded me a wonderful empathic relief (which a dipterist might not appreciate). Anyway, on my butterfly hunts I always preferred hiking to any other form of locomotion (except, naturally, a flying seat gliding leisurely over the plant mats and rocks of an unexplored mountain, or hovering just above the flowery roof of a rain forest); for when you walk, especially in a region you have studied well, there is an exquisite pleasure in departing from one's itinerary to visit, here and there by the wayside, this glade, that glen, this or that combination of soil and flora – to drop in, as it were, on a familiar butterfly in his particular habitat, in order to see if he has emerged, and if so, how he is doing.

There came a July day – around 1910, I suppose – when I felt the urge to explore the vast marshland beyond the Oredezh. After skirting the river for three or four miles, I found a rickety footbridge. While crossing over, I could see the huts of a hamlet on my left, apple trees, rows of tawny pine logs lying on a green bank, and the bright patches made on the turf by the scattered clothes of peasant girls, who, stark naked in shallow water, romped and yelled, heeding me as little as if I were the discarnate carrier of my present reminiscences.

On the other side of the river, a dense crowd of small, bright blue male butterflies that had been tippling on the rich, trampled mud and cow dung through which I trudged rose all together into the spangled air and settled again as soon as I had passed.

After making my way through some pine groves and alder scrub I came to the bog. No sooner had my ear caught the hum of diptera around me, the guttural cry of a snipe overhead, the gulping sound of the morass under my foot, than I knew I would find here quite special arctic butterflies, whose pictures, or, still better, nonillustrated descriptions I had worshiped for several seasons. And the next moment I was among them. Over the small shrubs of bog bilberry with fruit of a dim, dreamy blue, over the brown eye of stagnant water, over moss and mire, over the flower spikes of the fragrant bog orchid (the *nochnaya fialka* of Russian poets), a dusky little Fritillary bearing the name of a Norse goddess passed in low, skimming flight. Pretty Cordigera, a gemlike moth, buzzed all over its uliginose food plant. I pursued rose-margined Sulphurs, gray-marbled Satyrs. Unmindful of the mosquitoes that furred my forearms, I stooped with a grunt of delight to snuff out the life of some silver-studded lepidopteron throbbing in the folds of my net. Through the smells of the bog, I caught the subtle perfume of butterfly wings on my fingers, a perfume which varies with the species – vanilla, or lemon, or musk, or a musty, sweetish odor difficult to define. Still unsated, I pressed forward. At last I saw I had come to the end of the marsh. The rising ground beyond was a paradise of lupines, columbines, and pentstemons. Mariposa lilies bloomed under Ponderosa pines. In the distance, fleeting cloud shadows dappled the dull green of slopes above timber line, and the gray and white of Longs Peak.

I confess I do not believe in time. I like to fold my magic carpet, after use, in such a way as to superimpose one part of the pattern upon another. Let visitors trip. And the highest enjoyment of timelessness – in a landscape selected at random – is when I stand among rare butterflies and their food plants. This is ecstasy, and behind the ecstasy is something else, which is hard to explain. It is like a momentary vacuum into which rushes all that I love. A sense of oneness with sun and stone. A thrill of gratitude to whom it may concern – to the contrapuntal genius of human fate or to tender ghosts humoring a lucky mortal.

PENGUIN 60S

ISABEL ALLENDE · *Voices in My Ear*
NICHOLSON BAKER · *Playing Trombone*
LINDSEY BAREHAM · *The Little Book of Big Soups*
KAREN BLIXEN · *From the Ngong Hills*
DIRK BOGARDE · *Coming of Age*
ANTHONY BURGESS · *Childhood*
ANGELA CARTER · *Lizzie Borden*
CARLOS CASTANEDA · *The Sorcerer's Ring of Power*
ELIZABETH DAVID · *Peperonata and Other Italian Dishes*
RICHARD DAWKINS · *The Pocket Watchmaker*
GERALD DURRELL · *The Pageant of Fireflies*
RICHARD ELLMANN · *The Trial of Oscar Wilde*
EPICURUS · *Letter on Happiness*
MARIANNE FAITHFULL · *Year One*
KEITH FLOYD · *Hot and Spicy Floyd*
ALEXANDER FRATER · *Where the Dawn Comes Up Like Thunder*
ESTHER FREUD · *Meeting Bilal*
JOHN KENNETH GALBRAITH · *The Culture of Contentment*
ROB GRANT AND DOUG NAYLOR · *Scenes from the Dwarf*
ROBERT GRAVES · *The Gods of Olympus*
JANE GRIGSON · *Puddings*
SOPHIE GRIGSON · *From Sophie's Table*
KATHARINE HEPBURN · *Little Me*
SUSAN HILL · *The Badness Within Him*
ALAN HOLLINGHURST · *Adventures Underground*
BARRY HUMPHRIES · *Less is More Please*
HOWARD JACOBSON · *Expulsion from Paradise*
P. D. JAMES · *The Girl Who Loved Graveyards*
STEPHEN KING · *Umney's Last Case*
LAO TZU · *Tao Te Ching*
DAVID LEAVITT · *Chips Is Here*

PENGUIN 60s

LAURIE LEE · *To War in Spain*
PATRICK LEIGH FERMOR · *Loose as the Wind*
ELMORE LEONARD · *Trouble at Rindo's Station*
DAVID LODGE · *Surprised by Summer*
BERNARD MAC LAVERTY · *The Miraculous Candidate*
SHENA MACKAY · *Cloud-Cuckoo-Land*
NORMAN MAILER · *The Dressing Room*
PETER MAYLE · *Postcards from Summer*
JAN MORRIS · *Scenes from Havian Life*
BLAKE MORRISON · *Camp Cuba*
VLADIMIR NABOKOV · *Now Remember*
REDMOND O'HANLON · *A River in Borneo*
STEVEN PINKER · *Thinking in Tongues*
CRAIG RAINE · *Private View*
CLAUDIA RODEN · *Ful Medames and Other Vegetarian Dishes*
HELGE RUBINSTEIN · *Chocolate Parfait*
SIMON SCHAMA · *The Taking of the Bastille*
WILL SELF · *The Rock of Crack As Big As the Ritz*
MARK SHAND · *Elephant Tales*
NIGEL SLATER · *30-Minute Suppers*
RICK STEIN · *Fresh from the Sea*
LYTTON STRACHEY · *Florence Nightingale*
PAUL THEROUX · *Slow Trains to Simla*
COLIN THUBRON · *Samarkand*
MARK TULLY · *Beyond Purdah*
LAURENS VAN DER POST · *Merry Christmas, Mr Lawrence*
MARGARET VISSER · *More than Meets the Eye*
GAVIN YOUNG · *Something of Samoa*

and

Thirty Obituaries from Wisden · SELECTED BY MATTHEW ENGEL

READ MORE IN PENGUIN

For complete information about books available from Penguin and how to order them, please write to us at the appropriate address below. Please note that for copyright reasons the selection of books varies from country to country.

IN THE UNITED KINGDOM: Please write to *Dept. EP, Penguin Books Ltd, Bath Road, Harmondsworth, Middlesex UB7 0DA.*

IN THE UNITED STATES: Please write to *Consumer Sales, Penguin USA, P.O. Box 999, Dept. 17109, Bergenfield, New Jersey 07621-0120.* VISA and MasterCard holders call 1-800-253-6476 to order Penguin titles.

IN CANADA: Please write to *Penguin Books Canada Ltd, 10 Alcorn Avenue, Suite 300, Toronto, Ontario M4V 3B2.*

IN AUSTRALIA: Please write to *Penguin Books Australia Ltd, P.O. Box 257, Ringwood, Victoria 3134.*

IN NEW ZEALAND: Please write to *Penguin Books (NZ) Ltd, Private Bag 102902, North Shore Mail Centre, Auckland 10.*

IN INDIA: Please write to *Penguin Books India Pvt Ltd, 706 Eros Apartments, 56 Nehru Place, New Delhi 110 019.*

IN THE NETHERLANDS: Please write to *Penguin Books Netherlands bv, Postbus 3507, NL-1001 AH Amsterdam.*

IN GERMANY: Please write to *Penguin Books Deutschland GmbH, Metzlerstrasse 26, 60594 Frankfurt am Main.*

IN SPAIN: Please write to *Penguin Books S. A., Bravo Murillo 19, 1° B, 28015 Madrid.*

IN ITALY: Please write to *Penguin Italia s.r.l., Via Felice Casati 20, I–20124 Milano.*

IN FRANCE: Please write to *Penguin France S. A., 17 rue Lejeune, F–31000 Toulouse.*

IN JAPAN: Please write to *Penguin Books Japan, Ishikiribashi Building, 2–5–4, Suido, Bunkyo-ku, Tokyo 112.*

IN GREECE: Please write to *Penguin Hellas Ltd, Dimocritou 3, GR–106 71 Athens.*

IN SOUTH AFRICA: Please write to *Longman Penguin Southern Africa (Pty) Ltd, Private Bag X08, Bertsham 2013.*

BARRY
HUMPHRIES

LESS IS MORE PLEASE

PENGUIN BOOKS

PENGUIN BOOKS

Published by the Penguin Group. Penguin Books Ltd, 27 Wrights Lane, London W8 5TZ, England. Penguin Books USA Inc., 375 Hudson Street, New York, New York 10014, USA. Penguin Books Australia Ltd, Ringwood, Victoria, Australia. Penguin Books Canada Ltd, 10 Alcorn Avenue, Toronto, Ontario, Canada M4V 3B2. Penguin Books (NZ) Ltd, 182–190 Wairau Road, Auckland 10, New Zealand · Penguin Books Ltd, Registered Offices: Harmondsworth, Middlesex, England · This extract is from *More Please*, by Barry Humphries, first published by Viking 1992. Published in Penguin Books 1993. This edition published 1996 · The moral right of the author has been asserted · Typeset by Rowland Phototypesetting Ltd, Bury St Edmunds, Suffolk. Printed in England by Clays Ltd, St Ives plc · 10 9 8 7 6 5 4 3 2 1

Author's Note: The people portrayed in this book are real and the events described took place, but fictional names and descriptive detail have sometimes been used.

CONTENTS

Licking the Beaters

Mrs Flint was my very first teacher. I have thought of changing her name in case some litigious descendant recognizes his venerated great-grandmother, but I can find no better name for her than her real name; grey quartzy sharp-edged hard. She ran a small kindergarten in her own grey pebble-dashed Californian bungalow down the hill from our place, and her two best rooms, the lounge and dining-room to the right of her dark hallway, had been turned into a classroom for local tots. Edna, my first and favourite nanny, would escort me every morning down the steep pavement of Marlborough Avenue until after several twists and turns and carefully crossed, sparsely motored roads we arrived at Mrs Flint's front gate, already jammed with tricycles and mothers. Mrs Flint, wearing a large apron to keep the chalk off her faded if floral print dress, stood on the front step screwing her face into what she imagined to be a friendly and motherly grimace as she welcomed her little pupils and reassured departing parents. She was a good actress, this old battle-axe, for the mothers all went home fondly believing that their littlies were in wonderful hands in spite of the panic-stricken screams that most of Mrs Flint's pupils emitted as soon as they realized that they had been abandoned to her care. No sooner had the last mother gone and the drone of the last parental sedan faded up Orrong Crescent than Mrs Flint's true mineral nature asserted itself. Once she was alone with her infant charges the ingratiating smile of the kindly old widow who adored children quickly faded and she would swing around from her blackboard and exhibit to the class a very different and frightening countenance on which rage, spite and ignorance jostled for supremacy.

It always took a long time for the crying to stop at Mrs Flint's kindergarten. One little girl called Jocelyn cried all the time and no amount of cajolery could stop her. In the end Mrs Flint put her out to graze in the back yard where, still bawling, she executed endless circuits on her trike. Inside we sat at miniature tables on stools enamelled cherry-red, one of the most popular hues of the late thirties. Because the classroom occupied Mrs Flint's lounge and dining room there were a few of her more substantial pieces of furniture – a Genoa-velvet couch, a bookcase and a Jacobean-style dining table with matching sideboard – shoved against the wall to make room for our small chairs and tables. Mrs Flint made it very clear that if anyone so much as laid a curious finger on one of her trumpery treacle-coloured sticks they would be put out in the yard with the eternally blubbering Jocelyn.

Mrs Flint was no great reader; except for the *Pears Cyclopaedia*, a couple of Ethel M. Dells and a Netta Muskett, her bookshelves accommodated faded family snaps and gewgaws which she called her 'ordiments'. However, every morning, seated in one of her deeper fawn-and-russet Genoa-velvet lounge chairs, with her dress hitched up so we could see her surgical stockings, she read us a story. Her favourite was Hansel and Gretel and even the least imaginative child found a painful empathy with this tale and its themes of parental abandonment and persecution by a cannibalistic crone.

There was a mid-morning break and we all filed out the back to our trikes and lugubriously circled Mrs Flint's prickly lawn. When I first saw Doré's engraving of convicts dismally revolving in their bleak exercise yard, I had only to imagine them with gaily painted Cyclops tricycles and scooters between their shanks to be grimly reminded of playtime at Mrs Flint's.

One day two bikes rammed into each other just in front of me, and my friend Graham Coles fell off his seat and crashed to the ground, breaking his arm. There was a big fuss and Mrs Flint's face nearly ruptured itself, feigning expressions of compassion and concern. Poor Graham's arm wasn't set properly and it had to be operated on again. This operation was not successful however and Graham's arm never grew. Years later when we were no longer the friends we had been in childhood I would see him as he passed our house on his way to Scotch College, one sleeve especially shortened to accommodate his bonsai appendage.

Apart from her fawning attentions to our parents and nannies there was one other human being to whom Mrs Flint displayed an amiable demeanour. Her daughter Nursie. Over half a century later I can only assume that Nursie was a nurse and that she had a real name like everyone else. But Mrs Flint always called her Nursie and something resembling warmth crept into her cold dry voice when she announced Nursie's presence in the house. For Nursie came and went, and we glimpsed her but occasionally sitting at the linoleum-covered kitchen table having a cup of tea, as we filed out to the back verandah for our play lunch. She had plucked eyebrows and a blonde perm which stuck out in a wedge at the back like Garbo's in the last scene in *Queen Christina*, or like the 'art deco' windswept hair-do of the woman whose white glass profile appeared on top of Atlantic petrol pumps; a crude commercial descendant of Lalique's opaline car mascots.

Between sips of Robur tea and puffs on her Du Maurier, Nursie flashed us a flirtatious smile while Mrs Flint fussed about refilling her cup and fetching her ginger nuts and Marie biscuits as though she were a nice person pleased to see her daughter.

Mrs Flint was keen to show parents that their children didn't just listen to stories or ride their bikes in endless circles in her back yard, so she decided we must all learn to count. I must have been the slowest to acquire this doubtful skill, for I remember being kept back while the other children played. Alone amongst the chipped cherry-red stools while Mrs Flint, terribly close so that I could smell her damp surgical stockings and her odour of stale talcum, forced me to count and count and recount until, weeping, I finally stumbled to one hundred. When would Edna come to rescue me? I wondered, peering up towards the lozenged leadlight windows through which grown-ups could be seen on their way to the front porch. But on that dreadful day each shrill chirrup of the doorbell announced someone else's mother, so that I was alone with my tormentor and all those numbers for what seemed like an eternity before deliverance finally came. Since those early struggles with innumeracy – as I believe it is now called – I have shunned every form of mathematics, leaving the counting to accountants and trusted managers, a task they have often performed with a surprising display of imagination.

I am not certain at this distance in time whether, having counted to a century, I graduated from Mrs Flint's Dame School, or whether my mother, detecting my misery, rescued me. I may well have complained, for I remember my mother saying, in her defence, what a 'refined' woman she thought Mrs Flint to be. Already at four years of age I had begun to apprehend that refinement was very often an extenuating virtue; one that excused and eclipsed almost every other unappetizing trait. But it was hard for me to share this adult view of Mrs Flint's refinement. No doubt the hag had once patronized my mother with a long word or an unfamiliar locution – a verbal crooking of the pinky – and had thereafter acquired her dubious epithet.

I preferred to be at home anyway; pampered by Edna and spoilt by Pat Bagott, our gardener and handyman. Pat was my father's favourite employee, and in Australian society of this period he was that great rarity, a childless Roman Catholic. This may have been the main reason why my mother spoke more generously of him and his little wife than she customarily did of their more fecund co-religionists.

As Mrs Flint's saving grace had been refinement, the Bagotts' was their cleanliness, not an attribute my mother's family associated with the adherents of Rome. She had made a point of seeing where the Bagotts lived; in a flat working-class suburb far from our undulant and lawned oasis. And she had pronounced the dwelling 'spotless', '*small, but spotless*'. One of her favourite sayings was: 'You don't have to be well-off to be *particular*,' and she frequently attributed this apophthegm to her late mother, lending it a kind of genealogical veracity. Much as Field-Marshal Goering sought to confer Aryan status on the Jewish tenor Richard Tauber, so my mother spared Pat Bagott her usual strictures against Catholicism. Without knowing it, the spotless and particular Bagotts were granted a unique amnesty; in my mother's eyes at least they were honorary Protestants.

My father was a builder of sturdy suburban villas whose business reached its first peak of success in the years before the Second World War. He built houses in all the popular styles: mock Tudor, Spanish mission, neo-Georgian, Californian bungalow and moderne. In the very late thirties, if the client was especially rich and daring and my father able to procure enough glass building blocks and aubergine-coloured 'manganese' bricks, he would build them a 'jazz moderne' house with curved corner windows, a flat roof, a nautical-looking sun deck and *no front fence!* It is still odd to see in the suburban streets of Melbourne these once startling architectural hybrids; chubby colonial relations of their austere German cousins in Dessau and Stuttgart.

As a toddler, long before Mrs Flint's kindergarten, I would often be taken off by my father on his daily rounds visiting building sites. In that epoch before seat-belts I would roll around on the back seat of his streamlined putty-white Oldsmobile, or stand precariously on the hot grey leather clinging to a sturdy tassel. We would arrive at a 'job' and while my father strode fearlessly across the raw yellow joists remonstrating with brickies, or pored over flapping blueprints with the foreman, I would amuse myself with a drill and an offcut of Oregon pine. Sometimes we would arrive during the lunch break and I would see the men rolling their 'smokes' and making their billy tea over a mound of blazing wood chips on an improvised hearth. Just as the water in the blackened tin came to the boil Alec Gibson would open a sachet of wax paper his wife had packed with his doorstep sandwiches, and fling the contents of sugar and tea-leaves into the seething water.

I used to love watching the cement being mixed, as I enjoyed a similar process at home when my mother ran up a sponge. Fascinated, I watched the brickies laying a parapet, and, with deft trowels, slicing off the frills of the wet mortar. Alec warned me against getting too near the concrete mixer with a story about a nipper who had only the other day got too close to the grey-lipped maw of that relentlessly sloshing drum, and got sucked in. With a calloused finger he pointed to a small cement-encrusted boot lying amongst the builders' debris. 'That's all that's left of him, Bun,' said Alec lugubriously, 'so don't get too near that bloody doover, or *you'll* be a goner yesself!'

Alec and Pat Bagott and the other men called me 'Bun', which was probably short for currant bun; a reference to my innumerable moles. One day, at smoko, while we were sitting around on piles of bricks, eating our sandwiches and waiting for the billy to boil, Alec stood up, 'See you in a jiff, Bun, just going to strain the potatoes.' And he ambled off in the direction of the narrow galvanized iron dunny, screened with a hessian curtain. That night at dinner I rather pointedly left the table and on the way to the lavatory I called back to my mother,

'Just off to strain the potatoes.' When I returned there was an 'atmosphere' and I overheard my mother saying in the low voice children are not supposed to hear, '. . . and just make sure the more common element amongst your men watch what they say in front of little Barry, or who knows what he'll be coming out with next'.

The South Camberwell State School was a raw red-brick two-storey building in a small street off Toorak Road. It stood in an extensive asphalt wasteland, bounded by the palings of adjacent houses. This was the playground. Far away, against the back fence and partly shaded by a mutilated peppercorn, stood the only other structure in that desolate schoolground, the shelter shed. This was a sort of wooden box with one wall missing in which children presumably sheltered from the extremes of the Melbourne climate. At lunchtime on a wet day it would be packed with damp urchins delving into their sandwich tins and screaming at the tops of their voices. The noise in that confined space under a reboant tin roof was appalling, but worse was the overpowering and nauseating stench of gooey brown banana sandwiches and other nameless fillings. It did not surprise me in the least, when years later I learnt that the artless expression, 'Who opened their lunch?' was 1930s Australian slang for 'Who farted?' Only then did I realize that others before me had reeled back from the effluvia of cut lunches.

My parents sent me there for about a year until I was old enough to attend a nice Junior School. I had seen the brochure for Camberwell Grammar in my father's den. It had a sky-blue crinkly cover, embossed with the school's mitred crest, and glossy pages with pictures of some brand-new manganese brick buildings photographed from oblique angles to make them look more monumental than they actually were. It was supposed to be a 'very good school' and it charged *fees*. It catered for boys only, and mostly boys from 'comfortable homes'.

But Camberwell State, which I was forced to attend in the meantime, was free and co-ed. The hardships of life in Mrs Flint's back-yard jungle were nothing compared with the shrieking, thumping, yelling, wrestling maelstrom of human maggots into which I had been hurled.

Quickly I became aware of the gulf that divided me from them; the gulf that separated the Australian working class from the newly arisen 'affluent' middle class. It was wider, bleaker and more inimical than the grey tundra of the playground. In my effeminate little blue Aertex shirt which laced at the neck, pleated linen shorts, fawn cotton socks and leather sandals with side buckles, I felt uncomfortably alien to the other boys. Many of them wore scuffed and splitting sandshoes and a few even arrived at school barefoot. Our classroom was full of densely darned and threadbare maroon sweaters, patched britches, grubby lacunose stockings, scabby knees, bloody noses, verminous hair and ears erupting with bright pumpkin wax. The slatternly girls were no less alarming to a mollycoddled little Lord Fauntleroy from the Golf Links Estate.

The first form was presided over by a gorgon called Miss Jensen. She was the first woman I ever met with her hair in a bun, and she had a knack of making the chalk squeal on the blackboard. She favoured bottle-green 'twin sets' and fawn tweed skirts and she looked uncannily like Mrs Bun the Baker's wife in Happy Families. Miss Jensen and I took an instant dislike to one another.

We lived only about half a mile from the school, so I was mostly spared the ordeal of sandwiches in the shelter shed. Instead, punctually at 12.30, my father would collect me in the big putty-white Oldsmobile and drive me home for a peaceful lunch at my own little table on the lawn, or with my mother in the sun-room amongst her new cane furniture and shining brass knick-knacks. Everything in our house was new, or 'up-to-date' as they said in the thirties. We had a new Frigidaire with a light inside which went on when you opened the door. Every now and then it shuddered rather violently, as if from the cold. Most other people we knew still had ice-chests, and I rather envied them the iceman's visit as he shouldered those great glassy blocks up their sideways. On top of the fridge stood our new Sunbeam Mixmaster. This was a streamlined bullet-shaped appliance rather like a Buck Rogers spaceship, in the popular colour combination of cream and black. We had all the attachments and the brochure, but we only used it for juicing oranges and making cakes. When the twin whisks plunged into the bowl of glutinous sponge mixture my mother tweaked a mammiform control knob to the appropriate speed and the engine whirred into action, the whisks churning so that their blades seemed to vanish until they were just two chrome rods suspended in a fragrant yellow vortex. The kitchen filled with a miraculous aroma of heating machinery, compounded with vanilla essence. Once the Mixmaster was silenced and the whisks detached, I was allowed to lick off the ambrosial emulsion. Licking the beaters was one of the great privileges of an Australian childhood.

Our other modern appliance was a Radiola 'mantel model' wireless set. Chubbily zigguratish in moulded brown Bakelite, it had a vertically fluted front panel rather like the fascia of a modernistic building. Behind the organ-pipe grille could be glimpsed a curtain of sheeny brown cretonne through which the music and the voices shrilly filtered. 'The Girl on the Pink Police Gazette' and 'My Merry Oldsmobile' were popular airs of the period, and it seemed strange and inexplicable that the radio could be singing so intimately about our family car.

Come away with me Lucile
In my merry Oldsmobile,
Down the road of life we'll fly
Automobubbling you and I.
To the church we'll swiftly steal,
Then our wedding bells will peal,
You can go as far as you like with me,
In my merry Oldsmobile.

I had been given a toy submarine made in Japan, containing a clockwork mechanism which, when wound up, propelled it realistically along the bottom of the bath. One day I took it to school, a big mistake. It was one of those rare days when I didn't go home for lunch, so, avoiding the hellish shelter shed, I took my sub and my sandwiches to a peaceful corner of the playground. Soon I found myself encircled by a group of rough kids who demanded my submarine. A tussle ensued in which my lunch got trodden into the asphalt and as the jeering circle of larrikins drew closer and more threatening I picked up a handful of gravel ready to defend myself. The bullies fled, but they did not disperse. They must have formed a delegation to Miss Jensen because immediately after recess she hauled me out in front of the class for 'throwing stones', a heinous violation of the school rules. I denied doing any such thing, but the testimony of the smirking yahoos carried more weight than my tearful protestations, and I was pushed in the corner for the rest of the afternoon with a sign on my back: I AM A BULLY. Much later, when the class had been dismissed for the afternoon, Miss Jensen told me that if I persisted in denying my guilt she would take me to see Mr Fraser, the headmaster, a ginger-haired functionary whom I had privately nicknamed 'Duckface'. I stuck to my guns, however, and only at the entrance to his study, and threatened with imminent expulsion, did I finally break down and recant, confessing to a crime I had never committed. Grudgingly, clemency supervened, and I was allowed to go home, my heart pounding with shame and rage. For some reason which remains obscure, I never told my parents of this incident – perhaps I feared that they might share Miss Jensen's view of the matter.

Since then I have entertained fantasies of vengeance. Supposing Miss Jensen had been, say, twenty-five at the time, she might now, in 1992, be a sprightly seventy-seven-year-old living with her daughter, sitting peacefully knitting in some honeysuckled garden bower, or quietly watching television in a Melbourne suburb. For my purposes it would be more convenient if she were installed in a sunset facility or oldsters' terminary. There I could visit her, explaining to the nursing staff that I was a concerned relation who required a few moments' privacy with the titubating inmate. I would need very little time to attach the small placard, concealed under my raincoat, to the back of old Miss Jensen's bobbing matinée jacket.

Wilf

Uncle Wilf was my favourite uncle. He was married to Aunty Violet, my mother's oldest sister, who had once been a nurse and had tended victims of the Spanish influenza just after the First World War. Wilf had served in the Australian infantry in France and their house contained a number of souvenirs of those terrible battles. On their Arts and Crafts mantelpiece stood two gleaming brass shell-cases and, high up in a cupboard, Uncle Wilf kept a German helmet with a spike on it. Sometimes he showed us a sepia photograph taken from the pocket of a dead German soldier, perhaps the same soldier who no longer required the helmet. The picture showed a husband and wife, she seated with a certain wistful beauty, he in uniform standing stiffly at her side. In the background was the blurred hint of a bourgeois parlour – no doubt a tricked-up corner of the photographer's studio. They both gazed apprehensively at the lens as though it were about to go off like a rifle, but that would come a month or two later.

Uncle Wilf was the only person I knew who had served in the First World War, though casualties of that legendary catastrophe were often pointed out to me; legless lift drivers, blind newspaper sellers, and the door-to-door salesman from whom my mother bought our honey who always wore one stiff black glove.

 Wilf always marched on 25 April, that most important day

in the Australian calendar, Anzac Day, when a great cavalcade of Diggers walked in solemn procession to the Shrine of Remembrance. Every year we, and thousands of others, would line the roadside and cheer the old soldiers, many in uniform and others in their Sunday best blazing with medals, as the military bands played 'Tipperary', 'Pack Up Your Troubles' and 'Roses of Picardy'. At the end of that long procession came the wheelchairs and the stretchers and nurses leading the gassed and the blind.

Wilf and Vi had one son, who was a spastic, and my aunt and uncle were devoted to his welfare. John loved music and had a large collection of records which he would play loudly at family tea parties. No one listened to his carefully planned recitals, they only talked louder, though occasionally someone would glance over at him as he sat by the gramophone nodding his head to the music, his poor legs in chromium callipers.

'There's no doubt about John,' they would cluck. *'He loves his music.'*

Uncle Wilf worked for Imperial Chemical Industries and my father often took me to his office in the city where I would be given small sample jars of dye manufactured by the company. At home I experimented with these wonderful pigments: purple, fuchsia and gamboge, dropping a pinch or two into a full beaker, and watching the bright streamers of colour fall through the water and spread like tendrils, or making exotically hued potions in the new laboratory which my father had built for me at the back of the garage.

Wilf and my father adored each other, and the three of us would regularly lunch at the Wool Exchange Hotel near Uncle

Wilf's office. It was my first experience of a restaurant, and there was a pretty receptionist who always greeted the brothers-in-law flirtatiously and made a fuss over me as she led us between the rowdy lunchers to our special table. There were stiff, starched napkins, a cruet holding the indispensable bottle of Holbrook's Worcestershire sauce and, in the centre of the table, an oxidized nickel trumpet from which a few crumpled poppies bloomed on their hairy stems. The vegetable fritter with hot tomato sauce was one of the Wool Exchange's gastronomic specialities, as well as the more conservative T-bone steak and crumbed whiting.

It must have been during one of these lunches that the two men planned to build a weekend shack together at Healesville, a beauty spot about forty miles from town. Accordingly they bought thirty acres of virgin bush about a mile from the township, up a dusty track. There, in a small clearing with a blue view of Mount Riddell and the lavender-coloured foothills of the Great Divide, my father, assisted by Pat and Alec, built a house, known thereafter as 'the shack'. It was a rudimentary structure of weatherboard, asbestos sheeting and corrugated iron and there were none of the cosy amenities of Camberwell. No water, electricity or sewerage, so we had a galvanized-iron tank at the side of the house, spirit lamps and an outdoor dunny, built of split logs over a very deep hole. This was furnished with little more than a huge desiccated tarantula on the ceiling and, for the hygienic convenience of visitors, a mutilated Melbourne telephone book suspended by a string from a bent nail. This popular cubicle buzzed perpetually with the sound of voracious flies and reeked of some ammoniac pink powder which Papa Brown regularly ladled into the abyss.

Soon our shack in the bush became a regular weekend haven for all the relations. There were beds everywhere, and at night on my lumpy mattress in my little 'sleep-out', I could hear the adults in the living-room playing Whist and Mah-jong late into the night, smell Uncle Wilf's sweet Wayside Mixture and hear my father pumping up the kerosene lamps until the guttering mantles glowed white again. In the forties we acquired a battery-powered wireless set, and on Sunday evenings everyone listened to the Lux Radio Theatre. There was great excitement if the hour-long melodrama happened to star Thelma Scott, my mother's sole theatrical acquaintance, or Thelma's talented young friend, Coral Browne.

When war came I would lie awake in bed watching the lamplight ebb and flow through the crack under my door and hear those urgent, ominous news reports of far-away catastrophes. The voice of Winston Churchill crackled over the BBC World Service as my family sat gravely listening to the war in the silent Australian bush 13,000 miles from Westminster. There was so much distortion and explosive static on those shortwave broadcasts that I pictured Churchill himself standing at the very heart of the battlefield, perpetually under fire and growling his famous rhetoric through a lethal fusillade.

One night in about 1943 I heard them playing 'Sweet Spirit', a psychic parlour game in which I was never allowed to participate. An alphabetical circle was arranged on the table top and everyone put their finger on an upturned glass in the middle. They all took it in turns to ask the spirit questions, and there were always crescendos of laughter followed by, 'Shhh, you'll wake the children.' My father was regularly reproached for cheating. One night I heard a voice, I think it was Aunty Dorothy's, ask the spirit when Cliff Jones, Phyllis's brother, was coming home on leave, and there was a strange silence in the room as the glass, carrying everyone's fingers with it, darted from N to E to V to E to R. They never played that game again.

In the long summer vacation my father built a log fort for me and a red bark tree-house high up in a shaggy old eucalypt. My tree-house even had an old-fashioned battery-operated telephone connected to the main house, so that I could order cakes and sandwiches without ever having to leave my eyrie. Here I played for hours in my new Gene Autry cowboy suit with its fringed white kid chaps and my Gene Autry ivory-handled cap gun. Watching out for snakes, my young sister and I would explore the bush together, while back at the house cousin John played his portable gramophone, so that wherever we were we could hear from afar those wisps of tinny music like the horns of elfland faintly blowing. It was strange sitting on a mossy log in the Australian bush and listening to Fraser Simpson's incomparable Vocal Gems from *Toad of Toad Hall* or Richard Tauber's 'Dein ist mein ganzes Herz'. Especially strange, really, to hear the illicit language of the Enemy thrillingly wafted through the saplings and the sword grass and the yellow flowering acacias and the mauve bush orchids.

The hour drive to Healesville seemed, of course, interminable to a child. Camberwell was then on the outskirts of the metropolitan area and once past Box Hill we were in open country. Near Lilydale, my father always pointed out the long and impeccably shaved hedge of green privet that concealed from the road the vast estate of Dame Nellie Melba, and Coombe Cottage, the Australian diva's legendary home. Melba and Donald Bradman were the only famous Australians I had ever heard of, and it seemed an amazing coincidence that Melba's name should so closely resemble the city of her birth.

Half-way to the shack we crossed a billabong of the Yarra River on a low pontoon bridge, and there on a kind of island almost camouflaged amongst the tangled blackberries and the sloughed bark of the huge river gums was a small swagman's encampment; a few wretched humpies built from rusty kerosene tins and hessian bags. As our Oldsmobile rolled past, a starved yellow mongrel always started up and barked until we were out of sight. My father had only once pointed to this little camp, but thereafter our noses were pressed to the car windows whenever we approached the river bank in the hope that we might glimpse one of these legendary vagabonds boiling his billy, or stuffing a jumbuck in his tucker bag like the hero of that incomprehensible song 'Waltzing Matilda'.

Half a mile from the shack on the other side of the Don Road lived a real swagman called Smithy. Smithy dwelt in an improvised hovel of galvanized iron and sacking where chooks and dogs scrabbled in the dust. He had a wife somewhere in that kennel too, who was supposed to be, according to Uncle Wilf, 'as black as your hat'. Smithy was a lanky taciturn figure with a pointed Adam's apple, a grey 'Kitchener' moustache and an old digger's hat. He still wore the threadbare remnant of a khaki uniform and after Uncle Wilf befriended him he used to chop wood for us, and do odd jobs. Sometimes I would sit with the men at smoko and hear Smithy tell some of his old soldier's yarns. He had a great and touching nobility, like a peasant in a story by Turgenev. In September, before the morning mist cleared and the magpies were gargling in the tall saplings, Smithy would show us the paddocks where we could find the best and biggest mushrooms. They were the ones with the blue-pink gills underneath: the colour of milky cocoa.

If we were at Healesville at Christmas time, and the heat became unbearable, we would set off with rugs and picnic baskets to Badgers Creek. There, where no badger had ever set foot, amongst the pungent mosses, and sheltered by tall tree ferns, we splashed about in a dark green pool. Then we would perch on the bank watching the icy water purl and gurgle over rocks like emus' eggs, and sip raspberry vinegar from Bakelite cups, while Peter Dawson sang 'The Floral Dance' on John's wind-up phonograph.

There was a terrible week in 1939 when the great bushfires which raged throughout Victoria nearly got the shack. Wilf and my father drove back and forth from Healesville all day, through the smoke and under a dark copper sky, bringing linen and portable furniture to safety. The house and its surroundings, however, were spared, though it was a close one, and on the crest of Mount Riddell there was always, thereafter, a bald white patch of bleached burnt-out timber.

Those bush holidays provide the happiest memories of my childhood, and during the war the house was extended to furnish more bedrooms in case we decided to evacuate there when the bombs fell. For some reason it was felt that thirty-five miles from the General Post Office was a safe radius if the Japanese invaded Melbourne.

In the late 1930s the voice of Joseph Schmidt was always on the wireless, singing that evocative song of the period, 'A Star Fell from Heaven'. It was the voice of Europe before the Terror and, had I but known it, a Jewish voice. But the song which I most associate with the outbreak of war was 'South of the Border (Down Mexico Way)' crooned in the light tenor of Gene Autry. Whenever I am in Los Angeles, supping with my friend Roddy McDowall in Studio City, I gaze across his fence at the house next door where Gene Autry still lives, in the hope that I may catch a glimpse of my childhood idol.

Papa Brown, my maternal grandfather, had an ominous ditty in his music-hall repertoire.

> Tramp, tramp, the boys are marching
> Knock, knock, the bobby's at the door.
> If you don't let him in
> He will knock the door right in,
> And you won't see your daddy any more!

This cautionary refrain gave me terrible nightmares and Papa was forbidden by my mother to sing it ever again. Early in the war I must have overheard many discussions between my parents about whether or not my father should enlist. His younger brother, Dick, had joined the air force and my mother's brother was in the Australian Imperial Force, and I am sure my father, although he was just too old to be called up, had pangs of conscience about not doing 'his bit'. I can remember an argument between my parents once, when we drove past the Hawthorn recruiting station, but Wilf ultimately arranged for my father to do war work for ICI, building munition factories and nitroglycerine storage tanks at Deer Park, an outer Melbourne suburb. However, I am convinced the spectre of conscription must have hung over him during the early war years and I always feared that his father-in-law's minatory recruiting jingle would come true, and that my father might be snatched away by the army and I would never see him again.

When the war broke out he employed several very jolly Italians called the Angelo Brothers who created the terrazzo porches and bathroom floors in all his houses. They seemed to sing all the time as they worked and they wore paper hats made from Geelong Cement bags to keep off the sun. But one day they disappeared and were never spoken of again. Although they had probably lived in Australia for years and had barely heard of Mussolini they were interned for the duration of the war in some dismal concentration camp outside the city. There was also a German carpenter called Fritz whom my father liked, and an attempt was made to save him from the same fate as the Dagos. One day my father asked Fritz to come into his den, put his hand on the family Bible and swear allegiance to King George. Agog, I witnessed this touching if somewhat naïve ceremony but, alas, it failed to save poor old Fritz from his inevitable sequestration.

Unlike my mother, my father sometimes spoke to foreigners, and often told a story of one of his uncles back in Benalla who had befriended a German tradesman during the Great War when the rest of the town refused to talk to him. When he finally died he left Great-Uncle Frank a house and several thousand pounds.

I had embarked on philately and I already had a large collection of British stamps, including a Penny Black. When my grandparents went back to England for the coronation of King George VI, I steamed the stamps off their many letters and postcards. I also had an exciting German section in my album thanks to a funny old lady called Mrs Vennermark who lived a few doors down Marlborough Avenue in a tapestry-brick, neo-Tudor bungalow built for her by my father in 1938. Old Mrs Vennermark – though she was probably only about forty-five – spoke with a strange accent, which gave her an air of acerbity. Her house had quite a few 'teething problems' too, and I often heard her harsh voice on the telephone asking for my father. 'It's that Jewish woman making trouble again,' my mother would say. 'Why your father does business with them I'll never understand.' Mr Friedmann was another thorn in her side. He ran a local firm called the Suburban Timber Supply and although my father liked him, my mother was convinced that he was a cheat and a swindler. However, in spite of my mother's open hostility towards her, old Mrs Vennermark was very kind to me, giving me the stamps off all the letters she received from her family who were still in Germany. They were rather spectacular: most had swastikas on them and images of a bad-tempered-looking man with folded arms and a square moustache. I secretly hoped Mrs Vennermark's family would not come to Melbourne too soon or an important philatelic source might dry up. But as it happened she remained alone, and some time around 1940 the letters stopped.

My parents enjoyed a busy social life. Once a week they had a card night. Baize-topped bridge tables were erected in the 'best' room and my mother spent the whole day making sandwiches and cakes. Her specialities were matches – a delicious colonial millefeuille filled with jam and cream and covered with walnuts – and sponge fingers with passionfruit icing. The next morning we had what was left of the sandwiches toasted for breakfast and took the cakes to school in greaseproof paper.

When my mother took me into town on her shopping expeditions, we usually visited Mitzi of Vienna, her favourite dress shop. The proprietrix, whose creations my mother found irresistible, was another of those exotic arrivals of the late thirties whose companions had given Melbourne chocolates, coffee lounges and chamber music. We would also visit the Myer Emporium, where my mother had once worked as a modiste, before she married my father. I noticed her voice changed when she spoke to the shop assistants, as though she had to make it very clear that she and they were now separated by a great distance, and the gap was getting wider. I always felt uncomfortable when she spoke in that unreal drawl, but I was coming to believe that my mother was perhaps several women; or different things to different people, and there was a life within her which excluded me.

Sometimes we lunched at Myer's in the Mural Hall, which for suburban shoppers of this, or any, period was the height of grandeur. Frequently used for fashion parades and receptions, it was decorated with large pale neo-classical frescoes by Napier Waller, a Melbourne artist who had lost his right arm in the First World War and immediately began painting with his left. More often, however, we had our lunch at the Wattle Tea Rooms in Little Collins Street. The Wattle was a long room in the Arts and Crafts style, with leadlight windows on the street, and dark wainscot within. Plates, Toby jugs and knick-knacks stood on the sempiternal curio ledge, and there were chintzy banquettes to the left and right, and white linen tables down the middle. These dark varnished surroundings emphasized the bright floral dresses and hats of the women who, talced and toilet-watered, thronged the Wattle every day, so that the whole café resembled a conservatory. Women like stocks, in mauve and heliotrope, or puffed up in brighter speckled hues like calceolarias. Blue delphinium women nodded to each other across the room and there were old ladies too, like bunches of violets and boronia huddled behind their Denby Ware tea sets, or sitting alone pecking at asparagus rolls. There was, of course, no shortage of snapdragons.

In the centre of each table at the Wattle there were real flowers: gum-tips and luminous orange and yellow Iceland poppies in cut-glass vases, dropping their calyxes on the doilies as each new flower shook out its crumpled petals, the long hairy stems turning double-jointed in the water.

The speciality at the Wattle was Adelaide whiting, which all the ladies ordered if they didn't eat egg sandwiches or asparagus rolls. Afterwards there were scrumptious things on silver three-tiered cake stands: kisses, éclairs, butterfly cakes, neenish tarts, matches and lamingtons.

Sometimes, at the sound of too loud and imperious a voice at an adjacent table, or the appearance of a pink-cheeked man in a hound's-tooth jacket and corduroy trousers with perhaps, also, a spoilt child, behaving like a *little madam*, my mother, or one of the other seed-packets, would smile secretly at her neighbour and, with a roll of her eyes, mouth the mysterious initials, like a code: 'E.N.T.' The whisper ran around the Wattle; nudges and little moues were exchanged, serviettes would discreetly mask smiles as eyes swivelled in the direction of this rather stiff *loud* family. 'E.N.T. and no doubt about it I'm afraid, Coral!' I heard a tight-lipped Carnation exclaim to a Gladiolus. English Next Table.

Lou and Eric – my parents – belonged to the local tennis club and on Saturday afternoons I would sit in the small clubhouse with a book listening to the distant laughter from the mixed doubles and the soporific sounds of tennis floating in from the courts. After the tennis there was always an enormous tea dominated by something called a 'tennis cake'. They were carefree afternoons of perpetual sunshine which the war changed forever.

We lived quite close to the Camberwell Sports Ground and on Saturday afternoons, if I happened to be at home in bed sick, I would hear, borne with terrible clarity across the housetops, the spasmodic applause of the cricket fans and, worse, in winter, the frighteningly mindless roar of the football
 rabble. Long before I was ever forced by school authorities to

watch these horrible and pointless games, I had formed a lifelong aversion to them based solely on those first auditory impressions. Crowds have always frightened and appalled me unless they happen to be in a theatre during one of my engagements. Then the noise they make is benign; a great ecstatic whoosh like a fire going up a chimney or the word 'yes' chanted by a heavenly host.

My mother was always concerned about my health and the great bogy of my childhood was Infantile Paralysis. I was never quite sure how old one had to be to avoid this scourge, nor had I ever met a victim, but I willingly swallowed whatever my mother poured into a spoon and pressed to my lips. Usually it was just the sticky and delicious Saunder's Malt Extract. I had seen it advertised on a hoarding which depicted a muscular baby, decorously diapered, shouldering an enormous steel girder. A favourite tonic of my mother's was Hypol, which was a less palatable white emulsion of cod-liver oil. There was, however, one prophylactic against Infantile Paralysis and other ailments that always made me sick. It was the egg flip, a glass of milk into which a raw egg had been whisked. Threads and clots of albumen always wrapped themselves around my uvula like a tourniquet, and although I gagged horribly, favours were withheld until I drank the last drop.

The illnesses of my childhood, although brief, gave me time to lie in bed, reading and listening to the wireless. My mother put the Radiola set in my room on a table beside the bed, and between sips of barley water I would tweak the knurled Bakelite knob from station to station. Throughout the day there was a succession of what are now called soap operas. Many of them employed the same actors, so that it was disquieting to hear a familiar character in *Aunt Jenny's Real Life Stories* crop up again with a different name in *Dr Mack*, *Fred and Maggie Everybody*, *When a Girl Marries* and *Martin's Corner*. Somehow it gave all those radio melodramas a spooky homogeneity.

In the mornings, soon after *Daybreak Dan*, there was a popular programme of community singing; a type of entertainment that has almost died out. With Uncle Wilf, Aunty Vi and John, I once went to a recording of this show in a small radio auditorium in town. It was thronged with women, a few accompanied by their children. Some of the ladies had brought knitting, very often khaki socks on five needles, and others had colanders in their laps into which they absently shelled peas. Led by a radio 'personality' called Charlie Vaud, with Mabel Nelson at the piano, they all enthusiastically sang such wartime hits as 'Run Rabbit Run', 'We're Going to Hang Out Our Washing on the Siegfried Line', 'Hey, Little Hen', 'Berlin or Bust' and 'The White Cliffs of Dover'. There was a vaudeville interlude when two comedians called Edgley and Dawe capered before the microphone and a strange woman called Nellie Colley, dressed in top hat and tails and smoking a pipe, sang a comic song called 'Burlington Bertie'. It was my first enticing glimpse of the Music Hall.

There were humorous interludes on the radio: mostly records of pre-war British vaudeville comics like George Tilly, Sid Field, Cyril Fletcher, Jack Hulbert and Cicely Courtneidge and my favourite, Horace Kenny. I would lie there in the darkened room through measles, mumps, whooping cough and scarlet fever, with my calamine lotion and Vicks Vaporub, laughing at those wonderful old-fashioned jesters. In the voices of some of these radio comics I recognized with a start the northern intonations of my father's father, whose Lancastrian accent had hitherto seemed so unique and outlandish. Here on the wireless were men with similar voices, interrupted by explosions of laughter. I later wondered why so many of the funniest comedians came from the North of England and why the idea of a 'Kent comic' seemed so anomalous.

In the forties, yodelling was popular and there were many excruciating hillbilly programmes on the wireless, but in the afternoon the children's sessions began, and I would listen to rather arch transmissions of *Chums at Chatterbox Corner* and later, around teatime, *The Search for the Golden Boomerang*, which used as its signature tune the voluptuous hothouse melody of Tchaikovsky's 'Waltz of the Flowers'. By the end of the day the bedroom smelt strongly of my medicaments mingled with the aroma of hot Bakelite.

One morning, when I was about ten, I woke very early, and as I went to the lavatory I glanced down at the skirting board outside my bedroom door. I then got down on my hands and knees and looked at it more closely. There was a small wire staple fixed to the wood an inch or two above the carpet, through which was threaded a thin cord. There was another staple on the opposite side of the architrave, and more, as I discovered, at regular intervals between my bedroom and the door to my parents' room, into which, like Ariadne's thread, the string disappeared. It occurred to me that I could easily have tripped on this filament on my way to the bathroom, and it was a mere fluke that I had not.

That morning, I was alone with my father for a few minutes after he had made my mother's breakfast, and when I told him of my strange discovery he became agitated and evasive. Finally, swearing me to secrecy, he explained that for some weeks he and my mother had been disturbed in the middle of the night by Barbara's sleepwalking, so he had installed this ingenious system of trip cords which connected to a bell beside his bed. Thus, whatever the hour, he would be instantly alerted to my sister's noctambulations and steer her safely back to bed. I must say, he looked particularly haggard that morning so I assumed the mechanism had been working all too successfully over the past few weeks.

I could not help but admire my father's ingenuity, though only one detail puzzled me; the cord did not pass across my sister's bedroom door, but mine. A few weeks later I noticed the whole system had been dismantled without a trace, and my father looked considerably rested in the mornings. I assumed that my unconscious wanderings had come to an end.

My father had secured a valuable contract to build a sausage factory for Mr Prince of Prince's Sausages. I went along with him to the old meat works for his first discussions. The noise in the factory was deafening and there was an appalling and nidorous smell. Very fat men in overalls and gumboots sloshed around in pink water as machines masticated huge quivering swags and chandeliers of offal; mauve, crimson and magenta.

 At the other end dirty pipes extruded serpents and stools of bright pink mince which the brutish men aimed into endless frankfurter skins. I remember my father had to rush away to be sick and thereafter never ate another sausage in his life. At our children's parties we always had cocktail frankfurters – from another firm – which we dunked in sauce and washed down with raspberry vinegar. These lavish teas, usually a celebration of a birthday, were held on Saturday afternoons and were preceded by a matinée at the Rivoli Picture Theatre near the Camberwell Junction. After the candles had been blown out and the last frankfurter ground into a slice of bread and butter and hundreds and thousands, there were party games in the garden until the parents arrived to escort their invariably weeping children home to be sick. Uncle Wilf always turned up at my parties and would organize the activities, which sometimes got rather rough, and he would find himself playing 'Stacks on the Mill, More on Still' flat on his back on the lawn beneath a writhing pyramid of about fifteen small boys.

'Stacks on the mill,
More on still . . .'

chanted the children. My parents would exchange a glance and my mother once said, 'Poor Wilf. He loves children and he's only got John.'

Uncle Wilf always bought the latest parlour games which helped to fill in the long evenings after tea when we were up at Healesville. We loved Mah-jong until Wilf produced a pack of Belisha, a new card game inspired by British traffic signs. Each card had a picturesque view of England, Scotland or Wales painted in bright colours in a slightly primitive,

Lowry-ish style. Although the cars in the pictures looked quaintly out of date, the landscapes, as green as salads, and the castles and thatched cottages, filled me with a yearning to go there.

After the family weekend at the shack, we used to drive back from Healesville in rather a long convoy, stopping occasionally for the children to go behind bushes or for Aunt Ella to be sick, or sometimes stopping too for Uncle Wilf to get out of their grey Chev and lean for a while with his elbows on the roof and his head in his hands. We would stop our car a few yards ahead and my father would watch his brother-in-law in the rear-vision mirror. 'Wilf's getting more of those headaches,' he said. 'Time he had a check-up.' A few months later he did, and had to go to hospital for a 'minor operation', as my parents, with their usual prudery about illness, described the removal of a brain tumour. I spoke to him on the telephone soon after he came home from the Alfred Hospital but he didn't seem to know who I was. When he died, leaving no will, the house and the land at Healesville had to be sold to provide money for his widow and son. And we left the bush forever.

Not long after Wilf's funeral, which I was not allowed to attend, my father and I were driving to one of his more important jobs to deliver a precious cargo of plate glass which was roped to the open boot. My father was driving a little too fast and as we went over an unexpected hump in the road there was an ominous thump and a dull crash behind the car. My father pulled over to the side of the road and got out to examine the disaster. I had never heard him swear, but this time he stood looking at the shivered panes and released a litany of curses. Then he sat on the kerb and sobbed quietly for a while. I didn't know what to do, but I felt he wasn't just grieving over the glass.

Hats and Glads

Camberwell Grammar School had been built in the grounds of a large Victorian house in an older neighbouring suburb. The original gardens were still there, including two elephantine Moreton Bay fig trees and a tottering arbour, from which, in its season, wistaria mauvely dripped. There was also the inevitable Norfolk Island pine tree which every Victorian residence of any distinction seemed to possess. They rose like tall viridian fishbones over the suburban landscape and always denoted the presence of an interesting old house. Today, however, though many of the trees survive, their gardens are often subdivided and the houses demolished; replaced by nice 'units' and practical townhouses. Mr Tonkin, the magenta-nosed headmaster, lived in the original Victorian house in the school grounds that also accommodated a few wretched and dispossessed boarders on whom we well-fed, warmly housed day boys gazed with pity.

My teachers in the junior school were mostly women. But there was a bald and nervous little choirmaster called Mr Dennis who visited the school and led us all in rousing renditions of 'Nymphs and Shepherds', 'Bird of the Wilderness' (. . . blithesome and cumberless) and a muscular ditty called 'Clang, Clang, Clang on the Anvil' – a song that sounded particularly odd when rendered by boy sopranos. At home Purcell's 'Nymphs and Shepherds' became my earliest party turn, after my mother had overheard me singing it in the bath, and much to my embarrassment she insisted that I sing it to all the uncles and aunts at the next family Sunday tea party. I only agreed to this on condition I was allowed to perform behind the curtain, so that my voice was disembodied like those on the radio. Thereafter, if ever my parents wanted to cajole me into a song or recitation, they would have to say – and I wince to recall the words – *pretend to be the wireless*. Needless to say I have pretended to be the wireless on many occasions since.

After the persecutions by Miss Jensen at my former school, Camberwell Grammar was a blissful respite, though a boy called John Bromley, who seemed tall for his age and had soft white skin like a slug, used to push me over whenever he saw me, for no reason that I could ever understand. I learnt to avoid him . . .

Sometimes when Bromley's capricious bullying got too much for me I would, I am afraid, seek a victim of my own. There was a perfectly nice, but rather small lad called Gifford, whom I pushed over a couple of times, on one occasion causing his mother's beautifully cut sandwiches to scatter on the dusty playground. For years afterwards I experienced a sharp pang of guilt whenever I thought of this incident until, on a recent visit to Melbourne, I could bear it no longer and decided, half a century later, to make amends. By consulting the telephone directory I discovered that there was, in fact, a Bruce Gifford who was practising architecture in the city and to my delight he answered the telephone. I came quickly to the point, explaining that I was sorry about the sandwiches and hoped he was doing well and that there were no hard feelings. A wave of relief and absolution passed over me, though as I gently replaced the receiver, I could still hear his voice exclaiming, 'Who is this? Who *is* this?'

I loved history, art and English, but I was already having difficulty with arithmetic, which seemed to be the one subject in which my father hoped I might excel. Even then I may have been vaguely aware that he wanted me to become an architect; something better and grander than himself. If only he had known, he could have adopted little Gifford!

One morning, through the classroom window, we noticed a strange figure prowling around outside in the school playground. He wore floppy green trousers, a red shirt and a bow tie, and his hair was very long and wavy. We laughed delightedly at the sight of him; he was the oddest fellow any of us had ever seen. Miss Ewers left the classroom and went outside and we saw her talking to the peculiar stranger for a few minutes and shaking her head. They could both see our grinning faces pressed to the window and the weird man glanced at us nervously, but Miss Ewers did not seem to mind. She was blushing, and trying not to smile herself. Soon the stranger walked off towards the school gate and our teacher came back into the classroom. She sat at her desk and exploded with laughter. She was convulsed. 'Who was that, Miss?' we all asked, but Miss Ewers took some time to compose herself. 'He . . . wanted to know if we'd like him to give us theatre lessons at the school!' She could hardly get the words out before a further paroxysm. We were all laughing now and the

 weird man must have heard us through one of the open

windows. We could see him at the gate, gazing back at the school with a pale puzzled face. 'Who is he, Miss Ewers?' we piped in chorus. Miss Ewers had gone bright red. She looked very pretty with her eyes sparkling with tears. 'An actor,' she said at last, drying her eyes with a handkerchief, 'he said he was an actor!' Our peals of merriment must surely have reached him now as he closed the gate and trudged off towards the bus stop.

Sport was my greatest problem at school. I was always perfectly healthy and yet I could never see the point of games. Paradoxically, I attribute my excellent constitution and energy today to the fact that since school I have never engaged in more than a minute of athletic activity. We all had to traipse down to a horrible building called The Gym. Here were coarse unscalable ropes, parallel bars and porridge-coloured mattresses, stained and pinguid from generations of brilliantined scalps and sweaty somersaults. This torture chamber was presided over by a man called Scotty, one of those repulsive and nuggety Caledonians with pale sandy hair and white eyelashes that gave him the look of a near-albino. Scotty was perpetually dressed in a short-sleeved Aertex, briefs and tennis shoes, which we called 'sandshoes' and 'ordinary' people called 'runners'. Scotty's piggy little eye fell on me immediately when he saw the difficulty I had in executing a pointless somersault. Much given to jocular nicknames, he decided that mine should be 'Granny Humphries', a soubriquet which met with the ribald approval of my schoolfellows. Needless to say, on subsequent sports days at which I was a reluctant participant and in the tedious brutalities of egg, spoon and sack races, the air rang with shrill cries of 'Come on Granny! Come on Granny!' As the reader may imagine, I had little affection for Mr Scott, but I am happy to say that very many years later a terrible sadness befell him in which I played a decisive, if anonymous, role.

An unpleasant concomitant of Physical Training was the cold shower we were forced to endure in a dank concrete basement near the gym. There were no lights and no proper drainage system, so we had to splash around in the dark with black water up to our knees, for no good reason that I could comprehend, except that cold showers were supposed to be 'good for you'.

There was a tuck shop at the school where two women sold pasties and pies to boys whose mothers, unlike mine, could not be bothered to cut their sandwiches or lovingly pack their leather satchels with fruit and cakes. The savoury effluvium which wafted from the tuck shop daily at twelve o'clock percolated to every corner of the school, and as I chewed my bland sandwiches I sometimes wished I was just slightly neglected, as I hankered for a succulent pasty, haemorrhaging sauce.

It would not be long before we would all be officially urged to devour something called the 'Oslo lunch'. At the time I assumed this to be identical with the lunches eaten by schoolchildren in occupied Norway. It consisted of a carrot, a slice of brown bread (in Melbourne, in those days, this was white bread coloured brown), a piece of Kraft processed cheese still half-wrapped in foil and bearing a parent's thumb print, and half a pint of milk. For a short while in the early years of the war my mother followed this edict and daily packed this austere and unappetizing collation in my satchel. However, on the journey to school the milk bottle often leaked and by the end of the term most of our school bags reeked with the smell of raw leather, ink and rancid milk. Soon, and in spite of the war effort, I persuaded my mother to supply me with a normal lunch of spaghetti sandwiches and cakes.

At the beginning of the war with Japan, trenches were dug in the gardens of the old school house and we were issued with gas masks and strange black rubber gags which, if bitten on when the bombs fell, would prevent our teeth from shattering. We all had to bring money to school to pay for these prophylactics, but I horrified the Head and was made to feel shamefully unpatriotic when, before the whole school, I innocently asked whether we would get our money back if the Japs didn't bomb us. It was a solecism I was never allowed to forget.

Meanwhile the school grounds became a muddy maze of trenches, and strips of cellophane were pasted in lattice patterns all over the windows. On the wireless Vera Lynn optimistically sang:

> When the lights go on again
> All over the world . . .

Many of our neighbours in Christowell Street were happily building air-raid shelters in their back gardens. These were exciting subterranean dwellings upholstered with sandbags, but my father refused to disfigure our back lawn and constructed an elaborate, but barely bomb-proof, bunker under the stairs. Carpenters made large hardboard panels that could be fitted to the inside of our windows in the event of aerial bombardment, though how this could be done at high speed in an air raid, and in a house that must have had at least forty windows, is difficult to imagine. Fortunately it was never put to the test. The back garden was converted from flowers to vegetables and fruits, and in a short time we were producing our own carrots, parsnips, beans, potatoes, peas, lemons, peaches and apricots.

There was some confusion, certainly amongst children, as to which war we should be worrying about: the Hitler one or the Tojo one. However, most streets had a Fat for Britain depot.

It was popularly believed that fat, or its absence, would be a decisive factor in the outcome of the European war, and that the more fat we could send to England the better her chances of victory. The dripping from every Sunday roast in Melbourne was therefore carefully decanted into suitable containers – old Farex tins, glucose canisters and jam jars – and these, hygienically sealed, were left on the front porch of Mrs Long's Spanish Mission Home on the corner of Fairmont Avenue, whence they were presumably collected, consolidated and shipped to London. To this day I have never met a recipient or beneficiary of this lardy largesse, but the Japanese sank many Fat for Britain ships and it is strange to think of this greasy residue of a million Sunday joints lying in some coral dell at the bottom of the Pacific, waiting to produce the biggest dripping slick in history.

Our vicar, Canon P. W. Robinson, was a Londoner, and his sermons rambled on at some length about the threat to what was then called The Old Country and the safety of the King,

Queen and the little Princesses. To my father's disappointment, my mother always thought of some excuse for not going to church, though I knew that our sanctimonious vicar was the principal reason for her absence from Morning Prayer. My father, however, was a regular churchgoer, later a vestryman, and during the Offertory he would always slip a crunched-up pound note into the plate amongst everyone else's shillings, and insisted on saying Grace before meals: 'Forwhatweareabouttoreceivemaythe LordmakeustrulythankfulAmen.' This always embarrassed me when we had friends to stay, as my father's recitation usually caught them unawares mid-way through the first forkful. And sometimes, at night, I would see him through their half-open bedroom door – it was rarely closed – kneeling in prayer beside the bed. Canon Robinson took a great fancy to me and always patted my head vigorously after Sunday service. I had the uncomfortable feeling, later confirmed, that he envisaged some future for me in the Ministry, and at Sunday school he was always singling me out to read the lesson.

Sunday was the worst day of the week, because my father, with his north of England Methodist upbringing, forbade us to play with any other children on the Sabbath. Instead there were endless drives back and forth to St Mark's rather ugly buff-stuccoed nave, and the cold red-brick Sunday school beside it. In church, I liked the music, though I successfully resisted Canon Robinson's efforts to conscript me into the choir. However, the smell of everybody's 'Sunday Best'; the camphor, the talcum, hair oil and the toilet water, mingled with whatever disinfectant it was that the cleaners used, always made me feel like passing out as if I had inhaled carbon monoxide. Withal I struggled for some great faith; some transcendental religious experience. Great-Uncle Albert, always extolled to me as the most successful member of the Humphries family, had, back in Manchester, once written a seminal work, *The Holy Spirit in Faith and Experience* (Primitive Methodist Publishing Company, 1911), and though I attempted to read this book many times, it failed to yield up its mystery to me. Moreover, there was some evidence from its musty unopened appearance that previous readers had also abandoned their search for Truth amongst the closely printed pages.

Sunday lunch – or dinner as it was called – always consisted of a Roast; lamb, pork or beef. This was always cooked, as I still prefer it, until it was an attractive shade of grey. The roast was accompanied by potatoes, parsnips and pumpkin baked to a crisp, the pumpkin caramelized. This would be followed by tinned peaches or a steamed pudding in which apricot jam, golden syrup or sultanas were alternating constituents. Much as I looked forward to this meal throughout the tedious tracts of Canon Robinson's sermon, I dreaded the return home as well. For Sunday was the day that my parents usually had 'words'. It would be more truthful to say that they had no words at all, but there was a palpable atmosphere of tension which had no explicable origin. It may have been that my parents, to all appearances a happily married couple, found the prospect of one day in the week spent in each other's company unendurable. This oppressive atmosphere, which froze the heart of a child, may have had a purely gastric origin, as we consumed those large quantities of fat that would never find their way to Britain. Happily, the family's spirits lifted at last when we piled into the Oldsmobile and later the Buick and went for the traditional Sunday-afternoon spin.

There was nothing my parents enjoyed more than motoring around the new suburbs on the outskirts of the town looking at houses. For my father, the builder, it was an excursion of professional interest, and every now and then, as we drove down a brand-new street of villas, with their freshly planted lawns, bird baths and sickly silver birches, he might suddenly jam on the brakes and point an enraged finger at some crude, jerry-built imitation of one of his own designs. On the new roads, crescents and boulevards flanked by pristine triple-fronted cream-brick bungalows, other vehicles filled with gawking families also cruised. It was the thing everyone did on a Sunday afternoon, and it was called *Looking at the Lovely Homes*. On the hills of Ivanhoe and Eaglemont above the Yarra River, where the artists of the 1880s had painted their idyllic 'impressions', stood some of the grander new houses with tennis courts which especially interested my mother. Mostly of brick, the colour of milky tea, they had curved nautical-looking terraces, balconies and picture windows, with satin festoon or 'veil of tears' blinds; and if these were raised, as they often were by the proud owners, there might be a glimpse within of blond veneer and peach mirror, and prowling along the window sill just inside the glass, a lithe white marble puma.

The lovely homes bored me. As we glided along in our big chubby car past the raw new houses, still smelling of wet cement, admiring the azaleas and the 'crazy' stone work, the 'feature' chimneys and the names of the houses or their street numbers scribbled across the façades in duck-egg blue wrought-iron, I hankered for hovels. There was a place I had heard of called Dudley Flats, a low-lying wasteland to the west of Melbourne, where 'slums' and *really* poor people could be found.

I begged my parents to drive me there so that I could see them for myself. But we never visited the older suburbs of Melbourne, except when we went to see my mother's sister, Ella, who still lived in a dark Victorian house in Thornbury where her parents had once lived and my mother had grown up. It had ruby and Bristol-blue glass in the panels beside the front door and a long central corridor with a curtain half-way down, so that when the front door was opened, visitors were not afforded a vulgar view of the back yard. There was even an aspidistra in the front parlour which Ella washed with milk, and I once asked my father, in the presence of my aunt and uncle, if their house was a *real* hovel.

Sometimes on Sunday afternoons we would visit the Melbourne General Cemetery with my relations on my mother's side. After much wandering through the maze of granite obelisks and tottering tombstones, overrun with skeleton weed and lantana, we came to a grave that was better kept than the rest. It looked rather like a narrow bed of grey stone, covered with marble chips, and on the headstone was my grandmother's name. My mother removed the old stalks and put some fresh flowers in a little vase buried in the gravel. Aunty Elsie pulled out the weeds and we all just stood and shuffled, looking at the grave and trying to feel something. Around us were sadly neglected plots and even a few that had caved in, so that kneeling down and peering through the cracks you might just see the skeletons of other people's grandmothers.

To earn extra pocket money I often went shopping for my mother. There was a small parade of shops not far away in Camberwell Road, and although their proprietors, Mr Hall, the grocer, Mr Ryal, the chemist, and Mr Ernie Young, the butcher, all seemed to me to be of normal height, my mother always referred to them as diminutive. 'Barry, would you please go down the street and get me a half a pound of nice lean lamb chops from my little butcher. Oh, and while you're there, pop in and ask the little man in the chemist shop for a bottle of Hypol and some Buckley's Canadiol Mixture.' I always took a basket with an orange ten-shilling note and a ration book.

There seemed to be no great shortage of anything, though butterless recipes were popular, but I would stand on the sawdust floor of little Mr Young's butcher's shop while he put his bloodied thumbs in a pair of scissors and deftly snipped a few squares off our meat-ration book. Sometimes, if there was a big card night looming, I could pick up a sponge, a lemon meringue pie or a few fairy cakes from the Misses Longmire who had the 'homemade' cake shop at the end of the Parade. There was always a delicious smell in their shop, though it puzzled me, since everything was baked on the premises, that the Misses Longmire could, with a clear conscience, describe their confections as being homemade when they were so obviously baked in a shop.

If I were not running simple errands after school, I might be in my laboratory mixing quite dangerous combinations of sulphur and potassium permanganate over a spirit burner or practising a few magic tricks. I had always had a hankering to be a magician like the top-hatted, opera-cloaked gigolo called Mandrake who appeared regularly in a comic strip in my mother's *Women's Weekly*. Mandrake had only to 'gesture hypnotically' and people disappeared. That seemed to me to be the greatest gift imaginable; to make people and things vanish.

Sometimes, too, I might even play with my sister and her little friends, Maurine and Valerie. My mother had long ago whispered to me that Valerie was adopted, but never to say anything to her face because her adoptive parents had not yet told her. At the time this information intrigued and frightened me, since it occurred to me that I, like Val, might also be adopted and that my parents too could be keeping this a secret. It even occurred to me that my mother's confidences about Val's origins might be her way of preparing the ground for a confession of her own. It was true to say that her expressions of love for me were sometimes evasive or ambiguous. Once when I was quite young I asked her point-blank if she loved me and she seemed nonplussed and embarrassed. 'Well,' she replied evasively, 'naturally I love your father most of all, and then *my* mother and father, and after that, you and your sister, just the same.' It was clear from what she said that love had a strictly hierarchical structure, and was certainly not something that could be spontaneously experienced or bestowed. My unspoken adoption fears were not put to rest when my mother said, as she frequently did to others in my presence: 'Eric and I don't know *where Barry comes from*.' I have recorded this story as accurately as I can recollect it in order to show the warmer side of my mother's complex personality.

Every now and then there were special occasions; usually a wedding, or a dance at the tennis club. Weeks before these events my mother and I would drive to a distant suburb to the home of Miss Wilmot, my mother's dressmaker, and I would wait in the hall while she had another 'fitting'. These seemed to take forever, and from time to time, Miss Wilmot would put her head around the door and smile at me reassuringly, as if that were possible with a mouthful of pins. Taffeta was my mother's favourite fabric in that epoch; it was before the age of Thai silk. Taffeta was cool and it rustled and chafed upon itself, and before my mother's big night out it was, with a few drops of Bond Street perfume, the nicest textile to say your prayers against.

Once they went to a grand luncheon at the Town Hall, and my mother wore her best suit from Mitzi of Vienna, and a hat with a veil covered with fat black polka dots. Later I asked her what it was like. 'Lovely,' she replied. 'I'm pleased I went to a bit of trouble. It was all hats and glads.'

Gladioli, especially flesh-pink ones, were the floral symbols of respectability, success and thrusting, unquestioning optimism. They also seemed somehow to be the appropriate emblems of Mr Menzies, the reigning prime minister, who had such a nice 'speaking voice'. Never before had I heard a voice so described, and when my parents tuned in to the wireless to hear one of his public addresses I listened attentively to those sanctimonious, lah-di-dah tones, trying to detect why my parents had singled out this 'speaking voice' in particular. Did he have other more recondite voices, I wondered wickedly. A farting voice perhaps? Above all, Mr Menzies was extolled by my parents and their friends for his repartee and the swiftness with which he rebuked interjections from the Opposition supporters, whom he wittily described as 'that riff-raff at the back of the hall' to roars of laughter and applause.

His opponent, who was later victorious, was Mr Chifley, 'a pipe-smoking Labourite', who had once, Mrs Kendall whispered, 'been a *train driver*'. Certainly Mr Chifley had nothing which could be described as a 'speaking voice', and my father summed him up in three words, 'rough as bags'. 'Irish, too,' my mother added tartly. Since her only brother had married a Roman Catholic and been ostracized, my mother had little affection for the Irish. 'But didn't Nana's mother come from Ireland?' I asked ingenuously. '*Northern* Ireland, Barry,' she averred warmly, 'that's the nice part of Ireland, and don't you forget it.'

I sometimes think I might still bear the ugly scars of my early indoctrination, when I read absurdly Anglophobic accounts of the Gallipoli Campaign and sensationalist works of Australian history like Robert Hughes's *The Fatal Shore*, where the British are uniformly depicted as shits, and the Irish convicts as misunderstood scallywags and political prisoners. 'He would write that, wouldn't he,' I reflect, 'typical revisionist Mick that he is!' A modern manifestation of this persistent sectarian split in Australian life is the Republican Movement with its cant about patriotism. It is, of course, no such thing, but just another form of pommy-bashing. One has only to glance at the names of its most vociferous champions: Keating, Keneally, Doherty, O'Horne. It is no surprise that the Australian Republican flag is green.

Today I keep my sweaters in a toffee-coloured chest lined with camphor wood. It is densely and rather crudely carved with dragons and ovate oriental bas-reliefs which I remember in the greatest detail from my earliest childhood. It was bought by my grandparents in Colombo as they returned from the Coronation on the Orient Line, as, indeed, were thousands more identical chests purchased by other voyagers. It used to stand in our upstairs hallway and contained my mother's best things: her furs, rugs, table linen, wedding dress, and a gold meshed evening belt encrusted with imitation rubies, sapphires and emeralds.

When I was eleven I noticed in the window of a small second-hand shop near Camberwell Junction a pair of earrings that seemed to match my mother's belt perfectly. I covertly inquired the price which, though I no longer recall it, may have been quite expensive for such cheap paste, but over a long period, and by secretly slipping into the shop and leaving small amounts, I finally paid off the earrings, brought them home and carefully hid them. As her birthday approached I wrapped the earrings, speculating excitedly on the surprise and delight they would bring. I had not even breathed a word to my sister or father.

The great morning came and my father brought my mother breakfast in bed. It was then that I proudly presented my small package. I watched my mother's face carefully as she unwrapped it, but when the tissue paper parted and she saw the earrings, she did not smile. Instead her face darkened and she turned angrily to my father. 'Where did he get these, Eric?' my mother said sharply. 'I hope he didn't pay for these out of his own money?' My father looked confused, and speechless. 'Where did you get them?' my mother asked me. 'Not from that little rogue down at the Junction, I hope. How much did they cost?' I muttered a price. 'Daylight robbery,' exploded my mother. She thrust the earrings at my father. 'Eric?' she commanded. 'I want you to go straight down to that little Jew and tell him to give Barry his money back. And you can also tell him if he goes on overcharging children for rubbish like this I'll have him reported.' Needless to say, that was one of my mother's more memorable birthdays.

My father often used to bring home carnations as a peace offering for some nameless transgression, and I always found them unsympathetic flowers: prim, sharply budded, pinked and serrated blooms in ice-cream colours, with a scent that smelled sprayed-on. They still fill me with a remote dread. Always wrapped in a cone of pink or purple tissue paper, they often lay on the hall table for a long while, depending on the time my mother had set for my father's sentence. But in the end she would always drop them in a vase and say with a smile, 'Look at the lovely carnations your father has given me.' They had worked again.

My father insisted that my mother have domestic help. I had never quite recovered from the sudden departure of my first beloved nanny, Edna, who left without farewells or adequate explanations; although later there was a succession of domestics and housekeepers, they never meant the same to me. After my brother Michael was born my mother engaged a girl from the nearby Salvation Army home, euphoniously called Valmai Grubb. Although my mother admitted that the rest of Valmai's family were almost certainly 'ordinary', Valmai, she insisted, had a very kind heart and a sweet soft nature. Why otherwise would she cry so uncontrollably when rebuked? Valmai stayed a long time and was replaced by Mrs Lane, a woman of about sixty, who came from Welshpool and whom my mother described as 'very countrified'. They took an instant dislike to each other and my mother told me that as soon as she saw the down-trodden heels of Mrs Lane's shoes she knew that she should never have engaged her. On Mrs Lane's days off my mother would inspect the floor of the shower recess and with some satisfaction she always found it to be dry and the room filled with a cloying scent of Three Flowers talcum powder, Mrs Lane's preferred alternative to soap and water. In the mornings, as the housekeeper trudged up the stairs with my mother's breakfast tray, my sister and I often overheard her muttering under her frequently juniper-scented breath the malediction: 'I hate her, I hate her, *I hate her*.'

Having engaged a 'home help' who had quickly proved herself unsuitable, my mother found herself unable to dismiss her, so that thereafter Mrs Lane, having failed as a housekeeper, was retained – even became indispensable – as an example of incompetence and slovenliness. 'Look at the dust,' my mother would say with some satisfaction. 'It's that grub Mrs Lane. She thinks I don't notice.' My mother confided all her complaints about Mrs Lane to Mrs Shores, the woman who came to do the washing and ironing. Mrs Shores was a garrulous lady with a shrill laugh and a husband who enjoyed a drink. She laughed immoderately, though quite genuinely, at all my mother's sardonic jokes. Whenever Mrs Shores arrived my mother would hurry to impart to her Mrs Lane's latest outrage, at which Mrs Shores would burst into peals of incredulous hilarity. It began to look as though Mrs Lane would never be sacked, but be retained forever as a grim cabaret turn and an essential topic of conversation. Mrs Shores was another comic act on the same bill who frequently interrupted her tasks in the laundry to follow my amused parent from room to room gossiping; or she would stand in the kitchen recounting some long anecdote at the top of her voice, assuming my mother was listening in the adjacent sun-room. However my mother often went upstairs, or wandered into the garden to pick a few camellias, and after a wink at me would return to the house to find Mrs Shores still cheerfully soliloquizing.

Mr Dunt, the gardener, was another incompetent hired in order to provide my mother with anecdotes of incompetence. He was an old man, though perhaps little older than the author of this memoir, who arrived on a bicycle with a large pannier attached to the handlebars and who thereafter pottered about pruning the wrong things and digging up carefully planted bulbs. Mr Dunt had a special cup and saucer for his afternoon tea, from which we were forbidden to drink since it was rather uncertain as to where Mr Dunt might have been. It was only after a few years that my father noticed that small things were missing from his workshop behind the garage. The absence of an expensive electric exhaust fan finally aroused his suspicions and a telephone call was made to Mr Dunt's family who, sure enough, discovered a large haul of unused appliances, as well as hinges, nails, trowels and hammers, under the old man's bed. We never saw him again.

One day when I was about six my mother disappeared. My young sister and I were given no explanation of this terrible event and a kind family friend called Janet Ballantyne came to look after us. My father was rarely home, and seemed so stricken with anxiety that we were unable to demand an explanation. I would lie in bed feeling as though some calamity had taken place. Somehow it was even uncertain whether my mother would ever return. But she did. Perhaps she had only been absent for a few weeks, and quite recently I learnt that she had suffered a miscarriage and spent a period convalescing in hospital. My family were madly circumspect in matters to do with illness, sex and even reality, so that a misfortune combining all three taboos was veiled in absolute silence. To this day I can remember those feelings of childish desolation, so that if people close to me leave me now, even on shopping expeditions, I always need to know exactly where they are going, or that oppressive intimation of loss, with all its old force, comes back to me.

PENGUIN 60s

ISABEL ALLENDE · *Voices in My Ear*
NICHOLSON BAKER · *Playing Trombone*
LINDSEY BAREHAM · *The Little Book of Big Soups*
KAREN BLIXEN · *From the Ngong Hills*
DIRK BOGARDE · *Coming of Age*
ANTHONY BURGESS · *Childhood*
ANGELA CARTER · *Lizzie Borden*
CARLOS CASTANEDA · *The Sorcerer's Ring of Power*
ELIZABETH DAVID · *Peperonata and Other Italian Dishes*
RICHARD DAWKINS · *The Pocket Watchmaker*
GERALD DURRELL · *The Pageant of Fireflies*
RICHARD ELLMANN · *The Trial of Oscar Wilde*
EPICURUS · *Letter on Happiness*
MARIANNE FAITHFULL · *Year One*
KEITH FLOYD · *Hot and Spicy Floyd*
ALEXANDER FRATER · *Where the Dawn Comes Up Like Thunder*
ESTHER FREUD · *Meeting Bilal*
JOHN KENNETH GALBRAITH · *The Culture of Contentment*
ROB GRANT AND DOUG NAYLOR · *Scenes from the Dwarf*
ROBERT GRAVES · *The Gods of Olympus*
JANE GRIGSON · *Puddings*
SOPHIE GRIGSON · *From Sophie's Table*
KATHARINE HEPBURN · *Little Me*
SUSAN HILL · *The Badness Within Him*
ALAN HOLLINGHURST · *Adventures Underground*
BARRY HUMPHRIES · *Less is More Please*
HOWARD JACOBSON · *Expulsion from Paradise*
P. D. JAMES · *The Girl Who Loved Graveyards*
STEPHEN KING · *Umney's Last Case*
LAO TZU · *Tao Te Ching*
DAVID LEAVITT · *Chips Is Here*

PENGUIN 60s

LAURIE LEE · *To War in Spain*
PATRICK LEIGH FERMOR · *Loose as the Wind*
ELMORE LEONARD · *Trouble at Rindo's Station*
DAVID LODGE · *Surprised by Summer*
BERNARD MAC LAVERTY · *The Miraculous Candidate*
SHENA MACKAY · *Cloud-Cuckoo-Land*
NORMAN MAILER · *The Dressing Room*
PETER MAYLE · *Postcards from Summer*
JAN MORRIS · *Scenes from Havian Life*
BLAKE MORRISON · *Camp Cuba*
VLADIMIR NABOKOV · *Now Remember*
REDMOND O'HANLON · *A River in Borneo*
STEVEN PINKER · *Thinking in Tongues*
CRAIG RAINE · *Private View*
CLAUDIA RODEN · *Ful Medames and Other Vegetarian Dishes*
HELGE RUBINSTEIN · *Chocolate Parfait*
SIMON SCHAMA · *The Taking of the Bastille*
WILL SELF · *The Rock of Crack As Big As the Ritz*
MARK SHAND · *Elephant Tales*
NIGEL SLATER · *30-Minute Suppers*
RICK STEIN · *Fresh from the Sea*
LYTTON STRACHEY · *Florence Nightingale*
PAUL THEROUX · *Slow Trains to Simla*
COLIN THUBRON · *Samarkand*
MARK TULLY · *Beyond Purdah*
LAURENS VAN DER POST · *Merry Christmas, Mr Lawrence*
MARGARET VISSER · *More than Meets the Eye*
GAVIN YOUNG · *Something of Samoa*

and

Thirty Obituaries from Wisden · SELECTED BY MATTHEW ENGEL

READ MORE IN PENGUIN

LAURIE LEE

TO WAR IN SPAIN

PENGUIN BOOKS

PENGUIN BOOKS

Published by the Penguin Group. Penguin Books Ltd, 27 Wrights Lane, London W8 5TZ, England. Penguin Books USA Inc., 375 Hudson Street, New York, New York 10014, USA. Penguin Books Australia Ltd, Ringwood, Victoria, Australia. Penguin Books Canada Ltd, 10 Alcorn Avenue, Toronto, Ontario, Canada M4V 3B2. Penguin Books (NZ) Ltd, 182–190 Wairau Road, Auckland 10, New Zealand · Penguin Books Ltd, Registered Offices: Harmondsworth, Middlesex, England · The first extract is from *As I Walked Out One Midsummer Morning*, by Laurie Lee, first published by André Deutsch 1969. Published in Penguin Books 1971. The second extract is from *A Moment of War*, by Laurie Lee, first published by Viking 1991. Published in Penguin Books 1992. This edition published 1996. · Typeset by Rowland Phototypesetting Ltd, Bury St Edmunds, Suffolk. Printed in England by Clays Ltd, St Ives plc · 10 9 8 7 6 5 4 3 2 1

To War in Spain

I

Plucked from the Civil War by a British destroyer, I returned to my Gloucestershire village, amazed to see once more the depth of the grass and the weight of the leaves on the trees. But the pleasure of being home again, and receiving the traditional cosseting of the prodigal, was quickly replaced by misgivings. I'd been away two years, but was little the wiser for it. I was twenty-two, woolly-minded, and still naïve in everything, but I began to realize I'd come home too soon.

The Spanish War, seen close to within the local limits of an Andalusian village, was not what it had seemed to me at the time. As I learnt more about it from the newspapers – its scale and implications – I couldn't help feeling a private sense of betrayal.

Unlike so many of my age, for whom Spain in the Thirties represented one of the last theatres of political romanticism, I hadn't consciously chosen it as a Cause but had stumbled on it by accident, simply by happening to be there. Now I began to feel shameful doubts at having turned my back on events so easily, just when they were about to affect us all. I thought the least I could do was to give myself a second chance by returning to Spain as soon as I could.

It was a restless summer. I was penniless, without contacts, and totally ignorant of ways and means. Spain was over a thousand miles away and already sealed off by the hypocrisies of non-intervention. I might have given up the idea if I hadn't suddenly fallen in love, but the result of that experience, which went deeper than anything I'd known before, only made my situation all the more intolerable.

For me it was an hallucination of honour, no doubt a self-indulgence, irrelevant to events and certainly irrelevant to the girl. I told her my plans one evening as she sat twisting her hair with her fingers and gazing into my eyes with her long cat look. She wasn't impressed. Others may need a war, she said; but you don't, you've got one here. She bared her beautiful small teeth and unsheathed her claws. Heroics like mine didn't mean a thing. If I wished to command her admiration by sacrificing myself to a cause she herself was ready to provide one.

Of course, I tried to persuade her that I would be doing it for her, but this wasn't true, and she knew it. All the same, it was partly our entanglement that drove me, the feeling of over-indulgence and satiety brought on by too much easy and unearned pleasure. Guilt, too: she was married and had two young children, she was rich and demandingly beautiful, extravagantly generous with her emotions but fanatically jealous, and one who gave more than she got in love. For several days and nights our arguments swung back and forth, interspersed with desperate embraces, ending with threats of blackmail and bitter tears, with cries of 'Go, and you'll see me no more . . .'

With the help of another friend, I left London in the autumn and worked my way down through France, heading in the direction of the Pyrenees, planning, when the chances were right, simply to walk into the mountains and slip across the frontier alone. The Pyrenees, when I got there, were already touched with snow and looked grey and impregnable. Even so, I never doubted that I could get across. Winter was closing in like a cloak.

While I was waiting near the coast and making some rather slip-shod preparations, the girl suddenly turned up again, having driven out from England not in an attempt to dissuade

 me further but to present me instead with a

week of passionate farewell. A week of hysteria, too – embracing in ruined huts, on the salt-grass at the edge of the sea, gazing out at the windswept ocean while gigantic thunderstorms wheeled slowly round the distant mountains.

There were no more questions or arguments; the mountains were always in sight, and the girl made it clear she thought I was going to my death. Our love was more violent than ever, as though we accepted this as its end and wished to leave each other destroyed.

After we parted, I moved on to the little town of Perpignan, only about twelve miles from the Pyrenees. Perpignan, I'd been told, was swarming with Spanish Government agents eager to recruit volunteers and smuggle them over the mountains. Certainly the agents were there, but they must have thought me a doubtful proposition for my approaches were either blocked or met by evasions. When I mentioned the

International Brigade, the Spanish Consul was polite and said he had no knowledge of such a body. He appreciated my goodwill but assured me that he ran no excursions across the frontier: such junketings would be unthinkable and lawless. The war was a domestic matter, he said, and everything was going well; but if I really wished to help I should go back home.

I spent a couple of weeks in the town without breaking through this wall of equivocation, and finally I realized I would have to go it alone. The Pyrenees to the south, seen in the sharp winter air, began to look smaller and less noncommittal. So early in December I took a bus to Ceret in the foothills, where I spent my last snug night in an inn. Then next morning, at first light, I left the still sleeping village and started off up the mountain track.

Behind me, as I climbed, the gentle slopes of the foothills fell away to Perpignan and the sea, while before me the steep bulk of the

Pyrenees Orientales filled the sky with their sunlit peaks. I had about eight hours of daylight but was not too sure of my route, except that it must go up, over, and south. The fact that it was winter seemed to be the only thing in my favour, though I was still glad of the bright clear weather.

The track rose steeply among rocks that were diamond-crusted with ice, and I soon found the going tough. I was idiotically equipped for such a journey, having brought nothing that would help me, though plenty of stuff that wouldn't – no maps, no compass, no tent or ground-sheet, instead a rucksack loaded down with an assortment of books and papers, together with my violin, a folding camera, and a saucepan. I don't really know why I was carrying all this, except that it was all I had in the world.

Throughout the long clear morning I struggled up the mountain path, buffeted by icy winds from the north. The great peak of

Canigou stood away on my right, floating in the brilliant sky like an iceberg, and for much of the time, not having a compass, I was able to use it as a sighting post. By noon I'd climbed to about 3,000 feet, but the goat track grew more and more tortuous, so I decided to abandon it altogether and go straight up the mountain, still keeping Canigou on my right.

The way was tricky and hard, and I found myself stumbling on my knees and clawing at rock and tufts of frozen grass. By the middle of the afternoon I was sweating in the cold, slipping and scrambling over the broken slopes. But I was high up now, with a prickling across the back of my neck as I felt the whole of France plunging away behind me. Having been born and brought up at two hundred and fifty feet above sea-level, I was not used to such dizzying elevations.

Suddenly there was an ominous change in the atmosphere, an extra keenness of cold, and a curious glare and whitening of the sunlight. Looking down, I saw that the foothills had disappeared and had been replaced by a blanket of swirling vapour. The shining peak of Canigou began to switch on and off like a lighthouse, intermittently shuttered by racing clouds. Then the wind rose abruptly to a thin-edged wail, and I felt the first stinging bite of snow.

One moment I'd been climbing a mountain in a sparkle of sunshine; the next, the whole visible world had gone, and I was slapped to my knees and pinioned to a shelf of rock, head down in a driving gale. Gusts of snow swept round me, needling into my eyelids and piercing my clothes like powdered glass. The storm closed in and began scouring the mountain with an insane and relentless frenzy.

For a while I curled myself up and became just a ball of survival, mindlessly hugging the lee of a rock. I lay knee to chin, letting the storm ride over me; then I began to wonder what I was doing here. After all the boasting I'd done in summer fields back home, and in her Chanel-scented bed, what was I doing in France stuck to the face of a mountain alone in a winter blizzard? To lie freezing to death on the wrong side of the frontier was no way to go to a war. There was no point in staying where I was, so I started to move forward, crawling slowly on hands and knees. Distance, direction, movement, and balance were all fused by the driving snow; I may have advanced half a mile, or just a few yards, there was no longer any way of knowing. All I remember is the brightness of the ground, and being swept by waves of almost infantile pleasure, the delirious warmth of impending frostbite.

Then, by one of those long-shot chances, taken for granted at the time, I came upon a rough little stone-built shelter. It was half in ruins, and there was nothing inside it but straw, but I suppose it may have saved my life. Once

I'd bedded myself down, I heard the blizzard change gear, rising to an almost supersonic shriek, and for a couple of hours I lay motionless, curled deep in the straw, slowly and painfully thawing out.

Later it grew dark, and the anguish gradually eased as I built up a drowsy fug for myself. The sound of the wind settled down to a steady whine, soporific, like an electric motor. A pleasant comfort crept over me; I seemed to sense the feathersoft snow gathering in deep weightless drifts outside; a bosomy presence, invisible and reassuring, cushioning the naked rocks of the mountain. By now I was exhausted anyway, too drugged by the cold to move, even to attempt to build a fire; so I just lay, sniffing the damp warm smell of the straw, and presently I fell asleep.

Next morning the storm was over and the sun shone brilliantly again. I came out of the dark little hut to find the mountain transformed –

trees, rocks, and bushes thickly bolstered with snow and giving off a clean crispy smell, like starch. The French village below me was no longer in sight, but the slope above curved gradually away, smooth and bright, rising a few hundred yards then ending in a sharp blue line of sky.

Abandoning the cosy gully where I'd spent the night, I climbed unsteadily for an hour or so, ploughing through snowdrifts, stumbling over hidden rocks, and slithering about in my sodden shoes. It was a long cold struggle, and I'd had nothing to eat, but at least I was lucky to be on the move at all. Then suddenly there was no more climbing: the slope levelled and stopped, the sky plunged, and I was on top of the ridge.

The icy crests of the Pyrenees stretched east and west, flashing in the sun like broken glass on a wall, while before me, to the south, was

 what I had come to see – range after range of

little step-like hills falling away to the immensities of Spain . . .

But I was not over the mountains yet; there was still another ridge to cross, with a deep valley lying between. I could see a black frozen stream winding a thousand feet below me. I would simply have to go down and up again.

Crossing this mile-wide chasm took me the rest of the day – a vertical, trackless journey. Whipped by flurries of snow and bruising winds I slithered, slipped, and scrambled, seeing no living thing except a boy and a sheepdog who both fled when they saw me coming. Towards evening, very cold, and with a rime of frost on my eyelashes, I was about half-way up the second slope, when I came to a small mountain road, the first I'd seen for two days, winding bleakly among the trees. I sat and stared at it for a while, but it told me nothing; it could have been anywhere on earth - just an inscrutable little cart-track, half mud, half stones, as nameless as a peasant's face.

But darkness was coming now, and I was limp with hunger. I didn't fancy another night on the mountain. So I thought I'd better follow the road and see where it led me, even if it meant a clash with the frontier guards. The track wound upwards for half a mile through a thicket of pine trees and presently emerged in a little clearing. I saw roof-tops, a church, and a cluster of village lights. Then I smelt hot butter, and knew I was still in France.

Except for a hobbled horse and a couple of snarling dogs, the village street was empty. The low wooden houses, crudely thatched with bracken, had a look of dark Siberian squalor; but half-way up the street I saw the lights of a café shining warmly through steamed-up windows. I pushed open the door and entered
 a noisy room full of little men in sheep's-wool

coats. But when they saw me they froze as though I'd let in a blast of snow, and their conversation switched off abruptly.

What rough beast was this slouching towards the bar, dressed in a blanket and crumpled hat, coming out of the night like some ghost of winter, his hair and eyebrows white with frost? Nobody moved or spoke, except the old woman behind the bar who bobbed quickly out of sight as I approached her, and whose place was immediately taken by a huge-bellied man who began setting up bottles like a defensive wall.

I asked if I could have something to eat, and he repeated the question to the room, then, after a pause, nodded to an empty table. I slumped down in the chair, and presently he brought me some soup, which seemed to be a mixture of tar and onions. As I ate, the men watched me – rows of bright little faces wrapped to the ears in their fleece-lined collars. Some quietly shuffled their dominoes, others winked cryptically at one another, all seemed to be waiting for something to happen.

At last a committee of three detached themselves from the rest and came over and sat at my table. They were low-voiced and confidential, and one of them offered me a cigarette. I didn't have to answer, but they'd rather like to know: what exactly was I doing here? I'd come from Perpignan, hadn't I? I'd been seen there several times recently; also down in Ceret, a couple of days ago. It was hard on the mountain at this time of the year. I mustn't mind their curiosity.

They were a strange little trio but seemed harmless enough. One of them wore the look of a sleepy clown; the other had a Karl Marx beard, extravagantly bushy and white; the third was thin, like a weathered pole. But the warmth of the room, the soup, and their polite concern encouraged me to take a chance. I told them I

 was on my way to the 'south'. I had friends

there, I said – I wanted to join them, that was all. They asked a few more questions, then the fat clown smiled. 'Well, since you've got this far . . .' he said. He called for some brandy and poured me a glass. 'Drink it up, man. You're going to need it.'

I was lucky. It might just as easily have gone the other way, with an ignominious return to Perpignan. But it seemed I'd fallen on my feet among the very men who could help me: a cosy community of frontier anarchists. I don't know why they decided to trust me, or why they thought me worth the trouble, but clearly they'd made up their minds. The men put their heads together and held a brief discussion, then the thin one looked at his watch and nodded. 'It'll take us an hour,' he said, 'so as soon as you're ready. Better go before the moon comes up.'

He rose to his feet and wrapped a scarf round his long thin neck as though he was lagging a water pipe. The others helped me on with my bags and I was given some more brandy for the journey. The proprietor refused to be paid for the soup. Then the thin man said 'Come', and pushed open the door to admit a flurry of powdered snow, and we left the café to a murmur of benevolent farewells and a flourish of political salutes.

Once in the street, my companion glanced quickly at the sky, put out his cigarette, and rolled up his collar. 'Stay close, and say nothing,' he muttered briefly, then shot off up a narrow lane. I hurried after him, and we were out of the village immediately, climbing a steep and brutish path. The man raced on ahead of me, taking little goat-like leaps and dodging nimbly from rock to rock. I could see his tall gaunt figure bouncing against the hazy stars. He never bothered to check that I was still behind him.

 Easy enough for him, I thought: he was built

for these mountains while I'd been raised on very low hills. His legs were long and mine were short – I was also carrying a twenty-pound load. I did my best to keep with him but he soon outstripped me and I started to fall farther and farther back. I wanted to shout, 'Wait a minute!' but it didn't seem to be the thing to do. Instead, I began to indulge in a bit of carefree whistling.

That stopped him in the end. I found him perched on a rock waiting impatiently for me to catch up. 'Stop whistling,' he growled. 'Save it for the other side. This is no time for trivialities.' At least I was grateful for the halt, and the conversation. I asked him if he did this often. I must be mad, he said; it was the very first time, and by God he was sorry already.

He started climbing again while I went panting behind him, sweat trickling down my arms and legs. Brittle gusts of dry snow swept by on the wind, striking the face like handfuls of rice.

I felt engulfed by a contest that was growing too large for me; something I'd asked for but doubted that I could carry through. My companion ignored this, pushing ahead more relentlessly than ever, as though wishing to put me to the final test. That last half-hour was perhaps the worst I've known, casually unprepared as I was; ill-shod, badly clothed, and lumbered with junk, clawing my way up these icy slopes.

The point of collapse must have been near, but luckily I escaped it, for at last we reached the top of the rise. We were in a narrow pass flanked by slabs of rock which stood metallic and blue in the starlight. I seemed to sense a change in the air, a curious lifting of pressure before me as though some great obstacle had been rolled away. There was also a faint smell of charcoal, woodsmoke, and mules, and an indefinable whiff of pepper. My guide drew me into the shadows and gestured me to silence, sticking out his neck and sniffing the sky. We crouched in the darkness listening. We heard the wind, falling water, and what sounded like a distant gunshot.

'This is where I leave you,' said the Frenchman. He appeared a little more cheerful now. 'The frontier is between those rocks. Follow the path for half a kilometre and you'll come to a little farm. Knock on the door and you'll be among your friends.'

Suddenly it seemed too simple – after weeks of speculation and doubt, and these last two exhausting days – just a gap in the rocks a few hundred yards ahead of me, the tiny frontier between peace and war.

'Move slow and easy. There may be a few guards about but they shouldn't be too lively on a night like this. If you're challenged, drop everything and run like hell. Good luck, then; I can do no more.'

But there was no opposition. I just walked

towards the rocks and slipped between them as though on an evening stroll. A narrow path led downwards among the boulders. Then, after about half a kilometre, just as the Frenchman had said, I saw a little farmhouse and knocked on the door. It was opened by a young man with a rifle who held up a lantern to my face. I noticed he was wearing the Republican armband.

'I've come to join you,' I said.

'*Pase usted*,' he answered.

I was back in Spain, with a winter of war before me.

II

The young man slung his rifle over his shoulder and motioned me to enter the hut. A dark passage led to a smoky room. Inside, in a group, stood an old man and woman, another youth with a gun, and a gaunt little girl about eleven years old. They were huddled together like a family photograph fixing me with glassy teeth-set smiles. There was a motionless silence while they took me in – seeing a young tattered stranger, coatless and soaked to the knees, carrying a kit-bag from which a violin bow protruded. Suddenly the old woman said 'Ay!' and beckoned me to the fire, which was piled high with glowing pine cones.

I crouched, thawing out by the choking fumes, sensing deeply this moment of arrival.

I felt it first when threading through the high rocks of the frontier, when, almost by pressures in the atmosphere, and the changes of sound and scent, a great door seemed to close behind me, shutting off entirely the country I'd left; and then, as the southern Pyrenees fell away at my feet, this new one opened, with a rush of raw air, admitting all the scarred differences and immensities of Spain. At my back was the tang of Gauloises and slumberous sauces, scented flesh and opulent farmlands; before me, still ghostly, was all I remembered – the whiff of rags and woodsmoke, the salt of dried fish, sour wine and sickness, stone and thorn, old horses and rotting leather.

'Will you eat?' asked the woman.

'Don't be mad,' said her husband.

He cleared part of the table, and the old woman gave me a spoon and a plate. At the other end the little girl was cleaning a gun,
 frowning, tongue out, as though doing her

homework. An old black cooking-pot hung over the smouldering pine cones, from which the woman ladled me out some soup. It was hot, though thin, a watery mystery that might have been the tenth boiling of the bones of a hare. As I ate, my clothes steaming, shivering and warming up, the boys knelt by the doorway, hugging their rifles and watching me. Everybody watched me except for the gun-cleaning girl who was intent on more urgent matters. But I could not, from my appearance, offer much of a threat, save for the mysterious bundle I carried. Even so, the first suspicious silence ended; a light joky whispering seemed to fill the room.

'What are you?'

'I'm English.'

'Ah, yes – he's English.'

They nodded to each other with grave politeness.

'And how did you come here perhaps?'

'I came over the mountain.'

'Yes, he walked over the mountain . . . on foot.'

They were all round me at the table now as I ate my soup, all pulling at their eyes and winking, nodding delightedly and repeating everything I said, as though humouring a child just learning to speak.

'He's come to join us,' said one of the youths; and that set them off again, and even the girl lifted her gaunt head and simpered. But I was pleased too, pleased that I managed to get here so easily after two days' wandering among peaks and blizzards. I was here now with friends. Behind me was peace-engorged France. The people in the kitchen were a people stripped for war – the men smoking beech leaves, the soup reduced to near water; around us hand-grenades hanging on the walls like strings of onions; muskets and cartridge-belts piled in the corner, and open orange-boxes packed with sil-

 ver bullets like fish. War was still so local then,

it was like stepping into another room. And this was what I had come to re-visit. But I was now awash with sleep, hearing the blurred murmuring of voices and feeling the rocks of Spain under my feet. The men's eyes grew narrower, watching the unexpected stranger, and his lumpy belongings drying by the fire. Then the old woman came and took me by the elbow and led me upstairs and one of the boys followed close behind. I was shown into a small windowless room of bare white-washed stone containing a large iron bed smothered with goatskins. I lay down exhausted, and the old woman put an oil lamp on the floor, placed a cold hand on my brow, and left me with a gruff good-night. The room had no door, just an opening in the wall, and the boy stretched himself languidly across the threshold. He lay on his side, his chin resting on the stock of his gun, watching me with large black unblinking eyes. As I slipped into sleep I remembered I had left all my baggage downstairs; but it didn't seem to matter now.

I was awoken early next morning by the two armed brothers who were dressed for outdoors in ponchos of rabbit skin. They gave me a bucket of snow to wash in, then led me gingerly downstairs and sat me on a stool where the old lady poured me some coffee. The little girl, her hair brushed and shining already, was fitting ammunition into cartridge-belts. As I drank my coffee – which tasted of rusty buttons – she looked at me with radiant shyness.

'He came over the mountains,' she said perkily, nodding to herself.

The boys giggled, and the old man coughed.

They brought me my baggage and helped me sling it over my shoulders, and told me that a horse and cart were waiting for me outside.

'They sent it up from the town specially. They didn't want to keep you hanging about

. . . Well, not after you came all that way to join us.'

The boys half-marched me into the lane and the rest of the family followed and stood watching, blowing on their purple fingers. The old woman and child had bright shawls on their heads, while, for some reason, the old man wore a tall top hat.

The cart waiting in the lane resembled a rough-looking tumbril, and the driver had a cavernous, nervous face. 'Vamanos, vamanos, vamanos,' he kept muttering plaintively, giving me glances of sharp distaste.

The boys helped me into the back of the cart and climbed up after me.

'Here he is. The English one,' they said with ponderous jocularity.

The driver sniffed, and uncoiled his whip.

'Horse and cart,' said one of the brothers, nudging me smartly. 'We've got to save your legs. They must be half destroyed with all this walking over mountains. And what have we got if we haven't got your legs? You wouldn't be much use to us, would you?'

I was beginning to get a bit bored with all this levity, and sat there silent and shivering. The boys perched close beside me, one on each side, holding their guns at the ready, like sentries. Every so often they pointed them at me and nodded brightly. They appeared to be in a state of nervous high spirits. 'Vamanos!' snarled the driver, and shook up the reins crossly. The old man and his wife raised their hands solemnly and told me to go with God. The little girl threw a stone at the horse, or it may have been at me, but it hit the horse and caused it to start with a jerk. So we began to lumber and creak down the steep rocky lane, the brothers now holding me by either elbow. The Pyrenees stood high behind us, white and hard, their peaks colouring to the rising sun.
 The boys nodded towards them, grinning,

nudging me sharply again, and baring their chestnut-tinted teeth.

Through the iced winter morning, slipping over glassy rocks, we made our stumbling way down the valley, passing snow-covered villages, empty and bare, from which all life and sound seemed withdrawn. This chilling silence was surely not one of nature, which could be broken by a goat-bell or the chirp of a bird. It was as if a paralysing pestilence had visited the place, and I was to notice it on a number of occasions in the weeks to come. It was simply the stupefying numbness of war.

After an hour or so we came to a small hill town still shuttered by the shadow of rocks. A bent woman crept by, bearing a great load of firewood. A cat shot through a hole in a wall. I noticed that the brothers had suddenly grown tense and anxious, sitting straight as pillars, thin-lipped, beside me. Two militiamen, in khaki ponchos, came out of a doorway and marched ahead of us down the street. Even our driver perked up and began to look around him with what appeared to be an air of importance. The militiamen led us into the square, to the dilapidated Town Hall, from which the Republican flag was hanging. The brothers called out to a couple of sentries who were sitting on the steps, and one of them got up and went inside. Now for a proper welcome, I thought. I got down from the cart, and the brothers followed. Then four soldiers came out with fixed bayonets.

'We've brought you the spy,' said the brothers, and pushed me forward. The soldiers closed round me and handcuffed my wrists.

They put me in a cellar and left me for two days. I got a kind of soup the first day, and they forgot me the next – waiting and forgetting being just another part of the war. It was damp and very cold, the walls of the cellar limed with ice like spidery veins of lace. But luckily I'd been toughened up by the cottage bedrooms of home where the water in wash-basins froze solid in winter. The cell had a curious, narrow, coffin-like shape, and even had iron rings round the walls as though to lift it up from inside. There was one dim, yellow-coloured light-bulb hanging from the ceiling, but no furniture; I slept on the rocky floor.

Lying there, shivering, unvisited, well on into the third day, I was wondering idly what now might happen. This was not, after all, quite what I had expected. I had walked into a country at war uninvited and unannounced, and had found no comradely welcome, only suspicion and silence. I am surprised now how little surprised I was then, but I was soon to learn how natural this was.

Captain Perez was again not what I'd expected. He came for me in the late afternoon of the third day, opening my cellar door with a light whispering key. No whiskered revolutionary he, but a slim tailored dandy, a smart gleaming figure in elegantly belted uniform, and with riding boots so glazed and polished his legs appeared to be chocolate-coated. He smiled at me from the doorway, and held out a tin mug of coffee.

'Are you rested?' he asked, in a soft furry voice.

I took the coffee and drank it, hunched up on the floor, while he fetched in two chairs and placed them facing each other.

'Please sit down,' he said gently. 'Or, rather, stand up and sit down.' And he gave a sharp little affected laugh.

The officer seemed to have sleepy eyes and a lazy manner, but once seated in front of me his attitude became abrupt and clinical. How, where and why had I come to Spain? When I told him, he shook his head sadly.

 'No, señor! Not over the Pyrenees. Not with

all that circus equipment you were carrying. Books, cameras – and a violin, dear Jesus.' He laid a delicate warm hand on my knee. 'You know what we think, young friend? Not over the mountains – no. You came from the sea. You were landed by boat or submarine. From Bremen, was it? You mustn't be surprised that we know all this. We even know what you've come to do.'

He smiled with cream-faced satisfaction, shaking his head against my denials and explanations, and giving my knee another squeeze.

'But, comrade,' I said.

'Captain Perez,' he corrected.

'If you don't believe me, you've got my passport.'

'We've got dozens, dear boy. All of them phonies. And we've got an office that turns out twenty a day.' He looked at me solemnly. 'It was the violin that did it. And the German accent. You would never fool anyone, you know.'

He rose and went to the door, and clapped his hands. There was a heavy marching of feet. The four guards I'd seen earlier came tumbling into the cellar, so wrapped up there was scarcely space for the lot of us. But they circled me close in a friendly manner, trying to keep their bayonets out of each other's eyes.

'Go with them,' said the officer. 'They'll look after you.' And he stepped back into the passage to make room. As we went past him, he snapped a salute in farewell – shining, oiled and immaculate, the last of his kind I was to see in that war.

The guards marched me out into the courtyard and it was night already, with a freezing moon in the sky. The town was empty and silent, dark and shuttered, not even a child or dog could be heard. My guards clumped beside me, jogging me along by the elbows, relaxed now, puffing and whistling. They were all rather short, like Tartars; vapour billowed from their nostrils. The shortest one spun his rifle and grinned up in my face. 'Well,' he said. 'You come a long way to see us. Over the mountains? That's what we hear.' 'That's right,' I said. 'Well, we're nearly there,' he said. 'You won't have to march around much longer.'

Truly we didn't go far – down a short alley and into a rough moonlit scrapyard – till we came to a hole in the ground. The men cleared the snow round the edge, and raised a metal cover, and into the dark cavity they dropped me. It was not very deep – about six to eight feet, narrow, and walled with rock. 'Good-night, Rubio,' they called. 'Warmer down there than on the mountain tops. In this weather, you understand?' They lowered the iron cover over my head and secured it with heavy bolts. Then I heard them stamping away in the snow, and I was alone again.

The hole was wider at the bottom than at the top, and I curled up on some damp, mouldy straw. The darkness was absolute; I couldn't even see the stars through the grille. Drawing up my knees to my chin, and blowing on my fingers, I now began to consider my position. I was still not altogether surprised at what was happening to me. Indeed, I was letting it happen without question or protest. But since my arrival in Spain something quite unexpected had taken over, and I don't think I realized at that stage how sinister it might be, or what grave peril I had got myself into.

I knew I was not the only one to have wandered over the frontier to join the Republicans. There must have been other volunteers who arrived alone – but were they then always dropped into dark little holes like this? Could it be some sort of discipline to test us out, to prove our loyalty of mind?

I was cold and hungry now, and in this black

icy silence I began to get a sharpening taste of danger. No, thought I, this was clearly not a normal reception. The first two shivering days in the Town Hall cell may simply have been a matter of form. But then to have been cast headlong into this medieval pit seemed to suggest that I'd been picked out for something special.

But still my situation didn't disturb me too much, but rather injected me with a sharp sting of adventure. I was at that flush of youth which never doubts self-survival, that idiot belief in luck and a uniquely charmed life, without which illusion few wars would be possible. I felt the seal of fate on me, and a certain grim intoxication, alone in this buried silence. But macabre as things were, I had no idea then how very near to death I was . . .

It may have been a couple of days, or but a few hours, later that I heard the shuffle of returning feet overhead. The iron cover was removed; I saw a brief flash of stars, and another prisoner was dropped into the hole beside me. ‘Now you’ve got a committee!’ a voice called down, and the cover was lowered and bolted and the shuffling feet went away.

We stood close together in the darkness, each other’s prisoner now, and twin gaolers, in this tomb of rock. ‘They sent this for you,’ he said, and his hands found me blindly, and I took the hard piece of broken bread. There was just room for both of us if we lay down together; I couldn’t see him but at least the air grew warmer. For about a week we shared this black cave together, visited only at night by the guards overhead, who unbolted the manhole and briefly raised it while they lowered us bread, watered wine, and a bucket.

Strange being huddled so close and for so long to another human being whose face one was unable to see. I knew him to be young by

his voice and breath and the chance touch of

his hand when sharing food or wine. He also had a fresh wild smell about him, an outdoor smell, a mixture of pine and olives. I remember we slept a good deal, prey to an extraordinary lassitude, and, in the intervals, we talked. He was a deserter, he said; and seemed quite cheerful about it, laughing at the looking-glass differences between us. I was trying to get into the war, and he was trying to get out of it, and here we were, stuffed into the same black hole. I'd come over the mountains from France, and he'd been caught going the other way, and most certainly now, he said, we'd both be shot.

And why not, indeed? The deserter appeared quite fatalistic about it. Patiently, drowsily, with no complaint or self-pity, my companion explained the situation to me. The Civil War was eighteen months old, and entering a bitter winter. The Republican forces were in retreat and could afford to take no chances. Franco's rebels were better armed, and had powerful allies abroad, while our side had few weapons, few friends, almost no food, and had learned to trust no one but the dead. What could you expect them to do with a couple of doubtful characters like us? They couldn't afford to keep us, feed us, or even turn us loose. Even less could they afford the luxury of a trial. So it was thought safer, and quicker, that anyone under suspicion be shot, and this was being done regretfully as a matter of course.

My companion was called Dino, he said, and he was twenty-two years old, and he came from a little village in the Guadarramas. When his village had been burned by the Moors, in the early days, he'd run with his younger brother through the lines and become a dynamiter. They'd worked alone, and he'd seen his brother blown up when some of the fuses went wrong. He'd fought at Guadalajara, but didn't like that kind of warfare – mostly hanging about in ditches, then massacre and panic – so he'd taken off again and headed north for France. He'd been picked up twice, and had twice got away, but he reckoned they'd collared him now for good. He knew what to expect, yes sir. He'd seen quite a number of prisoners and deserters shot, and spoke of the Republicans' methods of execution – casual, informal, often good-humoured. Locked in the dark with Dino, and listening to him describe these scenes in his soft, joky voice, I drew steadily, as I thought, towards my hour, and wondered which of the two of us would be called out first.

When it came, it came suddenly, with us both half-asleep, the iron trap-door above raised with a swift muted action, and a low voice calling the young deserter's name, giving us just time enough for a quick fumbling handshake.

As they raised Dino towards the opening he lifted his arms, and I saw his face in a brief glimmer of moonlight. It was thin and hollow, his eyes huge and glowing, his long pointed countenance like an El Greco saint ascending. Finally two dark shapes pulled him through the narrow entrance, and the manhole was lowered again. I heard the clink of glasses, some moments of casual chatter, Dino's short laugh, then a pistol shot . . .

I'd been standing propped against the wall and listening, and now that it was over I slumped back on the straw. My hand touched the deserter's forage-cap, which he'd left behind. It was damp with sweat and still warm from his head.

A few days later, in the red light of dawn, the grille was dragged open and a voice called, 'Hey, Rubio! . . .' Arms reached down to help me, hands caught my wrists, and I was lifted bodily out of the sepulchre.

 My legs were shaking, but I put this down

to two weeks without exercise; and the dawn light stung my eyes. Was it my turn now? The courtyard glittered with snow; and the hurried preparations which I'd expected – the chair, the hand-cart, the plain wooden box, the sleepy officer with the bottle of coñac, the ragged soldiers lined up and looking at their feet – all were present. But not for me. Another young man sat bound to the chair, smoking furiously and chattering like a parrot.

But I was guided quickly across the yard and out into the lane, where two armed guards stood waiting beside a black battered car. They pushed me into the back seat and sat one on each side of me. A broad man in a hat sat up in front by the driver.

We drove fast and silently through the hunched unhappy town and out into the empty country. We climbed a poor bumpy road on to a desolate plateau across which the wind swept pink ruffles of snow. A plateau of scattered rock and thorn, and a few bent bushes, and the wide winter sky closing in.

It became hot and airless in the car, and the guards, in their heavy brown overcoats, began to steam like sweating horses. Their nostrils steamed too, and their noses shone, and dripped on the bayonets held between their knees.

They were an odd-looking couple, the guards – one small and clownlike, with bright blue chin, the other pink and chubby, a mother's boy. I tried to talk to them, but they wouldn't answer; though one whistled knowingly between his teeth. We drove fast, swaying together on the curves, along a road that was both empty and drear.

Where were we going, and what was in store for me? In spite of the guards' silence, I felt I knew this already. Something irrevocable had taken charge which could neither be reversed nor halted, some mad scrambling of language and understanding which had already misjudged my naïve reasons for being here. I didn't realize then how normal it was for anyone, if put through the right preliminaries, to be swamped by guilt.

Since my sudden arrest and imprisonment, which at first I'd been ready to accept as some light charade touched with military confusion, I felt myself sinking, more and more, into the hands of some obscure accusation against which I ceased to look for an answer.

As the sun rose higher and whitened the rocks, the landscape turned blank, as though over-exposed. And with the whistling guards on each side of me, and the bully-shouldered officer up front, I was sure I was on the road to my doom. As my eyes grew used to the light – after all, I'd been two weeks in darkness – I saw the landscape shudder into shape, grow even more desolate and brutal. Yet never more precious as it floated past me, the worn-out skin of this irreplaceable world, marked here and there by the scribbled signs of man, a broken thatched cabin, or a terraced slope. Every breath I took now seemed rich and stolen, in spite of the oil-fumed heat in the car. Even the two armed guards, grotesque and scruffy as they were, began to take on the power and beauty of fates, protectors or destroyers, who held one's thread of life in their hands.

We'd been driving, I guessed, for about an hour, when the officer suddenly straightened up and snapped his fingers, and we pulled off the road and stopped. The dead icy tableland crept with yellow mist, and seemed quite empty save for a clump of trees in the distance. I was ordered out of the car, one of the guards stuck a gun in my back, pointed to the trees and said, 'March!'

Why had they brought me all this way, I wondered. They could have done the job more snugly back in the jail. Yet the place seemed apt and fitting enough; no doubt they'd used it before. The officer was out of the car now, coughing and spitting, and he came and gave my shoulder a light little shove. 'Come on, Rubio,' he said. 'Come on, march – let's go.' So I put up my head and marched . . .

I saw the vast cold sky and the stony plain and I began to walk towards the distant trees. I heard the soldiers behind me slip the bolts on their rifles. This then, of course, could be the chosen place – the plateau ringed by rock, the late dawn on our breath, the empty silence around us, the little wood ahead, all set for quiet execution or murder. I felt the sharp edges of the stones under my thin-soled shoes. The guards behind me shuttled the bolts of their guns.

If my moment was coming – and I now felt certain it was – I told myself not to look back. My intentions were simple. If they gave me enough time, and I was able to reach the little wood ahead of them, that would be my last chance – and I'd make a break for it. The nearest wind-bent tree looked a thousand years old, its roots pouring over the rocks like wax. The guards were snuffling behind me. Would I reach it before they fired? Would I hear the blast before the thumping bullets hit me? Would I hear anything before the dark? I walked slowly, almost mincingly, trying not to appear to hurry. I reached the trees and prepared to run . . .

One of the guards came up behind me and took my arm. 'OK, Rubio,' he said. 'Sit down.' His comrade was already squatting under a tree and opening a tin of sardines with his bayonet. The officer and driver joined us, yawning and scratching, and we sat down in a circle together. They gave me sardines and some bread, and passed round a bottle of coñac, and as I looked at the food in my hand, and at the raw, safe landscape around me, I was seized by a brief spasm of uncontrollable happiness.

The soldiers stretched out their legs and began talking about football. The officer brushed down his clothes and rolled me a cigarette. He waved his hand at the scenery, the old trees and the rocks, and said it was his favourite spot for a picnic. They came here, he said, about twice a week. I asked him where we were going now.

'To Figueras, of course,' he said. They were going to drop me off at the barracks. 'We thought you'd rather ride than walk.'

But he was still responsible for me, he said, if I liked to think of it that way. But only till they'd delivered me to Brigade Headquarters, then he'd be clear of me. He looked at me oddly with his hazed, blue eyes, slightly mad, amused yet cold.

Why hadn't he explained all this before? The car, the armed guards, the remote stop in the hills. Had this been another test, or some daft Spanish joke? Was he really as harmless as he appeared to be? Would he have been equally amused if I'd made that dash through the trees? There's no doubt what would have happened then.

PENGUIN 60s

ISABEL ALLENDE · *Voices in My Ear*
NICHOLSON BAKER · *Playing Trombone*
LINDSEY BAREHAM · *The Little Book of Big Soups*
KAREN BLIXEN · *From the Ngong Hills*
DIRK BOGARDE · *Coming of Age*
ANTHONY BURGESS · *Childhood*
ANGELA CARTER · *Lizzie Borden*
CARLOS CASTANEDA · *The Sorcerer's Ring of Power*
ELIZABETH DAVID · *Peperonata and Other Italian Dishes*
RICHARD DAWKINS · *The Pocket Watchmaker*
GERALD DURRELL · *The Pageant of Fireflies*
RICHARD ELLMANN · *The Trial of Oscar Wilde*
EPICURUS · *Letter on Happiness*
MARIANNE FAITHFULL · *Year One*
KEITH FLOYD · *Hot and Spicy Floyd*
ALEXANDER FRATER · *Where the Dawn Comes Up Like Thunder*
ESTHER FREUD · *Meeting Bilal*
JOHN KENNETH GALBRAITH · *The Culture of Contentment*
ROB GRANT AND DOUG NAYLOR · *Scenes from the Dwarf*
ROBERT GRAVES · *The Gods of Olympus*
JANE GRIGSON · *Puddings*
SOPHIE GRIGSON · *From Sophie's Table*
KATHARINE HEPBURN · *Little Me*
SUSAN HILL · *The Badness Within Him*
ALAN HOLLINGHURST · *Adventures Underground*
BARRY HUMPHRIES · *Less is More Please*
HOWARD JACOBSON · *Expulsion from Paradise*
P. D. JAMES · *The Girl Who Loved Graveyards*
STEPHEN KING · *Umney's Last Case*
LAO TZU · *Tao Te Ching*
DAVID LEAVITT · *Chips Is Here*

PENGUIN 60s

LAURIE LEE · *To War in Spain*
PATRICK LEIGH FERMOR · *Loose as the Wind*
ELMORE LEONARD · *Trouble at Rindo's Station*
DAVID LODGE · *Surprised by Summer*
BERNARD MAC LAVERTY · *The Miraculous Candidate*
SHENA MACKAY · *Cloud-Cuckoo-Land*
NORMAN MAILER · *The Dressing Room*
PETER MAYLE · *Postcards from Summer*
JAN MORRIS · *Scenes from Havian Life*
BLAKE MORRISON · *Camp Cuba*
VLADIMIR NABOKOV · *Now Remember*
REDMOND O'HANLON · *A River in Borneo*
STEVEN PINKER · *Thinking in Tongues*
CRAIG RAINE · *Private View*
CLAUDIA RODEN · *Ful Medames and Other Vegetarian Dishes*
HELGE RUBINSTEIN · *Chocolate Parfait*
SIMON SCHAMA · *The Taking of the Bastille*
WILL SELF · *The Rock of Crack As Big As the Ritz*
MARK SHAND · *Elephant Tales*
NIGEL SLATER · *30-Minute Suppers*
RICK STEIN · *Fresh from the Sea*
LYTTON STRACHEY · *Florence Nightingale*
PAUL THEROUX · *Slow Trains to Simla*
COLIN THUBRON · *Samarkand*
MARK TULLY · *Beyond Purdah*
LAURENS VAN DER POST · *Merry Christmas, Mr Lawrence*
MARGARET VISSER · *More than Meets the Eye*
GAVIN YOUNG · *Something of Samoa*

and

Thirty Obituaries from Wisden · SELECTED BY MATTHEW ENGEL

READ MORE IN PENGUIN

For complete information about books available from Penguin and how to order them, please write to us at the appropriate address below. Please note that for copyright reasons the selection of books varies from country to country.

IN THE UNITED KINGDOM: Please write to *Dept. EP, Penguin Books Ltd, Bath Road, Harmondsworth, Middlesex UB7 ODA.*

IN THE UNITED STATES: Please write to *Consumer Sales, Penguin USA, P.O. Box 999, Dept. 17109, Bergenfield, New Jersey 07621-0120.* VISA and MasterCard holders call 1-800-253-6476 to order Penguin titles.

IN CANADA: Please write to *Penguin Books Canada Ltd, 10 Alcorn Avenue, Suite 300, Toronto, Ontario M4V 3B2.*

IN AUSTRALIA: Please write to *Penguin Books Australia Ltd, P.O. Box 257, Ringwood, Victoria 3134.*

IN NEW ZEALAND: Please write to *Penguin Books (NZ) Ltd, Private Bag 102902, North Shore Mail Centre, Auckland 10.*

IN INDIA: Please write to *Penguin Books India Pvt Ltd, 706 Eros Apartments, 56 Nehru Place, New Delhi 110 019.*

IN THE NETHERLANDS: Please write to *Penguin Books Netherlands bv, Postbus 3507, NL-1001 AH Amsterdam.*

IN GERMANY: Please write to *Penguin Books Deutschland GmbH, Metzlerstrasse 26, 60594 Frankfurt am Main.*

IN SPAIN: Please write to *Penguin Books S. A., Bravo Murillo 19, 1° B, 28015 Madrid.*

IN ITALY: Please write to *Penguin Italia s.r.l., Via Felice Casati 20, I-20124 Milano.*

IN FRANCE: Please write to *Penguin France S. A., 17 rue Lejeune, F-31000 Toulouse.*

IN JAPAN: Please write to *Penguin Books Japan, Ishikiribashi Building, 2-5-4, Suido, Bunkyo-ku, Tokyo 112.*

IN GREECE: Please write to *Penguin Hellas Ltd, Dimocritou 3, GR-106 71 Athens.*

IN SOUTH AFRICA: Please write to *Longman Penguin Southern Africa (Pty) Ltd, Private Bag X08, Bertsham 2013.*

PAUL

THEROUX

SLOW TRAINS TO SIMLA

PENGUIN BOOKS

PENGUIN BOOKS

Published by the Penguin Group. Penguin Books Ltd, 27 Wrights Lane, London W8 5TZ, England. Penguin Books USA Inc., 375 Hudson Street, New York, New York 10014, USA. Penguin Books Australia Ltd, Ringwood, Victoria, Australia. Penguin Books Canada Ltd, 10 Alcorn Avenue, Toronto, Ontario, Canada M4V 3B2. Penguin Books (NZ) Ltd, 182–190 Wairau Road, Auckland 10, New Zealand · Penguin Books Ltd, Registered Offices: Harmondsworth, Middlesex, England · These extracts are from *The Great Railway Bazaar*, by Paul Theroux, published in Penguin Books 1977. This edition published 1996. · Typeset by Rowland Phototypesetting Ltd, Bury St Edmunds, Suffolk. Printed in England by Clays Ltd, St Ives plc · · 10 9 8 7 6 5 4 3 2 1

CONTENTS

The Khyber Mail to Lahore Junction

Rashid, the conductor on the sleeping car, helped me find my compartment, and after a moment's hesitation he asked me to have a look at his tooth. It was giving him aches, he said. The request was not impertinent. I had told him I was a dentist. I was getting tired of the Asiatic inquisition: Where do you come from? What do you do? Married or single? Any children? This nagging made me evasive, secretive, foolish, an inventor of cock-and-bull stories. Rashid made the bed and then opened up, tugging his lip down to show me a canine gnawed with decay.

'You'd better see a dentist in Karachi,' I said. 'In the meantime chew your food on the other side.'

Satisfied with my advice (and I also gave him two aspirins), he said, 'You will be very comfortable here. German carriage, about fifteen years old. Heavy, you see, so no shaking.'

It had not taken long to find my compartment. Only three were occupied – the other two by army officers – and my name was on the door, printed large on a label. Now I could tell on entering a train what sort of a journey it would be. The feeling I had on the Khyber Mail was slight disappointment that the trip would be so short – only twelve hours to Lahore. I wished it were longer: I had everything I needed. The compartment was large, well lighted, and comfortable, with a toilet and sink in an adjoining room; I had a drop-leaf table, well-upholstered seat, mirror, ashtray, chrome gin-bottle holder, the works. I was alone. But if I wished to have company I could stroll to the dining car or idle in the passage with the army officers. Nothing is expected of the train passenger. In planes the traveller is condemned to hours in a tight seat; ships require high spirits and sociability; cars and buses are unspeakable. The sleeping car is the most painless form of travel. In *Ordered South*, Robert Louis Stevenson writes,

Herein, I think, is the chief attraction of railway travel. The speed is so easy, and the train disturbs so little the scenes through which it takes us, that our heart becomes full of the placidity and stillness of the country; and while the body is being borne forward in the flying chain of carriages, the thoughts alight, as the humour moves them, at unfrequented stations . . .

The romance associated with the sleeping car derives from its extreme privacy, combining the best features of a cupboard with forward movement. Whatever drama is being enacted in this moving bedroom is heightened by the landscape passing the window: a swell of hills, the surprise of mountains, the loud metal bridge, or the melancholy sight of people standing under yellow lamps. And the notion of travel as a continuous vision, a grand tour's succession of memorable images across a curved earth – with none of the distorting emptiness of air or sea – is possible only on a train. A train is a vehicle that allows residence: dinner in the diner, nothing could be finer.

'What time does the Khyber Mail get to Karachi?'

'Timetable says seven-fifteen in the night,' said Rashid. 'But we will be five and a half hours late.'

'Why?' I asked.

'We are always five and a half hours late. It is the case.'

I slept well and was awakened at six the following

morning by a Sikh with a steel badge pinned to his turban that read *Pakistan Western Railways.* His right eye was milky with trachoma.

'You wanting breakfast?'

I said yes.

'I coming seven o'clock.'

He brought an omelette, tea, and toast, and for the next half-hour I sprawled, reading Chekhov's wonderful story 'Ariadne' and finishing my tea. Then I snapped up the shade and flooded the compartment with light. In brilliant sunshine we were passing rice fields and stagnant pools full of white lotuses and standing herons. Farther on, at a small tree, we startled a pair of pistachio-green parrots; they flew up, getting greener as they rose. Looking out a train window in Asia is like watching an unedited travelogue without the obnoxious soundtrack; I had to guess at the purpose of activities – people patting pie-shaped turds and slapping them on to the side of a mud hut to dry; men with bullocks and submerged ploughs, preparing a rice field for planting; and at Badami Bagh, just outside Lahore, a town of grass huts, cardboard shelters, pup tents, and hovels of paper, twigs, and cloth, everyone was in motion – sorting fruit, folding clothes, fanning the fire, shooing a dog away, mending a roof. It is the industry of the poor in the morning, so busy they look hopeful, but it is deceptive. The position of their settlement gives them away; this is the extreme of poverty, the shantytown by the railway tracks.

The shantytown had another witness: a tall thin Indian of about twenty, with long hair, stood at the corridor window. He asked me the time; his London accent was unmistakable. I asked him where he was headed.

'India. I was born in Bombay, but I left when I was three or four. Still, I'm an Indian right the way through.'

'But you were brought up in England.'

'Yeah. I've got a British passport too. I didn't want to get one, after all they did to me. But an Indian passport is too much trouble. See, I want to go to Germany eventually – they're in the Common Market. It's easy with a British passport.'

'Why not stay in London?'

'You can stay in London if you like. They're all racialists. It starts when you're about ten years old, and that's all you hear – wog, nigger, blackie. There's nothing you can do about it. At school it's really terrible – ever hear about Paki-bashing? And I'm not even a Pakistani. They don't know the difference. But they're cowards. When I'm with me mate no one comes up and says nothing, but lots of times about ten blokes would start trouble with me. I hate them, I'm glad to be here.'

'This is Pakistan.'

'Same thing. Everyone's the same colour.'

'Not really,' I said.

'More or less,' he said. 'I can relax here – I'm free.'

'Won't you feel rather anonymous?'

'The first thing I'm going to do in India is get a haircut; then no one will know.'

It seemed a cruel fate. He spoke no Indian language, his parents were dead, and he was not quite sure how to get to Bombay, where he had some distant relatives who seldom replied to letters unless he enclosed money. He was one of those colonial anomalies, more English than he cared to admit, but uneasy in the only country he understood.

'In England they were always staring at me. I hated it.'

'I get stared at here,' I said.

 'How do *you* like it?' I could see he was reproaching me with my colour; after all, he was almost home.

I said, 'I rather enjoy it.'

'Sahib.' It was Rashid, with my suitcase. 'We are approaching.'

'He calls you sahib,' said the Indian. He looked disgusted. 'He's afraid of you, that's why.'

'Sahib,' said Rashid. But he was speaking to the Indian. 'Now, please show me your ticket.'

The Indian was travelling second class. Rashid evicted him from first as the train drew in.

At Lahore Junction I stepped out (Rashid was at my side apologizing for the train's being late) into a city that was familiar: it matched a stereotype in my memory. My image of the Indian city derives from Kipling, and it was in Lahore that Kipling came of age as a writer. Exaggerating the mobs, the vicious bazaar, the colour and confusion, the Kipling of the early stories and *Kim* is really describing Lahore today, that side of it beyond the Mall where processions of rickshaws, pony carts, hawkers, and veiled women fill the narrow lanes and sweep you in their direction. The Anarkali Bazaar and the walled city, with its fort and mosques, have retained the distracted exoticism Kipling mentions, though now, with a hundred years of repetition, it is touched with horror.

'Bad girls here,' said the *tonga* driver when he dropped me in a seedy district of the old city; but I saw none, and nothing resembling a Lahore house. The absence of women in Pakistan, all those cruising males, had an odd effect on me. I found myself staring, with other similarly idle men, at garish pictures of film stars, and I began to think that the strictures of Islam would quickly make me a fancier of the margins of anatomy, thrilling at especially trim ankles, seeking a wink behind a veil, or watching for a response in the shoulders of one of those shrouded forms. Islam's denials seemed capable of turning the most normal soul into a foot fetishist, and as if to combat this the movie posters lampooned the erotic: fat girls in boots struggling helplessly with hairy, leering men; tormented women clutching their breasts, Anglo-Indians (regarded as 'fast') swinging their bums and crooning into microphones. The men in Lahore stroll with their eyes upturned to these cartoon fantasies.

'They invite you out to eat,' an American told
 me. This was at the spectacular fort, and we were

both admiring the small marble pavilion, called *Naulakha* (Kipling named his house outside Brattleboro, Vermont, after it, because it was so expensive to build: 'naulakha' means 900,000). The American was agitated. He said, 'You finish eating and they start eyeballing your chick. It's always your chick they're after. The chick's strung out. "Gee, Mohammed, why don't you have any pockets in your *dhoti*?" "We are not having any pockets, miss" – that kind of crap. One guy – this really pissed me off – he takes me aside and says, "*Five minutes! Five minutes!* That's all I want with her!" But would he let me have *his* chick for five minutes? You've gotta be joking.'

The order in Lahore is in the architecture, the moghul and colonial splendour. All around it are crowds of people and vehicles, and their dereliction makes the grandeur emphatic, as the cooking fat and cow-dung makes the smells of perfume and joss-sticks keener. To get to the Shalimar Gardens I had to pass through miles of congested streets of jostling people with the starved look of predators. I shouldered my way through the venereal township of Begampura; but inside the gardens it is peaceful, and though it has been stripped of its marble, and the reflecting pools are dark brown, the gardens have the order and shade – a sense of delicious refuge – that could not be very different from that imagined by Shah Jahan, when he laid them out in 1637. The pleasures of Lahore are old, and though one sees attempts everywhere, the Pakistanis have not yet succeeded in turning this beautiful city into a ruin.

Ramadhan continued, and the restaurants were either closed or on emergency rations, eggs and tea. So I was forced into an unwilling fast too, hoping it wouldn't drive me crazy as it manifestly did the Afghan and Pakistani. Instead of somnolence, hunger produced excitable, glassy-eyed individuals, some of whom quick-marched from alleyways to clutch my sleeve.

'Pot – hashish – LSD.'

'LSD?' I said. 'You sell LSD?'

'Yes, why not? You come to my place. Also nice copper, silver, handicraft.'

'I don't want handicraft.'

'You want hashish? One kilo twenty dollar.'

It was tempting, but I preferred bottled mango juice, which was sweet and thick, and the curry puffs known as *samosas*. The *samosas* were always wrapped in pages from old school copybooks. I sat down, drank my juice, ate my *samosa*, and read the wrapper: '. . . the shearing force at any [grease mark] on the Beam is represented by the Vertical Distance between that Line and the Line CD.'

There were forty-seven tables in the dining room of Faletti's Hotel. I found them easy to count because I was the only diner present on the two evenings I ate there. The five waiters stood at various distances from me, and when I cleared my throat two would rush forward. Not wanting to disappoint them I asked them questions about Lahore, and in one of these conversations I learned that the Punjab Club was not far away. I thought it would be a good idea to have a postprandial snooker game, so on the second evening I was given directions by one of the waiters and set off for the club.

I lost my way almost immediately in a district adjacent to the hotel where there were no street lights. My footsteps roused the watchdogs and as I walked these barking hounds leaped at fences and hedges. I have not conquered a childhood fear of strange dogs, and, although the trees smelled sweet and the night was cool, I had no idea where I was going. It was ten minutes before a car approached. I flagged it down.

'You are coming from?'

'Faletti's Hotel.'

'I mean your country.'

'United States.'

'You are most welcome,' said the driver. 'My name is Anwar. May I give you a lift?'

'I'm trying to find the Punjab Club.'

'Get in please,' he said, and when I did, he said, 'How are you please?' This is precisely the way the posturing Ivan Turkin greets people in Chekhov's story 'Ionych'.

Mr Anwar drove for another mile, telling me how fortunate it was that we should meet – there were a lot of thieves around at night, he said – and at the Punjab Club he gave me his card and invited me to his daughter's wedding, which was one week away. I said I would be in India then.

'Well, India is another story altogether,' he said, and drove off.

The Punjab Club, a bungalow behind a high hedge, was lighted and looked cosy, but it was completely deserted. I had imagined a crowded bar, a lot of cheerful drinkers, a snooker game in progress, a pair in the corner plotting adultery, waiters with trays of drinks, and chits flying back and forth. This could have been a clinic of some kind; there was not a soul in sight, but it had the atmosphere – and even the magazines – of a dentist's waiting room. I saw what I wanted a few doors along a corridor: large red letters on the window read WAIT FOR THE STROKE, and in the shadows were two tables, the balls in position, ready for play under a gleaming rack of cues.

'Yes?' It was an elderly Pakistani, and he had the forlorn abstraction of a man interrupted in his reading. He wore a black bow tie, and the pocket of his shirt sagged with pens. 'What can I do for you?'

'I just happened to be passing,' I said. 'I thought I might stop in. Do you have reciprocal privileges with any clubs in London?'

'No, not that I know of.'

'Perhaps the manager would know.'

'I am the manager,' he said. 'We used to have an arrangement with a club in London – many years ago.'

'What was the name of it?'

'I'm sorry, I've forgotten, but I know the club is no longer in existence. What was it you wanted?'

'A game of snooker.'

'Who would you play with?' He smiled. 'There is no one here.'

He showed me around, but the lighted empty rooms depressed me. The place was abandoned, like Faletti's dining room with its forty-seven empty tables, like the district where there were only watch-dogs. I said I had to go, and at the front door he said, 'You might find a taxi over there, in the next road but one. Good night.'

It was hopeless. I had walked about a hundred yards from the club and could not find the road, though I was going in the direction he had indicated. I could hear a dog growling behind a near-by hedge. Then I heard a car. It moved swiftly towards me and screeched to a halt. The driver got out and opened the back door for me. He said the manager had sent him to take me back to my hotel; he was afraid I'd get lost.

I set off in search of a drink as soon as I got back to the hotel. It was still early, about ten o'clock, but I had not gone fifty yards when a thin man in striped pyjamas stepped from behind a tree. His eyes were prominent and lighted in the dusky triangle of his face.

'What are you looking for?'

'A drink.'

'I get you a nice girl. Two hundred rupees. Good fucking.' He said this with no more emotion than a man hawking razor blades.

'No thanks.'

'Very young. You come with me. Good fucking.'

'And good fucking to you,' I said. 'I'm looking for a drink.'

He tagged along behind me, mumbling his refrain, and then at an intersection, by a park, he said, 'Come with me – in here.'

'In there?'

'Yes, she is waiting.'

'In those trees?' It was black, unlighted and humming with crickets.

'It is a park.'

'You mean I'm supposed to do it there, under a tree?'

'It is a *good* park, sahib!'

A little farther on I was accosted again, this time by a young man who was smoking nervously. He caught my eye. 'Anything you want?'

'No.'

'A girl?'

'No.'

'Boy?'

'No, go away.'

He hesitated, but kept after me. At last he said softly, '*Take me.*'

A twenty-minute walk did not take me any closer to a bar. I turned, and, giving the pimps a wide berth, went back to the hotel. Under a tree in front three old men were hunched around a pressure lamp, playing cards. One saw me pass and called out, 'Wait, sahib!' He turned his cards face down and trotted over to me.

'No,' I said before he opened his mouth.

'She's very nice,' he said.

I kept walking.

'All right, only two hundred and fifty rupees.'

'I know where I can get one for two hundred.'

'But this is in your room! I will bring her. She will stay until morning.'

'Too much money. Sorry.'

'Sahib! There are expenses! Ten rupees for your sweeper, ten also for your *chowkidar*, ten for your bearer, *baksheesh* here and there. If not, they will make trouble. Take her! She will be very nice. My girls are experienced in every way.'

'Thin or fat?'

'As you like. I have one, neither thin nor fat, but like this.' He sketched a torso in the air with his fingers, suggesting plumpness. 'About twenty-two or twenty-three. Speaks very good English. You will like her so much. Sahib, she is a trained nurse!'

He was still calling out to me as I mounted the steps to the hotel's verandah. It turned out that the only bar in Lahore was the Polo Room in my hotel. I had an expensive beer and fell into conversation with a young Englishman. He had been in Lahore for two months. I asked him what he did for amusement. He said there wasn't very much to do, but he was planning to visit Peshawar. I told him Peshawar was quieter than Lahore. He said he was sorry to hear that because he found Lahore intolerable. He was bored, he said, but there was hope. 'I've got an application pending at the club,' he said. He was a tall plain fellow, who blew his nose at the end of every sentence. 'If they let me in, I think I'll be all right. I can go there in the evenings – it's a pretty lively place.'

'What club are you talking about?'

'The Punjab Club,' he said.

The Frontier Mail

Amritsar, two taxi rides from Lahore (the connecting train hasn't run since 1947), is on the Indian side of the frontier. It is to the Sikh what Benares is to the Hindu, a religious capital, a holy city. The object of the Sikh's pilgrimage is the Golden Temple, a copper-gilt gazebo in the centre of a tank. The tank's sanctity has not kept it from stagnation. You can smell it a mile away. It is the dearest wish of every Sikh to see this temple before he dies and to bring a souvenir back from Amritsar. One of the favourite souvenirs is a large multi-coloured poster of a headless man. Blood spurts from the stump of his neck; he wears the uniform of a warrior. In one hand he carries a sword, in the other he holds his dripping head. I asked nine Sikhs what this man's name was. None could tell me, but all knew his story. In one of the Punjab wars he was decapitated. But he was very determined. He picked up his head, and, holding it in his hand so that he could see what he was doing (the eyes of the severed head blaze with resolution), he continued to fight. He did this so that he could get back to Amritsar and have a proper cremation. This story exemplifies the Sikh virtues of piety, ferocity, and strength. But Sikhs are also very kind and friendly, and an enormous number are members of Lions Club International. This is partly a cultural misunderstanding, since all Sikhs bear the surname Singh, which means lion; they feel obliged to join.

Special underpants are required by the Sikh religion, along with uncut hair, a silver bangle, a wooden comb, and an iron dagger. And as shoes are prohibited at the Golden Temple, I hopped down the hot marble causeway, doing a kind of firewalker's tango, watching these leonine figures stripped to their holy drawers bathing themselves in the tank and gulping the green water, swallowing grace and dysentery in the same mouthful. The Sikhs are great soldiers and throughout the temple enclosure there are marble tablets stating the fact that the Poona Horse Regiment and the Bengal Sappers contributed so many thousand rupees. For the rest of the Indians, Gujaratis in particular, Sikhs are yokels, and jokes are told to illustrate the simplicity of the Sikh mind. There is the one about the Sikh who, on emigrating to Canada, is told that he must prove himself a true Canadian by going into the forest and wrestling a bear and raping a squaw. He sets out and returns a month later, with his turban in tatters and his face covered with scratches, saying, 'Now I must wrestle the squaw.' Another concerns a Sikh who misses his bus. He chases the bus, trying to board, and soon realizes he has run all the way home. 'I've just chased my bus and saved fifty paisas,' he tells his wife, who replies, 'If you had chased a taxi you could have saved a rupee.'

I had a meal at a Sikh restaurant after wandering around the city and then went to the railway station to buy my ticket on the Frontier Mail to Delhi. The man at Reservations put me on the waiting list and told me there was 'a 98 per cent chance' that I would get a berth, but that I would have to wait until half-past four for a confirmation. Indian railway stations are wonderful places for killing time in, and they are like scale models of Indian society, with its divisions of caste, class, and sex: SECOND-CLASS LADIES' WAITING ROOM, BEARERS' ENTRANCE, THIRD-CLASS EXIT, FIRST-CLASS TOILET, VEGETARIAN RESTAURANT, NON-

VEGETARIAN RESTAURANT, RETIRING ROOMS, CLOAKROOM and the whole range of occupations on office signboards, from the tiny one saying SWEEPER, to the neatest of all, STATION-MASTER.

A steam locomotive was belching smoke at one of the platforms. I crossed over and as I snapped a picture a Sikh appeared on the footplate and asked me to send him a print. I said I would. He asked me where I was going, and when I told him I was taking the Frontier Mail he said, 'You have so many hours to wait. Come with me. Get in this bogie' – he pointed to the first car – 'and at the first station you can come in here and ride with me.'

'I'm afraid I'll miss my train.'

'You will not,' he said. 'Without fail.' He said this precisely, as if remembering an English lesson.

'I don't have a ticket.'

'No one is having a ticket. They are all cheating!'

So I climbed aboard and at the first station joined him in the cab. The train was going to Atari, on the Pakistan border, sixteen miles away. I had always wanted to ride in the engine of a steam locomotive, but this trip was badly timed. We left just at sunset and as I was wearing my prescription sunglasses –

my other pair was in my suitcase in the station cloakroom – I could not see a thing. I held on, blind as a bat, sweating in the heat from the firebox. The Sikh shouted explanations of what he was doing, pulling levers, bringing up the pressure, spinning knobs, and dodging the coal shoveller. The noise and the heat prevented me from taking any pleasure in this two-hour jaunt, and I suppose I must have looked dispirited because the Sikh was anxious to amuse me by blowing the whistle. Every time he did it the train seemed to slow down.

My face and arms were flecked with soot from the ride to Atari. On the Frontier Mail this was no problem, and I had the enjoyable experience that humid evening of taking a cold shower, squatting on my heels under the burbling pipe, as the train tore through the Punjab to Delhi.

I returned to my compartment to find a young man sitting on my berth. He greeted me in an accent I could not quite place, partly because he lisped and also because his appearance was somewhat bizarre. His hair, parted in the middle, reached below his shoulders; his thin arms were sheathed in tight sleeves and he wore three rings with large orange stones on each hand, bracelets of various kinds and a necklace of white shells. His face frightened me: it was that corpselike face of lunacy or a fatal illness, with sunken eyes and cheeks, deeply lined, bloodless, narrow, and white. He had a cowering stare, and as he watched me – I was still dripping from my shower – he played with a small leather purse. He said his name was Hermann; he was going to Delhi. He had bribed the conductor so that he could travel with a European. He didn't want to be in a compartment with an Indian – there might be trouble. He hoped I understood.

'Of course,' I said. 'But do you feel all right?'

'I have been sick – four days in Amritsar I have been in the hospital, and in Quetta also. I was so nervous. The doctors take tests and they give me this medicine, but it does no good. I don't sleep, I don't eat – just maybe glass of milk and piece of bread. I fly to Amritsar from Lahore. I was so sick in Lahore – three days in hospital and in Quetta two days. I cross Baluchistan. Yazd, you know Yazd? It is a terrible place. Two nights I am there and I am on the bus two days from Teheran. I cannot sleep. Every five hours the bus stops and I take some tea and a little melon. I am sick. The people say, "Why you don't talk – are you angry?" But I say, "No, not angry, but sick –"'

This was the way he spoke, in long lisped passages, interrupting himself, repeating that he was sick in a voice that was monotonously apologetic. He was German and had been a sailor, a deck hand on a German ship, then a steward on a Finnish one. He had sailed for seven years and had been to the States – 'Yes, to every country,' he said, 'but only for a few hours.' He loved ships, but he couldn't sail any more. I asked why. 'Hepatitis,' he said, giving it a German pronunciation. He caught it in Indonesia and was in the hospital for weeks. He had never managed to shake it off: he still needed tests. He'd had one in Amritsar. 'People say to me, "Your face is sick." I know my face is sick, but I cannot eat.'

His face was ghastly, and he was trembling. 'Are you taking any medicine?'

'No.' He shook his head. 'I take this.' He opened the leather purse he had been smoothing with his scrawny fingers and took out a cellophane envelope. He peeled the cellophane away and showed me a wad of brown sticky stuff, like a flattened plug of English toffee.

'What is it?'

'Opium,' he said. 'I take it in little balls.'

His lisp made 'balls' moistly vicious.

'I am a yunk.' He broke off a piece of opium and rolled it between his fingers, slowly making it a pellet.

'A junkie?'

'Yes, I take needle. See my arms.'

He locked the compartment door and pulled the curtain across the window. He rolled up his left sleeve. His arm appalled me: each vein was clearly defined by dark bruised scars of needle marks, thick welts that made the veins into black cords. He touched his arm shyly, as if it didn't belong to him and said, 'I cannot get heroin. In Lahore I am not feeling so well. I stay in hospital but still I am weak and nervous. The people are making noise and it is so hot. I don't know what I can do. So I escape and I walk down the street. A Pakistani says to me he has some morphine. I go with him and he shows me. It is good – German morphine. He asks me for one hundred and fifty rupees. I give him and take an injection. That is how I get to Amritsar. But in Amritsar I get very sick and I cannot get any more of morphine. So I take this –' He patted his right pocket and took out a cake of hashish, roughly the size of the opium blob, but dry and cracked. 'Or I smoke this –' He withdrew a little sack of marijuana.

I told him that with his budget of drugs he was lucky to have got into India. At the border post I had seen an Indian customs official ask a boy to drop his jeans.

'Yes,' said Hermann. 'I am so nervous! The man asks me do I have pot and I say no. Do I smoke it? I say, yes, sometimes, but he doesn't look at my luggages. If I am nervous I can hide it in secret places.'

'Then I suppose you don't have anything to worry about.'

'No, I am hot and nervous always.'

'But you can hide your drugs.'

'I can even throw them away and buy more,' he said. 'But my arms! If they see my arms they know. I have to hide my arms always.' He pushed his sleeves up and looked again at the long dark scars.

He told me how it was that he had come to India. In Hanover, he decided to cure himself of his heroin habit. He registered as an addict and entered a rehabilitation centre – he called it 'The Release' – where he was given 700 Deutsche marks a month and a daily glass of methadone. In return for this he helped clean the centre. He never went out; he was afraid that if he did he would meet someone who'd sell him heroin. But an odd thing happened: by staying in he rarely spent his monthly allowance, and he found that at the end of a year he had saved quite a lot of money – enough to live on in India for six months or more. So he packed up and left, just like that, on a charter flight to Teheran, where his withdrawal symptoms began.

He had carried his dereliction to a derelict land. He was doomed, he stank of death, and his condition was not so different from that of the unfortunates who appeared at the railway stations we passed, gathering for the light and water. There are foreigners who, knowing they are wrecked, go to India to be anonymous in her decrepitude, to age and sicken in the *bustees* of the East. They are people, V. S. Naipaul wrote recently, 'who wish themselves on societies more fragile than their own . . . who in the end do no more than celebrate their own security'.

'I take this now.' He popped the pellet of opium into his mouth and closed his eyes. 'Then I take some water.' He drank a glass of water. He had already drunk two, and I realized that the Indian water would kill him if the drugs didn't. 'Now I sleep. If I don't sleep I take another opium.'

Twice during the night a match flared in the upper berth, lighting the fan on the ceiling. I heard the crackle of cellophane, the snap of the gummy opium in his fingers, and Hermann gulping water.

The signs in Amritsar Station (THIRD-CLASS EXIT, SECOND-CLASS LADIES' WAITING ROOM, FIRST-CLASS TOILET, SWEEPERS ONLY) had given me a formal idea of Indian society. The less formal reality I saw at seven in the morning in the Northern Railways Terminal in Old Delhi. To understand the real India, the Indians say, you must go to the villages. But that is not strictly true, because the Indians have carried their villages to the railway stations. In the daytime it is not apparent – you might mistake any of these people for beggars, ticketless travellers (sign: TICKETLESS TRAVEL IS A SOCIAL EVIL), or unlicensed hawkers. At night and in the early morning the station village is complete, a community so preoccupied that the thousands of passengers arriving and departing leave it undisturbed: they detour around it. The railway dwellers possess the station, but only the new arrival notices this. He feels something is wrong because he has not learned the Indian habit of ignoring the obvious, making a detour to preserve his calm. The newcomer cannot believe he has been plunged into such intimacy so soon. In another country this would all be hidden from him, and not even a trip to a village would reveal with this clarity the pattern of life. The village in rural India tells the visitor very little except that he is required to keep his distance and limit his experience of the place to tea or a meal in a stuffy parlour. The life of the village, its interior, is denied to him.

But the station village is all interior, and the shock of this exposure made me hurry away. I didn't feel I had any right to watch people bathing under a low faucet – naked among the incoming tide of office workers; men sleeping late on their *charpoys* or tucking up their turbans; women with nose rings and cracked yellow feet cooking stews of begged vegetables over smoky fires, suckling infants, folding bedrolls; children pissing on their toes; little girls, in oversized frocks falling from their shoulders, fetching water in tin cans from the third-class toilet;

and, near a newspaper vendor, a man lying on his back, holding a baby up to admire and tickling it. Hard work, poor pleasures, and the scrimmage of appetite. This village has no walls. I distracted myself with the signs, GWALIOR SUITINGS, RASHMI SUPERB COATINGS, and the film poster of plump faces that was never out of view, BOBBY ('A Story of Modern Love'). I was moving so quickly I lost Hermann. He had drugged himself for the arrival: crowds made him nervous. He floated down the platform and then sank from view.

I wondered whether I would find any of this Indian candour familiar enough to ignore. I was told that I should not draw any conclusions from Delhi: Delhi wasn't India – not the real India. Well, I said, I had no intention of staying in Delhi. I wanted to go to Simla, Nagpur, Ceylon – to wherever there was a train.

'There is no train to Ceylon.'

'There's one on the map.' I unrolled my map and traced the black line from Madras to Colombo.

'*Acha*,' said the man. He wore a colourful handloomed shirt and he waggled his head from side to side, the Indian gesture – like a man trying to shake water out of his ears – that means he is listening with approval. But the man, of course, was an American. Americans in India practise these affectations to endear themselves to Indians, who seem so embarrassed by these easily parodied mannerisms that (at the American embassy at least) the liaison men say, 'We're locking you into that programme,' while the American looking on says, '*Acha*,' and giggles mirthlessly.

I was being locked into a programme: lectures in Jaipur, Bombay, Calcutta, Colombo. Wherever, I said, there was a train.

'There is no train to Colombo.'

'We'll see,' I said, and then listened to one of those strange conversations I later found so common as to be the mainstay of American small talk in India: The American on His Bowels. After the usual greetings and pauses these people would report on the vagaries of their digestive tracts. Their passion was graceless and they were as hard to silence as whoopee cushions.

'I had a bad night,' one embassy man said. 'The German ambassador gave a party. Delicious meal – it always is. All kinds of wine, umpteen courses, the works. But, God, I was up at five this morning, sick as a dog. Tummy upset.'

'It's a funny thing,' said another man. 'You have a good meal at some dirty little place and you know you're going to pay for it. I just came back from Madras. I was fine – and I had some pretty risky meals. Then I go to some diplomatic thing and I'm doubled up for days. So there's no telling where you'll get it.'

'Tell Paul about Harris.'

'Harris! Listen,' said the man, 'there was a fella here. Harris. Press Section. Went to the doctor. Guess why? He was constipated. *Constipated!* In *India!* It got around the embassy. People used to see him and laugh like hell.'

'I've been fine lately,' said a junior officer, holding his end up, as it were. 'Knock on wood. I've had some severe – I mean, really bad times. But I figured it out. What I usually do is have yogurt. I drink tons of the stuff. I figure the bacteria in yogurt keeps down the bacteria in lousy food. Kind of an equalizing thing.'

There was another man. He looked pale, but he said he was bearing up. Kind of a bowel thing. Up all night. Cramps. Delhi belly. Food goes right through you. He said, 'I had it in spades. Bacillary. Ever have bacillary? No? It knocked me flat. For six days I couldn't do a thing. Running back and forth, practically living in the john.'

Each time the subject came up, I wanted to take the speaker by his hand-loomed shirt, and, shaking him, say, 'Now listen to me! There is absolutely nothing wrong with your bowels!'

The Kalka Mail for Simla

In spite of my dishevelled appearance, it was thought by some in Delhi to be beneath my dignity to stand in line for my ticket north to Simla, though perhaps this was a tactful way of suggesting that if I did stand in line I might be mistaken for an Untouchable and set alight (these Harijan combustions are reported daily in Indian newspapers). The American official who claimed his stomach was collapsing with dysentery introduced me to Mr Nath, who said, 'Don't sweat. We'll take care of everything.' I had heard that one before. Mr Nath rang his deputy, Mr Sheth, who told his secretary to ring a travel agent. At four o'clock there was no sign of the ticket. I saw Mr Sheth. He offered me tea. I refused his tea and went to the travel agent. This was Mr Sud. He had delegated the ticket-buying to one of his clerks. The clerk was summoned. He didn't have the ticket; he had sent a messenger, a low-caste Tamil whose role in life, it seemed, was to lengthen lines at ticket windows. An Indian story:

and still no ticket. Mr Nath and Mr Sud accompanied me to the ticket office, and there we stood ('Are you sure you don't want a nice cup of tea?') watching this damned messenger, ten feet from the window, holding my application. Bustling Indians began cutting in front of him.

'Now you see,' said Mr Nath, 'with your own eyes why things are so backwards over here. But don't worry. There are always seats for VIPs.' He explained that compartments for VIPs and senior government officials were reserved on every train until two hours before departure time, in case someone of importance might wish to travel at the last minute. Apparently a waiting list was drawn up every day for each of India's 10,000 trains.

'Mr Nath,' I said, 'I'm not a VIP.'

'Don't be silly,' he said. He puffed his pipe and moved his eyes from the messenger to me. I think he saw my point because his next words were, 'Also we could try money.'

'*Baksheesh*,' I said. Mr Nath made a face.

Mr Sud said, 'Why don't you fly?'

'Planes make me throw up.'

'I think we've waited long enough,' said Mr Nath.

'We'll see the man in charge and explain the situation. Let me do the talking.'

We walked around the barrier to where the ticket manager sat, squinting irritably at a ledger. He did not look up. He said, 'Yes, what is it?' Mr Nath pointed his pipe stem at me and, with the pomposity Indians assume when they speak to each other in English, introduced me as a distinguished American writer who was getting a bad impression of Indian Railways.

'Wait a minute,' I said.

'It is imperative that we do our utmost to ensure –'

'Tourist?' said the ticket manager.

I said yes.

He snapped his fingers. 'Passport.'

I handed it over. He wrote a new application and dismissed us. The application went back to the messenger, who had wormed his way to the window.

'It's a priority matter,' said Mr Nath crossly. 'You are a tourist. You have come all this way, so you have priority. We want to give favourable impression. If I want to travel with my family – wife, small children, maybe my mother too – they say, "Oh, no, there is a *tourist* here. Priority matter!"' He grinned without pleasure. 'That is the situation. But you have your ticket – that's the important thing, isn't it?'

The elderly Indian in the compartment was sitting cross-legged on his berth reading a copy of *Filmfare*. Seeing me enter, he took off his glasses, smiled, then returned to his magazine. I went to a large wooden cupboard and smacked it with my hand, trying to open it. I wanted to hang up my jacket. I got my fingers into the louvred front and tugged. The Indian took off his glasses again, and this time he closed the magazine.

'Please,' he said, 'you will break the air conditioner.'

'This is an air conditioner?' It was a tall box the height of the room, four feet wide, varnished, silent, and warm.

He nodded. 'It has been modernized. This carriage is fifty years old.'

'Nineteen twenty?'

'About that,' he said. 'The cooling system was very interesting then. Every compartment had its own unit. That is a unit. It worked very well.'

'I didn't realize there were air conditioners in the twenties,' I said.

'They used ice,' he said. He explained that blocks of ice were slipped into lockers under the floor – it was done from the outside so that the passengers' sleep would not be disturbed. Fans in the cupboard I had tried to open blew air over the ice and into the compartment. Every three hours or so the ice was renewed. (I imagined an Englishman snoring in his berth while at the platform of some outlying station Indians with bright eyes pushed cakes of ice into the lockers.) But the system had been converted: a refrigerating device had been installed under the blowers. Just as he finished speaking there was a whirr from behind the louvres and a loud and prolonged *whoosh*!

'When did they stop using ice?'

'About four years ago,' he said. He yawned. 'You will excuse me if I go to bed?'

The train started up, and the wood panelling of this old sleeping car groaned and creaked; the floor shuddered, the metal marauder-proof windows clattered in their frames, and the *whooshing* from the tall cupboard went on all night. The Kalka Mail

was full of Bengalis on their way to Simla for a

festival, the Kali *puja*. Bengalis, whose complexion resembles that of the black goddess of destruction they worship, and who have the same sharp hook to their noses, have the misfortune to live at the opposite end of the country from the most favoured Kali temple. Kali is usually depicted wearing a necklace of human skulls, sticking her maroon tongue out, and trampling a human corpse. But the Bengalis were smiling sweetly all along the train, with their baskets of food and neatly woven garlands of flowers.

I was asleep when the train reached Kalka at dawn, but the elderly Indian obligingly woke me up. He was dressed and seated at the drop-leaf table, having a cup of tea and reading the *Chandigarh Tribune*. He poured his tea into the cup, blew on it, poured half a cup into the saucer, blew on it, and then, making a pedestal of his fingers, drank the tea from the saucer, lapping it like a cat.

'You will want to read this,' he said. 'Your vice president has resigned.'

He showed me the paper, and there was the glad news, sharing the front page with an item about a Mr Dikshit. It seemed a happy combination, Dikshit and Agnew, though I am sure Mr Dikshit's political life had been blameless. As for Agnew's, the Indian laughed derisively when I translated the amount he had extorted into rupees. Even the black-market rate turned him into a cut-price punk. The Indian was in stitches.

In Kalka two landscapes meet. There is nothing gradual in the change from plains to mountains: the Himalayas stand at the upper edge of the Indo-Gangetic plain; the rise is sudden and dramatic. The trains must conform to the severity of the change; two are required – one large roomy one for the ride to Kalka, and a small tough beast for the ascent to Simla. Kalka itself is a well-organized station at the end of the broad-gauge line. Between the Himalayas and Kalka is the cool hill station of Simla on a bright balding ridge. I had my choice of trains for the sixty-mile journey on the narrow gauge: the toy train or the rail car. The blue wooden carriages of the train were already packed with pilgrims – the Bengalis, nimble at boarding trains, had performed the Calcutta trick of diving headfirst through the train windows and had got the best seats. It was an urban skill, this somersault – a fire drill in reverse – and it left the more patient hill people a bit glassy-eyed. I decided to take the rail car. This was a white squarish machine, with the face of a Model-T Ford and the body of an old bus. It was mounted low on the narrow-gauge tracks and had the look of a battered limousine. But considering that it was built in 1925 (so the driver assured me), it was in wonderful shape.

I found the conductor. He wore a stained white uniform and a brown peaked cap that did not fit him. He was sorry to hear I wanted to take the rail car. He ran his thumb down his clipboard to mystify me and said, 'I am expecting another party.'

There were only three people in the rail car. I felt he was angling for *baksheesh*. I said, 'How many people can you fit in?'

'Twelve,' he said.

'How many seats have been booked?'

He hid his clipboard and turned away. He said, 'I am very sorry.'

'You are very helpful.'

'I am expecting another party.'

'If they show up, you let me know,' I said. 'In the meantime, I'm putting my bag inside.'

'It might get stolen,' he said brightly.

'Nothing could please me more.'

'Wanting breakfast, sahib?' said a little man with a push-broom.

I said yes, and within five minutes my breakfast was laid out on an unused ticket counter in the middle of the platform, tea, toast, jam, a cube of butter, and an omelette. The morning sunlight struck through the platform, warming me as I stood eating my breakfast. It was an unusual station for India: it was not crowded, there were no sleepers, no encampment of naked squatters, no cows. It was filled that early hour with the smell of damp grass and wildflowers. I buttered a thick slice of toast and ate it, but I couldn't finish all the breakfast. I left two slices of toast, the jam, and half the omelette uneaten, and I walked over to the rail car. When I looked back, I saw two ragged children reaching up to the counter and stuffing the remainder of my breakfast into their mouths.

At seven-fifteen, the driver of the rail car inserted a long-handled crank into the engine and gave it a jerk. The engine shook and coughed and, still juddering and smoking, began to whine. Within minutes we were on the slope, looking down at the top of Kalka Station, where in the train yard two men were winching a huge steam locomotive around in a circle. The rail car's speed was a steady ten miles an hour, zigzagging in and out of the steeply pitched hill, reversing on switchbacks through the terraced gardens and the white flocks of butterflies. We passed through several tunnels before I noticed they were numbered; a large number 4 was painted over the entrance of the next one. The man seated beside me, who had told me he was a civil servant in Simla, said there were 103 tunnels altogether. I tried not to notice the numbers after that. Outside the car, there was a sheer drop, hundreds of feet down, for the railway, which was opened in 1904, is cut directly into the hillside, and the line above is notched like the skidway on a toboggan run, circling the hills.

After thirty minutes everyone in the rail car was asleep except the civil servant and me. At the little stations along the way, the postman in the rear seat awoke from his doze to throw a mailbag out the window to a waiting porter on the platform. I tried to take pictures, but the landscape eluded me: one vista shifted into another, lasting only seconds, a dizzying displacement of hill and air, of haze and all the morning shades of green. The meat-grinder cogs working against the rack under the rail car ticked like an ageing clock and made me drowsy. I took out my inflatable pillow, blew it up, put it under my head, and slept peacefully in the sunshine until I was awakened by the thud of the rail car's brakes and the banging of doors.

'Ten minutes,' said the driver.

We were just below a wooden structure, a doll's house, its window boxes overflowing with red blossoms, and moss trimming its wide eaves. This was Bangu Station. It had a wide complicated verandah on which a waiter stood with a menu under his arm. The rail-car passengers scrambled up the stairs. My Kalka breakfast had been premature; I smelled eggs and coffee and heard the Bengalis quarrelling with the waiters in English.

I walked down the gravel paths to admire the well-tended flower beds and the carefully mown lengths of turf beside the track; below the station a rushing stream gurgled, and signs there, and near the flower beds, read NO PLUCKING. A waiter chased me down to the stream and called out, 'We have juices! You like fresh mango juice? A little porridge? Coffee-tea?'

We resumed the ride, and the time passed quickly as I dozed again and woke to higher mountains, with fewer trees, stonier slopes, and huts perched more precariously. The haze had disappeared and the hillsides were bright, but the air was cool and a fresh breeze blew through the open windows of the rail car. In every tunnel the driver switched on orange lamps, and the racket of the clattering wheels increased and echoed. After Solon the only people in the rail car were a family of Bengali pilgrims (all of them sound asleep, snoring, their faces turned up), the civil servant, the postman, and me. The next stop was Solon Brewery, where the air was pungent with yeast and hops, and after that we passed through pine forests and cedar groves. On one stretch a baboon the size of a six-year-old crept off the tracks to let us go by. I remarked on the largeness of the creature.

The civil servant said, 'There was once a *saddhu* – a holy man – who lived near Simla. He could speak to monkeys. A certain Englishman had a garden, and all the time the monkeys were causing him trouble. Monkeys can be very destructive. The Englishman told this *saddhu* his problem. The *saddhu* said, "I will see what I can do." Then the *saddhu* went into the forest and assembled all the monkeys. He said, "I hear you are troubling the

Englishman. That is bad. You must stop; leave his garden alone. If I hear that you are causing damage I will treat you very harshly." And from that time onwards the monkeys never went into the Englishman's garden.'

'Do you believe that story?'

'Oh, yes. But the man is now dead – the *saddhu*. I don't know what happened to the Englishman. Perhaps he went away, like the rest of them.'

A little farther on, he said, 'What do you think of India?'

'It's a hard question,' I said. I wanted to tell him about the children I had seen that morning pathetically raiding the leftovers of my breakfast, and ask him if he thought there was any truth in Mark Twain's comment on Indians: 'It is a curious people. With them, all life seems to be sacred except human life.' But I added instead, 'I haven't been here very long.'

'I will tell you what I think,' he said. 'If all the people who are talking about honesty, fair play, socialism, and so forth – if they began to practise it themselves, India will do well. Otherwise there will be a revolution.'

He was an unsmiling man in his early fifties and had the stern features of a Brahmin. He neither drank nor smoked, and before he joined the civil service he had been a Sanskrit scholar in an Indian university. He got up at five every morning, had an apple, a glass of milk, and some almonds; he washed and said his prayers and after that took a long walk. Then he went to his office. To set an example for his junior officers he always walked to work, he furnished his office sparsely, and he did not require his bearer to wear a khaki uniform. He admitted that his example was unpersuasive. His junior officers had parking permits, sumptuous furnishings, and uniformed bearers.

'I ask them why all this money is spent for nothing. They tell me to make a good first impression is very important. I say to the blighters, "What about *second* impression?"'

'Blighters' was a word that occurred often in his speech. Lord Clive was a blighter and so were most of the other viceroys. Blighters ask for bribes; blighters try to cheat the Accounts Department; blighters are living in luxury and talking about socialism. It was a point of honour with this civil servant that he had never in his life given or received *baksheesh*: 'Not even a single paisa.' Some of his clerks had, and in eighteen years in the civil service he had personally fired thirty-two people. He thought it might be a record. I asked him what they had done wrong.

'Gross incompetence,' he said, 'pinching money, hanky-panky. But I never fire anyone without first having a good talk with his parents. There was a blighter in the Audit Department, always pinching girls' bottoms. Indian girls from good families! I warned him about this, but he couldn't stop. So I told him I wanted to see his parents. The blighter said his parents lived fifty miles away. I gave him money for their bus fare. They were poor, and they were quite worried about the blighter. I said to them, "Now I want you to understand that your son is in deep trouble. He is causing annoyance to the lady members of this department. Please talk to him and make him understand that if this continues I will have no choice but to sack him." Parents go away, blighter goes back to work, and ten days later he is at it again. I suspended him on the spot, then I charge-sheeted him.'

I wondered whether any of these people had tried to take revenge on him.

'Yes, there was one. He got himself drunk one
 night and came to my house with a knife. "Come

outside and I will kill you!" That sort of thing. My wife was upset. But I was angry. I couldn't control myself. I dashed outside and fetched the blighter a blooming kick. He dropped his knife and began to cry. "Don't call the police," he said. "I have a wife and children." He was a complete coward, you see. I let him go and everyone criticized me – they said I should have brought charges. But I told them he'll never bother anyone again.

'And there was another time. I was working for Heavy Electricals, doing an audit for some cheaters in Bengal. Faulty construction, double entries, and estimates that were five times what they should have been. There was also immorality. One bloke – son of the contractor, very wealthy – kept four harlots. He gave them whisky and made them take their clothes off and run naked into a group of women and children doing *puja*. Disgraceful! Well, they didn't like me at all and the day I left there were four *dacoits* with knives waiting for me on the station road. But I expected that, so I took a different road, and the blighters never caught me. A month later two auditors were murdered by *dacoits*.'

The rail car tottered around a cliffside, and on the opposite slope, across a deep valley, was Simla.

Most of the town fits the ridge like a saddle made entirely of rusty roofs, but as we drew closer the fringes seemed to be sliding into the valley. Simla is unmistakable, for as *Murray's Handbook* indicates, 'its skyline is incongruously dominated by a Gothic Church, a baronial castle and a Victorian country mansion'. Above these brick piles is the sharply pointed peak of Jakhu (8,000 feet); below are the clinging house fronts. The southerly aspect of Simla is so steep that flights of cement stairs take the place of roads. From the rail car it looked an attractive place, a town of rusting splendour with snowy mountains in the background.

'My office is in that castle,' said the civil servant.

'Gorton Castle,' I said, referring to my handbook. 'Do you work for the Accountant General of the Punjab?'

'Well, I *am* the A.G.,' he said. But he was giving information, not boasting. At Simla Station the porter strapped my suitcase to his back (he was a Kashmiri, up for the season). The civil servant introduced himself as Vishnu Bhardwaj and invited me for tea that afternoon.

The Mall was filled with Indian vacationers taking their morning stroll, warmly dressed children, women with cardigans over their saris, and men in tweed suits, clasping the green Simla guide-book in one hand and a cane in the other. The promenading has strict hours, nine to twelve in the morning and four to eight in the evening, determined by mealtimes and shop openings. These hours were fixed a hundred years ago, when Simla was the summer capital of the Indian empire, and they have not varied. The architecture is similarly unchanged – it is all high Victorian, with the vulgarly grandiose touches colonial labour allowed, extravagant gutters and porticoes, buttressed by pillars and steelwork to prevent its slipping down the hill. The Gaiety Theatre (1887) is still the Gaiety Theatre (though when I was there it was the venue of a 'Spiritual Exhibition' I was not privileged to see); pettifogging continues in Gorton Castle, as praying does in Christ Church (1857), the Anglican cathedral; the viceroy's lodge (Rastrapati Nivas), a baronial mansion, is now the Indian Institute of Advanced Studies, but the visiting scholars creep about with the diffidence of caretakers maintaining the sepulchral stateliness of the place. Scattered among these large Simla buildings are the bungalows – Holly Lodge, Romney Castle, The Bricks,

Forest View, Sevenoaks, Fernside – but the inhabitants now are Indians, or rather that inherited breed of Indian that insists on the guidebook, the walking stick, the cravat, tea at four, and an evening stroll to Scandal Point. It is the Empire with a dark complexion, an imperial outpost that the mimicking vacationers have preserved from change, though not the place of highly coloured intrigues described in *Kim*, and certainly tamer than it was a century ago. After all, Lola Montez, the *grande horizontale*, began her whoring in Simla, and the only single women I saw were short red-cheeked Tibetan labourers in quilted coats, who walked along the Mall with heavy stones in slings on their backs.

I had tea with the Bhardwaj family. It was not the simple meal I had expected. There were eight or nine dishes: *pakora*, vegetables fried in batter, *poha*, a rice mixture with peas, coriander, and turmeric; *khira*, a creamy pudding of rice, milk, and sugar; a kind of fruit salad, with cucumber and lemon added to it, called *chaat*; *murak*, a Tamil savoury, like large nutty pretzels; *tikkiya*, potato cakes; *malai* chops, sweet sugary balls topped with cream; and almond-scented *pinnis*. I ate what I could, and

 the next day I saw Mr Bhardwaj's office in Gorton

Castle. It was as sparely furnished as he had said on the rail car, and over his desk was this sign:

> I am not interested in excuses for delay;
> I am interested only in a thing done.
>
> *Jawaharlal Nehru*

The day I left I found an ashram on one of Simla's slopes. I had been interested in visiting an ashram ever since the hippies on the Teheran Express had told me what marvellous places they were. But I was disappointed. The ashram was a ramshackle bungalow run by a talkative old man named Gupta, who claimed he had cured many people of advanced paralysis by running his hands over their legs. There were no hippies in this ashram, though Mr Gupta was anxious to recruit me. I said I had a train to catch. He said that if I was a believer in yoga I wouldn't worry about catching trains. I said that was why I wasn't a believer in yoga.

Mr Gupta said, 'I will tell you a story. A yogi was approached by a certain man who said he wanted to be a student. Yogi said he was very busy and had no time for man. Man said he was desperate. Yogi did not believe him. Man said he would commit suicide by jumping from roof if yogi would not take him on. Yogi said nothing. Man jumped.

'"Bring his body to me," said yogi. Body was brought. Yogi passed his hands over body and after a few minutes man regained his life.

'"Now you are ready to be my student," said yogi. "I believe you can act on proper impulses and you have shown me great sincerity." So man who had been restored to the living became student.'

'Have you ever brought anyone to life?' I asked.

'Not as yet,' said Mr Gupta.

Not as yet! His guru was Paramahansa Yogananda, whose sleek saintly face was displayed all over the bungalow. In Ranchi, Paramahansa Y. had a vision. This was his vision: a gathering of millions of Americans who needed his advice. He described them in his *Autobiography* as 'a vast multitude, gazing at me intently' that 'swept actorlike across the stage of consciousness . . . the Lord is calling me to America . . . Yes! I am going forth to discover America, like Columbus. He thought he had found India; surely there is a karmic link between these two lands!' He could see the people so clearly, he recognized their faces when he arrived in California a few years later. He stayed in Los Angeles for thirty years, and, unlike Columbus, died rich, happy and fulfilled. Mr Gupta told me this hilarious story in a tone of great reverence, and then he took me on a tour of the bungalow, drawing my attention to the many portraits of Jesus (painted to look like a yogi) he had tacked to the walls.

'Where do you live?' asked a small friendly ashramite, who was eating an apple. (Simla apples are delicious, but, because of a trade agreement, the whole crop goes to Poland.)

'South London at the moment.'

'But it is so noisy and dirty there!'

I found this an astonishing observation from a man who said he was from Kathmandu; but I let it pass.

'I used to live in Kensington Palace Gardens,' he said. 'The rent was high, but my government paid. I was the Nepalese ambassador at the time.'

'Did you ever meet the queen?'

'Many times! The queen liked to talk about the plays that were on in London. She talked about the actors and the plot and so on. She would say, "Did you like *this* part of the play or that one?" If you hadn't seen the play it was very difficult to reply.

But usually she talked about horses, and I'm sorry to say I have no interest at all in horses.'

I left the ashram and paid a last visit to Mr Bhardwaj. He gave me various practical warnings about travelling and advised me to visit Madras, where I would see the real India. He was off to have the carburettor in his car checked and to finish up some accounts at his office. He hoped I had enjoyed Simla and said it was a shame I hadn't seen any snow. He was formal, almost severe in his farewell, but, walking down to Cart Road, he said, 'I will see you in England or America.'

'That would be nice. I hope we do meet again.'

'We will,' he said, with such certainty I challenged it.

'How do you know?'

'I am about to be transferred from Simla. Maybe going to England, maybe to the States. That is what my horoscope says.'

PENGUIN 60s

ISABEL ALLENDE · *Voices in My Ear*
NICHOLSON BAKER · *Playing Trombone*
LINDSEY BAREHAM · *The Little Book of Big Soups*
KAREN BLIXEN · *From the Ngong Hills*
DIRK BOGARDE · *Coming of Age*
ANTHONY BURGESS · *Childhood*
ANGELA CARTER · *Lizzie Borden*
CARLOS CASTANEDA · *The Sorcerer's Ring of Power*
ELIZABETH DAVID · *Peperonata and Other Italian Dishes*
RICHARD DAWKINS · *The Pocket Watchmaker*
GERALD DURRELL · *The Pageant of Fireflies*
RICHARD ELLMANN · *The Trial of Oscar Wilde*
EPICURUS · *Letter on Happiness*
MARIANNE FAITHFULL · *Year One*
KEITH FLOYD · *Hot and Spicy Floyd*
ALEXANDER FRATER · *Where the Dawn Comes Up Like Thunder*
ESTHER FREUD · *Meeting Bilal*
JOHN KENNETH GALBRAITH · *The Culture of Contentment*
ROB GRANT AND DOUG NAYLOR · *Scenes from the Dwarf*
ROBERT GRAVES · *The Gods of Olympus*
JANE GRIGSON · *Puddings*
SOPHIE GRIGSON · *From Sophie's Table*
KATHARINE HEPBURN · *Little Me*
SUSAN HILL · *The Badness Within Him*
ALAN HOLLINGHURST · *Adventures Underground*
BARRY HUMPHRIES · *Less is More Please*
HOWARD JACOBSON · *Expulsion from Paradise*
P. D. JAMES · *The Girl Who Loved Graveyards*
STEPHEN KING · *Umney's Last Case*
LAO TZU · *Tao Te Ching*
DAVID LEAVITT · *Chips Is Here*

PENGUIN 60s

LAURIE LEE · *To War in Spain*
PATRICK LEIGH FERMOR · *Loose as the Wind*
ELMORE LEONARD · *Trouble at Rindo's Station*
DAVID LODGE · *Surprised by Summer*
BERNARD MAC LAVERTY · *The Miraculous Candidate*
SHENA MACKAY · *Cloud-Cuckoo-Land*
NORMAN MAILER · *The Dressing Room*
PETER MAYLE · *Postcards from Summer*
JAN MORRIS · *Scenes from Havian Life*
BLAKE MORRISON · *Camp Cuba*
VLADIMIR NABOKOV · *Now Remember*
REDMOND O'HANLON · *A River in Borneo*
STEVEN PINKER · *Thinking in Tongues*
CRAIG RAINE · *Private View*
CLAUDIA RODEN · *Ful Medames and Other Vegetarian Dishes*
HELGE RUBINSTEIN · *Chocolate Parfait*
SIMON SCHAMA · *The Taking of the Bastille*
WILL SELF · *The Rock of Crack As Big As the Ritz*
MARK SHAND · *Elephant Tales*
NIGEL SLATER · *30-Minute Suppers*
RICK STEIN · *Fresh from the Sea*
LYTTON STRACHEY · *Florence Nightingale*
PAUL THEROUX · *Slow Trains to Simla*
COLIN THUBRON · *Samarkand*
MARK TULLY · *Beyond Purdah*
LAURENS VAN DER POST · *Merry Christmas, Mr Lawrence*
MARGARET VISSER · *More than Meets the Eye*
GAVIN YOUNG · *Something of Samoa*

and

Thirty Obituaries from Wisden · SELECTED BY MATTHEW ENGEL

READ MORE IN PENGUIN

For complete information about books available from Penguin and how to order them, please write to us at the appropriate address below. Please note that for copyright reasons the selection of books varies from country to country.

IN THE UNITED KINGDOM: Please write to *Dept. EP, Penguin Books Ltd, Bath Road, Harmondsworth, Middlesex UB7 ODA.*

IN THE UNITED STATES: Please write to *Consumer Sales, Penguin USA, P.O. Box 999, Dept. 17109, Bergenfield, New Jersey 07621-0120.* VISA and MasterCard holders call 1-800-253-6476 to order Penguin titles.

IN CANADA: Please write to *Penguin Books Canada Ltd, 10 Alcorn Avenue, Suite 300, Toronto, Ontario M4V 3B2.*

IN AUSTRALIA: Please write to *Penguin Books Australia Ltd, P.O. Box 257, Ringwood, Victoria 3134.*

IN NEW ZEALAND: Please write to *Penguin Books (NZ) Ltd, Private Bag 102902, North Shore Mail Centre, Auckland 10.*

IN INDIA: Please write to *Penguin Books India Pvt Ltd, 706 Eros Apartments, 56 Nehru Place, New Delhi 110 019.*

IN THE NETHERLANDS: Please write to *Penguin Books Netherlands bv, Postbus 3507, NL-1001 AH Amsterdam.*

IN GERMANY: Please write to *Penguin Books Deutschland GmbH, Metzlerstrasse 26, 60594 Frankfurt am Main.*

IN SPAIN: Please write to *Penguin Books S. A., Bravo Murillo 19, 1° B, 28015 Madrid.*

IN ITALY: Please write to *Penguin Italia s.r.l., Via Felice Casati 20, I–20124 Milano.*

IN FRANCE: Please write to *Penguin France S. A., 17 rue Lejeune, F–31000 Toulouse.*

IN JAPAN: Please write to *Penguin Books Japan, Ishikiribashi Building, 2–5–4, Suido, Bunkyo-ku, Tokyo 112.*

IN GREECE: Please write to *Penguin Hellas Ltd, Dimocritou 3, GR–106 71 Athens.*

IN SOUTH AFRICA: Please write to *Longman Penguin Southern Africa (Pty) Ltd, Private Bag X08, Bertsham 2013.*

PAUL

THEROUX

DOWN THE YANGTZE

PENGUIN BOOKS

PENGUIN BOOKS

Published by the Penguin Group. Penguin Books Ltd, 27 Wrights Lane, London W8 5TZ, England. Penguin Books USA Inc., 375 Hudson Street, New York, New York 10014, USA. Penguin Books Australia Ltd, Ringwood, Victoria, Australia. Penguin Books Canada Ltd, 10 Alcorn Avenue, Toronto, Ontario, Canada M4V 3B2. Penguin Books (NZ) Ltd, 182–190 Wairau Road, Auckland 10, New Zealand · Penguin Books Ltd, Registered Offices: Harmondsworth, Middlesex, England · **This book was first published under the title *Sailing Through China* by Michael Russell (Publishing) Ltd in 1983.** This edition published 1995 · Typeset by Datix International Limited, Bungay, Suffolk. Printed in England by Clays Ltd, St Ives plc · 10 9 8 7 6 5 4 3 2 1

There is no Yangtze River. The name is unknown to most Chinese, who call it Ta Jian, 'Great River', or Chang Jiang, 'Long River', unless they live above Chungking – there, the swift silt-filled waters are referred to as Chin-sha Jiang, 'The River of Gold Sand'. That is only a misnomer now. As recently as fifty years ago, in the winter months when the level dropped, the Chinese squatted at its edge and panned for gold, sluicing the mud and gathering gold dust. European travellers reported seeing washer-women wearing thick gold bangles, made of the metal that had been carried from where the river – let us call it the Yangtze – rises in Tibet.

But it has more moods than names. 'I am careful to give the date of each day's notes,' Archibald Little wrote in *Through the Yangtse Gorges* (1887). 'The river varies so wonderfully at different seasons that any description must be carefully understood only to apply to the day upon which it is written.' Captain Little was overwhelmed by it; he compared it to the Mississippi and the Amazon; he said it was indescribable. It has in many stretches a violent magnificence. It is subject to murderous floods, and its winter level creates rapids of such turbulence that the river captain steers his ship through the foam and travels down the tongue of the rapid, praying that no junk will lie in its path, as it is impossible for him to stop or reverse. But it is not all so dramatic. Its four divisions are like four separate rivers: above Chungking, it is mythic and still associated with gold and landslides; the Upper River (Chungking–Yichang) is the wildest – here are the gorges and the landscape of China's Walter Scottish classic, *The Romance of the Three Kingdoms*; the Middle River (Yichang–Wuhan) is serene and a mile wide; the Lower River (Wuhan–Shanghai) is slow and sticky yellow and populous.

I sailed 1,500 miles downstream, from Chungking to Shanghai. Every mile of it was different; but there were 1,200 miles I did not see. It crosses ten provinces, 700 rivers are joined to it – all Yangtze statistics are hopelessly huge and ungraspable; they obscure rather than clarify. And since words can have a greater precision than numbers, one day I asked a Chinese ship captain if he thought the river had a distinct personality.

He said, 'The mood of the river changes according to the season. It changes every day. It is not easy. Navigating the river is always a struggle against nature. And there is only one way to pilot a ship well.' He explained – he was smiling and blowing smoke out of his nostrils – 'It is necessary to see the river as an enemy.'

 Later, a man told me that in the course of one afternoon

he had counted nine human corpses bobbing hideously down the river.

The Yangtze is China's main artery, its major waterway, the source of many of its myths, the scene of much of its history. On its banks are some of its greatest cities. It is the fountainhead of superstition; it provides income and food to half the population. It is one of the most dangerous rivers in the world, in some places one of the dirtiest, in others one of the most spectacular. The Chinese drink it and bathe in it and wash clothes in it and shit in it. It represents both life and death. It is a wellspring, a sewer and a tomb; depthless in the gorges, puddle-shallow at its rapids. The Chinese say if you haven't been up the Great River, you haven't been anywhere.

They also say that in the winter, on the river, the days are so dark that when the sun comes out the dogs bark at it. Chungking was dark at nine in the morning, when I took the rattling tin tram on the cog railway that leads down the black crags which are Chungking's ramparts, down the sooty cliffs, past the tenements and billboards ('Flying Pigeon Bicycles', 'Seagull Watches', 'Parrot Accordions') to the landing stage. A thick sulphurous fog lay over the city, a Coketown of six million. The fog had muffled the morning noises and given the city an air of frightening solemnity. It also stank like poison. Doctor Ringrose, who was from Leeds, sniffed and said, 'That is the smell of my childhood.'

There were thirty-three of us, including Ringrose. The others were American, most of them millionaires, many of them multi-millionaires. 'If you have two or three million,' one of them told me in the dreary city of Wanxian, 'you're not a millionaire – you're just getting by.' Another enlarged on this. Not to be a poor millionaire you needed twenty-five million. 'If you have twenty-five,' she said crisply, 'you're all right.' But Lurabelle Laughlin, from Pasadena, had inherited fifty million dollars. Her husband Harry told me this. He said Lurabelle could buy and sell every person on board our ship. He wasn't being malicious, only factual. 'And I'm not too badly off myself,' he said.

'I hate walking,' Mrs Ver Bryck told me. Mrs Ver Bryck, another oil heiress, hailed from Incline, Nevada. 'I never walk. I've been everywhere and didn't have to walk. I pay so I don't have to walk. And stairs are my bugbear. But you look like a walker, Paul. Are you going to walk and do all that crappy-ola?'

I cherish the memory of Ami Ver Bryck and Lurabelle Laughlin walking from the tramway at Chungking across the muddy paving, on the foreshore, with hundreds of Chinese in baggy blue suits, watching in utter silence. Lurabelle's mink coat was golden, made from thirty-five creatures of the 'tourmaline' variety; Ami's was a rich glossy mahogany. And here was Bea Brantman, also in mink. 'This is my football coat,' she cried. 'I wear it to all the games.' Bea and her husband, who was known to everyone as Big Bob, had eleven children. Big Bob said, 'I guess they'd put me in jail for that in China! Watch out, Bea, it's kind of slippery here. It looks more like an ocean than a river. You can't even see the other side.'

It was a good companionable crowd, and though it seems a contradiction to say so, these millionaires represented a cross-section of American society. Some had inherited their money, some had got it from divorce settlements, or had married into it, or had made it from nothing. One had made it from brokering, another from gun accessories, another from burglar alarms, four were oil fortunes, one was advertising, others didn't say. Some struck me as rather stupid, with their cowboy novels and their remarks about building condominiums near Hankow or Yichang and all the talk about Connecticut. Some were very smart about Chinese history or porcelain and talked intelligently about why they disliked Norman Mailer, and they knew the various dates in the Cultural Revolution. They were Democrats and Republicans, Jewish and Christian, they came from all over the United States. Interestingly, they never argued among themselves, no one was ever on the outs, and the spouses never fought. All of them had travelled before. Half had already been to China once and knew their way around Inner Mongolia. The rest were novices and called Mao 'Mayo', and confused Thailand with Taiwan, and Fuji with Fiji. They were as tenacious and practical as the Chinese, and just as ethnocentric, but much funnier, and better at cards.

We boarded *Tung Fang Hong* ('The East is Red') – *Number 39* and were soon under way. Because of the construction of locks and a dam at Yichang, we would travel down river in two ships: the MS *Kun Lun* awaited us just below Yichang. *Number 39* and the *Kun Lun* were the same size, built to carry 900 people. But they had been specially chartered by the Lindblad Tour Company. There were, as I say, only thirty-three of us, and a crew of 102. No hardships for us, and it seemed at times, though we were travelling through the very heart of the country, that China was elsewhere.

My mind kept going back to my first impression of China, and my disbelief. We had left the frenzy, the scavengers, the free-for-all of Hong Kong and were heading towards the hills – so blurred and blue you might mistake them for clouds. China began there, on those bare hillsides. There were voices behind me.

'Look, Jack.'

'Yeah.'

'Lush vegetation.'

But for an hour, until the train reached the Chinese border at Lo Wu, it was not lush. It was still farming country, dusty fields and skinny crops, as far as my eye could see.

Mrs Ver Bryck was saying to me, 'I've been everywhere, more than once.' I took her to be well over seventy. In fact, she was just sixty-two. She chain-smoked. She had a shopping bag full of cartons of cigarettes. In another shopping bag she kept her supply of vodka. On this Express to Canton, she told me how much she liked the Chinese. She loathed Italians – they controlled all the gambling in Nevada, she said. She despised the Japanese – they had charged her $410 for a room in Tokyo a few days before. It was the Royal Suite, but she had not asked for it, and she had spent only twelve hours in it. That was $34 an hour. She looked out the window at the cabbages, the lettuce, the beans, and at the culverts and ditches. 'Look how they work,' she said. 'I love the Chinese.'

Just before Lo Wu there was a fence – coils of barbed wire about twenty feet high – and then, as the train penetrated The People's Republic of China, billboards by the side of the trains advertising 'Ginseng Bee Secretion' and 'Tiensin Shoes and Slippers' and 'Marlboro Cigarettes'. And inside the train, on a television set that had been showing a Chinese travelogue about Kweilin, there were commercials for 'Rainbow Brand' television sets and 'Ricoh' watches – men and women dancing sedately and all of them wearing Ricoh watches. It was all a flatter, duller version of Hong Kong commercialism, this communist parody of advertising; and it was a bit sad, because it was the imperfect mimicry of the Hong Kong vulgarity which was in turn an imitation of American crassness. It was saddest of all because it was unconvincing.

And it bore no relation at all to what was going on

outside the train window. There in Kwantung Province everyone was harvesting rice. The train tracks were surrounded by paddy fields. Some of the rice was already tied into bunches, and the rest was being gathered by hand or threshed. They threshed it the old way, by whipping the rice grains into a basket. The people worked in groups, never alone. In one field, about eighty people were working in the heat, and this was the beginning of my disbelief. It was rural; I did not want to think how primitive this method was.

The land looked scraped – no trees, only tiny houses, or huts, and cultivation everywhere. In places there were small stands of scrub pine or tall weedy eucalyptus trees. But there was no shade. The people working in the dazzling dust had black cloth fringes sewn to their coolie hats to keep off the sun. Some were yoked to huge watering cans, and they looked like miniature crucifixions in the mass of these bald hills.

That was the other strange thing: it was not lush. It was hot, even tropical, but the hills were naked, bald, scarred with plough-marks and paths. I saw an old man whipping a buffalo's wrinkled back with a stick to beat him out of a ditch.

The first town, an hour out of Lo Wu, was a railway junction named Tang t'ou-hsia. Outside it was a brickworks. Men and women were making bricks in the old way here, out of mud and straw, clumping them out of brick moulds and stacking them into a cathedral shape which they turned into a furnace. Sweltering, the brick-bakers stoked the fire. All the houses in this area were made of these liver-coloured bricks.

'What do you think?' Mrs Ver Bryck asked.

'Rustic,' I said. 'Very nice.'

But it was mournfully backward: no cars, no tractors, no threshing machines, no metal – only farming by hand, and brickmaking. I saw no livestock – no pigs, no chickens. It was like all the pictures I had seen of old China: the same baggy smocks and sandals and straw hats, the same laborious agriculture, the same simplicity.

On the television set in the train a film of singing soldiers began to roll. They were well-dressed soldiers and as they sang a pretty girl in a red dress skipped through fields and past a waterfall. Outside the train, people were harvesting rice, sweating their guts out in the brickworks; and there were soldiers there, too, standing by the tracks in their flimsy uniforms, looking too small to be soldiers, and wearing baggy pants.

Later, I could tell how important a person was by the way his blue suit fitted him.

The 'Blue Danube' was playing on the ship's loudspeakers as *Number 39* swung between the sampans and the fishing smacks and the burdened ferries. The captain greeted us in the lounge and told us the current was moving at two metres per second and added, 'As your captain, I am responsible for your safety, so please don't worry about it.'

Captain Liu was sixty. He had a narrow, flat-backed head and bristly hair and a seeping wound in his left eye and large spaces between his teeth. He had always worked on the river. His father had been a tracker on a junk, rowing and towing junks upstream. Captain Liu himself had started out as a steward, serving food on a Chinese riverboat, at the age of fifteen. 'I was the "boy" as they say in English, but I worked my way up to captain. I never went to school. You can't learn about this river in a school. You can only learn it by being on the bridge.'

This is true; and not much has been written about the Yangtze. But before I left London I had been given a list of twenty-eight landmarks on the Upper River, patiently typed by Captain A. R. Williamson, who spent nearly thirty years sailing up and down the river. Captain Williamson is ninety, living in vigorous retirement in Hove, and is one of the historians of the river. I was lucky in meeting him and lucky to have a detailed list of things to look out for – towns, cliffs, pagodas, rapids and shrines. It was Captain Williamson's list that convinced me that, though a great deal has changed in China ('China,' Premier Deng has promised, 'will be a modern power by the year 2000'), little on the Yangtze has altered. The cities are bigger and filthier, the rapids have been dynamited, there are more ships; but the river today is essentially the river Captain Williamson travelled on in 1920, and Archibald Little sailed on in 1886, and the Abbé David botanized on in the 1860s, and Italian missionaries proselytized on in the seventeenth and eighteenth centuries. The river and the ways of many of the river dwellers are as old as China. There is a painting in the Shanghai Museum of junks and sampans on a river, by Zhang Zheduan. Those vessels have the same sails, mats, rigging, rudders and oars as ones I saw on the Yangtze the other day. But it is a Sung Dynasty painting, 1,000 years old.

A half hour below Chungking, Captain Williamson's notes said, was a large Buddha in a shrine at the top of a long flight of steps. The niche was there, and the steps; but the Buddha was gone. In Captain Williamson's day, all upbound junks fired strings of firecrackers on passing the Buddha, 'in gratitude for safe passage'. Veneration has become political in China: there were no firecrackers, though there were dozens of passing junks.

Mottled hills appeared in the mist on both sides of the river, and here, just above Chang Shou, the river narrowed to about seventy-five feet. The ship slowed to negotiate this rocky bottleneck and gave me time to study the hills; Abbé David saw fortifications on the tops of these hills. In his *Diaries* is a wonderful account of his Yangtze trip. He wrote, 'These are refuges in times of trouble for the country people, where they can go with their possessions and be safe from the depredations of rebels and brigands.' Banditry was widespread on the Yangtze from the earliest times, and the 1920s and '30s were especially terrible, as warlords' armies fought their way towards Chungking; there was no peace on the river until 1949, when a brooding bureaucracy with parrot slogans took over.

Now, every inch of these hills was farmland: it is the agricultural overstrain of China. On the steepest slopes were terraces of vegetables. How was it possible to water the gardens on these cliff-faces? I looked closely and saw a man climbing up the hillside, carrying two buckets on a yoke. He tipped them into a ditch and, without pausing further, started down the hill. No one is idle on the Yangtze. In the loneliest bends of the river are solitary men breaking rocks and smashing them into gravel. You might think they would sit down and rest (who is watching?), or soak their feet in the shallows. It is killing work. But they go on hammering, and the sound I associate with these hidden stretches of the Upper River is the sound of hammers and chisels, a sound like the sweetest chimes.

In 1937 Captain Williamson saw only the city walls of Chang Shou from the river. Today there are no city walls, and Chang Shou (the name means 'Long Life') is one of the nightmare cities of the river. It burst through its old walls and sprawled across the banks, blackening three hillsides with chimneys and factories and blocks of workers' flats. 'Looks like Pittsburgh,' someone said. But Chungking had looked like Pittsburgh, and so did six others downstream. Yellow froth streamed from pipes and posterns, and drained into the river with white muck and oil and the suds of treated sewage and beautifully coloured poison. And on a bluff below the town, there was an old untroubled pagoda, still symmetrical, looking as if it had been carved from a piece of laundry soap. These pagodas have a purpose. They are always found near towns and cities and, even now in unspiritual China, serve a spiritual function, controlling the *Feng-shui* ('Wind-water') of a place: they balance the female influences of the *Yin* ('Darkness') and the male influence of the *Yang* ('Light'). The Chinese say they no longer believe in such superstitious malarkey, but the visible fact is that most pagodas survived the Cultural Revolution. Anything that a fanatical Red Guard left intact must be regarded as worthy, if not sacred. The pagodas on the Yangtze bluffs remain pretty much as they always were.

It was near Chang Shou, about noon on that first day, that I saw a sailing junk being steered to the bank, and the sail struck, and five men leaping onto the shore with towlines around their waists. They ran ahead, then jerked like dogs on a leash, and immediately began towing the junk against the current. These are trackers. They are mentioned by the earliest travellers on the Yangtze. They strain, leaning forward, and almost imperceptibly the sixty-foot junk begins to move upstream. There is no level towpath. The trackers are rock-climbers: they scamper from boulder to boulder, moving higher until the boulders give out, and then dropping down, pulling and climbing until there is a reach on the river where the junk can sail again. The only difference – but it is a fairly large one – between trackers long-ago and trackers today is that they are no longer whipped. 'Often our men have to climb or jump like monkeys,' wrote a Yangtze traveller, in the middle of the last century, of his trackers, 'and their backs are lashed by the two chiefs, to urge them to work at critical moments. This new spectacle at first revolts and angers us, but when we see that the men do not complain about the lashings we realize that it is the custom of the country, justified by the exceptional difficulties along the route.' Captain Little saw a tracker chief strip his clothes off, jump into the river, then roll himself in sand until he looked half-human, like a gritty ape; then he did a demon dance, and howled, and whipped the trackers, who – scared out of their wits – willingly pulled a junk off a sandbank.

The trackers sing or chant. There are garbled versions of what they say. Some travellers have them grunting and groaning, others are more specific and report the trackers yelling, 'Chor! Chor!' – slang for 'Shang-chia' or 'Put your shoulder to it'. I asked a boatman what the trackers were chanting. He said that they cried out 'Hai tzo! Hai tzo!' over and over again, which means 'Number! Number!' in Szechuanese, and is uttered by trackers and oarsmen alike.

'When we institute the Four Modernizations,' he added – this man was one of the minuscule number who are members of the Chinese Communist party – 'there will be no more junks or trackers.'

One day I was standing at the ship's rail with Big Bob. We saw some trackers, six of them, pulling a junk. The men skipped from rock to rock, they climbed, they hauled the lines attached to the junk, and they struggled along the steep rocky towpath. They were barefoot.

Brantman winced. It was a wince of sagacity, of understanding: Yes, it said, I now see what this is all about. Then he spoke, still wincing a little.

'The profound cultural differences between people!'

I looked at him. He was nodding at the trackers scampering among the rocks on the shore.

'They don't care about television,' he said.

I said, 'That's true.'

'Huh?' He was encouraged. He was smiling now. He said, 'I mean, they couldn't care less if the Rams are playing tomorrow.'

The Los Angeles Rams were Big Bob's favourite football team.

'Am I right, or not?'

'You're right, Bob,' I said. 'They don't care about television or the Rams.'

The junks and these trackers will be on the river for some time to come. Stare for five minutes at any point on the Yangtze and you will see a junk, sailing upstream with its ragged, ribbed sail; or being towed by yelling, tethered men; or slipping downstream with a skinny man clinging to its rudder. There are many new-fangled ships and boats on the river, but I should say that the Yangtze is a river of junks and sampans, fuelled by human sweat. 'Still, there is nothing lovelier than a junk with a following wind (the wind blows upstream, from east to west – a piece of great meteorological luck and a shaper of Chinese history), sailing so well that the clumsy vessel looks as light as a waterbird paddling and foraging in the muddy current.

That image is welcome, because there is little birdlife on the Yangtze – indeed, China itself is no place for an ornithologist. It is hard to say if the absence of trees is the reason for the scarceness of birds; or is it the use of powerful insecticides, or the plain hunger of the people who seem to kill anything that moves? Apart from a few kites and hawks, and some feeble sparrows, the only wild ground-dwelling creature I saw in China was a rat, and in twenty-two trips on the Yangtze a Lindblad guide told me he had only seen one wild thing, a small snake. No wonder the Chinese stared at mink coats and alligator handbags! Abbé David saw very few birds on the Yangtze
 in the 1860s and, as a naturalist, he was looking hard for

them. He put it down to the wilful destruction of animals by the Chinese, and his reflection on this has proved to be prophetic: 'A selfish and blind preoccupation with material interests has caused us to reduce this cosmos, so marvellous to him with eyes to see it, to a hard matter-of-fact place. Soon the horse and the pig on the one hand and wheat and potatoes on the other will replace hundreds of thousands of animals and plants given us by God.'

Down the Yangtze the awful prediction has been fulfilled. You expect this river trip to be an experience of the past – and it is. But it is also a glimpse of the future. In a hundred years or so, under a cold uncolonized moon, what we call the civilized world will all look like China, muddy and senile and old-fangled: no trees, no birds, and shortages of fuel and metal and meat; but plenty of pushcarts, cobblestones, ditch-diggers, and wooden inventions. Nine hundred million farmers splashing through puddles and the rest of the population growing weak and blind working the crashing looms in black factories.

Forget rocket-ships, super-technology, moving sidewalks and all the rubbishy hope in science fiction. No one will ever go to Mars and live. A religion has evolved from the belief that we have a future in outer space; but it is a half-baked religion – it is a little like Mormonism or the Cargo Cult. Our future is this mildly poisoned earth and its smoky air. We are in for hunger and hard work, the highest stage of poverty – no starvation, but crudeness everywhere, clumsy art, simple language, bad books, brutal laws, plain vegetables, and clothes of one colour. It will be damp and dull, like this. It will be monochrome and crowded – how could it be different? There will be no star wars or galactic empires and no more money to waste on the loony nationalism in space programmes. Our grandchildren will probably live in a version of China. On the dark brown banks of the Yangtze the future has already arrived.

It struck me that many of the American passengers were sedentary types. One man said to me, 'Back home, my wife and I lead a very sedimentary life.' I knew what he meant. And this was a kind of sedentary travel. Nor did these armchair travellers read books. They didn't talk about books – they talked about places. Many of their sentences began, 'When we were in Kenya . . .' Or it might be Tierra del Fuego or Inner Mongolia: they were well travelled. For facts they seldom referred to books, or their reading, but nearly always to their travel. They had seen crime in Korea, or an election in Costa Rica, or poverty in Turkey. To me they said, 'You've got a big race problem.' It wasn't personal; they meant England – I lived there.

Most of them had discovered that if you had enough money and time you did not have to read. You could discover things for yourself – or, rather, be told about them by a National Guide. In the corporate lives that they led they had become used to people telling them things, filling them in on a situation. In China we had 'briefings'. They loved 'briefings'. You sat there and someone with a briefcase gave you the low-down – facts, figures, a little history – and you interrogated him for ten minutes. Then it was over. It was so much easier than reading, so much more reassuring. But, of course, as travellers we were regarded as big and busy; in a sense the commune workers and the people in factories and the sailors on the Yangtze ships were working for us.

One of us was not busy. She was an armchair traveller who spent all her time seated, usually soaking herself in whisky.

'I've known a lot of women like her,' a man told me. 'A hell of a lot of women. I've met them on trips like this. They go to Mongolia. They go to Pago-Pago. Peru. Sri Lanka. And they never do anything. We had one with us on the Galapagos trip. She never got off the ship! Can you imagine going to the Galapagos and not getting off the ship? It was a twenty-eight-day trip!'

'Why do you suppose she came here?' I asked.

'To drink. Haven't you seen her? She's having a grand time. She's got a whole box full of whisky sours. She stays in the hotel and drinks while we're at the communes. The only thing is – she's got to drink them warm. She doesn't trust the ice. It's got germs in it – that's what she thinks. When it melts, the germs swim into her whisky-sour.'

Later, he said, 'I'll make a prediction. I'll bet you she never gets off the boat on the Yangtze. She'll just sit there, drinking her whisky sours.'

He was right. But sometimes I was grateful for this old woman's company – at night, in the lounge of the *Tung Fang Hong – Number 39*, after everyone had gone to bed. By half past nine nearly everyone was in bed, except this woman and me, drinking and playing gin rummy.

One night she looked across the table and said, 'I was rotten spoiled,' and she smiled. 'My daughter was rotten spoiled. And I'm going to make goddam sure that my granddaughter is rotten spoiled.'

Sixty-five miles below Chungking, at Fooling, I was joined at the rail by one of the passengers, a stockbroker. We talked about the price of gold and the delinquent bullion market as, on the shore, small tent camps of Chinese sifted gravel and lugged it in buckets to waiting sampans. We passed gardens and talked about land deals and Washington real estate.

'Timber,' he said. 'This is a very good time to buy timber. Something like Weyerhauser. The slump in building has meant the stock's depressed. But you can't go wrong with timber. What you want is a well-managed company, with a good product and a good record.'

There was a commune on the next hill: vegetables, a factory, chimney, huts, a brickworks. We watched it pass.

He told me the American stock market was vastly underrated. Then the dinner gong rang.

We were soon at Feng Tu. Abbé David: 'Very pretty because of its pagodas, towers and the green hills around it.' Captain Williamson: 'One hill is said to be haunted.' Nothing had been torn down, but a certain amount had been added: it was a sullen agglomeration of scorched factories and workers' flats under a weeping corona of smog.

'It certainly looks haunted to me,' I said to the Political Commissar on our ship. The Political Commissar is the labour relations man. If there is slackness in the galley or the engine room on a Chinese ship, the Political Commissar reminds the workers of their duties. Ours was Comrade Sun; he had been working on the river since 1950 ('just after Liberation'), when he was seventeen. He knew the hills and temples of Feng Tu very well.

No, he said, it was not haunted.

'There are no ghosts,' says a Chinese pamphlet entitled *Stories about Not Being Afraid of Ghosts*. 'Belief in ghosts is a backward idea, a superstition and a sign of cowardice. This is a matter of common sense today among the people. But while there are no demons . . . there are many things which resemble them – imperialism, reactionaries, difficulties and obstacles in work, for example.' Comrade Sun was a member of the Party: he agreed with this pamphlet.

We talked about river superstitions. It was not easy. He did not want to give me the idea that people today were silly enough to believe any of this stuff. But I pestered him for frights and beliefs.

'There was an old belief,' he said. 'that if a fish jumped out of the water onto the deck of a ship you could not eat it. Fish often jumped on to the junks. They still do, when they're swimming upstream. Such fish were regarded as demons.'

'Did they throw the fish back?' I asked.

'No. They had to take it ashore. Dig a hole. Then bury it.'

'What do they do now?'

'Eat them.'

I had read of another belief of the junk sailors, that when the wind died they stood on the deck and whistled, to call the wind, so that they would not have to go ashore and tow the boat. Whistling up a wind may once have been a practice among old British sailors – the idea occurs in *Macbeth.* It struck me as a weird and attractive superstition. Comrade Sun said, yes, long ago it was believed that if you whistled the wind would rise. Then he smiled. 'I don't think it does any good at all.'

That evening, our ship, *Number 39*, anchored below the remote town of Shibao Block (Shih Pao Chai, or 'Precious Stone Castle'). This is one of the most unusual – and probably least spoiled – places in China. It is a perfect butte, a hundred feet high, which once had a monastery on top and now has a bare temple. The way to the top is up a staircase in an eleven-storey red pavilion built against the perpendicular side of the rock. Amazingly, it remains just as it was described by travellers a hundred years ago, and the view from the top is a reminder that there are towns in China with no factories, little mechanization, and only the oldest methods of ploughing and planting. The town at the base of the rock is a labyrinth of slimy alleys and muddy streets, and cobblestone passageways that look like the wynds of Edinburgh. And shops: carpenters, bakers, weavers of funeral wreaths, fruitsellers. Just outside the town an old man led a blindfolded buffalo trampling around in circles, to soften the mud for the making of bricks and roof tiles.

I had brought a snapshot to Shibao Block. It was one of Captain Williamson's and it showed the town through the simple eye of a box camera in 1927. The townsfolk were interested. They called the mayor, Comrade Lu, and examined the snapshot. They found it very odd. It was clearly their town, and yet one house was not where it should be. This snapshot was the past: they had never seen an old picture of the town. The mayor asked to be photographed holding the picture.

'Please take his picture,' the interpreter said. 'He is a big potato.'

He meant it as the highest praise.

•

Nearly the whole town of Shibao Block saw us off: silent faces staring at Howard Buhse's red golfer's cap and Ira Weinstein's foot-long telephoto lens and Lurabelle's mink and Jerry McCarthy's whirring cine camera and old Mr Chase's tape-recorder (he recorded everything, even the sound of the ship's engines) and the pinks and blues of the ladies' $350 synthetic 'ultra-suede' dresses and my yellow suede shoes. We were bizarre. There was not a sound, not a murmur from the hundreds of people on the shore.

There were more watchers downstream at Wanxian, a city more nightmarish than Chungking – mud, rain, black streets, broken windows, smoke, and every housefront wearing a film of soot. It was once a city of great beauty, and famous for its perfectly poised *Feng-shui*. But the bluffs and hills that were praised are now covered with factories, the most shocking a silk filiature plant, where 1,300 women and girls were losing their health in the dim light, making silk thread from soaked cocoons. It was a sweat shop, all these women sacrificed to the manufacture of hideously patterned bolts of silk in garish colours. They worked quickly, silently, with ruined hands, to the racket of the jolting looms.

In the days that followed, we passed through the gorges. Many people come to the Yangtze for the gorges alone: they excite themselves on these marvels and skip the rest
 of the river. The gorges are wonderful, and it is almost

impossible to exaggerate their splendour; but the river is long and complicated, and much greater than its gorges, just as the Thames is more than what lies between Westminster and Greenwich.

The great gorges lie below Bai De ('White King City'), the lesser gorges just above Yichang. Bai De was as poisonous-looking as any of the other cities, but as soon as we left it the mountains rose – enormous limestone cliffs on each side of the river. There is no shore: the sheer cliffs plunge straight into the water. They were formed at the dawn of the world, when the vast inland sea in western China began to drain east and wear the mountains away. But limestone is a curious substance. It occurs in blocks, it has cracks and corners; and so the flow zigzagged, controlled by the stone, and made right angles in the river. Looking ahead through the gorges you see no exit, only the end of what looks like a blind canyon.

FROM
CAPTAIN WILLIAMSON'S NOTES

Pa Yang Hsia (Eight Cliffs Gorge): *About twelve miles below Wanhsien, the river flows through plateaux of sandstone for about five miles. On the left bank, three Buddhas are carved in the cliff-face and when the river falls low enough the little figures are cleaned and repainted.*

Yun Yang Hsien: *This city is on the left bank about 145 miles above Ichang. Opposite the city is a picturesque temple which is said to contain a magic bell.*

Bai De (White King City): *Below this important city the scene changes dramatically, as the river hence to Ichang – 110 miles – winds its way through gorges in the mountainous regions which lie athwart its course.*

Feng Hsiang Hsia (Wind-box Gorge): *Below Bai De is one of the most picturesque of the gorges, four miles long, precipitous sides, 700–800 feet in places. At the upper entrance to this gorge, off the left bank, is the isolated Goose Tail Rock – the summit about 80–90 feet above the river at winter level. Below the Goose Tail, the square holes of 'Meng Liang's Ladder' can be seen zigzagging up the right-hand cliffs, on the right bank, while further down the gorge, in a niche high up on the left-bank cliffs, can be seen the ends of the 'wind boxes'.*

Wu Shan Hsien: *Below the Wind-box Gorge is an open ten-mile reach . . . end of the reach is Wu Shan Hsien, the easternmost city in Szechuan – a picturesque, romantic city, with its walls and drum towers – situated immediately above the entrance to the longest gorge of the river.*

Wu Shan Hsia (Wu's Mountain Gorge): *Wu* (*witch*) *was a legendary wizard who dwelt on the mountain at the first reach of this gorge and is credited with blowing a twenty-*

five-mile gap through the mountains to permit the river to pass.

Kuei Chou (now called Zi Gui): *Picturesque small town on the left bank behind low prongs of projecting reefs.*

Niu Kan Ma Fei Hsia (Ox-liver and Horse-lung Gorge): *Situated below Kuei Chou, this gorge is four miles long on a bend in the river. It takes its name from a rocky outcrop on the cliff face on the left bank.*

Teng Ying Hsia (Lampshine Gorge): *This gorge is about eight miles long. At the end of the gorge the river turns abruptly left into the Yellow Cat Gorge.*

Huang Mao Hsia (Yellow Cat Gorge): *In the bend is a large smooth round rock which, because of its appearance, is called the Sleeping Pig. This last of the gorges is about eight miles long, and at its lower end the river emerges into open country and reaches the port of Ichang.*

After seeing the great gorges of the Upper Yangtze it is easy to believe in gods and demons and giants.

There are *graffiti* on the gorges. Some are political ('Mankind Unite to Smash Capitalism'), some are poetic ('Bamboos, flowers and rain purify the traveller'), while other scribbled characters give the gorge's name or its history, or they indicate a notable feature in the gorge. 'Wind-box Gorge' is labelled on the limestone, and the wind-boxes have painted captions. 'Meng-liang's Ladder', it says, at the appropriate place. These are the zigzag holes that Captain Williamson mentioned in his notes; and they have a curious history. In the second century AD the Shu army was encamped on the heights of the gorge. The Hupeh general, Meng-liang, had set out to conquer this army, but they were faced with this vertical gorge wall, over 700 feet high. Meng-liang had his men cut the ladder-holes in the stone, all the way to the top of the gorge, and his army ascended this way, and they surprised the enemy camp and overwhelmed them, ending the domination of Shu. (In 1887 Archibald Little wrote, 'The days are long past since the now effeminate Chinese were capable of such exertions . . .')

The wind blows fiercely through the gorges, as it does in New York between skyscrapers; and it is a good thing, too, because the junks can sail upstream – there is little room here for trackers. On the day I passed through, the sky was leaden, and the wind was tearing the clouds to pieces, and the river itself was yellow-brown or viscous and black, a kind of eel-colour. It is not only the height of the gorges, but the narrowness of the river – less than a hundred yards in places – which makes it swift, sixty metres per second in the narrower places. The scale gives it this look of strangeness, and fills it with an atmosphere of ominous splendour – the majestic cliffs, the thousand-foot gorge walls, the dagger-like pinnacles, and the dark foaming river below, and the skinny boatmen on their vessels of splinters and rags.

Archibald Little wrote, 'I rejoiced that it had been my good fortune to visit the Yangtse Gorges before the coming stream of European tourists, with the inevitable introduction of Western innovation in their train, should have destroyed all their old world charm.' The cities, certainly, are black and horrific, but the gorges are changeless and completely unlike anything I had ever seen before. In other landscapes I have had a sense of deterioration – the Grand Canyon looks as if it is wearing away and being sluiced, stone by orange stone, down the Colorado River. But the gorges look powerful and permanent, and make every person and artefact look puny. They will be here long after Man has destroyed himself with bombs.

It is said that every rock and cliff has a name. 'The Seated Woman and the Pouncing Lion', 'The Fairy Princess', and – less lyrically – 'The Ox-liver and Horse-lung Gorge' (the organs are boulder-formations, high on the cliff-face). The Yangtze is a river of precise nomenclature. Only simple, wild places, like the volcanic hills of south-west Uganda, are full of nameless topography; naming is one of the features of Chinese civilization and settlement. I asked the pilot of our ship if it was so that every rock in the Yangtze had a name. He said yes.

'What is the name of that one?' I asked quickly, pointing out of the window.

'That is Pearl Number Three. Over there is Pearl Number Two. We shall be coming to Pearl Number One in a few minutes.' He had not hesitated. And what was interesting was that these rocks looked rather insignificant to me.

One of the millionaires said, 'These gorges come up to expectations. Very few things do. The Taj Mahal did. The Pyramids didn't. But these gorges!'

We passed Wushan. There was a funeral procession making its way through the empty streets, beating drums and gongs, and at the front of the procession three people in white shrouds – white is the Chinese colour of mourning – and others carrying round paper wreaths, like archery targets. And now we were in the longest gorge, twenty-five miles of cliffs and peaks, and beneath them rain-spattered junks battling the current.

At one time, this part of the Yangtze was filled with rapids. Captain Williamson's list of landmarks noted all of them. They were still in the river, breaking ships apart, in 1937. But the worst have been dynamited away. The most notorious was the Hsin Lung Tan, a low-level rapid caused by a terrific landslide in 1896. It was wild water, eighty feet wide, but blasting opened it to 400 feet, and deepened it. Thirty years ago, only the smallest boats could travel on the river during the winter months; now it is navigable by even the largest throughout the year.

Our ship drew in below Yellow Cat Gorge, at a place

called Dou Shan Tuo ('Steep Hill Village'). We walked to the road and took a bus to the top of the hill. Looking across the river at the pinnacles called 'The Three Daggers', and at the sun pouring honey into the deep cliffs, one of the passengers said with gusto, 'What a place for a condominium!'

The MS *Kun Lun* is by any standards a luxurious ship. She is popularly known as 'Mao's yacht' because in the 1950s and early '60s she was used to take visiting dignitaries up and down the Yangtze. Any number of prominent Albanians can boast that they slept in one of the *Kun Lun*'s sumptuously carpeted suites and danced in the lounge or got stewed to the gills in the sixty-foot-wide club room. The idea for the fancy ship was Jiang Qing's – Chairman Mao's third wife and now the celebrated political criminal of the Gang of Four. She had the guts of a river ship torn out and she redecorated it in the style of Waldorf Astoria Ming – art deco and lotus blossoms – and did not stint on the curtains or the blue bathtubs. The Gregorys (Fred and Merial) had a rat in their room, but never mind – Raymond Barre of France once slept in their suite.

The chief feature of this wilderness of antimacassars is space: wide passageways, large cabins, huge lounges, and sofas on which seven can sit comfortably and catch up on the *Peking Review* or listen to 'News About Britain' or

'The Book Programme' on the World Service of the BBC – there are two gigantic 'Spring Thunder' brand shortwave radios on board. You hardly notice the grand piano, the bar is so big. For this reason, the *Kun Lun* was 'criticized' during the Cultural Revolution; she was turned over to the people and more or less raped. Cots and bunks were crammed into the suites, and for four years the proletariat used her as an ordinary river ship. When the Lindblads found her a few years ago she was in mothballs. Mr Lindblad made a deal with the China Travel Service: he would fix her up, restore her to her original splendour if he was allowed to use her for tours. The scheme was agreed upon, and now the *Kun Lun* is afloat once again, as great an anachronism, as large a contradiction, as could possibly be found in the People's Republic.

We transferred from *Number 39* to the *Kun Lun.* We were on the Middle River now, and there were no complaints. Or rather, not many. I did hear a shrill drunken voice moan one evening, 'I hate Chinese food. Once a month, maybe. Not more than that. But every damned day? I can't eat the stuff.'

And another night, Mrs Ver Bryck looked at me tipsily and said, unprovoked and unbidden, 'Of course I'm happier than you are. I've got more money.'

We stayed two days at Wuhan. The river had become wider, the banks lower and flatter; but the cities had grown more interesting. We watched a thyroidectomy at a hospital at Wuchang, the patient anaesthetized by four acupuncture needles in her hands, and a little voltage; and in the early morning I prowled the streets of Hankow and noted that free markets had sprung up – until this year such improvisatory capitalism was forbidden. At six o'clock one morning I saw my first Chinese beggar, and on the next corner a trio of child acrobats balancing plates on their heads and doing handstands, and then passing the hat. New Hankow looked something like old Hankow.

At night in Hankow and Canton and other hot places where the windows were open I could hear people playing Mah Jong, the sounds of the tiles clicking like castanets and the chatter of the players. It has not been outlawed, and the various types of Chinese chess – *xiang qi*, which has certain similarities to our own chess game, and *wei qi*, which is the same as the Japanese game *go* – are actually encouraged. In alleys, sitting on overturned crates, Chinese men can often be seen playing cards, the game they call 'Aiming High'. In Hankow and Wuhan I saw gamblers throwing dice in the shadows, playing dominoes, and arguing over cards.

The suggestion that the Chinese might be gambling was always sharply denied. Gambling is seen as one of the worst things that a person could do, and there was such shock expressed when the subject came up that I was certain the urge to gamble was still strong.

'Games should be played just for fun,' Comrade Wu

said. And he told me the story of the man who gambles away his money, his food, his radio, and is finally forced to use his wife to give value to a wager – and he loses the bet and his wife.

But there are all sorts of stakes. In Shanghai four men were squatting in an alleyway, playing cards. There was a bottle of home-made gin and pile of clothes-pins near the men. Each time someone lost a hand of cards he had to put a clothes-pin on his ear and take a swig of gin. The drunkest of them had a cluster of clothes-pins on his ear, and looked a complete jackass, which was of course the point – the others were laughing at him.

Public humiliation was a sort of teaching technique. A gambler paid his debt by submitting to humiliation. But if the gamblers were caught by the authorities they would be punished with another form of humiliation.

I had asked Comrade Wu what happened to people who were found gambling.

'Oh, it is very bad,' he said. 'They pay a fine, some are even put into prison. We *educate* them!'

'Educate' is said with force. It is discipline, a humiliation, and I seldom heard the word 'education' in China without its sounding like a hard smack in the face.

At Suchow primary school the headmistress said that they never used corporal punishment. They 'educated' people who used corporal punishment, 'and if a teacher cannot learn to teach patiently, and resorts to hitting, he is criticized'.

She made 'criticized' sound like a whipping. It was another form of discipline, a refinement of humiliation. A person, one of the billion, was criticized by being singled out and exposed. He was severely questioned by the various members of his block or commune and made publicly to show his contrition.

This, in effect, was what the Gang of Four trial was all about: it was public humiliation. The trial was its own punishment – it did not need any sentences at the end. Dragging someone out of a mob, singling out an individual, demanding that a student stand up while the others remain seated – these are the worst things that can happen to someone who values his anonymity and sees himself as part of the powerful Chinese army of workers. Isolated, the person loses his power and is humiliated and weakened by the gaze of the mob. In the nineteenth century it was done with the 'cangue' – those wooden collars that thieves were made to wear.

It is hard to disentangle education from discipline, since both are imposed and carry penalties. Education is learning English, but education is also learning your place. Education might be a discussion with neighbours because of a misdemeanour – it is a telling off, and the offender is given a few books of Mao or Lenin to read. Education might also be a 'struggle session' or something similar with the local committee – 'Change your ways or else', and many books of Mao or Lenin to read. But education also means a pig farm in Inner Mongolia, a farm in Shenyang or Ganzi province – long days slopping the hogs or planting trees, and studying Communist texts at night. In China, the most extreme form of education is prison.

At Lu Shan, a hill station above the Yangtze port of Jiujang, Harry Laughlin pointed to one of the millionaires walking up a hill and said, 'He's captious – that's what we call his type.'

Harry, a millionaire too, sometimes described himself as an educator. He had taught psychology – never mind his two Mercedes (or Lurabelle's Rolls).

'He's insecure,' Harry said, as we walked along the stony path to the pagoda. 'Notice how he's always alone? He's trying to prove something. He always walks ahead, always apart from the group. See, he wants to show us his ass. Very interesting. He's making a statement there.'

I had thought that the odd-man-out was Mr Clark, because he was almost eighty-two and kept stepping on his camera. Or he would look up and smile and say, 'I lost my pen. I had that pen for years.' He became friendly with Dr Ringrose, and then I decided Dr Ringrose – 'Ring-nose', one of the New York ladies called him – was the odd-man-out. He was a cancer doctor from Calgary, but originally from Leeds. He had some Yorkshire traits –
 downrightness, unsmiling humour, practicality – but also

a sense of grievance. He dressed like a camper. He was a bachelor; he was very intelligent; and he was a pedant. He boasted about his travels and his books. In that grey guest house at Lu Shan he said, 'I have six thousand books. People in Calgary are amazed.'

Lu Shan was a quiet gloomy place, paradise for the Chinese who visit there. It is the opposite of every other Chinese city I had seen. It was cool, not crowded, nor elbow-bumping. The Chinese did not seem to notice Lu Shan's smell or its decrepitude. It was exotic – they made movies there, because the landscape – the piney backdrop, with cliffs and peaks and deep valleys – was the classical Chinese topography. The package tours from Shanghai and Nanjing to Lu Shan cost thirty to forty *yuan*, about a month's wage.

The Chinese went in groups marvelling at the azaleas and dwarf cedars and the lone pines and waterfalls they recognized from scroll paintings. The rhododendrons were tall bushy trees. The architecture was very English-looking – stone bungalows and stone shops, and a large stone church. The Catholic church had been turned into a movie theatre (a bust of Chairman Mao in the foyer) and that month they were showing *She*, a love story. On the hill paths there were little signs carved in Chinese characters in the grey stone. 'Share happiness, share difficulties' – the slogan of a Chinese general in the 1920s. Near a stone seat, the motto: 'Sitting here and dreaming here'.

In the early morning Lu Shan resembled every hill station I had ever seen, from Simla and Fraser's Hill, to the ones above Medan in Sumatra, and Surabaya. The people had rosy cheeks, the pine trees dripped, the stone bungalows were dark and dampstained, and the low cloud and fog settled over the mission steeples and villa roofs until their outlines were faintly pencilled in the mist. The gloom in the place was the same gloom I had noticed in other hill stations, perhaps a result of the fact that such places were entirely a European invention, the architecture English and unmanageable, and the inheritors rather baffled by the layout. The Lu Shan Guest House had English virtues – fine banisters and light fittings and solid walls. But the rooms smelled of damp, the lights did not work, and the whole place had lost its ornaments – no pictures, no plants. The previous occupants had moved out, the new occupants – being poor – could not furnish the house properly.

In Lu Shan I listened to our Comrade Tao question one of the millionaires' wives about life in America.

Mr Tao asked, 'Is rent very high in America?'

'I've never paid rent,' the American lady said.

This surprised Mr Tao. He said, 'What about food? You must spend ten or twenty dollars a week on food.'

'Twenty dollars is nothing,' the lady said.

In China it was almost a month's salary.

'Do you have a bicycle?' the Chinese man asked.

'Yes, I do, but I only use it for fun.'

'A bicycle for fun!' he said. 'What about a car – do you have one?'

'Yes.'

'What kind is it?'

This was a difficult question. The lady could not answer. She said, 'Actually, I have four cars.'

Comrade Tao seemed to swallow something very large, and he blinked and squinted at the lady, who had become self-conscious and was saying, 'There's a Chevy convertible, but I can't really use it in bad weather. I usually take one of the smaller ones – they're easier to park, and you save gas. And the others . . .'

Comrade Tao stared.

But the lady had seen her mistake and tactfully changed the subject to azaleas.

Near Lu Shan was a nursery and botanical garden. I asked what effect the Cultural Revolution had had on the operation of the botanical garden and the nursery. The director said, 'All my greenhouses were destroyed for being bourgeois.'

There were faint traces of huge 'big character' slogans on the façade of the Lu Shan Guest House. No one would translate them for me, and two Chinese men denied seeing them.

The millionaires on the Yangtze were always polite, always

sociable and always stayed off contentious topics. 'Don't talk to So-and-so about politics,' Jerry McCarthy said. 'No way! Don't mention the Equal Rights Amendment.' Occasionally I heard people issue warnings like this; it meant that a contentious topic had been discovered and was to be avoided in the future. In this way an atmosphere of agreement was maintained.

But when they played games they played to win. I played gin rummy with one of them and he spent the whole time badgering me, mocking me, telling me what I was doing wrong, predicting my discards. He was actually very angry at one point, and after about eight games, when it was clear that I had beaten him, he cursed and stomped away.

The next day he followed me around the deck saying, 'The shill . . . the gin rummy expert . . . the novice,' and he demanded that I play him again.

'This time we'll play for a dollar a point, just to keep up your concentration. What do you say, Paulie-boy? What about it? A rematch! Come on!'

He was not happy until he had beaten me three nights in a row, and then he refused to play me again on the pretext that it was a waste of his time. So I played gin rummy with the ladies from New York, who proved exhausting opponents.

I played Scrabble, and that was worse. I had never played such unenjoyable Scrabble in my life. And the fact was that most of the Scrabble players cheated, or tried to slip non-words by me. One lady insisted that adze was spelled 'adz'. There was no English dictionary on our ship, and she claimed that if there had been she would have been vindicated. Another Scrabble player claimed that 'yo' was a word. When I challenged her, she said, 'Yo-ho-ho!'

They were also full of odd information. The paint on an airplane fuselage weighs between 150 and 400 pounds – there was a fuel economy in flying unpainted planes. I was told that by one of our millionaires while we were touring Nanjing. 'And did you know that Robert Redford is really very short?' a lady said one day. 'No bicycle in China has gears but every one of them has a lock,' a man said. Observant!

I discovered the term for yogurt in Chinese was *suan niu nai.* (Cheese does not exist in China.) I ordered some and was eating it with pleasure, when Doctor Ringrose said, 'We put yogurt on certain forms of skin cancer.'

And they asked questions, sometimes the damnedest questions. Before we went ashore at Hankow a lady asked the Chinese tour leader, 'What shall I wear?' She meant what style of dress.

At the thermos-bottle factory, Mr Clark asked the American guide, 'How many pounds per square inch is the pressure on that glass blowing apparatus?'

At the Wuhan Conservatory, Mr Jones asked, 'What is

the name of that instrument?' He was told it was a harp, but he wanted its Chinese name. The musician looked at him and said loudly '*Zhong*!'

People asked how much water flowed through a particular spot on the Yangtze, and what the depth was, and the width, and the population here and there ('Four or five million' was a frequent answer to many different questions). I decided that demanding statistics was a way of getting their money's worth – why else would someone pay $10,000 to sail through China?

At Hubei Medical College Hospital one of the millionaires gazed at an electrical transformer hooked up to some acupuncture needles that were inserted into a patient's wrists.

'How much voltage?' he asked.

He was told.

'Is that a.c. or d.c.?' he asked.

He was told, and satisfied that it was d.c., he walked away.

All over the river people were fishing, some with hooks and lines, others with circular weighted nets, or curtains of nets which they trailed behind their sampans, or the complicated tentlike nets in bamboo frames that Abbé David saw raised and lowered in Shashi. They caught tiny fish – sardine-sized, and they kept even the minnows. More modern methods might have emptied the Yangtze of all its fish, but Comrade Sun had told me that some men still fished with trained cormorants and otters.

The river had widened again: on this stretch of the river I was seldom able to see the far bank, and we sailed to Jiujang in a heated mist, glad for the night at Lu Shan ('The road is very twisty,' Mr Chen said, 'but we have a good driver and he will not go bananas'). In both Jiujang and Lu Shan, people could be seen fighting for cinema tickets. The same films were playing in both places, *The Great Dictator* and *City Lights*, starring China's favourite actor, Cha-Li Zhuo Bi-lin.

On our way to Nanjing, I talked to the *Kun Lun*'s captain. Like Captain Liu of *Number 39*, he had worked his way up to captain, from steward, by on-the-job training, and had never gone to naval college. 'There is no reason for a man to remain a steward his whole life. I tell my men – "Work hard and there will be promotions for you."'

I asked him what the difficulties were in navigating on the Yangtze.

'Two main ones,' he said. 'From December to March, the water is very low and the channel is narrow. This makes things difficult, because there is so much other traffic on the river. The second is the weather. There is fog and mist from October to April, and sometimes it is impossible to see what lies ahead. Radar is often no help. To avoid getting into an accident, some nights we anchor until the weather clears.'

I said that it seemed that very little had changed on the Yangtze. People fished in the old way; they sailed and rowed and towed wooden junks; they watered their fields carrying buckets on yokes; and right back there at Jiujang, women were washing clothes, clubbing bundles of laundry and thrashing it in the muddy water. They crossed the river in rusty ferries and still drowned by the score when the river was in flood.

The captain reminded me of the Four Modernizations and said that with the smashing of the Gang of Four, things would improve. How ironic, I thought: the leader of the Gang of Four had probably sat in this very cabin; she was certainly responsible for its decor. 'Before Liberation, this river was different. The foreigners were very careless. They ran rampant. The Chinese people hated and feared them, because they had a reputation for not stopping for a junk or a sampan, or they might swamp a small boat in their wake. It made them unpopular. The gunboats were the worst of all. The foreigners were disliked for the way they used the river – Japanese, French, Italian, English, American. But things are different now.'

We went ashore at Nanjing. The Gang of Four trial had started. We were encouraged to watch it, by the China Travel Service guides: it reminded me of Hate Week in *1984*, and the defendants looked sick and crazy after four years in prison. I ended up playing gin rummy with Harry Laughlin, who said he was dying to get back to Pasadena.

Above Sun Yat-Sen's mausoleum in Nanjing, there was a slogan which was translated in my guidebook as 'The world belongs to the people'.

I mentioned this to Mr Gregory, one of the Connecticut millionaires. Mr Gregory said President Carter was stupid. Mr Gregory was also an authority on semi-precious stones, and he told me that he had owned more than twenty Cadillacs. He had the security and burglar alarm business and one day he told me, 'I think it's about time the world started to be afraid of America again.' He often said something at dinner and the whole table of ten went silent. Then someone would smile at a big bowl and say, 'Now what do you suppose *that* is?'

'The world belongs to the people,' Mr Gregory said. Then he breathed hard. 'Well, that's not true.'

'Why not?'

'The world belongs to *some* people, but not *the* people.'

He was speaking of the world as it ought to be, not as it was.

'No, sir, not *the* people.'

Later I came across a different translation, without the loaded word 'people'. 'The world belongs to everyone,' it said.

I mentioned this to Mr Gregory.

'That's better,' he said. 'That's true.'

He liked everyone, but he certainly didn't think much of the people.

Slogans were often a problem. At the Xiao Ying Primary School in Nanjing, a slogan which had been painted on a wall at the time of the Cultural Revolution had read, 'Never Forget Class Struggle'. Half of it had been obliterated. It read, 'Never Forget'.

Then there were the Four Modernizations: Defence, Science and Technology, Industry, and Agriculture. At school, children were taught the Five Loves: Love Work, Love People, Love Neighbours, Love Science, Love Public Property. In the mid-1970s the Eight Antis were to be supported, and it was patriotic and comradely to be Anti-Intellectual, Anti-Western, Anti-Bourgeois, Anti-Capitalist-Roader, Anti-Revisionist, Anti-Traditional, Anti-Confucian, and Anti-Imperialist.

It was important to remember that the Four News were different from the Four Modernizations, and that the Four Olds were especially pernicious. I never discovered what the Four Olds were.

Slogans of an abusive nature had been removed from the building façades in western China, but many of Chairman Mao's picturesque phrases still remained lettered on the walls of certain buildings, and it was one of the pleasures of China to hear these translated by our guides. 'Yes, it says, "Despicable American Imperialists and Their Running Dogs Must Never be Allowed . . ."'

The name of the oldest restaurant in Suchow, The Pine and Crane (perhaps 300 years old?), was thought to be too bourgeois during the Cultural Revolution, so it was changed to The East is Red Restaurant. Recently it has been changed back to The Pine and Crane. Heavenly Park, an ancient garden, was changed to Workers' Park, but it has also reverted to its original name.

Many slogans seemed to me to be defacing public property. In China anyone would write anything anywhere: 'Love Public Property' might be scrawled on a fine building. Slogans were merely a form of public *graffiti*. In the Yangtze Gorges some of the *graffiti* were very old, but I came across more recent stuff. I went to the formal garden in Suchow called The Garden of The Master of Nets. It had been laid out in the year 1140. In The Pavilion of the Accumulated Void (it is a Taoist concept), the rosewood walls are covered with *graffiti* – for example, 'Li Han Ming Came Here on His Travels 1980'.

We were often invited to admire buildings or objects by the Chinese. Look at this Catholic church! they would say. Look at this jade suit made for a nobleman! Look at these tombs! Their explanations were very brief – a date, an anecdote, a name; and then on to the next sight.

But there were always signs near these sights, and I discovered that the signs were usually different from the explanations we received. I asked the Chinese guides to translate these signs. They did so with great reluctance, but the experience was illuminating for me.

Caption under a photograph of a Catholic church in

Canton, built in 1861: 'In order to build this church people were forced to move away. The citizens felt very angry. People were not allowed to build residences around this church. No person was allowed to look through the windows of this church.'

Caption under a photograph of a Catholic church in Nanjing, built in the 1850s: 'American imperialism took preaching as its cover. All over China they erected churches like this and carried out destructive activities. In 1853, in Shanghai, the Small Sword Society echoed the Tai-Ping rebels. They occupied Shanghai, country and city. The American missionaries joined up with the Ching Dynasty troops and attacked the Small Sword Society troops, and the church acted as a stronghold. After the Ching troops lost, the American missionaries escorted them to safety at the American Embassy.'

Sign next to the jade burial suit (Han Dynasty, AD 25–220) in the Nanjing Museum: 'The feudal rulers exploited the workers before birth, oppressed the labouring peoples, and even after death wanted to wear the blood and sweat of the labouring peoples, as represented by the jade suit. They planned to preserve their corpses. This reflects the tremendous waste of the feudal rulers and reveals the limitless exploitative nature of the feudal rulers.'

Inscription on the Ming Tombs outside Peking: 'The real landlords of this 40 sq. kms. were the peasants. But after the Emperor selected this site, the imperial troops came in like mad animals. They destroyed the orchards and razed the villages. They used military might to expel the labouring peasants, who had been here for centuries, and they occupied the site.

'The numerous peasant families remembered this with malice. They took everything they owned and left behind their destroyed lives.

'After the tombs were established, this area was labelled "Off Limits". If one of the Masses came here he was caned 100 strokes; if he grabbed a handful of earth he was executed.

'This is the background of the feudalistic ruling classes' oppression of the peasantry . . .'

These explanations are for the Chinese. Foreigners were given different explanations, or none at all. At the churches, the jade suit, and the Ming Tombs, there was always a Chinese to say, 'Isn't it pretty?'

At Suchow I took the Shanghai Express, the last part of my sail through China. There were policemen at Suchow station barking orders at the people streaming in. The policemen were rather nasty-looking. I had seen such men be very rough in China, at times manhandling cyclists and pedestrians. Now they were barking orders at the travellers, telling them which platform to go to, how to line up and look sharp.

Within a few minutes we were out of the ancient city of

Suchow and had lost sight of the canals and the city moat. We travelled across the vegetable fields of Jiangsu. The last hills I had seen were south of Nanjing. Long ago, this plain through which the Shanghai Express was passing was part of the Pacific Ocean: the Yangtze had extended China's land mass and swelled its estuary into several new provinces, over millions of years.

The soil did not look fertile – Chinese soil seldom did. The gardens were oblongs, stretching to the horizons on both sides of the train. This was Chinese topography, the vegetable plot. When there were hills they had vegetables on them. When there was a riverbank it was a riverbank with vegetables. A valley, a plain, whatever – it always looked the same, slightly exhausted and orderly with cabbages.

Someone said, 'Look, a pig!'

Because there were so few animals to be seen, a pig or a goat caused great interest, and a dog – those rare crosseyed mongrels – was a sensation. The Chinese did not grow flowers except in pots, in parks and for special occasions. The Chinese were practical, unspiritual, materialistic, baffled and hungry, and these qualities had brought a crudity and a terrible fatigue to their country. In order to stay alive they had to kill the imagination; the result was a vegetable economy and a monochrome culture.

Shanghai was commercial, but the advertising often puzzled me: 'Dragonfly Cotton Shoes! They Are Stylish and Cheap!' 'Rado Watch! Styleproof, Scratchproof, Timeproof!' and 'Aero Tennis Racket – Indeformable!'

I decided to have a look at the Antique Exchange. On the way there I met a Chinese man who had worked for the US Navy during the war. He had a perfect American accent. He summed up for me the years since Liberation: 'The first ten years were bad, the next ten years were okay, but the past ten years have been terrible. I don't know how we got through them. It was the Cultural Revolution. Boy, that was terrible.'

I asked him whether he thought there would be another cultural revolution.

'Sure,' he said.

'Why?'

'Mao said so. Another one. And one after that. Just one after the other.'

The Antique Exchange is where the Chinese sell family treasures to the government, so that they can be resold in the government antique shops and Friendship Stores (which are full of valuable and pretty museum pieces).

On the high stool of a darkened room sits a skinny Chinese man, with yellow protruding teeth and wire-frame glasses. He is sitting cross-legged on the stool, and he wears a skullcap, and he puffs a cigarette by the light of a dim lamp. He points, raises a long fingernail, and beckons a man forward.

The man steps into the light, carrying a canvas bag. He

wears a loose army uniform and slippers. He begins to take crockery out of the bag – rice bowls, plates, dishes.

'No, no, no –' The smoker waves this pretty stuff away.

The soldier takes out a stone lion.

'No –'

The soldier puts the lion away, and takes out more rice bowls.

'No –'

The soldier takes out a blue porcelain jar, about ten inches high, luminous and lovely even in this bad light.

The skinny man stops smoking. He sets the jar aside.

There is nothing else. The man shifts on his stool and writes a chit. There is no bargaining: the antique is assigned a price. The soldier puts the rejected stuff into his bag, takes his slip of paper and collects some money.

'They buy things for ten bucks, they sell them for a hundred bucks,' a Chinese man told me in Shanghai. Shanghai was full of English speakers, full of slang from the Second World War.

What interested me was that this smoky seedy interior was a government bureau. But it was the old China. Outside it, a sign in Chinese said: 'Sell Your Old Plates, Bronzes and Carvings for Cash'. Of course, this is capitalism in the service of the state, buying up heirlooms to sell to tourists, but the old man, the back room, the shelves of cracked porcelain and the dusty bronzes, and the pitiful prices, the pawnshop gloom – it all looked as old as China.

The antique shop prices were very high, but most of the merchandise deserved to be in museums. How long, I wondered, would these treasures be available to tourists?

Not everyone saw these objects as treasures. There was a New York lady, Dorothy Hirshon, who would squint at an item on the shelf and say, 'That's the ugliest thing in China.'

One night after dinner, at about nine o'clock, I went for a walk down a dark street. I had been walking only about ten minutes when I was greeted ('Good evening, sir') by three young men, Comrade Ma, Comrade Lu and Comrade Wee. They wanted to practise their English. I said that I had been reading the supernatural stories of Pu Sung-ling, his *Strange Tales of Liao-chai.* I asked them whether they believed in ghosts. They found this very funny.

'I don't believe in ghosts,' Comrade Ma said.

I asked him why not.

'I never see one.'

I said, 'So there are no ghosts in China?'

'No,' Comrade Lu said.

'What about your ancestors?' I asked.

Comrade Ma said, 'They are under the ground.'

I asked them whether they celebrated the Ching Ming Festival by exploding firecrackers in the graveyards. They said they didn't celebrate it at all.

'Overseas Chinese do that.'

We were passing a railway embankment where, behind a row of trees, there were young people kissing. They embraced standing up, in the shadowy side of the tree trunks. I called attention to it.

Comrade Ma said, 'Since the Gang of Four were smashed there is now kissing. From 1949 until the Gang of Four there was no kissing. Now there is kissing. Even on television there is kissing.'

'Did the Gang of Four kiss?'

'Oh, yes. But inside their houses!' Comrade Ma said. The others laughed. They regarded Ma as a great wit.

I asked whether they themselves kissed girls.

Comrade Ma said, 'Comrade Lu has a darling. He kisses. I have two darlings. I kiss them.'

I said, 'Indoors or outdoors?'

'Only married people can kiss indoors, in a room. We kiss over there. In the trees. Sometimes in the park. In the park, at night, you can put your hands around the girl – and other places. Ha-ha! Also other things. But it is very stony on the ground – too many rocks!'

'Mister Paul,' Comrade Wee said. 'What is the proper way to kiss?'

He had told me earlier that he was a printer. This inspired me. I said that kissing was like printing. You printed your lips on the girl's lips – not too hard. They laughed and said, yes, that's what they thought it was like.

 I asked them when they planned to get married. They

said when they were about thirty-five or so. They were twenty-six and twenty-seven, and each earned 50 *yuan* ($30) a month.

The trial of the Gang of Four had recently started, so I asked, 'Are the Gang of Four guilty?'

'Oh, yes. Guilty.'

'But not Chairman Mao, eh?' I said. 'Chairman Mao was a great man, right?'

Comrade Ma smiled at me and said, 'Maybe.'

Comrade Wee said, 'Do you think so?'

'I don't know,' I said.

'You are very clever!'

We talked about the Yangtze. The people there, they said, had different clothes and different 'hairs'. This topic provoked Comrade Lu to tell me that his father lived in Surinam – in South America, of all places. But he hated it. 'Too many Negroes.' Hong Kong was better, Lu said.

Comrade Ma told me that he had a bicycle, a TV and a radio. I said that he had everything, apparently.

'No. I want to go to Hong Kong.'

They all agreed: they all wanted to go to Hong Kong. But they had never been outside Shanghai. They lived with their parents, and would go on living with them until they married. I asked whether they regarded themselves as revolutionaries. No, they said, they were workers.

'I don't want to be a revolutionary,' Comrade Ma said.

Had they been in the army?

'There are too many people in the army,' Comrade Lu said. 'They like the army. It is better than farming. Harvesting rice is hard work. It is easier to be a soldier.'

They were cheery, candid fellows, and we continued walking the dark streets of Shanghai, talking about everything.

What about sports? I asked.

'Table tennis,' Comrade Ma said.

'Badminton,' Comrade Lu said.

'I take' – Comrade Wee glanced nervously at the others – 'I take cold showers.'

In Shanghai, as in other cities in China, the air was bad, it stank, it was dark brown. There were people in the streets, mobs of them, because their rooms were so small and crowded. The streets were free. There is little sign of money, no sign of wealth. Small ugly coins and filthy paper rags are money – it is worthless stuff. The people have clean faces and they observe a kind of ragged order. One can only compare this to the anarchy and distress of India. Here there are scarcely any beggars; there is little apparent violence. Most people are dressed exactly the same. They all wear shoes.

There is a powerful silence in these streets, and the junkyard smell – dust and old rags – is not the smell of death but of illness. Motor traffic would make these cities uninhabitable, but in a crude way the people have made motors unnecessary. The people seldom talk – their silence is the most amazing thing.

For these billion people this is probably the only system that would work. Under capitalism, five per cent would be conspicuously rich, and the rest rather poor or very poor, the starving and begging society of China's past. A non-begging society is a good thing – more than that, it is unique. Now, the people ask for nothing. They get very little. If there were disorder here, even a slight amount, I had the impression there would be catastrophe.

Any change in China would be for the worse, which is a pity because it seemed so bad when I sailed through it. Would it always be these people in cheap cotton clothes, walking through the streets, carting the steel rods that are used for these awful buildings, saying nothing? The air pollution gives China the look of existing in a permanent sunset. It worried me that China might never be better than it is now, and that water might always be scarce, clothes always rationed, food never plentiful, houses always tiny, and the hard work never done.

Author's Note

This trip was taken in November 1980, when the hard-line Maoists were still in control and Hua Guofeng was Party Chairman. The reformers in the government, among them Deng Xiaoping, had not yet consolidated their power. China had hardly changed since the end of the Cultural Revolution in 1976. The Chinese still wore their revolutionary clothes, blue boiler suits and cloth slippers; their motto was 'Serve the People', though they were already sick of saying it. China is a different country now.

PENGUIN 60s

MARTIN AMIS · *God's Dice*
HANS CHRISTIAN ANDERSEN · *The Emperor's New Clothes*
MARCUS AURELIUS · *Meditations*
JAMES BALDWIN · *Sonny's Blues*
AMBROSE BIERCE · *An Occurrence at Owl Creek Bridge*
DIRK BOGARDE · *From Le Pigeonnier*
WILLIAM BOYD · *Killing Lizards*
POPPY Z. BRITE · *His Mouth will Taste of Wormwood*
ITALO CALVINO · *Ten Italian Folktales*
ALBERT CAMUS · *Summer*
TRUMAN CAPOTE · *First and Last*
RAYMOND CHANDLER · *Goldfish*
ANTON CHEKHOV · *The Black Monk*
ROALD DAHL · *Lamb to the Slaughter*
ELIZABETH DAVID · *I'll be with You in the Squeezing of a Lemon*
N. J. DAWOOD (TRANS.) · *The Seven Voyages of Sindbad the Sailor*
ISAK DINESEN · *The Dreaming Child*
SIR ARTHUR CONAN DOYLE · *The Man with the Twisted Lip*
DICK FRANCIS · *Racing Classics*
SIGMUND FREUD · *Five Lectures on Psycho-Analysis*
KAHLIL GIBRAN · *Prophet, Madman, Wanderer*
STEPHEN JAY GOULD · *Adam's Navel*
ALASDAIR GRAY · *Five Letters from an Eastern Empire*
GRAHAM GREENE · *Under the Garden*
JAMES HERRIOT · *Seven Yorkshire Tales*
PATRICIA HIGHSMITH · *Little Tales of Misogyny*
M. R. JAMES AND R. L. STEVENSON · *The Haunted Dolls' House*
RUDYARD KIPLING · *Baa Baa, Black Sheep*
PENELOPE LIVELY · *A Long Night at Abu Simbel*
KATHERINE MANSFIELD · *The Escape*

PENGUIN 60s

GABRIEL GARCÍA MÁRQUEZ · *Bon Voyage, Mr President*
PATRICK MCGRATH · *The Angel*
HERMAN MELVILLE · *Bartleby*
SPIKE MILLIGAN · *Gunner Milligan, 954024*
MICHEL DE MONTAIGNE · *Four Essays*
JAN MORRIS · *From the Four Corners*
JOHN MORTIMER · *Rumpole and the Younger Generation*
R. K. NARAYAN · *Tales from Malgudi*
ANAÏS NIN · *A Model*
FRANK O'CONNOR · *The Genius*
GEORGE ORWELL · *Pages from a Scullion's Diary*
CAMILLE PAGLIA · *Sex and Violence, or Nature and Art*
SARA PARETSKY · *A Taste of Life*
EDGAR ALLAN POE · *The Pit and the Pendulum*
MISS READ · *Village Christmas*
JEAN RHYS · *Let Them Call It Jazz*
DAMON RUNYON · *The Snatching of Bookie Bob*
SAKI · *The Secret Sin of Septimus Brope*
WILL SELF · *Scale*
GEORGES SIMENON · *Death of a Nobody*
MURIEL SPARK · *The Portobello Road*
ROBERT LOUIS STEVENSON · *The Pavilion on the Links*
PAUL THEROUX · *Down the Yangtze*
WILLIAM TREVOR · *Matilda's England*
MARK TULLY · *Ram Chander's Story*
JOHN UPDIKE · *Friends from Philadelphia*
EUDORA WELTY · *Why I Live at the P. O.*
EDITH WHARTON · *Madame de Treymes*
OSCAR WILDE · *The Happy Prince*
VIRGINIA WOOLF · *Killing the Angel in the House*

READ MORE IN PENGUIN